A·N·N·U·A·L EDITIONS

Early Childhood Education

Twenty-Sixth Edition

05/06

EDITOR

Karen Menke Paciorek

Eastern Michigan University

Karen Menke Paciorek is a professor and program coordinator of early childhood education at Eastern Michigan University in Ypsilanti. Her degrees in early childhood education include a B.A. from the University of Pittsburgh, a M.A. from George Washington University, and a Ph.D. from Peabody College of Vanderbilt University. She co-edits, with Joyce Huth Monro, *Sources: Notable Selections in Early Childhood Education* and is the editor of *Taking Sides: Clashing Views on Controversial Issues in Early Childhood Education* (McGraw-Hill/Dushkin). She has served as president of the Michigan Association for the Education of Young Children and the Michigan Early Childhood Education Consortium. She presents at local, state, and national conferences on curriculum planning, guiding behavior, preparing the learning environment, and working with families. She currently serves on the school board for the Northville Public Schools, Northville, Michigan and on the Board of Directors for Wolverine Human Services.

Joyce Huth Munro

National Association for the Education of Young Children

Joyce Huth Munro is Coordinator of the Associate Degree Program Accreditation at the National Association for the Education of Young Children in Washington, DC. She has been an administrator and professor at colleges in Kentucky, South Carolina, and New Jersey. She is a frequent presenter on curriculum planning and professional development at national and regional early childhood conferences. In addition to editing *Annual Editions* and *Sources: Notable Selection in Early Childhood Education* for McGraw-Hill/Dushkin, Munro has authored a professional development text and on-line course for the ETS PATHWISE series. She holds a M.Ed. from the University of South Carolina and a Ph.D. from Peabody College of Vanderbilt University.

McGraw-Hill/Dushkin

2460 Kerper Blvd., Dubuque, IA 52001

Visit us on the Internet
http://www.dushkin.com

Credits

1. **How the World Treats Young Children**
   Unit photo—© Getty Images/Ryan McVay
2. **Child Development and Families**
   Unit photo—© Getty Images/Buccina Studios
3. **Educational Practices**
   Unit photo—© Getty Images
4. **Guiding and Supporting Young Children**
   Unit photo—© Getty Images/Photodisc Collection
5. **Curricular Issues**
   Unit photo—© Getty Images/David Buffington

Copyright

Cataloging in Publication Data
Main entry under title: Annual Editions: Early Childhood Education. 2005/2006.
1. Early Childhood Education—Periodicals. I. Menke Paciorek, Karen, *comp.* II. Munro, Joyce H.   Title: Early Childhood Education.
ISBN 0–07–311253-4   658'.05   ISSN 0272–4456

Twenty-Sixth Edition

Cover image © Photodisc/Getty Images/Photodisc/Eyewire/Getty Images
Printed in the United States of America   1234567890QPDQPD98765   Printed on Recycled Paper

Editors/Advisory Board

Members of the Advisory Board are instrumental in the final selection of articles for each edition of ANNUAL EDITIONS. Their review of articles for content, level, currentness, and appropriateness provides critical direction to the editor and staff. We think that you will find their careful consideration well reflected in this volume.

Preface

In publishing ANNUAL EDITIONS we recognize the enormous role played by the magazines, newspapers, and journals of the public press in providing current, first-rate educational information in a broad spectrum of interest areas. Many of these articles are appropriate for students, researchers, and professionals seeking accurate, current material to help bridge the gap between principles and theories and the real world. These articles, however, become more useful for study when those of lasting value are carefully collected, organized, indexed, and reproduced in a low-cost format, which provides easy and permanent access when the material is needed. That is the role played by ANNUAL EDITIONS.

Twenty-six years ago the profession of early childhood education was just beginning to take shape as schools around the country were beginning to offer a degree in the new field. A collection of readings was developed to help the new professionals understand the abilities and needs of young children. This annual reader is used today at over 550 colleges and universities. For twenty-six years we have worked diligently to bring you the best and most significant articles in the field. We realize this is a tremendous responsibility to provide a thorough review of the current literature—a responsibility we take seriously. Our goal is to provide the reader with a snapshot of the critical issues facing professionals in early childhood education.

Early childhood education is an interdisciplinary field that includes child development, family issues, educational practices, behavior guidance, and curriculum. *Annual Editions: Early Childhood Education 05/06* brings you the latest information in the field from a wide variety of recent journals, newspapers, and magazines. In selecting articles for this edition, we were careful to provide you with a well-balanced look at the issues and concerns facing teachers, families, society, and children. There are three themes found in readings chosen for this twenty-sixth edition of *Annual Editions: Early Childhood Education.* They are: (1) the attention placed on achievement standards whether from professional organizations or states, (2) the continued focus on early literacy experiences being critical for young children prior to public school entry age, and (3) with the release of year forty data from the High/Scope Perry Preschool Study there exists a vast amount of research that supports the need for quality early childhood programs for all children, but especially children at risk. It is especially gratifying to see issues affecting children and families covered in magazines other than professional association journals. The general public needs to be aware of the impact of positive early learning and family experiences on the growth and development of children.

Continuing in this edition of *Annual Editions: Early Childhood Education* are selected World Wide Web sites that can be used to further explore topics addressed in the articles. We have chosen to include only a few high-quality sites. Students are encouraged to explore these sites on their own, or in collaboration with others, for extended learning opportunities.

Given the wide range of topics included, *Annual Editions: Early Childhood Education 05/06* may be used by several groups: undergraduate or graduate students, professionals, parents, or administrators who want to develop an understanding of the critical issues in the field.

The selection of readings for this edition has been a cooperative effort between the two editors and the advisory board members. We appreciate the time the advisory board members have taken to provide suggestions for improvement and possible articles for consideration. We couldn't produce this book without the assistance of many. The production and editorial staff of McGraw-Hill/Dushkin ably support and coordinate our efforts. In addition, we appreciated the expert work by Eastern Michigan University graduate student Kim Schemansky.

To the instructor or reader interested in the history of early childhood care and education programs throughout the years, we invite you to view our other book, also published by McGraw-Hill/Dushkin. *Sources: Notable Selections in Early Childhood Education,* 2nd edition (1999) is a collection of 46 writings of enduring historical value by influential people in the field. All of the selections are primary sources that allow you to experience firsthand the thoughts and views of these important educators. Also available is the first edition of *Taking Sides: Clashing Views on Controversial Issues in Early Childhood Education.* This book is also published by McGraw-Hill/Dushkin and edited by Karen Menke Paciorek. Eighteen controversial issues facing early childhood professionals or parents have been selected. The book can be used in a seminar or issues course.

We are grateful to readers who have corresponded with us about the selection and organization of previous editions. Your comments and articles sent for consideration are welcomed and will serve to modify future volumes. Take time to fill out and return the postage-paid article rating form on the last page. You may also contact either of us at *kpaciorek@emich.edu or jmunro@naeyc.org.*

We look forward to hearing from you.

Karen Menke Paciorek
Editor

Joyce Huth Munro
Editor

Contents

UNIT 1
How the World Treats Young Children

The concepts in bold italics are developed in the article. For further expansion, please refer to the Topic Guide and the Index.

UNIT 2
Child Development and Families

The concepts in bold italics are developed in the article. For further expansion, please refer to the Topic Guide and the Index.

UNIT 3
Educational Practices

The concepts in bold italics are developed in the article. For further expansion, please refer to the Topic Guide and the Index.

UNIT 4
Guiding and Supporting Young Children

The concepts in bold italics are developed in the article. For further expansion, please refer to the Topic Guide and the Index.

The concepts in bold italics are developed in the article. For further expansion, please refer to the Topic Guide and the Index.

UNIT 5
Curricular Issues

The concepts in bold italics are developed in the article. For further expansion, please refer to the Topic Guide and the Index.

The concepts in bold italics are developed in the article. For further expansion, please refer to the Topic Guide and the Index.

Topic Guide

This topic guide suggests how the selections in this book relate to the subjects covered in your course. You may want to use the topics listed on these pages to search the Web more easily.

On the following pages a number of Web sites have been gathered specifically for this book. They are arranged to reflect the units of this *Annual Edition*. You can link to these sites by going to the DUSHKIN ONLINE support site at *http://www.dushkin.com/online/*.

ALL THE ARTICLES THAT RELATE TO EACH TOPIC ARE LISTED BELOW THE BOLD-FACED TERM.

World Wide Web Sites

The following World Wide Web sites have been carefully researched and selected to support the articles found in this reader. The easiest way to access these selected sites is to go to our DUSHKIN ONLINE support site at *http://www.dushkin.com/online/*.

AE: Early Childhood Education 05/06

The following sites were available at the time of publication. Visit our Web site—we update DUSHKIN ONLINE regularly to reflect any changes.

General Sources

Children's Defense Fund (CDF)
http://www.childrensdefense.org

At this site of the CDF, an organization that seeks to ensure that every child is treated fairly, there are reports and resources regarding current issues facing today's youth, along with national statistics on various subjects.

Connect for Kids
http://www.connectforkids.org

This nonprofit site provides news and information on issues affecting children and families, with over 1,500 helpful links to national and local resources.

National Association for the Education of Young Children
http://www.naeyc.org

The NAEYC Web site is a valuable tool for anyone working with young children. Also see the National Education Association site: *http://www.nea.org*.

U.S. Department of Education
http://www.ed.gov/pubs/TeachersGuide/

Government goals, projects, grants, and other educational programs are listed here as well as many links to teacher services and resources.

UNIT 1: How the World Treats Young Children

Child Care Directory: Careguide
http://www.careguide.net

Find licensed/registered child care by state, city, region, or age of child at this site. Site contains providers' pages, parents' pages, and many links.

Early Childhood Care and Development
http://www.ecdgroup.com

This site concerns international resources in support of children to age 8 and their families. It includes research and evaluation, policy matters, programming matters, and related Web sites.

Global SchoolNet Foundation
http://www.gsn.org

Access this site for multicultural education information. The site includes news for teachers, students, and parents as well as chat rooms, links to educational resources, programs, and contests and competitions.

Goals 2000: A Progress Report
http://www.ed.gov/pubs/goals/progrpt/index.html

Open this site to survey a progress report by the U.S. Department of Education on the Goals 2000 reform initiative. It provides a sense of educators' future goals.

Mid-Continent Research for Education and Learning
http://www.mcrel.org/standards-benchmarks

This site provides a listing of standards and benchmarks that include content descriptions from 112 significant subject areas and documents from across 14 content areas.

The National Association of State Boards of Education
http://www.nasbe.org/

Included on this site is an extensive overview of the No Child Left Behind Act. There are links to specific state's plans.

UNIT 2: Child Development and Families

Administration for Children and Families
http://www.dhhs.gov

This site provides information on federally funded programs that promote the economic and social well-being of families, children, and communities.

The AARP Grandparent Information Center
http://www.aarp.org/grandparents

The center offers tips for raising grandchildren, activities, health and safety, visitations, and other resources to assist grandparents.

All About Asthma
http://pbskids.org/arthur/grownups/teacherguides/health/asthma_tips.html

This is a fact sheet/activity book used to educate children about asthma. It gives tips on how to decrease asthma triggers within your house or school. It has both English and Spanish versions of some of the materials.

Changing the Scene on Nutrition
http://www.fns.usda.gov/tn/Healthy/changing.html

This is a free toolkit for parents, school administrators, and teachers to help change the attitudes toward health and nutrition in their schools.

I Am Your Child
http://www.iamyourchild.org

Rob Reiner's I Am Your Child Foundation features excellent information on child development.

Internet Resources for Education
http://web.hamline.edu/personal/kfmeyer/cla_education.html#hamline

This site, which aims for "educational collaboration," takes you to Internet links that examine virtual classrooms, trends, policy, and infrastructure development. It leads to information about school reform, multiculturalism, technology in education, and much more.

The National Academy for Child Development
http://www.nacd.org

The NACD, an international organization, is dedicated to helping children and adults reach their full potential. Its home page presents links to various programs, research, and resources into such topics as learning disabilities, ADD/ADHD, brain injuries, autism, accelerated and gifted, and other similar topic areas.

www.dushkin.com/online/

National Safe Kids Campaign
http://www.babycenter.com

This site includes an easy-to-follow milestone chart and advice on when to call the doctor.

Zero to Three
http://www.zerotothree.org

Find here developmental information on the first 3 years of life—an excellent site for both parents and professionals.

UNIT 3: Educational Practices

Canada's Schoolnet Staff Room
http://www.schoolnet.ca/home/e/

Here is a resource and link site for anyone involved in education, including special-needs educators, teachers, parents, volunteers, and administrators.

Classroom Connect
http://www.classroom.com/login/home.jhtml

A major Web site for K–12 teachers and students, this site provides links to schools, teachers, and resources online. It includes discussion of the use of technology in the classroom.

The Council for Exceptional Children
http://www.cec.sped.org/index.html

Information on identifying and teaching gifted children, attention deficit disorders, and other topics in disabilities and gifted education may be accessed at this site.

National Resource Center for Health and Safety in Child Care
http://nrc.uchsc.edu

Search through this site's extensive links to find information on health and safety in child care. Health and safety tips are provided, as are other child-care information resources.

Online Innovation Institute
http://oii.org

A collaborative project among Internet-using educators, proponents of systemic reform, content-area experts, and teachers who desire professional growth, this site provides a learning environment for integrating the Internet into educators' individual teaching styles.

Make your own Web page
http://www.teacherweb.com

Easy step by step directions for teachers at all levels to construct their own web page. Parents can log on and check out what is going on in their child's classroom.

UNIT 4: Guiding and Supporting Young Children

Child Welfare League of America (CWLA)
http://www.cwla.org

The CWLA is the United States' oldest and largest organization devoted entirely to the well-being of vulnerable children and their families. Its Web site provides links to information about issues related to morality and values in education.

You Can Handle Them All
http://www.disciplinehelp.com

This site describes different types of behavioral problems and offers suggestions for managing these problems.

Tips for Teachers
http://www.counselorandteachertips.com

This site includes links for various topics of interest to teachers such as behavior management, peer mediation, and new teacher resources.

UNIT 5: Curricular Issues

Association for Childhood Education International (ACEI)
http://www.acei.org/

This site, established by the oldest professional early childhood education organization, describes the association, its programs, and the services it offers to both teachers and families.

Early Childhood Education Online
http://www.umaine.edu/eceol/

This site gives information on developmental guidelines and issues in the field, presents tips for observation and assessment, and gives information on advocacy.

International Reading Association
http://www.reading.org

This organization for professionals who are interested in literacy contains information about the reading process and assists teachers in dealing with literacy issues.

PE Central
http://www.pecentral.org

Included in this site are developmentally appropriate physical activities for children, also containing one section dedicated to preschool physical education. It also includes resources and research in physical education.

Phi Delta Kappa
http://www.pdkintl.org

This important organization publishes articles about all facets of education. By clicking on the links in this site, for example, you can check out the journal's online archive, which has resources such as articles having to do with assessment.

Reggio Emilia
http://www.ericdigests.org/2001-3/reggio.htm

Through ERIC, link to publications related to the Reggio Emilia approach and to resources, videos, and contact information.

Teacher Quick Source
http://www.teacherquicksource.com

Originally designed to help Head Start teachers meet the child outcomes, this site can be useful to all preschool teachers. Domains can be linked to developmentally appropriate activities for classroom use.

Teachers Helping Teachers
http://www.pacificnet.net/~mandel/

Basic teaching tips, new teaching methodologies, and forums for teachers to share experiences are provided on this site. Download software and participate in chats. It features educational resources on the Web, with new ones added each week.

Tech Learning
http://www.techlearning.com

An award-winning K–12 educational technology resource, this site offers thousands of classroom and administrative tools, case studies, curricular resources, and solutions.

Awesome Library for Teachers
http://www.neat-schoolhouse.org/teacher.html

Open this page for links and access to teacher information on everything from educational assessment to general child development topics.

www.dushkin.com/online/

Future of Children
http://www.futureofchildren.org

Produced by the David and Lucille Packard Foundation, the primary purpose of this page is to disseminate timely information on major issues related to children's well-being.

Prospects: The Congressionally Mandated Study of Educational Growth and Opportunity
http://www.ed.gov/pubs/Prospects/index.html

This report analyzes cross-sectional data on language-minority and LEP students and outlines what actions are needed to improve their educational performance. Family and economic situations are addressed plus information on related reports and sites.

Busy Teacher's Cafe
http://www.busyteacherscafe.com

This is a website for early childhood educators with resource pages for everything from worksheets to classroom management.

The Educators' Network
http://www.theeducatorsnetwork.com

A very useful site for teachers at every level in every subject area. Includes lesson plans, theme units, teacher tools, rubrics, books, educational news, and much more.

Technology Help
http://www.apples4theteacher.com

This site helps teachers incorporate technology into the classroom. Full of interactive activities children can do alone, with a partner, or for full group instruction in all subject areas.

Grade Level Reading Lists
http://www.gradelevelreadinglists.org

Recommended reading lists for grades kindergarten - eight can be downloaded through this site.

We highly recommend that you review our Web site for expanded information and our other product lines. We are continually updating and adding links to our Web site in order to offer you the most usable and useful information that will support and expand the value of your Annual Editions. You can reach us at: *http://www.dushkin.com/annualeditions/.*

UNIT 1

How the World Treats Young Children

Unit Selections

Key Points to Consider

- If our nation wants to make high-quality preschool education a priority, what are some challenges we face?

- How much emphasis should be placed on academics in a preschool program?

- What is the role of play in the learning and development of a four-year-old?

- How are social disadvantage and poverty related to low achievement of young children?

- In your local school, do you see evidence among children that school is becoming more stressful?

- What are some of the benefits to children and their families of statewide universal pre-K programs?

 **Links: www.dushkin.com/online/**
These sites are annotated in the World Wide Web pages.

Child Care Directory: Careguide
http://www.careguide.net

Early Childhood Care and Development
http://www.ecdgroup.com

Global SchoolNet Foundation
http://www.gsn.org

Goals 2000: A Progress Report
http://www.ed.gov/pubs/goals/progrpt/index.html

Mid-Continent Research for Education and Learning
http://www.mcrel.org/standards-benchmarks

The National Association of State Boards of Education
http://www.nasbe.org/

The value of early childhood education is receiving unprecedented attention from public officials and policy-making groups. There are several reasons for increased attention. One is that the nation is learning that high quality programs are beneficial for young children's long-term development. Another reason is the compelling evidence from brain research that children are born learning. Yet, despite new information on the importance of early childhood, we still tend to hold onto cultural traditions about who young children are and how to care for them. This dichotomy between information and tradition results in an impasse when it comes to creating national policy related to young children. And professionals in the field are faced with the dilemma of how to convince legislators, community leaders, and business people to make the political and monetary investment needed for new research and more high quality programs.

This unit, "How the World Treats Children," includes articles that lay out national issues related to early education today. The unit begins with "Starting Right" and ends with "The 'Failure' of Head Start." In both articles, the authors describe the positive impact of preschool education and write convincingly of the need for comprehensive national policies. Also included are articles such as, "Life Way After Head Start," a *New York Times Maga-*

zine article on the impact of preschool—not just on test scores in later grades but on life long opportunities for success.

One of the most controversial issues we face in early childhood education nationally is the race achievement gap. In "Class and the Classroom," the author contends that traditional beliefs prevent us from solving our national educational challenge. Rothstein challenges us to analyze again the ways that poverty, social class, and income affect learning. He points to research that shows a pervasive "culture of under achievement" among lower class black children, a culture that is difficult to change. This author calls for a comprehensive approach to closing the achievement gap that includes more quality preschool programs, as well as infant and toddler care, health care services, and affordable housing. These large-scale economic changes must be combined with school reform in order to address the gap effectively.

The editors of this *Annual Editions* take great pleasure in finding articles on early childhood education from non-education sources. One such article, from *American Scientist,* is Henry Petroski's speech at a conference sponsored by the national Aeronautics and Space Administration. In his speech, Petroski describes the connection between children's play and engineering. He asserts if one wants to observe the future engineers of the world, they need only to watch young children at play.

Two articles in this unit examine the trend of high stakes testing and its effects on young children. "Ready to Learn" and "Too Soon to Test" deal with the conflicting opinions of professionals and policy makers on academics in preschool. At issue is whether young children should be held accountable for academic skills through traditional methods testing. When children arrive at school on test days displaying signs of stress, professional's question the wisdom of high stakes approaches to teaching and learning. Many experts warn of consequences later in life. There are those who would say school should not be fun, the purpose is to work hard and get ahead. This is one of our national cultural norms. Yet, we know that young children are more productive in school when it is a supportive and cooperative environment and where approaches to teaching and learning are developmentally effective.

The editors hope you gain benefit from reading the articles and reflecting on the important issues facing early childhood education today.

Starting Right

Building on proven strategies to promote development in very young children.

BY JOAN LOMBARDI

IN THE MID-1990S, NEWSSTANDS ACROSS THE COUNTRY BRIMMED WITH MAGAZINES touting new research on brain development, and the "science" of early-childhood development was championed from the East Room to the hearing room, from the boardroom to the living room. Yet almost a decade later, there is still a significant gap between what we know about the earliest years of life and the public policies that support families with infants and toddlers in the United States.

Why the gap? There is no simple answer; rather a combination of factors has left this country without a coherent family policy—and lagging far behind virtually all other advanced nations when it comes to support for families with children under age 3. Perhaps the strongest influence has been the cultural tradition that considers the care of very young children the sole responsibility of their parents. Any attempts to develop policies that are perceived as "interfering" with this responsibility have been taboo. Even a policy to give parents time off during the critical first year of a baby's life has been stubbornly hard to win.

Yet the sense that parents must "go it alone" is not the only thing that stands in the way of change. Traditional thinking on education still has not fully embraced the concept that children are "born learning," despite compelling evidence from the newest brain research. Similarly, our policies do not fully reflect what science teaches about the vitally important contribution of parents and caregivers to a child's education. Education reform has focused much more on what goes on inside the school building and much less on what goes on at home and in the community.

Strategies to promote the healthy development of and early education for our youngest children—starting well before school age—should be the next frontier of educa-

tion reform. We need a more cohesive set of policies that can support the earliest forms of education while respecting the range of choices parents make for their families. Along with access to prenatal and early health care, such policies would address parental leave and preparation for parenthood for all families; improved child care for working families; and access to comprehensive early-childhood services for expectant parents, babies, and toddlers at greatest risk.

IT IS WIDELY RECOGNIZED that parents need time and support to be with their newborn baby to establish the strong early bonds that lead to positive and healthy relationships. Indeed, while most industrialized countries guarantee paid parental leave, the United States is not among them. The closest we've come to a national response—the Family and Medical Leave Act of 1993—provides 12 weeks of unpaid leave and covers only about 60 percent of private-sector employees, and only about 45 percent are both covered and eligible.

Predictably, low-income working families are least likely to benefit because they can rarely afford to take unpaid leave, have jobs with the least flexibility, and have the hardest time finding quality infant care and reliable transportation. Welfare reform in the 1990s only compounded the problem, allowing states to require women with children under age 1 to participate in work activities, while funding for child care in the past few years has failed to keep up with demand.

In recent years, advocates for family and medical leave have turned to the states. In 2002, California became the first state in the nation to enact paid family leave, expanding the state disability insurance program to provide up to six weeks of partial wage-replacement benefits to workers who take time off to care for a new baby or seriously ill family member. According to the National Partnership for Women and Families, five states (and Puerto Rico) have state-administered Temporary Disability Insurance systems (or require employers to offer them). Such systems provide partial wage replacement to employees who are temporarily disabled for medical reasons, including pregnancy or birth-related medical reasons. Efforts to enact paid leave have been introduced in more than two dozen states.

One innovative solution, the At-Home Infant Care (AHIC) program, was pioneered by Minnesota and Montana in response to the lack of good infant care. AHIC gives low-income families a partial subsidy so they can remain home to care for their very young children. Minnesota families could participate if they were eligible for child-care assistance and had children under age 1. In Montana, eligibility was set at 150 percent of poverty for families with children under age 2. Parents reported both developmental and financial benefits. Despite the promise and interest in this model, though, tight budgets have hampered its progress.

Most children under age 3 have working parents. It is well-established that the quality of the infant and toddler care on which millions of these parents depend each day can affect a child's well-being. Despite this knowledge, affordable, high-quality care remains out of reach for many working parents—particularly low-income ones, whose children could benefit most from the enrichment a good program might provide. Families with very young children have the fewest child-care options and pay the highest price for care. Quality is stretched thin due to low wages, high turnover, and limited training opportunities for providers. Child-care resource and referral agencies across the country receive more calls from parents seeking affordable, quality infant care than any other type of child care. Even when child-care assistance is available, it most often does not cover the full cost of quality care.

If we are indeed committed to making top-notch education a priority for the nation's youngest children, it must start well before they reach the preschool door.

In an effort to address this national need, Congress has appropriated an additional $100 million each year since 1998 to improve the quality of infant care through the nation's main child-care program, the Child Care and Development Block Grant (CCDBG). With these funds, states have been launching new strategies, creating innovative training and credentialing for infant- and toddler-care providers, expanding family child-care networks, and developing supports for "family, friends and neighbor care"—the type most often used by parents of very young children and by low-income families. While all these efforts are important, they are only initial steps forward; much more is needed to make high-quality infant care the national priority it deserves to be.

The early Head Start program was designed with this challenge in mind. Added to the Head Start program in 1994, it was designed to offer comprehensive health, family-support, and education services to expectant parents and infants and toddlers living in poverty. In fiscal year 2003, Early Head Start served nearly 62,000 children under age 3 in more than 650 programs across the country. Services are delivered through home visits, center-based programs, or a combination of the two.

So far, the results have been promising. A rigorous evaluation of Early Head Start has shown positive impacts on children's cognitive, language, and social-emotional development—and, importantly, solid effects on their parents, too. Results were stronger when programs started during pregnancy and when standards were carefully implemented.

As is too often the case, though, too few are helped: Early Head Start still serves only 3 percent of the more than 2 million poor children under age 3 nationwide. And with poverty among very young children growing, expansion of services to infants and toddlers is more important than ever. With more and more states investing in preschool programs, the logical next step for Head Start is to expand downward. Because we know that most children enter the program already behind in language development and other skills important for school readiness, we simply can't afford to wait to start them on the right road.

There are more than 11 million infants and toddlers living in the United States. If we are indeed committed to making top-notch education a priority, it must start well before they reach the preschool door. And it must bridge partisan and ideological differences that have impeded progress for far too long. The next Congress and administration can start by expanding the Family and Medical Leave Act to provide benefits to more families, and by providing incentives to states to experiment with paid leave and programs like the At-Home Infant Care model. Reauthorization of both Head Start and the CCDBG provide important opportunities for change, too. The funding set aside for infants and toddlers in the CCDBG should be authorized and expanded, and each state should be required to have a plan to ensure better care for babies and toddlers. Head Start programs across the country should be allowed to serve expectant parents and children under age 3 if that is what their communities need.

These steps can lay the foundation of a compassionate agenda, can lead to long-term benefits, and are the most basic elements of a comprehensive approach to education reform—a goal that everyone can embrace.

JOAN LOMBARDI *is the director of The Children's Project in Washington, D.C. She served as a deputy assistant secretary for children and families and the associate commissioner of the Child Care Bureau during the Clinton administration.*

Investing in Preschool

Money spent on early childhood education is money well spent

By Gerald W. Bracey

"There are problems we do not know how to solve, but this is not one of them." *Washington Post* columnist David Broder wrote in January 2002. "The evidence that high-quality education beginning at age 3 or 4 will pay lifetime dividends is overwhelming. The only question is whether we will make the needed investment."

This statement stands in rather stark contrast to one by educational psychologist Arthur Jensen in 1969: "Compensatory education has been tried, and it apparently has failed." Apparently, the operative word in Jensen's comment was "apparently."

The years between the Jensen and Broder statements have produced a great deal of evidence about the effects of early childhood education, and the evidence is indeed overwhelming. It is also less well-known than it ought to be, and it certainly has not had the policy of influence it should have. The three major, well-controlled studies of early childhood education differ in some respects but produced highly similar results. In addition, long-term positive outcomes have been found from Head Start. A careful look at these research findings will show why it pays to provide preschool education to all children.

The Perry Preschool study

The best known and longest term of these studies is referred to as the High/Scope Perry Preschool Project. From 1962 through 1965, 123 African-American children whose parents applied to a preschool program in Ypsilanti, Mich., were randomly assigned to either receive preschool or not (the program did not have room for all applicants).

Random assignment is important in research design. It does not guarantee that the groups will be the same, but it eliminates any systematic bias—only chance differences will occur. Fifty-eight children were assigned to the experimental group, 65 to the control group.

Children who entered the program in 1962 received one year of preschool at age 4. In subsequent years, children received two years of the program at ages 3 and 4. All 123 students re-

ceived the same sequence of tests and interviews over the years. Testers, interviewers, and subsequent teachers did not know whether the children had been in the experimental group or the control group.

The parents were screened for socioeconomic status, and the children were given the Stanford-Binet IQ test. The children had IQs between 60 and 90 and no evidence of physical handicap. The parents had completed 9.4 years of school, on average, and only 20 percent had completed high school—fewer than the average for all African Americans, which was 33 percent. The half-day program lasted for eight months and included weekly 90-minute home visits by project staff.

The Perry project used a curriculum developed at the High/Scope Educational Research Foundation based on the concepts of Jean Piaget and other theorists who view children as active learners. The teachers rarely assessed specific knowledge, as might happen in a classroom using direct instruction; instead, they asked questions that allowed children to generate conversations with adults.

Instruction focused on what the curriculum developers considered 10 categories of key preschool experiences: creative representation, language and literacy, social relations and personal initiative, movement, music, classification, seriation (creating series and patterns), number, space, and time. The school day included individual, small-group, and large-group activities.

The study so far has looked at the children as they moved through school and at ages 19 and 27. A study of the adults at age 40 is in progress.

What the Perry study found

By the time they were 19, the students who attended preschool had higher graduation rates and were less likely to have been in special education. They also scored higher on the Adult Performance Level Survey, a test from the American College Testing Program designed to provide simulations of real-life situations. Researchers estimated that—in constant 1981 dollars—A K-12 education cost $34,813 for preschoolers and $41,895 for those who had not attended preschool.

By the time the students turned 27, some 71 percent of the preschool group had attained a high school diploma or GED, compared to 54 percent of the control group. Forty-two percent of the preschool children reported making more than $2,000 a month, compared to only 6 percent of those in the control group. Thirty-six percent of the preschoolers, but only 13 percent of the control group, owned their own homes. The preschool group had longer and more stable marriages.

Preschool did not turn the kids into angels, but it made them more at ease in society. The control group's females had an out-of-wedlock birth rate of 85 percent, compared to 57 percent of the preschool group. Control group members suffered twice as many arrests as preschoolers, and five times as many of the control group (35 percent) had been arrested five or more times. Two females in the control group had been murdered.

At the time, researchers estimated a cost-benefit ratio of $7.16-to-$1—that is, considering the cost of the preschool vs. the cost of special education, retention in grade, and incarceration and considering other benefits of preschool, the public saved more than $7 for every $1 invested in preschool. In contrast, between 1958 and 1981, the Dow Jones Industrial Average had little more than doubled, and from 1962 to 1985 it rose by only 64 percent.

The Chicago study

A similar cost-benefit ratio emerged from a later study, the Chicago Child-Parent Center Program (CPC). In 2001, when the preschoolers were 21, researchers estimated that, factoring in the participants' reduced crime rates (17 percent vs. 25 percent for those in the control group), higher high school completion rates (61 percent vs. 52 percent), and fewer special education placements (14 percent vs. 25 percent)—plus a significant difference in retentions in grade—the program had returned $47,549 to the public.

The one-year program cost $6,788 per child in constant 1998 dollars, yielding a ratio of almost precisely 7-to-1 ($47,549-to-$6,788). An intervention program initiated after children had begun school returned a much smaller amount.

The CPC study was much larger than the High/Scope Perry Preschool Project, consisting of 989 children who received preschool education, 179 who began kindergarten with no preschool, and 374 who were enrolled in other preschool programs. However, students in the CPC were not randomly assigned.

Because the CPC program was offered in 20 centers, it was more diffuse than the Perry program. Initially, teachers had wide latitude over what materials to incorporate, although later they all incorporated a program developed through the Chicago Board of Education. This program emphasized three general areas of development: body image and gross motor skills, perceptual-motor and arithmetic skills, and language. The language skills taught ranged from the auditory discrimination of sounds to building sentences to story comprehension and verbal problem solving. Arthur Reynolds, the senior researcher in the

project, classified seven of the 20 centers as teacher oriented, 10 as child oriented, and three as giving equal emphasis to teacher-initiated and child-initiated activities.

Both the Perry and CPC projects emphasized parent involvement with the children. Project staff made home visits, and parents often accompanied children on field trips.

The Abecedarian study

Researchers at the University of North Carolina, Chapel Hill, conducted the third study, called the Abecedarian Project. It differed from the first two in that it identified children at birth, and those who participated in the study received full-day day care for 50 weeks a year.

Early interventions consisted of "age-appropriate" adult-child interactions, such as talking to children, showing them toys or pictures, and offering infants a chance to react to sights or sounds in the environment. As children grew older, the content of the interactions became more conceptual and skill oriented and, for older preschoolers, more group oriented. Some students participated in the program only until school began; some until age 8. A school-only intervention was also available to another group of children once they reached kindergarten or first grade. For this group, parents were provided with activities and encouraged to use them with their children.

The children in a separate control group were not completely left to fend for themselves. Researchers supplied them with iron-rich formula, reducing the possibility that differences in nutrition could affect brain growth. Social work and crisis intervention services were also available to control-group families. If assessments indicated developmental lags, the family was referred to a relevant agency for follow-up. A number of families sent their children to other preschool programs available in the area. It seems likely that these various programs provided at least some members of the control group benefits similar to those provided by the Abecedarian program. This means that any differences between the preschool and non-preschool group are smaller than they would be if the control group had attended no program at all.

Of the 111 children in the original study, 104 took part in a follow-up at age 21 (four children had died, one had been withdrawn from the study, one had developed a severe physical condition that prevented inclusion, and one declined to take part).

Young adults who had received preschool intervention had completed more years of schooling (12.2 vs. 11.6), but this was largely due to the high number of females, who are less likely to drop out of school than males. More were still in school (42 percent vs. 20 percent), and more had enrolled in four-year colleges (35.9 percent vs. 13.7 percent). Forty-seven percent of the preschool group had skilled jobs, such as electrician, compared to 27 percent of the controls. Those in the preschool group were less likely to smoke or use marijuana but no less likely to use alcohol or indulge in binge drinking. Cocaine use was denied by virtually all participants in both groups.

Tests administered at ages 8, 12, 15, and 21 showed that the program paid off in both reading and mathematics. Specifically, for children who participated for eight years, the program had a large impact on reading, ranging from an effect size of 1.04 at age 8 to .79 at age 21. Effect sizes for math ranged from .64 at age 8 to .42 at age 21. (An "effect size" is a metric for analyzing the impact of a program or intervention. The greater the effect size, the greater the impact.)

For those receiving only a preschool intervention, the effect sizes in reading ranged from .75 at age 8 to .28 at age 21. For math, the impact grew over time, being .27 at age 8 and .73 at age 21. Smaller effect sizes were seen for those who had been in a school-only program. In reading the effect size ranged from .28 at age 8 to .11 at age 21. Math effects went from .11 to .26 over the same period.

What about Head Start?

Some have discounted the results from these three studies because they are model programs and perhaps cannot be generalized or because they consider the effects small. In their controversial book *The Bell Curve,* Richard J. Herrnstein and Charles Murray managed to dismiss the studies on both counts—and to dismiss Head Start at the same time. After concluding that Head Start programs neither raise intelligence nor display "sleeper effects" (higher graduation rates, less crime, improved employability), the authors had this to say: "Perry Preschool resembled the average Head Start program as a Ferrari resembles the family sedan.... The effects [from Perry Preschool] are small and some of them fall short of statistical significance. They hardly justify investing billions of dollars in run-of-the-mill Head Start programs."

Several rejoinders to the Herrnstein-Murray contentions are available. One can point to longer-term effects now displayed by the three programs (*The Bell Curve* was published in 1994). Or one can point to the effect sizes produced by the Abecedarian and Perry projects (effect sizes have not been published for the CPC program). Not even Herrnstein (were he alive) or Murray would call those effects small.

(Labeling an effect size small, medium, or large is a matter of judgment—there is no formula for such a calculation, no point decisively dividing middle from small or large from middle. Most would call the preschool-only treatment effects in the Perry project "moderate.")

One can also point to studies that show that "run-of-the-mill" Head Start programs, as varied as they might be, do produce long-term results. Researchers looking at such outcomes found that white students who attended Head Start were more likely to finish high-school and attend four-year college. The trend for African-American students was not significant, although they were less likely to have had run-ins with the law. For both races, there also appeared to be a spillover effect to younger siblings. The young brothers and sisters of students who attended Head Start do slightly better in school and are significantly less likely to have been arrested.

The lack of a significant achievement trend for African American students themselves could be discouraging. However, the same researchers found in another study that African

Americans who attended Head Start also attended schools that had lower test scores than did other African Americans. For whatever reason, this was not true for white students. Thus, the implication is that long-term effects are not seen for African Americans because of the quality of their schooling after Head Start—not because Head Start itself is ineffective. In connection with other findings of preschool effects, this result points to the need to provide for high-quality preschool experiences for minority children while simultaneously improving their schools.

Taken together, the focused research and the Head Start research affirm Broder's conclusion. We know how to provide these services, but we're not doing it. According to *Cellblocks or Classrooms? The Funding of Higher Education and Corrections and Its Impact on African-American Men,* a study released in August 2002 by the Washington-based Justice Policy Institute, the increase in state spending on corrections between 1985 and 2000 was twice what it was on higher education ($20 billion vs. $10.7 billion). And, the study reported, there are now more African-American men in jail than in colleges and universities.

Something as remote from adulthood as preschool affects the odds of landing in jail in favor of both the individual and society. And that's not all. About the same time as the Justice Policy Institute study was released, *The New York Times* reported a side-effect of welfare reform: the "no-parent family." Many more mothers now have jobs, but this leaves their children with no caretakers. The kids are shuttled around to relatives and friends. Obviously these children could benefit from good preschool programs. The question is, as Broder asked, do we have the will to make the investment?

Gerald W. Bracey (gbracey@erols.com) is an associate with the High-Scope Educational Research Foundation and an associate professor of education at George Mason University, Fairfax, Va.

Resources

Bernstein, Nina. Side Effect of Welfare Law: The No-Parent Family," *New York Times,* July 29, 2002.

Berrueta-Clement, John B., Lawrence J. Schweinhart, W. Steven Barnett, Ann S. Epstein, and David P. Weikart. *Changed Lives: The Effects of the Perry Preschool Program on Youths Through Age 19.* Ypsilanti, Mich.: High/Scope Educational Research Foundation, 1984.

Campbell, Frances A., Craig T. Ramey, Elizabeth Pungello, Joseph Sparling, and Shari Miller-Johnson. "Early Childhood Education: Young Adult Outcomes for the Abecedarian Project." *Applied Developmental Science,* vol. 6, 2002, pp. 42-57.

Campbell, Frances A., Elizabeth P. Pungello, Shari Miller-Johnson, Margaret Burchinal, and Craig T. Ramey. "The Development of Cognitive and Academic Abilities: Growth Curves from an Early Childhood Experiment." *Developmental Psychology,* vol. 37, 2001, pp. 231-242.

Currie, Janet, and Duncan Campbell. "School Quality and the Longer-Term Effects of Head Start," *Journal of Human Resources,* Fall 2000, pp. 755-774.

Garces, Eliana, Duncan Thomas, and Janet Currie. "Longer-Term Effects of Head Start." National Bureau of Economic Research,

Working Paper 8054, December 2000. www.nber.org/papers/w8054.

Justice Policy Institute. *Cellblocks or Classrooms? The Funding of Higher Education and Corrections and Its Impact on African American Men.* Washington, D.C.: Justice Policy Institute, August 2002. www.justicepolicy.org.

Reynolds, Arthur J., Judy A. Temple, Dylan L. Robertson, and Emily A. Mann. "Age 21 Benefit-Cost Analysis of the Chicago Child-Parent Center Program." Paper presented to the Society for Prevention Research, Madison, Wis., May 31-June 2, 2001.

Reynolds, Arthur J., Judy A. Temple, Dylan L. Robertson, and Emily A. Mann. "Long-Term Effects of an Early Childhood Intervention on Educational Achievement and Juvenile Arrest. *Journal of the American Medical Association,* May 9, 2001.

Schweinhart, Lawrence J., Helen V. Barnes, and David P. Weikart. *Significant Benefits: The High/Scope Perry Preschool Study Through Age 27.* Ypsilanti, Mich.: High/Scope Educational Research Foundation, 1993.

Preschool: The Most Important Grade

Research findings confirm the long-term benefits of early education and offer some options for integrating the existing patchwork of U.S. public and private preK programs into a uniform system that provides a high-quality early education to all young children.

W. Steven Barnett and Jason T. Hustedt

The early education system in the United States has recently experienced tremendous growth, a trend that has enabled most children to gain access to some sort of early education program. Unfortunately, U.S. preschool education programs are generally mediocre and inconsistent, and the best programs are too expensive for most U.S. families to afford. A recent *USA Today* article declared that

> We can, and should, be creating a preschool system that would be good enough for everyone. Public preschools should be built the same way we constructed our highway system: the same road available to all Americans, rich and poor. (Merrow, 2002)

The Status of U.S. Early Education

Three-fourths of young children in the United States participate in a preschool program. These programs operate under a wide range of auspices, from private organizations to public schools and Head Start, a federal government education initiative that has provided children from low-income families with free access to early education programs since 1965. Until recently, most statewide early education programs followed Head Start's lead and targeted children of low socioeconomic status or children who were otherwise "at risk." In the past decade, however, states have developed more options for children from middle- and upper-income families to receive a free preschool education.

In 1995, Georgia introduced the first statewide universal preK program, a model that offers a free preschool education to all 4-year-old children, regardless of family income. New York and Oklahoma soon followed with their own universal preK programs, and in 2002, Florida voters approved a constitutional amendment stipulating that all 4-year-olds in the state be offered a free preK education by 2005. As the early education movement continues to gather steam and as universal preK programs take shape across the country, it is important to take stock of what we know about the long-term benefits and implementation of education for young children.

The Benefits of Early Education

Research has established that preschool education can produce substantial gains in children's learning and development (Barnett, 2002), but researchers disagree about whether such gains are permanent. Most research on early education has focused on its effects on the IQ scores of economically disadvantaged children and has found few preschool programs that have produced lasting IQ score gains (Barnett, 1998). Even the more effective programs tend to show positive results in the short rather than long term.

But studies also find that preschool education produces persistent gains on achievement test scores, along with fewer occurrences of grade retention and placement in special education programs (Barnett & Camilli, 2002). Other long-term benefits from preschool education include increased high school graduation rates and decreased crime and delinquency rates.

Recent research has shown that preschool education is a sound investment—academically, socially, and economically. Three studies—which examined the High/Scope Perry Preschool program, the Abecedarian Early Childhood Intervention program, and the Title I Chicago Child-Parent Centers—provide comprehensive evidence that academic and other benefits from preschool education can yield economic benefits that far outweigh the costs of intensive, high-quality preschool programs (Barnett, 1996; Masse & Barnett, 2002; Reynolds, Temple, Robertson, & Mann, 2002). These studies identified several long-term economic benefits of early education, finding that both former preschool participants and taxpayers can benefit from public investments in preschool education. For example, former preschool participants were less likely to cost taxpayers money in the long term for such public services as

- Schooling—Participants were less likely to be retained in grade or placed in special education.
- Welfare—As adults, participants were more likely to get better jobs and earn more money.
- The criminal justice system—Participants were less likely to break laws or participate in other delinquent acts.

These positive effects have far-reaching benefits. Although preschool education research has largely focused on the benefits of early education for children in poverty, several child care studies indicate that high-quality, effective early education programs improve the learning and development of all children (Shonkoff & Phillips, 2000). And problems that we tend to associate with students from low-income families—grade retention and high drop-out rates, for example—are more common among middle-class students than we often assume. For example, more than 1 in 10 children in the middle three quintiles of the U.S. income distribution are retained in grade, and the same proportion drop out of high school (National Center for Education Statistics, 1997). High-quality preschool programs might reduce such problems for middle-class students by 25 to 50 percent, again saving taxpayers' money in the long term.

The three successful programs discussed above, however, all had higher standards for education than do most typical early education programs today, many of which hire underqualified teachers and pay those teachers salaries that average less than half of a public school teacher's salary (Barnett, 2003). Teachers from each of the successful programs had credentials and received compensation equivalent to those of public school teachers. In addition, each program had relatively small class sizes and strong education goals. Unfortunately, current state child care standards are extremely low. Head Start requires that only half of its teachers have a two-year college degree, and even some state universal preK programs have lower standards for teacher qualifications than do public schools.

New Evaluations of Head Start

Head Start's research record shows consistent evidence of positive effects, but questions remain about the extent to which that research generalizes across variations both in different Head Start programs and in the children and families that Head Start serves. In recent years, research studies have attempted to provide more information on the services that these programs offer and on the progress of the programs' participants.

Shortly after the inception of Early Head Start—a program established in 1994 that seeks to improve the long-term outcomes of infants and toddlers in poverty by providing comprehensive services to both the children and their parents—the Administration on Children, Youth, and Families funded a multisite, randomized trial to evaluate Early Head Start and its effects on children and families. Recently released results (Love et al., 2002) comparing 2- and 3-year-old Early Head Start participants and their parents with a control group of demographically equivalent nonparticipant children and parents suggest that this program has a variety of positive im-

pacts. Participants earned higher scores on assessments of cognitive and language development and were less aggressive than were nonparticipants. Early Head Start parents achieved positive outcomes as well: They gained self-sufficiency through job training and education activities and improved on parenting assessments. Although effects were relatively small, the broad range of effects suggests that they might be important in the aggregate.

In 2002, data collection began for a large-scale, randomized experimental study to provide a similar look at the longitudinal effects of Head Start, mandated by the U.S. Congress as part of the program's 1998 reauthorization. The results of this study will provide stronger, more conclusive findings about Head Start's effects on children and families than current research such as the Family and Child Experiences Survey (FACES) (Zill et al., 2001). FACES tells us that Head Start children remain significantly behind their more advantaged peers, particularly in vocabulary. But FACES cannot tell us how much they gain from participating in Head Start.

Ongoing State Programs

As state initiatives for early education have grown, researchers have turned greater attention toward integrating existing preschool programs into more uniform state programs. Typically, universal preK and other broad state programs seek to build on and combine existing private and public programs into a more coordinated system with consistent standards. A recent study by the Center for the Child Care Workforce (Bellm, Burton, Whitebook, Broatch, & Young, 2002) examined large, publicly funded preK initiatives under way in Georgia, New York, Texas, California, and Chicago. Although only the Georgia program currently provides universal, statewide access to preK programs, comparisons across these programs help illuminate implementation issues that will become important as more states move toward universal preK.

Recent research has shown that preschool education is a sound investment—academically, socially, and economically.

The study found that a two-tiered system emerged wherever public and private programs participated together. Teachers in preK programs sponsored by public schools

were better educated, earned higher salaries, and had lower turnover in their jobs than teachers in privately operated programs. Private program providers voiced concern that teachers took private program positions only as stepping stones to more lucrative jobs in the public schools. Head Start directors frequently voiced similar concerns, because their teachers earn roughly half the salary of public school teachers. Substantial evidence shows that all of these advantages for public programs lead to higher education quality and improved learning and development for children (Barnett, 2003). States must face the challenge of successfully developing a universal preK program that delivers uniformly high-quality education services to all children by mixing publicly and privately operated programs funded with federal, state, and local government dollars.

Implications for the Future

As universal preK becomes more popular in the United States, we will need to clarify and refine the role of Head Start. With an annual budget of more than $6 billion, Head Start is by far the largest source of public funds for preschool education, employing one in five U.S. preschool teachers. Head Start has accumulated substantial expertise over the years in meeting the needs of at-risk children and families. But because Head Start targets children in poverty and is subject to an extensive list of federal standards regulating such factors as program governance, performance, and accountability, it will be difficult to integrate it into a state system serving all children.

To respond to the increasing availability of universal preK programs, Head Start could shift its focus to provide specialized services to children ages 3 and younger from low-income families. In states or communities that already provide all children with access to free universal preK, Head Start could use its resources more effectively by providing children in poverty with appropriate education preparation *before* they enter a preK program. This change can be accomplished within existing federal legislation; whereas current law mandates that Head Start provide a wide variety of services to low-income parents and their children, it does not mandate that the program focus primarily on 4-year-olds. In fact, Head Start already serves many 3-year-olds and even younger children.

Another option is for Head Start to merge with state universal preK programs. Such a move would permit states to incorporate Head Start funding, expertise, staff, and facilities into universal preK, thereby reducing costs to the state and making maximum use of existing resources. Local or state education agencies could make contracts with Head Start and provide a partial payment for each child eligible for Head Start (allowing Head Start to meet higher state requirements for teacher qualifications, for example) and a full payment for each child ineligible for Head Start (allowing Head Start to become a more socially integrated program).

Although some states already contract with Head Start as part of their state preK programs, others do not. Some modification or waiver of federal Head Start regulations is necessary to enable Head Start to effectively operate under contracts with state programs. For example, Head Start policy councils and local boards of education constitute potentially incompatible governance structures. To avoid such problems, the federal government could raise the education standards of Head Start and provide sufficient funds for Head Start to meet state preK standards. These changes could be conducted uniformly or on a state-by-state basis, and would allow Head Start to effectively "merge" without accepting state or local funds and governance.

Other ways to merge Head Start with state universal preK might provide even greater flexibility. One solution would be to allow Head Start dollars to follow the child to any program participating in universal preK (public or private) chosen by the parents. Another option would be for Head Start to begin providing supplemental services to Head Start-eligible children attending universal preK programs while withdrawing from the provision of direct classroom services. These children would then receive the advantages associated with participating in both Head Start and universal preK.

All of these approaches would address a longstanding issue for Head Start, which is that its eligibility requirements effectively isolate children in poverty from their more economically advantaged peers. A challenge for each of the approaches, especially the most flexible approach, is to ensure that Head Start and state preK standards are maintained or raised where necessary for more effective early education. These options would also require changes in federal legislation, and the 2003 reauthorization of Head Start provides an opportunity for creative thinking about how Head Start might best respond to the trend toward universal preK.

The Most Important Grade

Senator Zell Miller, the former governor of Georgia, has called preschool "the most important grade." The U.S. public agrees, judging from the steadily growing attendance rates and state movements toward universal preK, including the overwhelming support that passed Florida's universal preK ballot initiative in 2002. Many research studies have confirmed preschool's positive effects on school readiness and school success, especially for our most disadvantaged children.

Yet preschool will fulfill its promise only if educators take on the hard work of developing and implementing sound policy. This challenge will require higher standards, greater accountability, and increased public funding. It will also require creative new approaches to move from the current uneven patchwork of private and public programs to uniformly and highly effective universal preK programs that provide a high-quality early education for every child in the United States.

References

Barnett, W. S. (1996). *Lives in the balance: Age 27 benefit-cost analysis of the High/Scope Perry Preschool Program.* Ypsilanti, MI: High/Scope Press.

Barnett, W. S. (1998). Long-term effects on cognitive development and school success. In W. S. Barnett & S. S. Boocock (Eds.), *Early care and education for children in poverty: Promises, programs, and long-term results* (pp. 11–44). Albany, NY: SUNY Press.

Barnett, W. S. (2002). Early childhood education. In A. Molnar (Ed.), *School reform proposals: The research evidence* (pp. 1–26). Greenwich, CT: Information Age Publishing, Inc.

Barnett, W. S. (2003). Better teachers, better preschools: Student achievement linked to teacher qualifications. *Preschool Policy Matters* (No. 2). New Brunswick, NJ: National Institute for Early Education Research, Rutgers University.

Barnett, W. S., & Camilli, G. (2002). Compensatory preschool education, cognitive development, and "race." In J. M. Fish (Ed.), *Race and intelligence: Separating science from myth* (pp. 369–406). Mahwah, NJ: Erlbaum.

Bellm, D., Burton, A., Whitebook, M., Broatch, L., & Young, M. P. (2002). *Inside the preK classroom: A study of staffing and stability in state-funded prekindergarten programs.* Washington, DC: Center for the Child Care Workforce.

Love, J. M., Kisker, E. E., Ross, C. M., Schochet, P. Z., Brooks-Gunn, J., Paulsell, D., Boller, K., Constantine, J., Vogel, C., Fuligni, A. S., & Brady-Smith, C. (2002). *Making a difference in the lives of infants and toddlers and their families: The impacts of Early Head Start. Executive summary.* Washington, DC: Administration on Children, Youth, and Families, U.S. Department of Health and Human Services.

Masse, L. N., & Barnett, W. S. (2002). *A benefit-cost analysis of the Abecedarian Early Childhood Intervention.* New Brunswick, NJ: National Institute for Early Education Research, Rutgers University.

Merrow, J. (2002, July 17). European preschools should embarrass USA. *USA Today*, p. 15A.

National Center for Education Statistics. (1997). *Dropout rates in the United States: 1995.* Washington, DC: U.S. Department of Education.

Reynolds, A., Temple, J., Robertson, D., & Mann, E. (2002). *Age 21 Cost-benefit analysis of the Title I Chicago Child-Parent Centers.* Madison, WI: University of Wisconsin (Institute for Research on Poverty Discussion Paper #1245-02).

Shonkoff, J., & Phillips, D. (Eds.). (2000). *From neurons to neighborhoods: The science of early child development.* Washington, DC: National Academies Press.

Zill, N., Resnick, G., Kim, K., McKey, R. H., Clark, C., Pai-Samant, S., Connell, D., Vaden-Kiernan, M., O'Brien, R., & D'Elio, M. A. (2001). *Head Start FACES: Longitudinal findings on program performance. Third progress report.* Washington, DC: Administration on Children, Youth, and Families, U.S. Department of Health and Human Services.

W. Steven Barnett (sbarnett@nieer.org) is Director and **Jason T. Hustedt** (jhustedt@nieer.org) is an assistant research professor at the National Institute for Early Education Research, 120 Albany St., Ste. 500, New Brunswick, NJ 08901; http://nieer.org.

From *Educational Leadership*, April 2003, pp. 54-57. Reprinted with permission of the Association for Supervision and Curriculum Development. © 2003 by ASCD. All rights reserved. The Association for Supervision and Curriculum Development is a worldwide community of educators advocating sound policies and sharing best practices to achieve the success of each learner. To learn more, visit ASCD at www.ascd.org

Life *Way* After Head Start

A new study turns up some surprising midlife benefits of preschooling for poor children

By David L. Kirp

The power of education to level the playing field has long been an American article of faith. Education is the "balance wheel of the social machinery," argued Horace Mann, the *first great advocate of public schooling*. "It prevents being poor." But that belief has been undermined by research findings—seized on ever since by skeptics—that federal programs like Head Start, designed to benefit poor children, actually have little long-term impact.

Now evidence from an experiment that has lasted nearly four decades may revive Horace Mann's faith. "Lifetime Effects: The High/Scope Perry Preschool Study Through Age 40," was released earlier this week. It shows that an innovative early education program can make a marked difference in the lives of poor minority youngsters—not just while they are in school but for decades afterward. The 123 participants in this experiment, says David Ellwood, dean of the Kennedy School of Government at Harvard and an architect of the Clinton administration's original welfare reform plan, "may be the most powerfully influential group in the recent history of social science."

The life stories of the Perry students have been tracked since they left preschool in the 1960's. Like so much in education research, the findings have been known mainly in professional circles. But this latest dispatch from the field, confirming the remarkable and enduring impact of a long-ago experience, should alter the way we understand preschool and, maybe, the way society invests in the future.

The study began without fanfare in the fall of 1962, several years before Head Start was conceived. In the mostly blue-collar town Ypsilanti, Mich., 21 3- and 4-year-old children started preschool. All of them, as well as 37 more youngsters who enrolled over the next three years, were black. They came from poor families, and the South Side neighborhood, with its rundown public housing and high crime rates, was a rough place to grow up.

Based on past experience, it was a near certainty that most of these kids would fail in school. During the previous decade, not a single class in the Perry elementary school had ever scored above

the 10th percentile on national achievement tests, while across town, in the school that served the children of well-off professionals, no class had ever scored below the 90th percentile.

The reformers who developed the High/Scope Perry model hoped that exposure at an early age to a program emphasizing cognitive development could rewrite this script. Most children attended Perry for two years, three hours a day, five days a week. The curriculum emphasized problem-solving rather than unstructured play or "repeat after me" drills. The children were viewed as active learners, not sponges; a major part of their daily routine involved planning, carrying out and reviewing what they were learning. Teachers were well trained and decently paid, and there was a teacher for every five youngsters. They made weekly home visits to parents, helping them teach their own children. "The message was, 'Read to your child,'" one woman, whose daughter went to Perry in 1962, remembered. "If you read the newspaper, put your child on your lap, read out loud and ask her, 'What did I just read?' When you take her to the grocery store, have her count the change."

Even though prosperous children had thrived in similar settings for well over a century, 3-year-olds from poverty backgrounds had never had the same chance. Leading developmental psychologists cautioned against the idea. Such an intellectually rigorous regime, they argued, could actually harm such children by asking too much of them.

Leading psychologists cautioned against rigorous preschools, arguing that they could harm poor children by asking too much of them.

David Weikart, the moving force behind Perry Preschool, was not convinced. The experts had a theory but no evidence, and Weikart decided to conduct an experiment. From a group of 123 South Side neighborhood children, 58 were randomly assigned to the Perry program, while the rest, identical in virtually all respects, didn't attend preschool. Random assignment is the research gold standard because the "treatment"—in this case, preschool—best explains any subsequent differences between the two groups.

Early results were discouraging. In reading and arithmetic, the preschoolers' achievement scores at 7 and 8 weren't much better than the control group's, and while the preschoolers' IQ scores spiked, that difference soon disappeared. Those results were consistent with the dispiriting conclusion of a 1969 nationwide evaluation of Head Start. That study's key finding—that the boost in test scores recorded by Head Start children faded by second grade—was widely interpreted to mean that Head Start and, by implication, most other early childhood education programs for poor kids, were a waste of time.

But in Ypsilanti the researchers didn't give up. They collected data every year from age 3 through 11, then at ages 14, 15, 19, 27 and now 40—an astonishingly long time span in the research annals. Just as astonishingly, they have kept track of 97 percent of the surviving group. "I've found people on the streets, gone to crack houses where there were AK-47's," said Van Loggins, a gym teacher who coached many of the participants when they were teenagers and who has been interviewing them for 25 years. "I'm bilingual—ghetto and English."

Not only has the Perry study set records for longevity, but it also asks the truly pertinent question: what is the impact of preschool, not on the test scores of 7-year-olds but on their life chances? The answer is positive—a well-designed program really works.

As they progressed through school, the Perry children were less likely to be assigned to a special education class for the mentally retarded. Their attitude toward school was also better, and their parents were more enthusiastic about their youngsters' schooling. Their high-school grade point average was higher. By age 19, two-thirds had graduated from high school, compared with 45 percent of those who didn't attend preschool.

Most remarkably, the impact of those preschool years still persists. By almost any measure we might care about—education, income, crime, family stability—the contrast with those who didn't attend Perry is striking. When they were 27, the preschool group scored higher on tests of literacy. Now they are in their 40's, many with children and even grandchildren of their own. Nearly twice as many have earned college degrees (one has a Ph.D.). More of them have jobs: 76 percent versus 62 percent. They are more likely to own their home, own a car and have a savings account. They are less likely to have been on welfare. They earn considerably more—$20,800 versus $15,300—and that difference pushes them well above the poverty line.

The crime statistics reveal similarly significant differences. Compared with the control group, fewer preschoolers have gone on to be arrested for violent crimes, drug-related crimes or property crimes. Only about half as many (28 percent versus 52 percent) have been sentenced to prison or jail. Preschool also seems to have affected their decisions about family life. More of the males in the Perry contingent have been married (68 percent versus 51 percent, though they are also more likely than those who didn't attend Perry to have been married more than once) and almost twice as many have raised their own children (57 percent versus 30 percent). These men report fewer serious complaints about their health and are less likely to use drugs.

The newest report attaches a dollar-and-cents figure to this good news. Economists estimate that the return to society is more than $250,000 (calculated in 2000 dollars) on an investment of just $15,166—that's 17 dollars for every dollar invested.

There are no miracles here. Not everyone who attended Perry became a model citizen—the crime figures alone make that plain—and some of those who didn't attend preschool have fared well. But because their opportunities are so constricted, the odds are stacked against kids who grow up in neighborhoods like Ypsilanti's South Side. Bluntly put, these are the children of whom we expect the least—and overall, the life histories of the control group confirm those expectations.

By contrast, many of those who went to Perry found their way to more stable lives. One graduate, a sales manager, has moved back to the South Side neighborhood, where he devotes much of his time to his church group, "giving back" to the community. "I'm still using the discipline of school," he said. "The harder you work in school or in life, the more you get out of it." One Perry alum said that when she was in her mid-20's, living on welfare and "borrowing" from her mother, she "woke up one day to decide that was just wrong. I apologized to my mother and went to work in the factory. When I had the money, I bought Mom all new living room furniture. I stopped dating the wrong kind of guys, and eventually I got married." Now she's a union leader, and when she had children of her own, there was no doubt they'd go to preschool.

The contrast between those who attended Perry and those who didn't is striking.

Why did Perry have such an impact? Though the data can't provide a definitive answer, a plausible interpretation is that the experience proved to be a timely intervention, altering the arc of these children's lives. Preschool gave them the intellectual tools to do better in school. When they succeeded academically, they became more committed to education, and so they stayed on. Then, because a diploma opened up new economic opportunities, crime proved a less appealing alternative.

The strategy first developed at Perry is now packaged as the High/Scope curriculum and is widely used across the nation. Other well-conceived preschool initiatives have also generated impressive long-term results, including the Chicago school district's Child-Parent Center Program, which brings mothers and relatives into the schools, and the Carolina Abecedarian Project, in which intervention begins during the very first weeks of an infant's life and carries on until kindergarten.

These successes have given ammunition to those who champion expanded preschool opportunities—not just for poor children but for all children. Oklahoma and Georgia have been leaders in the movement for universal prekindergarten, and two years ago, Florida became the first state to pass a constitutional amendment requiring "high quality" preschool for all 4-year-olds. "I testified in Florida," said Evelyn Moore, one of the original teachers at Perry Preschool, who is now president of the National Black Child Development Institute. "The research has been vital in getting people to understand why early childhood education matters." Give us the child to age 7, the Jesuits say, and we'll give you the man. Give us the child at age 3, these findings suggest, and with quality preschool it's possible to work wonders.

David L. Kirp is a professor of public policy at the University of California at Berkeley and the author of "Shakespeare, Einstein and the Bottom Line: The Marketing of Higher Education."

ready to learn

What the Head Start debate about early academics means for your schools

By Kathleen Vail

the 4-year-olds at the Margaret H. Cone Head Start Center live in one of the most depressed and crime-plagued neighborhoods in Dallas. Most come from single-parent families, and many of their mothers and fathers did not graduate from high school.

But when these children leave the center, they're ready for elementary school. And they do some astonishing things when they get to Julia C. Frazier Elementary, a K-3 school that has earned exemplary ratings for the past two years despite a 97 percent poverty rate.

By third grade, the Cone graduates outscore their peers on local and national reading tests. In 2002-03, 90 percent of the third-grade Cone graduates at Frazier read at or above grade level on the national Stanford-9 exam. Two years ago, every Cone graduate third-grader passed the Texas assessment tests in reading and math.

How can children from such overwhelming poverty score so high on these standardized tests? Cone's literacy enrichment program, developed a decade ago, is at least partly responsible. LEAP, as it is called, does not focus on worksheets for 4-year-olds or require children to learn concepts and skills before they are developmentally ready.

"I don't want to push any child," says Nell Carvell, who designed the program and now serves as the director of the Language Enrichment Activities Program and Head Start Initiatives at Southern Methodist University in Dallas. "I do think that's inappropriate. But if you give them an opportunity under guidance to play with these things, it's amazing how much they learn."

An academic jumpstart

How much kids should be able to learn at 4 years old is at the heart of the reauthorization debate for Head Start, the federal program that helps about 1 million of the nation's poorest and most vulnerable children prepare for school. The Bush administration's proposal to emphasize literacy and academic skills in Head Start has raised new questions

and renewed old battles about how young children learn—and when they should be required to show it on a test.

Is this academic jumpstart good for kids? Should 3- and 4-year-olds be held accountable for their literacy skills? Or is the push for early achievement another signal that social and emotional development is taking a backseat to testing? Child advocates and early education professionals offer conflicting opinions. And caught in the middle of the debate are school districts whose preschool programs are performing the eternal juggling act between academics and the development of the whole child.

At least 40 states offer a prekindergarten program for 4-year-olds, mostly for low-income families and mostly modeled on Head Start. Two high-profile states, California and Florida, have proposed offering universal preschool for 4-year-olds, regardless of their families' economic status.

When Carvell developed LEAP a decade ago, teaching literacy and reading skills to children as young as 3 and 4 was unheard of in preschool programs. But groundbreaking brain research during the 1980s and '90s changed perceptions and beliefs about what very young children can learn.

This research, paired with the standards and high-stakes testing movement, has resulted in a pushed-down curriculum of sorts. Kindergartners who once finger painted, built with blocks, and napped through their days now are expected to learn the same concepts and skills that first-graders once did.

"What has happened in the face of this emphasis on literacy is that people have become negative about play" says Edward Zigler, a Yale University professor who is known as the father of Head Start. "Kindergartens no longer have blocks and dress-up corners. They see children playing as wasting time. That is a serious mistake."

Some child advocates and early childhood education professionals, however, applaud the increased academic emphasis for children served by Head Start. These children, they say, are exactly the ones who need an early introduction to reading and math concepts.

Deborah Stipek, dean of Stanford University's School of Education and author of *Motivated Minds: Raising Children to Love Learning,* says research shows that middle-class 4-year-olds outscore low-income 5-year-olds on cognitive skills. "Low-income kids start way behind," she says. "They don't catch up. It's foolish to say we don't need to worry about it."

Zigler and most other early childhood education professionals agree young children can benefit from exposure to early reading and math concepts. But some worry the emphasis on academics will edge out what is known about developmentally appropriate teaching. In preschool and kindergarten, much of the teaching looks like fun and games to adults, promoting the perception that children aren't learning.

But they are. "We have known for 75 years that an important determiner of growth and development is play," says Zigler, director of Yale's Center in Child Development and Social Policy. "Play is the work of children."

The importance of play

When Nell Carvell was asked to develop a literacy and phonics program for 4-year-olds, she found few precedents to draw on. She began by testing the children at Cone and found most were about 18 months behind developmentally in oral language. They were weak on vocabulary and weren't aware of sentence structure.

Carvell's curriculum was designed to address those areas while keeping the kids' attention. She brought posters of children doing different activities so the kids could talk about them and emphasized literature by putting multicultural, hardback books in the classroom. "They hadn't seen books in their home, so these books should hold up and look good," she says.

"I tried to make it fun," says Carvell, noting that the children played matching games and wrote letters in sand.

Making learning fun by including play is an important element in teaching young children. Early childhood professionals say it's nearly impossible to separate social, emotional, and cognitive learning in young children. As a result, educators say that programs are doomed to fail if they require young children to act like older kids—sitting at desks or in rows for long periods of time, writing on worksheets, or listening to instruction in large groups. Treating young children like small middle-schoolers ignores much of what is known about the under-7 crowd and how they learn.

"If we try to structure preschool and kindergarten with a formalized approach to reading, social studies, and math, there's a school of thought that believes a large number of children would be hindered," says Mary Mindess, professor of early childhood education at Lesley University in Cambridge, Mass., and coordinator of the New England Kindergarten Conference. "There is a real

danger in losing a lot of kids and danger in not producing the kind of thinking that is successful in today's world."

Barbara Warash, director of West Virginia University's Child Development Laboratory, says parents at her play-based preschool now ask for proof that their children are learning. "They agree in theory that play is important, but they say, 'Could you just throw in the worksheets, so I can see what they are learning?'" says Warash. "Worksheets are visible, tangible items. But they can't see that when their children are playing restaurant, the child is pointing out the letter D on the cereal boxes."

Research shows that certain types of play, especially role-playing, are the foundation for all types of intellectual, social, and emotional development. Focusing solely or even narrowly on academics often asks "too much and too little of children," says Barbara Willer of the National Association for the Education of Young Children, in Washington, D.C.

"If you provide meaningful opportunities for children, they can take on much greater depth than the drill-and-kill [worksheet]," says Willer, the association's deputy executive director. "If you're narrowly focused on letter recognition, you lose the opportunity for vocabulary building and broad base of language."

Not all play is created equal, however. W. Steven Barnett, director of the National Institute for Early Education Research, a nonpartisan think tank at Rutgers University, cautions that if play means recess, then it's not the kind of play that helps children acquire skills and knowledge.

"That's not what experts mean. They mean deeply engaged in role-play in which teachers are engaged and there is reciprocal activity between teachers and among kids," says Barnett. "Play is wasted if kids aren't learning."

The whole child

Children won't learn if they're hungry. They won't learn if a tooth hurts, or if they're angry all the time, or if they simply don't have any adults to connect with. This is true of all children, but especially of very young children.

It is also one of the basic tenets of Head Start, which was originally conceived as an anti-poverty program during the Lyndon Johnson era. Since the program was launched in 1965 as part of Johnson's Great Society initiative, parent involvement and social services have been at its core.

"We must help families through a myriad of problems," says Sarah Greene, executive director of the National Head Start Association, a nonprofit membership organization in Alexandria, Va. "It's just as important as what you do with that child."

Child advocates and early childhood educators are concerned that the Bush plan to increase academics in Head Start will force out or diminish other elements of the program, including social and health services and emphasis on social and emotional development.

"Most everyone knows that young children need to be challenged academically, and they need to be exposed to literacy, letters and sounds, and literature at an early age—science, math, and social studies, too," says Samuel Meisels, president of the Erikson Institute, a graduate school of child development in Chicago. However, Meisels says, you can't teach cognitive concepts without also teaching social and emotional skills: "We really need to have an emphasis on all areas of development."

Zigler, who administered the Head Start program at the federal level in the 1970s, says the move toward an academic focus goes against the program's fundamental purpose.

"There wasn't any early intervention program before Head Start," he says. "All they had were the usual nursery school programs, designed for middle-class kids.

"The two hallmarks of Head Start are parent involvement and comprehensive services," Zigler adds. "You can't just teach phonemics if the kids are abused. I don't care how phonemics are taught, they won't learn it."

G. Reid Lyon, chief of the child development and behavior branch of the National Institute of Child Health and Human Development, says that the administration is not trying to do away with Head Start's nonacademic elements. "We are trying to recommend that we provide kids with integrated programs for social, emotional, and cognitive [skills]," he says.

Zigler and others say the new Head Start testing program, which assesses about 550,000 4-year-olds with standardized tests twice a year, will show only how well centers are doing with the academic part of the program. The testing also raises concerns about whether the scores will be used punitively.

"All they measure are cognition, literacy, and numeracy," says Zigler. "Where is comprehension? They will assess the value of the centers on the basis of testing—not if the centers helped parents get jobs or a child inoculated. That's too narrow."

Greene agrees. "They are only assessing in language and literacy, not looking at the other areas," she says. "I don't think it's the best way to find out how our kids and teachers are doing."

The impact on school districts

The increased emphasis on early academics in preschool has been reflected in an explosion in the number of all-day kindergartens. According to U.S. Census data, about 60 percent of kindergartners were in full-day programs in 2000. That percentage has more than tripled since 1974. But as school districts face a severe budget pinch, some feel universal preschool and full-day kindergarten are luxuries, not necessities.

Full-day programs that combine academics with social and emotional development are crucial but costly, early childhood advocates say. Many feel that academics taught in developmentally inappropriate ways could make children feel like failures at the age of 5.

"If the push-down curriculum demands that kindergartners are exposed to the same expectations and skills

the preschool teacher gap

Educating young children in developmentally appropriate ways requires the best, most experienced teachers. But those teachers tend to work elsewhere. After all, the early childhood education profession is not known for being a high-paying or well-respected career.

Improving the quality of teaching is one of the key goals in Congress' proposed reauthorization of Head Start, the federal preschool program. A House bill that passed in July would require all Head Start teachers to have associate degrees; by 2008, half would have to have bachelor's degrees.

That's an admirable goal, say many in the Head Start and early childhood education community, but it's unlikely to be reached without extra money to attract and retain good teachers. The starting salary for a Head Start teacher is $18,000, compared to $30,000 for the average kindergarten teacher.

And there's another problem: One of Head Start's goals is to raise families out of poverty, and mothers of students are often hired to be teachers. From a social standpoint, it's commendable practice. But few of these mothers have associate degrees, let alone bachelor's degrees. So from an educational perspective, some observers are worried that the practice could hamper the teaching of cognitive skills.

W. Steven Barnett, director of the National Institute for Early Education Research at Rutgers University, cites research showing that a 3-year-old in a family where both parents went to college uses as many words as an adult in a family receiving welfare.

"You don't take those parents and turn them into preschool teachers," says Barnett. "We want to give all kids access to the culture, language, and knowledge about how the world works that well-educated people have. The notion that you can do that without well-educated teachers is misguided."

Teachers with less experience often rely on scripted or "teacher-proof" curricula that can result in children receiving less-than-desirable instruction. But Barnett says scripted curricula prevent teachers from individualizing instruction, following the student's interests, and teaching children to be responsible for their own learning.

"The notion that you can hand a teacher a script is like the notion that we can run all the kids through the same process," he says. "You will lop off the bottom kids and lop off kids at the top because they will be bored. That just doesn't work."

Instead of scripts, says Amy Wilkins, executive director of the Trust for Early Education in Washington, D.C., preschool teachers need more training. "In our child-care centers are lots of child-generated teachable moments," she says, "but we don't have the curriculum in place to take advantage of the learning opportunities that the children present." —K.V.

development, we already see a group of youngsters in jeopardy," says Jacqueline Haines, director of training and clinic services for the Gesell Institute, a child development research center in New Haven, Conn.

Carol Seefeldt, an early childhood education professor at the University of Maryland and author of *Guidelines for Pre-Kindergarten Learning and Teaching,* says she is concerned that children "aren't learning to think, and they are learning that a lot of school is useless."

"I worry that they are being turned off to learning," she says. "It's almost like we want to create an underclass. If we want them to drop out of high school, fail them when they are 4."

Edward Miller, who serves on the board of the Alliance for Childhood, an advocacy group in Waldorf, Md., attributes the reading problems that many children experience to "the unrealistic expectation that they will start reading at an early age." He notes that, until relatively recently, reading instruction did not start until first grade in many schools.

"Now children are supposed to start to read in kindergarten," Miller says. "It has a counterproductive effect. The child picks up on the idea that something is wrong. He gets anxious and hates the idea of reading."

Doris Fromberg, an education professor at Hofstra University and author of *Play and Meaning in Early Childhood Education,* visits 10 to 15 kindergarten classes a year. Increasingly, she sees time for imaginative play being cut in favor of rote learning.

"The opportunity to have in-depth conversations is a marker of literacy," Fromberg says. "If you are exhorted to be quiet and come up with a single correct answer, what you learn is how to satisfy adults and guess at what the adults want, rather than learning for its own sake."

In some states, the push-down curriculum has had other noticeable impacts. Fromberg says some kindergarten teachers have left the field because they are "very distressed" about the heavy emphasis on academics. And a number of parents have started "red-shirting" their kindergarten-age children, preferring to hold them back a year rather than have them face academic requirements at the age of 5.

The Gesell Institute, for example, encourages parents who have children with summer birthdays to give the kids another year until enrolling them in kindergarten. "We think children should be quite mature when they go to kindergarten," Haines says. "It's another reason why our kindergartens need to be flexible. Some of those youngsters won't be as old as other children chronologically, and they deserve success and a positive experience as much as other youngsters have."

A tough standard

Despite what brain research has found about young children's impressive capacity to learn, says Walter S. Gilliam of the Yale University Child Study Center, there is "a lot of normal variability in what age they can get prerequisite skills."

Children "can't read until they can verbally remember letters, recognize letters, pair with the visual, and synthesize letters and sounds," Gilliam says. "It's lots of different skills. If they haven't quite developed, they won't get it. Children are ready to do certain things at different times."

Jeff Poe does not have that luxury. A kindergarten teacher for 10 years at Millard Elementary School in Fremont, Calif., he has to teach his students how to write a paragraph by the end of the year. A tough standard? Yes, says Poe, but his students meet it even though they come to class for only half a day.

Last year, 18 of Poe's 20 students scored "exceeds expectations" on the writing sample, and the other two met the state criteria for passing. That's no small feat for a class in a district where many students show up for kindergarten speaking no English.

Poe, who also taught first grade for 10 years, does not object to the standards. Still, he admits that he used to have more time to work on readiness, socialization, and fine and gross motor skills. Because of the time restrictions, Poe depends heavily on parents to teach their children the nonacademic skills, and he wishes the district could afford full-day kindergarten.

"It would give us back that piece of the day where we can do music and physical education and the other things," he says.

Kathleen Vail is senior editor of American School Board Journal.

Class and the Classroom

Even the best schools can't close the race achievement gap

BY RICHARD ROTHSTEIN

The achievement gap between poor and middle-class black and white children is widely recognized as our most important educational challenge. But we prevent ourselves from solving it because of a commonplace belief that poverty and race can't "cause" low achievement and that therefore schools must be failing to teach disadvantaged children adequately. After all, we see many highly successful students from lower-class backgrounds. Their success seems to prove that social class cannot be what impedes most disadvantaged students.

Yet the success of some lower-class students proves nothing about the power of schools to close the achievement gap. In every social group, there are low achievers and high achievers alike. On average, the achievement of low-income students is below the average achievement of middle-class students, but there are always some middle-class students who achieve below typical low-income levels. Similarly, some low-income students achieve above typical middle-class levels. Demography is not destiny, but students' family characteristics are a powerful influence on their relative average achievement.

Widely repeated accounts of schools that somehow elicit consistently high achievement from lower-class children almost always turn out, upon examination, to be flawed. In some cases, these "schools that beat the odds" are highly selective, enrolling only the most able or most motivated lower-class children. In other cases, they are not truly lower-class schools—for example, a school enrolling children who qualify for subsidized lunches because their parents are graduate students living on low stipends. In other cases, such schools define high achievement at such a low level that all students can reach it, despite big gaps that remain at more meaningful levels.

It seems plausible that if *some* children can defy the demographic odds, *all* children can, but that belief reflects a reasoning whose naiveté we easily recognize in other policy areas. In human affairs where multiple causation is typical, causes are not disproved by exceptions. Tobacco firms once claimed that smoking does not cause cancer because some people smoke without getting cancer. We now consider such reasoning specious. We do not suggest that alcoholism does not cause child or spousal abuse because not all alcoholics are abusers. We un-

derstand that because no single cause is rigidly deterministic, some people can smoke or drink to excess without harm. But we also understand that, on average, these behaviors are dangerous. Yet despite such understanding, quite sophisticated people often proclaim that the success of some poor children proves that social disadvantage does not cause low achievement.

Partly, our confusion stems from failing to examine the concrete ways that social class actually affects learning. Describing these may help to make their influence more obvious—and may make it more obvious why the achievement gap can be substantially narrowed only when school improvement is combined with social and economic reform.

The reading gap

Consider how parents of different social classes tend to raise children. Young children of educated parents are read to more consistently and are encouraged to read more to themselves when they are older. Most children whose parents have college degrees are read to daily before they begin kindergarten, but few children whose parents have only a high school diploma or less benefit from daily reading. And, white children are more likely than black children to be read to in their prekindergarten years.

A 5-year-old who enters school recognizing some words and who has turned the pages of many stories will be easier to teach than one who has rarely held a book. The second child can be taught, but with equally high expectations and effective teaching, the first will be more likely to pass an age-appropriate reading test than the second. So the achievement gap begins.

If a society with such differences wants all children, irrespective of social class, to have the same chance to achieve academic goals, it should find ways to help lower-class children enter school having the same familiarity with books as middle-class children have. This requires rethinking the institutional settings in which we provide early childhood care, beginning in infancy.

Some people acknowledge the impact of such differences but find it hard to accept that good schools should have so difficult a time overcoming them. This would be easier to understand if Americans had a broader international perspective on education. Class backgrounds influence *relative* achievement everywhere. The inability of schools to overcome the disadvantage of less-literate homes is not a peculiar American failure but a universal reality. The number of books in students' homes, for example, consistently predicts their test scores in almost every country. Turkish immigrant students suffer from an achievement gap in Germany, as do Algerians in France, as do Caribbean, African, Pakistani, and Bangladeshi pupils in Great Britain, and as do Okinawans and low-caste Buraku in Japan.

An international reading survey of 15-year-olds, conducted in 2000, found a strong relationship in almost every nation between parental occupation and student literacy. The gap between the literacy of children of the highest-status workers (such as doctors, professors, and lawyers) and the lowest-status workers (such as waiters and waitresses, taxi drivers, and mechanics) was even greater in Germany and the United Kingdom than it was in the United States.

After reviewing these results, a U.S. Department of Education summary concluded that "most participating countries do not differ significantly from the United States in terms of the strength of the relationship between socioeconomic status and literacy in any subject." Remarkably, the department published this conclusion at the same time that it was guiding a bill through Congress— the No Child Left Behind Act—that demanded every school in the nation abolish social class differences in achievement within 12 years.

Urging less-educated parents to read to children can't fully compensate for differences in school readiness. Children who see parents read to solve their own problems or for entertainment are more likely to want to read themselves. Parents who bring reading material home from work demonstrate by example to children that reading is not a segmented burden but a seamless activity that bridges work and leisure. Parents who read to children but don't read for themselves send a different message.

How parents read to children is as important as whether they do, and an extensive literature confirms that more educated parents read aloud differently. When working-class parents read aloud, they are more likely to tell children to pay attention without interruptions or to sound out words or name letters. When they ask children about a story, the questions are more likely to be factual, asking for names of objects or memory of events.

THE ACHIEVEMENT GAP CAN BE SUBSTANTIALLY NARROWED ONLY WHEN SCHOOL IMPROVEMENT IS COMBINED WITH SOCIAL AND ECONOMIC REFORM.

Parents who are more literate are more likely to ask questions that are creative, interpretive, or connective, such as, "What do you think will happen next?" "Does that remind you of what we did yesterday?" Middle-class parents are more likely to read aloud to have fun, to start conversations, or as an entree to the world outside. Their children learn that reading is enjoyable and are more motivated to read in school.

The conversation gap

There are stark class differences not only in how parents read but in how they converse. Explaining events in the broader world to children at the dinner table, for example, may have as much of an influence on test scores as early reading itself. Through such conversations, children develop vocabularies and become familiar with contexts for reading in school. Educated parents are more likely to engage in such talk and to begin it with infants and toddlers, conducting pretend conversations long before infants can understand the language.

Typically, middle-class parents ask infants about their needs, then provide answers for the children. ("Are you ready for a nap now? Yes, you are, aren't you?") Instructions are more likely to be given indirectly: "You don't want to make so much noise, do you?" This kind of instruction is really an invitation for a child to work through the reasoning behind an order and to internalize it. Middle-class parents implicitly begin academic instruction for infants with such indirect guidance.

Yet such instruction is quite different from what policymakers nowadays consider "academic" for young children: explicit training in letter and number recognition, letter-sound correspondence, and so on. Such drill in basic skills can be helpful but is unlikely to close the social class gap in learning.

Soon after middle-class children become verbal, their parents typically draw them into adult conversations so the children can practice expressing their own opinions. Being included in adult conversations this early develops a sense of entitlement in children; they feel comfortable addressing adults as equals and without deference. Children who ask for reasons, rather than accepting assertions on adult authority, develop intellectual skills upon which later academic success in school will rely. Certainly, some lower-class children have such skills and some middle-class children lack them. But, on average, a sense of entitlement is based on one's social class.

Parents whose professional occupations entail authority and responsibility typically believe more strongly that they can affect their environments and solve problems. At work, they explore alternatives and negotiate compromises. They naturally express these personality traits at home when they design activities in which children figure out solutions for themselves. Even the youngest middle-class children practice traits that make academic success more likely when they negotiate what to wear or to eat. When middle-class parents give orders, the parents are more likely to explain why the rules are reasonable.

But parents whose jobs entail following orders or doing routine tasks show less sense of efficacy. They are less likely to encourage their children to negotiate over clothing or food and more likely to instruct them by giving directions without extended discussion. Following orders, after all, is how they themselves behave at work. Their children are also more likely to be fatalistic about obstacles they face, in and out of school.

Middle-class children's self-assurance is enhanced in after-school activities that sometimes require large fees for enrollment and almost always require parents to have enough free time and resources to provide transportation. Organized sports, music, drama, and dance programs build self-confidence and discipline in middle-class children. Lower-class parents find the fees for such activities more daunting, and transportation may also be more of a problem. Organized athletic and artistic activities may not be available in their neighborhoods, so lower-class children's sports are more informal and less confidence-building, with less opportunity to learn teamwork and self-discipline. For children with greater self-confidence, unfamiliar school challenges can be exciting. These children, who are more likely to be from middle-class homes, are more likely to succeed than those who are less self-confident.

Homework exacerbates academic differences between these two groups of children because middle-class parents are more likely to help with homework. Yet homework would increase the achievement gap even if all parents were able to assist. Parents from different social classes supervise homework differently. Consistent with overall patterns of language use, middle-class parents—especially those whose own occupational habits require problem solving—are more likely to assist by posing questions that break large problems down into smaller ones and that help children figure out correct answers. Lower-class parents are more likely to guide children with direct instructions. Children from both classes may go to school with completed homework, but middle-class children are more likely to gain in intellectual power from the exercise than lower-class children.

Twenty years ago, Betty Hart and Todd Risley, two researchers from the University of Kansas, visited families from different social classes to monitor the conversations between parents and toddlers. Hart and Risley found that, on average, professional parents spoke more than 2,000 words per hour to their children, working-class parents spoke about 1,300, and welfare mothers spoke about 600. So by age 3, the children of professionals had vocabularies that were nearly 50 percent greater than those of working-class children and twice as large as those of welfare children.

Deficits like these cannot be made up by schools alone, no matter how high the teachers' expectations. For all children to achieve the same goals, the less advantaged would have to enter school with verbal fluency that is similar to the fluency of middle-class children.

The Kansas researchers also tracked how often parents verbally encouraged children's behavior and how often they reprimanded their children. Toddlers of professionals got an average of six encouragements per reprimand. Working-class children had two. For welfare children, the ratio was reversed—an average of one encouragement for two reprimands. Children whose initiative was encouraged from a very early age are more likely, on average, to take responsibility for their own learning.

The role model gap

Social class differences in role modeling also make an achievement gap almost inevitable. Not surprisingly, middle-class professional parents tend to associate with, and be friends with, similarly educated professionals. Working-class parents have fewer professional friends. If parents and their friends perform jobs requiring little academic skill, their children's images of their own futures are influenced. On average, these children must struggle harder to motivate themselves to achieve than children who assume, on the basis of their parents' social circle, that the only roles are doctor, lawyer, teacher, social worker, manager, administrator, or businessperson.

Even disadvantaged children usually say they plan to attend college. College has become such a broad rhetorical goal that black eighth-graders tell surveyors they expect to earn college degrees as often as white eighth-graders do. But despite these intentions, fewer black than white eighth-graders actually graduate from high school four years later; fewer enroll in college the following year; and fewer still persist to get bachelor's degrees.

This discrepancy is not due simply to the cost of college. A bigger reason is that while disadvantaged students say they plan to go to college, they don't feel as much parental, community, or peer pressure to take the courses or to get the grades they need to become more attractive to college admission offices. Lower-class parents say they expect children to get good grades, but they are less likely to enforce these expectations, for example with rewards or punishments. Teachers and counselors can stress doing well in school to lower-class children, but such lessons compete with children's own self-images, formed early in life and reinforced daily at home.

As John Ogbu and others have noted, a culture of underachievement may help explain why even middle-class black children often don't do as well in school as white children from seemingly similar socioeconomic backgrounds. On average, middle-class black students don't study as hard as white middle-class students and blacks are more disruptive in class than whites from similar income strata.

This culture of underachievement is easier to understand than to cure. Throughout American history, many black students who excelled in school were not rewarded for that effort in the labor market. Many black college graduates could find work only as servants or Pullman car porters or, in white-collar fields, as assistants to less-qualified whites. Many Americans believe that these practices have disappeared and that blacks and whites with similar test scores now have similar earnings and occupational status. But labor market discrimination continues to be a significant obstacle—especially for black males with high school educations.

Evidence for this comes from employment discrimination cases, such as the prominent 1996 case in which Texaco settled for a payment of $176 million to black employees after taped conversations of executives revealed pervasive racist attitudes, presumably not restricted to executives of this corporation alone. Other evidence comes from studies that find black workers with darker complexions have less success in the labor market than those with identical education, age, and criminal records but lighter complexions.

Still more evidence comes from studies in which blacks and whites with similar qualifications are sent to apply for job vacancies; the whites are typically more successful than the blacks. In one recent study where young, well-groomed, and articulate black and white college graduates, posing as high school graduates with identical qualifications, submitted applications for entry-level jobs, the applications of whites with criminal records got positive responses more often than the applications of blacks with no criminal records.

So the expectation of black students that their academic efforts will be less rewarded than the efforts of their white peers is rational for the majority of black students who do not expect to complete college. Some will reduce their academic efforts as a result. We can say that they should not do so and, instead, should redouble their efforts in response to the greater obstacles they face. But as long as racial discrimination persists, the average achievement of black students will be lower than the average achievement of whites, simply because many blacks (especially males) who see that academic effort has less of a payoff will respond rationally by reducing their effort.

The health and housing gaps
Despite these big race and social class differences in child rearing, role modeling, labor market experiences, and cultural characteristics, the lower achievement of lower-class students is not caused by these differences alone. Just as important are differences in the actual social and economic conditions of children.

Overall, lower-income children are in poorer health. They have poorer vision, partly because of prenatal conditions and partly because, even as toddlers, they watch too much television, so their eyes are poorly trained. Trying to read, their eyes may wander or have difficulty tracking print or focusing. A good part of the over-identification of learning disabilities for lower-class children may well be attributable to undiagnosed vision problems that could be easily treated by optometrists and for which special education placement then should be unnecessary.

Lower-class children have poorer oral hygiene, more lead poisoning, more asthma, poorer nutrition, less-adequate pediatric care, more exposure to smoke, and a host of other health problems. Because of less-adequate dental care, for example, they are more likely to have toothaches and resulting discomfort that affects concentration.

Because low-income children live in communities where landlords use high-sulfur home heating oil and where diesel trucks frequently pass en route to industrial and commercial sites, they are more likely to suffer from asthma, leading to more absences from school and, when they do attend, drowsiness from lying awake at night, wheezing. Recent surveys in Chicago and in New York City's Harlem community found one of every four children suffering from asthma, a rate six times as great as that for all children.

In addition, there are fewer primary-care physicians in low-income communities, where the physician-to-population ratio is less than a third the rate in middle-class communities. For that reason, disadvantaged children—even those with health insurance—are more likely to miss school for relatively minor problems, such as common ear infections, for which middle-class children are treated promptly.

Each of these well-documented social class differences in health is likely to have a palpable effect on academic achievement; combined, their influence is probably huge.

The growing unaffordability of adequate housing for low-income families also affects achievement. Children whose families have difficulty finding stable housing are more likely to be mobile, and student mobility is an important cause of failing student performance. A 1994 government report found that 30 percent of the poorest children had attended at least three different schools by third grade, while only 10 percent of middle-class children had done so. Black children were more than twice as likely as white children to change schools this often. It is hard to imagine how teachers, no matter how well trained, can be as effective for children who move in and out of their classrooms as they can be for those who attend regularly.

Differences in wealth are also likely to be important determinants of achievement, but these are usually overlooked because most analysts focus only on annual family income to indicate disadvantage. This makes it hard to understand why black students, on average, score lower than whites whose family incomes are the same. It is easier to understand this pattern when we recognize that children can have similar family incomes but be of different economic classes. In any given year, black families with low income are likely to have been poor for longer than white families with similar income in that year.

White families are also likely to own far more assets that support their children's achievement than are black families at the same income level, partly because black middle-class parents are more likely to be the first generation in their families to have middle-class status. Although the median black family income is about two-thirds the median income of white families, the assets of black families are still only 12 percent those of whites. Among other things, this difference means that, among white and black families with the same middle-class incomes, the whites are more likely to have savings for college. This makes white children's college aspirations more practical, and therefore more commonplace.

Narrowing the gaps
If we properly identify the actual social class characteristics that produce differences in average achievement, we should be able to design policies that narrow the achievement gap. Certainly, improvement of instructional practices is among these, but a focus on school reform alone is bound to be frustrating and ultimately unsuccessful. To work, school improvement must combine with policies that narrow the social and economic differences between children. Where these differences cannot easily be narrowed, school should be redefined to cover more of the early childhood, after-school, and summer times, when the disparate influences of families and communities are now most powerful.

Because the gap is already huge at age 3, the most important new investment should no doubt be in early childhood programs. Prekindergarten classes for 4-year-olds are needed, but they barely begin to address the problem. The quality of early childhood programs is as important as the existence of such programs themselves. Too many low-income children are parked before television sets in low-quality day-care settings. To narrow the gap, care for infants and toddlers should be provided by adults who can create the kind of intellectual environment that is typically experienced by middle-class infants and toddlers. This requires professional caregivers and low child-adult ratios.

After-school and summer experiences for lower-class children, similar to programs middle-class children take for granted, would also be needed to narrow the gap. This does not mean remedial programs where lower-class children get added drill in math and reading. Certainly, remediation should be part of an adequate after-school and summer program, but only a part. The advantage that middle-class children gain after school and in summer comes from the self-confidence they acquire and the awareness of the world outside that they develop through organized athletics, dance, drama, museum visits, recreational reading, and other activities that develop inquisitiveness, creativity, self-discipline, and organizational skills. After-school and summer programs can be expected to narrow the achievement gap only by attempting to duplicate such experiences.

TO WORK, SCHOOL IMPROVEMENT MUST COMBINE WITH POLICIES THAT NARROW THE SOCIAL AND ECONOMIC DIFFERENCES BETWEEN CHILDREN.

Provision of health-care services to lower-class children and their families is also required to narrow the achievement gap. Some health services are relatively inexpensive, such as school vision and dental clinics. A full array of health services will cost more, but it cannot be avoided if we truly intend to raise the achievement of lower-class children.

The connection between social and economic disadvantage and an academic achievement gap has long been well known. Most educators, however, have avoided the obvious implication: Improving lower-class children's learning requires ameliorating the social and economic conditions of their lives. School board members—who are often the officials with the closest ties to public opinion—cannot afford to remain silent about the connection between school improvement and social reform. Calling attention to this link is not to make excuses for poor school performance. It is only to be honest about the social support schools require if they are to fulfill the public's expectation that the achievement gap will disappear.

Richard Rothstein is a research associate of the Economic Policy Institute and a visiting professor at Teachers College, Columbia University.

He is the author most recently of *Class and Schools: Using Social, Economic, and Educational Reform to Close the Black-White Achievement Gap* (The Economic Policy Institute and Teachers College Press, 2004), on which this article is based. *Class and Schools* includes full bibliographic citations supporting the many claims and generalizations made in this article.

From *American School Board Journal*, October 2004, pp. 17-21. Copyright © 2004 by Richard Rothstein. Reprinted by permission of the author. rr2159@columbia.edu

Too Soon to Test

*When it comes to kindergarten screening,
research raises warning signs*

By Susan Black

It's a rite of passage: Parents start calling in September to ask about preparing their 4- and 5-year-olds for kindergarten screening in the spring. "No matter how I reassure them and explain that screening is not a test," an elementary school principal told me, "many parents are anxious that their children won't be ready for kindergarten."

Parents have a right to be worried, and so do school boards and others involved in setting policies and determining practices for this annual event. On the surface, kindergarten screening appears innocuous—little more than greeting new students and their parents, checking their vision and hearing, and recording their knowledge of such things as numbers and letters.

But kindergarten screenings aren't always what they seem—or what they should be. In a recent large-scale study in New York state, Virginia Costenbader and her research team at the University of Rochester found that many schools are replacing developmental screening—used to identify possible problems in such areas as language, motor skills, and social-emotional growth—with readiness screening—used to determine whether or not children possess the cognitive and behavioral skills schools say they need to enter and succeed in kindergarten.

Especially troubling, says Costenbader, is the fact that the most commonly used standardized screening instruments are not psychometrically sound and do not accurately predict students' success in the early grades. The positive predictive value of many widely used screening measures hovers around 50 percent—meaning that only about half of the children with low scores on their screening actually turn out to have academic trouble. When I showed this finding to a superintendent, he said, with a hint of irony, "We could save a lot of money by rolling the dice."

Developmental or 'maturational'?

The National Education Goal that "all children will start school ready to learn," adopted as part of the national education agenda in 1990, outlined three objectives for schools and communities:

1. Provide disadvantaged and disabled children with access to high-quality and developmentally appropriate preschool programs designed to help prepare them for school.
2. Recognize that parents are their children's first teachers and encourage them to spend time daily to help preschool children learn; provide parents with training and support to teach their children.
3. Improve prenatal health systems to reduce the number of low-birth-weight babies and ensure that children receive the nutrition and health care they need to arrive at school with healthy minds and bodies.

But over the past decade, the concept of school readiness has drifted from the original goal and objectives, says Gilbert Gredler, a professor of school psychology at the University of South Carolina. Gredler's studies record a significant shift from a developmental perspective, in which schools adapt their curriculum to kindergartners, to a maturational perspective, in which schools insist that kindergartners must be ready for the curriculum.

"Readiness to learn" often implies that children aren't learners before they enter school, a concept that offends early childhood experts. In a commentary on school readiness, Lilian Katz describes the "spectacular learning" that occurs—especially in language and motor development—from birth to the time children reach school age. Most infants and children learn at astonishing rates, Katz contends, but she acknowledges that what they learn, how they learn, and how much they learn depend to a great extent on their physical and emotional well-being and their home environment.

Schools should not penalize children who spend their first years of life without benefits of stimulating developmental experiences, says Katz, who has written extensively about early childhood education and child development. Instead, she says schools should find ways to respond to the "wide range of experiences, backgrounds and needs of the children who are starting school."

Red-shirting kindergartners

IT'S HARD TO SAY what the "right" age is to begin kindergarten. According to the U.S. Department of Education, almost two-thirds of entering kindergartners are between the ages of 5 years and 5 years 8 months. About one-quarter are almost 6 years old; another 9 percent are still 4 years old, and 4 percent are over six.

And, the department says, 9 percent or more of the children eligible to enroll in kindergarten are "red-shirted"—that is, held out for a year to give them extra time for intellectual development and social maturity.

Some schools encourage red-shirting, especially for children they deem unready to sit still for long periods, follow complex directions, and complete considerable homework. Some parents request red-shirting, hoping that buying time for their children will ensure their success in kindergarten and later.

Who's being red-shirted? The 1997 National Household Education Survey, conducted by the National Center for Education Statistics (NCES), found that many children whose birth dates fall close to their school's cutoff date for kindergarten enrollment are granted delayed entrance.

But the statistics tell a more complicated story. Red-shirting is fairly common in affluent communities, especially among children attending private schools. Overall, boys and non-Hispanic white children are more likely to be red-shirted.

The benefits of red-shirting are mostly speculative, but a 1993 NCES study indicated that students whose school entrance was delayed for a year were less likely to receive negative evaluations from their teachers or to be retained in first or second grade. A repeat survey, conducted in 1995, found no differences between students, who were held out or retained and other first- and second-graders.

But Robert Byrd of the University of California, Davis, says delaying school entrance often leads to delayed problems.

Byrd's study, published in *Pediatrics,* found that students who started school later had more behavioral problems, especially when they reached adolescence. At age 17, Byrd reports, 16 percent of students with delayed kindergarten entrance demonstrated extreme behavior problems, compared to 7 percent of students who entered on time.

Red-shirting also affects the demographics of kindergarten, as Sandra Crosser points out in a 1998 ERIC Digest prepared for the Clearinghouse on Elementary and Early Childhood Education. In effect, Crosser says, red-shirting adds more 6-year-olds to the kindergarten classroom mix. As a result, the youngest children could be as much as two years younger than the oldest students.

This age spread, she says, presents "a real danger" that teachers will expect the youngest children to keep up to an advanced curriculum that's well beyond their reach. Crosser projects that red-shirting will lead to kindergarten programs that are developmentally inappropriate for the young children they are meant to serve.

Sources

Byrd, Robert et al. "Increased Behavior Problems Associated with Delayed School Entry and Delayed School Progress." *Pediatrics,* pp. 654-661, 1997.

Crosser, Sandra. "He Has a Summer Birthday: The Kindergarten Entrance Age Dilemma." ERIC Digest, 1998. www.ed.gov/databases/ERIC_Digests/ed423079.html.

West, Jerry, and others. "Children Who Enter Kindergarten Late or Repeat Kindergarten: Their Characteristics and Late School Performance." *Education Statistics Quarterly, 2001.* http://nces.ed.gov/pubs2001/quarterly/fall/elem_kindergarten.html.

Misusing readiness tests

Both the National Association for the Education of Young Children (NAEYC) and the American Academy of Pediatrics (AAP) have taken strong stands on the use—or misuse—of school readiness tests.

Misusing the concept of readiness NAEYC says, places the burden of proof on 5-year-olds instead of on the schools. NAEYC stands by its position statement on school readiness, issued in 1995, which advises schools to base readiness screening and kindergarten instruction on three factors: (1) diversity and possible inequity of children's early life experiences; (2) wide variation in young children's development and learning; and (3) the degree to which schools' expectations of children entering kindergarten are reasonable, appropriate, and supportive of their individual differences.

AAP's policy, also adopted in 1995, says school readiness tests often are used inappropriately. Children are most likely to be wrongly identified, AAP officials say, if schools administer screening instruments without adequate knowledge of child development and testing procedures, or if they use screening scores to diagnose children with learning disabilities or other problems. All children are entitled to an education in schools where the great variability in early childhood development is understood and supported, AAP's policy states.

New approaches

Some states and school districts are rethinking kindergarten screening and the notion of readiness. Maryland, for example, has begun collecting baseline information on all kindergartners' social, physical, linguistic, and cognitive skills. Baseline information for the 2001-02 school year shows that teachers judged 49 percent of entering kindergartners as "fully ready to do kindergarten work." Forty-four percent were rated as "approaching readiness" and in need of targeted support to meet expectations, and 7 percent were rated as "developing readiness" and in need of considerable support to succeed in kindergarten.

The Maryland Model for School Readiness—which focuses on helping pre-kindergarten and kindergarten teachers with family communication, curriculum, instruction, and assessment—avoids conventional readiness testing. Instead, teachers observe, record, and evaluate their students twice a year in seven areas: social and personal development; language and literacy; mathematical thinking; scientific thinking; social studies; the arts; and physical development and health. For each assessment area, teachers rate children as proficient, in process, or needing development.

Teachers are expected to use their observations to support and challenge children's learning by modifying instruction, grouping students according to learning needs, and providing support for individual students on an as-needed basis. But the observational data teachers collect is never used to place children in special programs.

Resistance to school readiness testing is also apparent in some local school districts. Wisconsin's Middleton-Cross Plains Area School District, for example, describes its all-day kindergarten as a "relaxed, unhurried experience" that allows children and teachers time for a variety of learning experiences, including music, art, and physical education, and ongoing screening and assessments. The district's policy, posted on its Web site (www.mcpasd.k12.wi.us/home.cfm), informs parents that children do not need to be ready for school—the school needs to be ready for the child. Screening includes mail-in packets, filled out by parents, that help determine which children might be eligible for support programs, and a number to call if parents have concerns about their child's development.

Are your schools ready?

About 4 million children will be eligible to enter kindergarten in 2003. They'll arrive at your school's doorway taking baby steps. But before they show up for kindergarten screening, I suggest that you and other school officials take a few giant steps to get ready for your youngest students:

1. Examine your kindergarten screening policies and practices and replace those that don't measure up to research on developmentally appropriate practice.

2. Study and review psychometric problems with standardized screening instruments.

3. Develop school-community partnerships for school readiness based on the three objectives attached to the national readiness goal.

4. Develop school readiness positions similar to those adopted in Maryland schools and in Shrewsbury and Middleton-Cross Plains.

5. Make sure your teachers will be ready for kindergartners with appropriate curriculum, instruction, and assessments that match students' developmental states.

Steps like these will help ensure that kindergarten, as it was originally conceived by Friedrich Wilhelm Froebel in the 1840s, lives up to its promise and remains a learning garden for all children.

Susan Black, an *American School Board Journal* contributing editor, is an education research consultant in Hammondsport, N.Y.

Selected references

Black, Susan. "The Children's Garden." *American School Board Journal,* September 1997, pp. 35-37.

"Children Entering School Ready to Learn: School Readiness Baseline Information." Executive Summary. Maryland State Department of Education, February 2002.

Costenbader, Virginia, and others. "Kindergarten Screening: A Survey of Current Practice." *Psychology in the Schools,* July 2000, pp. 323-332.

Gredler, Gilbert. "Issues in Early Childhood Screening and Assessment." *Psychology in the Schools,* 1997, pp. 98-106.

Gredler, Gilbert. *School Readiness: Assessment and Educational Issues.* Brandon Vt.: Clinical Psychology Publishing Co., 1992.

"The Inappropriate Use of School Readiness Tests." Policy Statement: American Academy of Pediatrics. *Pediatrics,* March 1995, pp. 437-438. www.aap.org/policy/00694.html.

Katz, Lilian. "Readiness: Children and Schools." ERIC Clearinghouse on Elementary and Early Childhood Education, 1991. http://ericeece.org/pubs/digests/1991/katz91.html.

"NAEYC Position Statement on School Readiness." National Association for the Education of Young Children, 1998. www.ed.gov/databases/ERIC_Digests/ed423079.html.

Zill, Nicholas, and Jerry West. *Entering Kindergarten: A Portrait of American Children When They Begin School: Findings from the Condition of Education, 2000.* U.S. Department of Education, National Center for Education Statistics, NCES 2001-035, 2001.

OVERBURDENED OVERWHELMED

*Schools—and life—are more
stressful than ever, and students
are feeling the strain*

By LAWRENCE HARDY

In the elementary and middle schools of Rockingham County, N.C., a rural district north of Greensboro, administrators have to discard as many as 20 test booklets on exam days because children vomit on them.

"Kids [are] throwing up in the middle of the tests," says Dianne Campbell, the district's director of testing and accountability. "They cry. They have to be removed. The stress is so much on the test that they can't handle it."

It's not just tests that are stressing students. Across the country, school nurses, psychologists, counselors, and others concerned about children's mental health say that schools in general have become more stressful places and that many students can't handle the pressure.

What are we doing to our children? Why are we making them sick? What is it about our families, our communities, and particularly our schools that has made their lives so stressful? And what can we do to help?

While there are few studies on stress among K-12 students, two recent surveys show a disturbing trend at the college level. In one of the studies, released in February by the journal *Professional Psychology: Research and Practice*, the counseling center at Kansas State University found that the percentage of students being treated for depression at the center had doubled between 1989 and 2001. The study, one of the most extensive of its kind, followed a 2001 national survey in which more than 80 percent of college counselors said they believed the number of students seeking help for serious psychological problems had increased over the past five years.

And the trend appears to be starting before college. At the K-12 level, school health experts say they are seeing more student stress, much of it coming from outside school. High divorce rates, a sluggish economy, and the rapid pace of society have all put unprecedented pressure on families—and on kids.

Fear of failure

These societal pressures are difficult enough without schools contributing to the problem, but some observers say that's exactly what's happening. Students are stressed by the climate of schools that have grown too large and impersonal and by the unintended effects of the nation-wide effort to raise standards. Parents complain about a glut of homework in the early grades, about elementary school students having to sit through hours of testing, about kindergartens morphing from places where children learned to love school to the start of what could become a grueling 13-year marathon.

"Young children, even first-graders, know where they stand in the achievement hierarchy," says Rhonda S. Weinstein, a psychology professor at the university of California, Berkeley, and author of *Reaching Higher: The Power of Expectations in Schooling.* Rather than creating classrooms that develop talent, Weinstein says, "We magnify minor differences and make them salient."

This relentless sorting is not helping our students, Weinstein says: It undercuts self-esteem and increases the fear of failure. As the late John Holt, the eminent teacher and education writer, wrote in 1964, "Adults destroy the intellectual and creative capacity of children ... above all by making them afraid, afraid of not doing what other people want, of not pleasing, or making mistakes, of failing, of being *wrong.*"

Almost three decades later, that fear has not abated.

Intolerable levels of stress

In numerous interviews with professionals in education and mental health—including school nurses, counselors, and psychologists—*ASBJ* found near-unanimous agreement that too many students are suffering from intolerable levels of stress. Of course, much of this stress comes from family and societal factors that are beyond the school's control. But instead of creating schools that are refuges from outside stress, these professionals say, we have too often constructed environments that only add to them.

"It's about as rough as I've seen it in a number of years of talking to schools," says Randy Compton, executive director of the School Mediation Center in Boulder, Colo. "It's hard out there."

Adds Michael Klonsky, director of the Small Schools Workshop at the University of Illinois, Chicago: "The pressures on students are tremendous."

That's certainly the case in Rockingham County. In North Carolina, students are tested in grades three through eight as part of a process that can determine whether they will be promoted. For Rockingham, that's about 7,500 students. "I probably have, during a three-day period, about 15 or 20 cases where kids get sick during the test," Campbell says. "That's a pretty high rate. As the tests start, they literally fall apart. It would break your heart."

Campbell believes in testing as a diagnostic tool, and she says the teachers in Rockingham try their best not to transfer the pressure they feel to the kids. "Even though you feel the pressure, don't put it on your kids," she says. "There's a fine line between making them feel responsible and making them feel overstressed."

Stress and pressure—both external and self-imposed—affect kids all along the achievement spectrum. For high-achieving students, it's harder than ever to get into a top college or a state's flagship university. In part that's because of the sheer number of students competing for a limited supply of spots. At Berkeley, for example, where admissions officers refer to this generation as "Tidal Wave II," it's almost twice as hard to gain acceptance as it was 10 years ago, the admission rate having dropped from 42.9 percent in 1992 to 23.9 percent last year.

Increased anxiety

Low-performing students, especially those from poorer areas, face a different challenge—simply staying in school. And being held back a grade raises the stakes. Numerous studies show that grade retention doesn't help students' academic success and may even increase dropout rates, yet between 1980 and 1992 the number of students retained increased from about 20 percent to nearly 32 percent, according to a 1995 study by Melissa Roderick. Anecdotal evidence suggests the rates have increased further since 1992—and will continue to increase—as more states require high-stakes tests for promotion and graduation.

What impact is this retention—and the threat of it—having on students' emotional well-being? Without any national studies to draw on, we can't be sure, but some indications suggest it increases the level of anxiety. Con-

sider a 1987 study in which Kaoru Yamamoto, of the University of Colorado at Denver, and Deborah A.

Byrnes, of Utah State University, examined how stressful various events were in the lives of 558 elementary school children. For sixth-graders, fear of grade retention was the third-highest stressor, right behind losing a parent and going blind.

Rose Paolino is a counselor at Bailey Middle School in West Haven, Conn., where a large number of students receive free or reduced-price lunches. Lying just across the river from New Haven, the city shares many of the social and economic problems of its larger neighbor. Many of Paolino's students come from single-parent homes and don't have the emotional resiliency of their peers from intact families, Paolino says. She says her caseload has nearly doubled in six years.

"The social-emotional has to come before the academic, and it will always be that way," Paolino says. "Until a child is established socially and emotionally, you can forget about the academics."

Too much, too soon

How much of this stress can be blamed on schools and how much on our fast-paced, fractured society? It's hard to say. With anytime access to cable TV, the Internet, and other kinds of media, kids are no longer shielded from what goes on in the world. They're forced to grow up fast—or, at least, to appear to grow up fast. And a large part of that stepped-up pace of development is facing sexual pressures at an earlier age.

"Some girls will say, 'I'm a lesbian' to keep the boys off them and not be pressured so much," says Brenda Melton, a counselor at Alamo Achievement Center, an alternative school in San Antonio, and president of the American School Counselor Association.

A school may teach values or abstinence or problem-solving skills, but Britney Spears teaches something else. A generation ago, if you skipped school, your neighbor or your relative down the street might report you, and your parents and the teacher would have a talk. Now, your parents are both working, your neighbor doesn't know you, and there is no relative down the street.

Schools also can't control a child's reaction to world events, and the world of late has seemed a strange and treacherous place. Several school nurses and counselors say that Sept. 11, the war in Afghanistan, and the possibility of war in Iraq all cause stress for their students.

Sandra Gadsden, a school nurse in the Worthington Public Schools near Columbus, Ohio, tells of a fourth-grader who came into her office complaining of a stomach ache and saying his eyes were "feeling funny."

"His mother had the television on, and he heard all this rattling about war in Iraq," Gadsden says. "He told me he's afraid our country will go to war. He's 9 years old."

'A Complete Pressure Cooker'

AFTER MORE THAN 40 years as a psychologist in Philadelphia, Irwin Hyman is adamant about the stresses facing his patients, saying they are the worst he's ever seen.

"What we're doing is taking some of our brightest students and some of the most motivated and putting them through a complete pressure cooker," says Hyman, a Temple University school psychologist and coauthor of *Dangerous Schools: What We Can Do About the Physical and Emotional Abuse of Our Children.*

Hyman says the new education act has just added to the pressure. "No Child Left Behind puts pressure on school boards," he says "School boards put pressure on the superintendent. The superintendent puts pressure on the teachers. And the victims are the kids."

Some psychologists are particularly concerned about the stresses facing younger children and the consequences of such policies as reducing or eliminating recess and making kindergarten more academic.

"If you can't have a wonderful, joyous kindergarten experience, what's life all about?" asks Ted Feinberg, assistant executive director of the National Association of School Psychologists in Bethesda, Md.

Feinberg recalls an e-mail message he received from a mother whose daughter was in an accelerated kindergarten class. Noting that her child was having difficulty and had just been diagnosed with what Feinberg calls "a newly created syndrome," the woman asked if perhaps the problem might be that her daughter wasn't ready for such an intensive academic experience after all. When Feinberg stated the obvious—that, yes, the accelerated kindergarten might be causing the problem—the mother admitted, "I thought that all along."

Feinberg tells another story: About 12 years ago, when he was a school psychologist, he was conducting kindergarten screenings for 4-year-olds and was asked by a parent what was on the "test."

"She wanted to have a copy of the test so she could prep her child," Feinberg said. "God help us if we have to have test prep courses to prepare children for kindergarten."—*L.H.*

But most of her students' concerns are closer to home. They often involve their parents' expectations and the fear that they cannot meet them. "I've had children tell me, 'My mother says I won't get into a good college if I don't do well on the test,'" Gadsden says.

And these children are in elementary school.

Parent pressure

Sometimes, parental expectations and school pressure combine to put needless strain on children. More than a year ago, on a state testing day, a third-grader walked into Gadsden's office carrying with her a terrible odor of skunk. It turned out that the girl's dog had been sprayed by a skunk and then jumped on her.

"I had to come up with a plan very quickly to 'de-skunk' her" so she could take the test, Gadsden recalls.

The cafeteria didn't have any tomato juice, a common antidote for skunk musk, so Gadsden doused the girl with catsup, rinsed it off, and put a stocking cap over her wet head. She later recalled the note that had been sent home with the students, telling parents to make sure their children got a good night's sleep and a nourishing breakfast before the test. This test, the note seemed to say, was extremely important.

"This mother didn't have the confidence to say, 'Testing isn't all *that* important,'" Gadsden says.

Obviously, this mother thought the test was more essential than helping her daughter rid herself of an embarrassing and unpleasant odor. But other parents in Worthington are questioning the wisdom of frequent testing and the other academic demands being placed on their children. And they've asked Gadsden to lead a stress-reduction group for interested students.

One of those parents, Pam Nylander, was concerned about her 13-year-old daughter Brittany, a seventh-grader who has juvenile diabetes. A straight-A student, Brittany was staying up too late to finish her homework, and Nylander was worried about her health. She talked to other parents and found their children were also doing homework late into the night, so they approached the school about their concerns.

Of course, it's not all the school's fault. Parents need to limit their children's outside activities, Nylander says, but that, too, can be hard. There was a time a generation ago when students could do well in school, take up a sport, play an instrument, and participate in a youth group—and still have free time.

Not anymore. Noting that her daughter is an accomplished pianist, Nylander says, "If she wanted to, she could be in five music competitions in the next three months." The same is true of the increasingly competitive world of athletics, whether school sponsored or run by a club.

"Everybody has raised the bar on their expectations for these kids for everything," Nylander says, "and it's very difficult to strike a balance."

One school district that is trying to strike a balance is the Adams 12 Five Star Schools in Thornton, Colo. More than two years ago, the district convened the first of 89 focus groups to ask residents what they wanted for the school system and its students. What the district found, says Superintendent Jim Christensen, is "that they have higher expectations and more expectations than just the test scores."

The result is a plan for "Educating the Whole Child" in which students will be assessed according to eight traits. The district says students should be competent, creative, productive, healthy, ethical, successful, thoughtful, and good citizens.

Christensen, who has been working on ways to assess these traits, says the main goals are motivating students and involving their parents. "It really focuses on getting the students, the parents, and the teacher on the same page," Christensen says "so that [the student's] competence can be enhanced through these traits."

EARLY EDUCATION

Henry Petroski

Children are born engineers. Everything they see, they want to change. They want to remake their world. They want to turn over, crawl, and walk. They want to make words out of sounds. They want to amplify and broadcast their voice. They want to rearrange their clothes. They want to hold their air, their water, their fire, and their earth. They want to swim and fly. They want their food, and they want to play with it too. They want to move dirt and pile sand. They want to build dams and make lakes. They want to launch ships of sticks. They want to stack blocks and cans and boxes. They want to build towers and bridges. They want to move cars and trucks over roads of their own design. They want to walk and ride on wheels. They want to draw and paint and write. They want to command armies and direct dolls. They want to make pictures out of pixels. They want to play games—computer games. They want to talk across distance and time. They want to control the universe. They want to make something of themselves.

Grown-up engineering, which is as old as civilization, maintains the youth, vigor and imagination of a child. This is why, when presented to children on their own terms, the excitement of engineering is immediately apparent and fully comprehendible. No child is too young to play and therefore to engage in engineering, albeit of a primitive kind. We all did so as children ourselves, when we divided our own toys and games—and sometimes even imaginary friends to enjoy them with us. The idea of playfulness is embedded in engineering through the concepts of invention and design. Not that engineering is frivolous; rather, the heart of the activity is giving the imagination its head, reining it in only to check impossible or dangerous dreams and to turn ideas into reality.

Children do experience the essence of engineering in their earliest activities, yet there is seldom any recognition that this is the case. They may hear the word "engineer" only in connection with railroad locomotives and have no idea that their playful activity could become a lifelong profession. Engineers themselves are understandably reluctant to equate their professional activity with mere child's play. After all, they studied long and hard to master esoteric knowledge of atoms and molecules, stresses and strains, heat and power, currents and voltages, bits and bytes. They manipulate equations, not blocks. They use computers for serious modeling and calculation, not for fun and games. They design and build real towers and bridges that test the limits of reliability and safety, not toy ones that totter and fall down with little consequence.

These regimens learned in college and put into practice are important and serious, but they are still not essential to comprehending the profession's fundamental activity: design. Design is rooted in choice and imagination—and play. Thus the essential idea of engineering can readily be explained to and understood by children.

Sharing the Joy

Much has been said and written about the declining numbers of and disappointing lack of diversity among college students majoring in engineering. Among the factors cited to explain this paucity are the lack of exposure of high school students to the very idea of engineering and the fact that many have insufficient mathematics and science background to gain entrance to engineering school, even if they do identify the profession as a possible career. This is unfortunate, for the ideas of engineering should be integrated into the curricula not only of high schools but also of middle and primary schools. Our children are being done a disservice by not being exposed properly throughout their education to engineering activities identified as such. After all, even preschool children have the prerequisites in their play for appreciating exactly what engineering is: design. Indeed, design is ubiquitous throughout their school day, even in their before- and after-school activities. It need only be pointed out to them that they are designing something, and therefore being engineers of sorts, in virtually everything that they do.

According to Nicholson Baker in his novel, *The Mezzanine*, "Shoes are the first adult machines we are given to master." As children, we learn to tie our shoes even before going to school. This is no mean accomplishment, as most of us may remember, and its execution is by no means as rigidly codified among classmates as the alphabet they are drilled in school. There are different ways to tie a shoelace, as we readily learn when we help different children unknot theirs. This is a manifestation of the fact that the steps in tying a knot or bow can vary from family to family in ways that the order of the letters in the alphabet cannot. Most children learn from their parents how to tie a shoe, and in their teaching role the parents often have to relearn the process themselves from a different point of view. That there are different tying techniques is characteristic of the fact that tying a shoe is a design problem—and design problems seldom if ever have unique solutions. Each individual child may be taught to tie shoes in a prescribed way, but that is not to say that it is the only way or even the best way. The lessons that can come of such an observation are beneficial not only for introducing students to design but also for augmenting lessons in diversity.

Opportunities in the Everyday

The idea of tying a shoe, and the related problem of lacing one up, can be turned into playful educational activities that expose students to the idea of design and thereby to engineering. A recent article in the *New York Times'* "Science Times" described how Burkard Polster, a mathematician at Monash University, calculated that there are over 40,000 distinct ways to lace up a shoe with two rows of six eyelets each. In true academic mathematic fashion, Dr. Polster extended his research by viewing the laced shoe as a pulley system to determine which lacing pattern was most effective in performing its function. He also determined the lacing that could be effected with the shortest lace. The combinatorial mathematics used by Polster make the problem as he approached it unsuitable for school children, of course, but that is not to say that the practical problem itself cannot be used to advantage in the elementary-school classroom. How much fun could children have redesigning the lacings of their shoes into imaginative patterns and learning by doing that there is more than one way to solve a problem? Being told by the teacher that a mathematician calculated that there were exactly 43,200 different ways they could have solved the problem can only add to the wonder of the lesson.

Elementary school students might also be asked if they could imagine how Polster got the idea of counting how many ways there are to lace a shoe. Telling them that he did so after learning that two physicists from the University of Cambridge calculated how many ways there were to knot a necktie provides yet another opportunity to describe a commonplace problem in design. Even if the children are not in uniform—and the teacher, too, is dressed casually—the tie-knotting problem is at least one they might take home to tackle with their families. It would also expand the vocabulary of professions to which the children are exposed. To their knowledge that mathematicians can have fun counting shoe lacing patterns, the students can add the mental note that physicists can have fun counting tie knottings. To this can be added the observation that if mathematicians and physicists have such fun counting things, imagine how much fun engineers have in designing things that can be counted.

(As an aside to teachers and others, the word "science" is in fact a misnomer when it actually refers to engineering. Science, strictly speaking, does not include engineering, an activity distinguished by its domination by design. Engineers design things, such as patterns of shoe lacings; scientists analyze things, such as counting how many lacings can be designed. These are distinctly different activities, even though the object of their attentions can be common. Journalists and others often use the term "science" as a convenient shorthand to include "engineering," but it verbally subsumes engineering into an activity whose fundamental objectives are of another kind altogether. This use of "science" essentially keeps "engineering" out of the vocabulary of children, who consequently do not learn about all the possible ways there are to have fun with shoelaces, neckties, and so much more—including real towers, bridges, automobiles, airplanes, power plants, computers, and everything designed and made.)

An after-school snack provides further opportunities for children to learn that design means that there is not just one way to do something. Consider the problem of designing a method for eating an Oreo cookie with a glass of milk. Different children (and adults) employ different techniques. Those with big enough mouths might just pop the whole thing in. Most will eat the cookie in steps, some taking a bite at a time, as if it were a real sandwich. Others proceed by first twisting or prying off one side of the cookie to expose the cream. Some will eat the separated top right away; others put it aside and attack the cream first. Even this allows for variations: Some lick the cream off, and others scrape it off with their teeth; some use their top and others use their bottom teeth. After finishing the cream, those who put the top aside still have another choice to make: whether to eat the top or bottom next. All along, the glass of milk on the table has allowed for further variations on the process, for the cookie may be dunked or not before each bite. Countless everyday activities, in school or out, provide ample opportunities to introduce young children to design and therefore to engineering. .

Invention—within Bounds

Design pervades the lives of children and adults alike; virtually nothing that we do goes untouched by it. We design our own approaches to the everyday things of life, such as lacing our shoes, knotting our ties, and eating our cookies. But we also design our own procedures for washing our hands, taking a shower, putting on our clothes. As I recall, in one episode of *All in the Family*, Archie Bunker's son-in-law, Mike, watches Archie put on his shoes and socks. Mike goes into a conniption when Archie puts the sock and shoe completely on one foot first, tying a bow to complete the action, while the other foot remains bear. To Mike, if I remember correctly, the right way to put on shoes and socks is first to put a sock on each foot and only then put the shoes on over them, and only in the same order as the socks. In an ironic development in his character, the politically liberal Mike shows himself to be intolerant of differences in how people do common little things, unaccepting of the fact that there is more than one way to skin a cat or put on one's shoes.

At times we do prescribe how certain everyday things are done, even though there might be countless ways to vary the procedure. This is especially the case in more formal social situations, where doing things too individually might detract from the formality or, in some instances, even prove to be repulsive to polite society. Thus, we have manners and social protocols. Arbitrary as they sometimes seem, such things as table manners and restraint in creativity at the table obviate distractions that otherwise might make eating with others, especially strangers, a less than pleasant experience. Imagine a business lunch where the group of people around the table ate with the individuality that children show when eating cream-sandwich cookies. As many ways to eat a sandwich as there might be, there are also practical reasons beyond decorum for following a customary procedure. By keeping the sandwich intact and bringing it to the mouth in the conventional way, we demonstrate one of the sandwich's design features: The fingers are kept free of mustard and mayonnaise, which in turn means that the outside of the drink glass remains relatively tidy throughout the meal and that after lunch the business associates can shake hands without feeling they are washing dishes.

We discover as children, sometimes with the guidance of an adult but often by our own devices, preferred ways to proceed with all sorts of social and recreational activities. There are many ways to design a ball game, and the plethora includes the supplemental use of bats, rackets, bases, baskets, goalposts, nets, and more. But when two or more people participate in any game, they must agree on which implements to allow and which rules to follow. Otherwise what transpired would hardly be a game as we know it. Imagine a player on a tennis court serving a football with a baseball bat across a volleyball net to an opponent with a lacrosse stick. Only an agreed-upon set of rules is likely to produce a recreational activity that is not chaotic. If the objective is to have a friendly, or even a fiercely competitive game, it must proceed according to rules of a rigid design. Even the game of solitaire is only truly played by sticking to the rules. Engineers must certainly stick to the rules of physics, chemistry, and the other sciences.

Putting together a jigsaw puzzle is an activity that can be done alone or in a group. Either way, it provides another fine example of how many ways there are to achieve an objective—forming a single picture out of hundreds of pieces of various colors and shapes. Theoretically, it is possible to solve the puzzle by arbitrarily choosing a piece and then trying to fit each of the remaining pieces to it. Systematically trying each piece in each orientation on each side of the starter piece would lead eventually to a match, and the procedure could be followed to completion. I know of no one who works jigsaw puzzles in this tedious and unimaginative way, however, because one of the implicit challenges is to finish the puzzle as efficiently as possible. Most people look for edge and corner pieces first, completing the periphery before tackling the more amorphous middle. If nothing else, this way there are fewer pieces to contend with. As many ways as there might be to complete a puzzle, the preferred way is the most efficient way.

Making Engineering Evident

Teachers cannot be faulted for failing to promote engineering if they have not been exposed to it themselves. Engineering is not taught in every teacher's college, and it is not a required field of study even in most full-service universities. It is certainly possible to get a bachelor of arts or science—and a teaching certificate—without appreciating that engineering is a profession every bit as noble, rewarding, and satisfying as medicine and law. The absence of even the playful rudiments of engineering in the curriculum is unfortunate, as I have learned from doctors and lawyers who have expressed a disappointment that they were not exposed more to engineering while in school themselves.

I compare engineering design to making sand castles or lacing up shoes or eating cookies or designing toys not to trivialize it but to humanize it. The conventional wisdom, among the general population, as well as among many teachers of children, is that engineering is a cold, dehumanizing and unsatisfying career. Those who hold such a view are not likely to have met or spoken with engineers who enjoy what they do. They are no longer children playing with blocks or building castles on the beach, of course, but many of them retain a certain childlike fascination with the elemental structure of the world and with what can be done with timber and concrete and steel—or with atoms and molecules and microbes. They know that what they have fun designing and building and overseeing is essential to the smooth working of civilization. We should all learn this as children.

Bibliography

Baker, Nicholson. 1990. *The Mezzanine: A Novel*. New York: Vintage Books.

Chang, Kenneth. 2002. Seeking perfection in shoe lacing, with 43,200 choices. *New York Times*, December 10, p. D3.

Fink, Thomas M., and Yong Mao. 1999. Designing tie knots by random walks. *Nature* 398:31–32.

Polster, Burkard. 2002. Mathematics: What is the best way to lace your shoes? *Nature* 420:476.

The 'Failure' of Head Start

By John Merrow

Head Start has failed. The federal preschool program for 4-year-olds was supposed to "level the playing field" for poor children, and it has not done that.

Educationally and linguistically, poor children are behind from the beginning. Parents with professional jobs speak about 2,100 words an hour to toddlers; those in poverty only about 600. Not surprisingly, a 5-year-old child from a low-income home has a 5,000-word vocabulary, while a middle-class child already knows 20,000 words.

One reason for its failure was the misguided practice at some Head Start centers, where teaching the alphabet was actually banned, in favor of teaching social skills. But the dominant reason for the persistent gap is the fervor with which middle- and upper-middle-class parents embrace preschool.

These parents enroll their own children in preschool because they know that 3- and 4-year-olds are ready and eager to learn. Seventy-six per cent of 4-year-olds from households with an annual income of more than $50,000 are enrolled. The National Center for Education Statistics reports that twice as many 3- to 5-year-olds from families with incomes above $75,000 are enrolled, compared with children whose parents make $10,000 a year.

By contrast, fewer than half of children whose families fall below the poverty line attend preschool, not because their parents don't want them to, but because we haven't created enough Head Start programs. To serve all the eligible children, we'd need twice as many as we have. Once again, we're talking the talk when it comes to helping poor children, but not walking the walk. And, largely for that reason, the gap will not only not disappear, it will grow.

We ought to be embarrassed about our approach to preschool. Most industrialized countries provide free, high-quality preschool for 3-, 4-, and 5-year-olds, regardless of family income. Almost all 4-year-olds in England, Luxembourg, and the Netherlands go to public school; 70 percent of German, Danish, and Greek 4- year- olds go to public school; and over 90 percent of 4- and 5-year-olds in Italy and Spain are in public school.

We're the opposite: a patchwork nonsystem with weakly trained, poorly paid staff members. The quality ranges from excellent to abysmal, the tuition from $15,000 to zero, the teachers' salaries from $45,000 a year with benefits to as low as $8 or $9 per hour, with no benefits.

I've just spent seven weeks driving around Europe, visiting lots of small towns and villages. Every small town I visited in France had a sign, prominently placed, pointing the way to the local école maternelle, the town's preschool. Had I stopped to look, I would have found every 3- and 4- year- old from the village at the school.

A few months earlier, I visited three écoles maternelles in very different neighborhoods in Paris. The school serving poor children was virtually identical to those serving middle-class and upper- middle-class children. All three schools were staffed with well-trained, well- paid teachers, because all école maternelle teachers must have master's degrees, and all are paid at the same rate as elementary school teachers. Today in France, 100 percent of children ages 3 through 5 attend preschool, most in public programs.

In the United States, preschool is a seller's market, and even well-off parents have to endure "preschool panic," because there's not enough quality to go around. One of the families in our forthcoming PBS documentary on the subject moved from New York City to France while we were filming. The parents had been forced to choose between career opportunities for themselves and a decent preschool for their sons. Today, while both parents are struggling to develop their careers in France, their children are in sound educational programs.

Today preschool is on a lot of state agendas. According to the Child Care Action Campaign, 42 states now have some form of "preschool initiative." However, that phrase encompasses everything from legislative proposals to real programs, and only Georgia, New York, Oklahoma, and the District of Columbia have genuine programs that provide free preschool for a substantial number of children.

Georgia is at the head of the preschool class. Its program currently serves more than 63,000 4-year-olds. In toto, 70 percent of Georgia's 4-year-olds are now in some form of publicly subsidized preschool. The Georgia program is the brainchild of former Gov. Zell Miller, now a U.S. senator, who believes that "preschool is more important than the 12th grade in high school." Georgia requires districts to offer prekindergarten and pays the bill—$240 million a year—with money from its lottery and with federal Head Start funds. New York and Oklahoma are leaving it up to school districts to decide whether they will provide such services, with the state paying the bills. But states are hard-pressed for funds these days, and so, for example, New York's legislature has put up less than half the money needed to establish programs across the state.

Creating high-quality programs is proving to be difficult. No state is starting from scratch, of course, which means that any new program must be grafted on to what exists. And what exists is a hodgepodge of programs: Some are run for profit, some are staffed with trained, well-paid teachers, some are storefront operations where a TV set is the caregiver, and so on. Some Head Start programs are excellent, but others are woeful. One evaluation of Head Start found that some children began knowing just one letter of the alphabet, A, and left nine months later without having learned B.

President Bush says he wants to change that, but his proposal is flawed. To improve literacy skills, he plans to give 2,500 Head Start teachers four days of training in early-literacy instructional techniques, after which they are supposed to pass on what they learned to the other 47,000 Head Start teachers. Critical reaction was immediate. A spokesman for U.S. Rep. George Miller, D- Calif., told reporters, "The idea that you would be able to create reading specialists among Head Start teachers with four days of training is absurd."

Moreover, the president's budget won't allow Head Start to grow, even though the program misses more than half of eligible children.

I BELIEVE THAT WE'RE OPERATING FROM THE WRONG PREMISE. Instead of relying on income-based programs like Head Start that are supposed to help the poor, we ought to be creating a system that would be good enough for the well-off. Create something that's good enough for those with money, but make it available to everyone. Design a preschool system the way we built our Interstate highway system. We didn't create separate highways for rich and poor. Instead, we built an Interstate system that was good enough for people behind the wheel of a Cadillac or a Lexus, a Corvette or a Mercedes, and there were no complaints from those driving a Chevy or a Ford.

We know that good preschools have long-term benefits for children, and we ought to recognize that as a nation.

Creating universal, free, high-quality preschool will be difficult, complicated, and costly: By one estimate, it would cost $30 billion a year to run programs just for those 3- and 4-year-olds from families making less that $30,000 a year. For all 3- and 4-year-olds, "The cost could easily be $100 billion," according to Ron Haskins of the Brookings Institution. However, we know that good preschools have long-term benefits for children, and we ought to recognize that as a nation.

It took 50 years for the United States to be able to compete as a peer in soccer's World Cup with Italy, Mexico, Portugal, France, Germany, Sweden, and other long-established powers. We cannot afford to take that long to catch up in the world of preschool education.

John Merrow's documentary "The Promise of Preschool" appeared on PBS. He is the author of Choosing Excellence *(Scarecrow Press, 2001) and an education correspondent for "The NewsHour with Jim Lehrer."*

UNIT 2

Child Development and Families

Unit Selections

Key Points to Consider

- How can parents become more involved and interested in their children's education?

- Why has childhood obesity become such an epidemic in our country today?

- What strategies are most successful for helping homeless children be successful in school?

- How can teachers and parents assist children effected by the divorce of their parents?

- What are some of the issues related to allergies facing school personnel?

- Describe the four types of emotional competence children can develop.

- What skills developed during the preschool years will be of most assistance as children grow and develop throughout life?

 **Links: www.dushkin.com/online/**
These sites are annotated in the World Wide Web pages.

Administration for Children and Families
http://www.dhhs.gov

The AARP Grandparent Information Center
http://www.aarp.org/grandparents

All About Asthma
http://pbskids.org/arthur/grownups/teacherguides/health/asthma_tips.html

Changing the Scene on Nutrition
http://www.fns.usda.gov/tn/Healthy/changing.html

I Am Your Child
http://www.iamyourchild.org

Internet Resources for Education
http://web.hamline.edu/personal/kfmeyer/cla_education.html#hamline

The National Academy for Child Development
http://www.nacd.org

National Safe Kids Campaign
http://www.babycenter.com

Zero to Three
http://www.zerotothree.org

The articles in this section represent many diverse families and issues surrounding young children today. Two of the articles focus on issues affecting affluent families and two articles are geared to professionals who work with children who come from families not able to provide their children with the resources or support they need to fully grow and learn beginning at an early age. Twenty years ago, women thought having a rewarding career and family would be an attainable goal. In an article from *Time*, Claudia Wallis reports some mothers are now finding that the job with a corner office comes with a huge price tag, often requiring four nights a week away from home. Some women are fortunate and have a very supportive spouse or partner who is the consistent stay at home parent. Others are finding it impossible to manage a career and a family without that support and are leaving the corporate world to stay at home while their children are still in school. Many of these mothers are seeking jobs that do not require unrealistic demands for travel or time. They are choosing to start their own consulting or other businesses of-

ten drawing from their work in the corporate world. As demographers study trends on a variety of fronts the spending influence of preschoolers and tweens, those 8-12, has emerged as a powerful force. Margaret Magnarelli writes in *Parents* that this age group, children 4-12, is responsible for hundreds of billions of dollars of purchases made in one of three ways. First, they spend $35.6 million of their own money each year on items they want. Second, they have great influence over family purchases by reciting lines from advertisements or ensuring a certain brand is purchased, and third, they are the recipients of billions of dollars of gifts and other items purchased for them by their parents. Tweens alone have $260 billion in purchasing power and when the age group from 4-8 is added that power is even greater. On the other end of the spectrum there are more and more homeless children in schools and educators must be prepared to meet their needs. Almost 20 years after the passage of the Education of Homeless Children and Youth Program of the 1987 Stewart B. McKinney Homeless Assistance Act the issue remains at the top of the crisis list for educators in predominately low income districts. Kevin Swick provides strategies for helping homeless children be successful in school. All families can benefit from parent education, but particularly low income parents with limited support. In a special issue on Early Childhood, *The American Prospect* includes the article "Leave No Parent Behind" by Dick Mendel. The article addresses the ever growing needs of families in poverty, Mendel reports a combination of programs serving both at risk preschoolers and their parents are successful in helping the children compete in school and life.

Issues related to the health of young children continued to emerge this year. Included are articles that reflect the new interest in children's health and well being. As in the previous edition of *Annual Editions: Early Childhood Education,* the editors found numerous articles on childhood obesity. Childhood obesity is noticeable every time one enters a fast food restaurant and hears a child order a meal by its number on the menu because they are so familiar with the selection at that particular restaurant. It is also evident on a playground where children just sit on the sideline not wanting to participate with their peers due to body image. In "Childhood Obesity: The Caregiver's Role," Bernadette

Haschke provides many suggestions for educators to follow which will help children develop appropriate eating habits and an active lifestyle. Parents and educators must work together to promote healthy living. Teachers should also participate in healthy living activities. We are powerful role models in the lives of young children.

Parents may want academic skills to be the focus of their child's early learning experiences, but when asked what skills will best prepare their child to be successful in life, there may be a different answer. In "Skills for School Readiness—and Life." the Texas Workforce Commission outlines six important attitudes and behaviors for success throughout life. The teachers' role in providing for the development of independence, compassion, trust, creativity, self-control, perseverance, and resilience is critical.

The collaboration of families, the community, and school personnel will enable children to benefit from the partnership these three groups bring to the educational setting. Our hope is every child will have a strong network of support in their home, their community, and school which will enable them to be successful lifelong learners and contributors to society.

Leave No Parent Behind

The most effective child-development programs work with kids *and* their parents.
When, then, do we leave so many parents behind?

By Dick Mendel

Forty years ago, as Marian Wright Edelman and her fellow pioneers at the Child Development Group of Mississippi were organizing sharecroppers, fending off Jim Crow, and cobbling together a model for the nation's Head Start program, Betty Hart and Todd Risley were up in Kansas City working on an early childhood program of their own. First, Hart and Risley designed a state-of-the-art preschool curriculum for children at the Turner House in Kansas City's impoverished Juniper Gardens neighborhood. The children made rapid progress, but when they were tested a year later, their vocabularies again lagged far behind those of better-off children. Hart and Risley tried other teaching strategies: an Afrocentric approach, field trips, structured discussions to help children integrate new experiences into their daily conversation. These efforts failed, too.

So Hart and Risley delved deeper into children's lives. For more than two years, the professors and their team paid monthly visits to 42 children as young as 7 months old—some from families on welfare, others from working-class and professional homes. They recorded every word spoken by child or parent, every gesture, every question. The results showed a contrast starker than Hart and

Risley ever imagined: By age 3, upper-income toddlers not only had vocabularies twice as large as the welfare children; they also had bigger vocabularies than the welfare *parents*. The data explained why: Affluent parents spoke an average of 487 words to their children every hour, compared with 301 words for working-class parents and 176 words for welfare parents. Extrapolated over the first four years of life, that meant well-to-do kids heard an astonishing *30 million* more words than kids from the poorest families. What's more, affluent parents showered their children with encouragement, while welfare parents—reflecting the greater stress in their lives—offered less praise and more frequent criticism. By third grade, the children's success in school mirrored their vocabulary growth at age 3, which closely tracked the levels of positive stimulation by their parents. In fact, differences in parenting during the first three years were far more powerful predictors of children's success in third grade than socioeconomic status.

Hart and Risley weren't the first to suggest that parents play a crucial role in their children's success, of course. But their eye-opening data raise an important question: How can we hope to leave no

child behind if we do not first help disadvantaged parents give their children richer and more positive support in the early years?

The question resonates further when you consider the success of efforts like Phyllis Levenstein's Parent-Child Home Program. Beginning in the mid-1960s, Levenstein trained visitors to go into the homes of new parents and help teach them positive parenting strategies. Twice weekly for the better part of two years, these visitors went to the homes of 2- and 3-year-olds, bringing gifts for the child and sitting with the parent and child while modeling positive parenting behaviors. The strategy worked, and it continues to work with more than 4,000 children each year at 139 sites nationwide. In South Carolina, a 2002 study found that a mostly African American group of first-graders who had participated in the program as tots scored above the state and district averages for school readiness and far above the averages for other poor children. A long-term follow-up in Pittsfield, Massachusetts, found that at-risk children who took part in the program had an 84-percent high-school-graduation rate, compared with 53 percent for eligible children who didn't participate.

Some scholars have questioned the research on Levenstein's program, and most other research has suggested more moderate benefits from home-visiting programs. But a mountain of evidence shows that combining parental support with high-quality child care offers the most powerful approach for erasing the school-readiness gap facing poor children.

• The Perry Preschool Program, pioneered in 1962 in Ypsilanti, Michigan, offered two years of high-quality preschool plus weekly home visits. The program's impact was so powerful that, at age 27, participating children's average earnings were almost twice that of a control group. Participants were three times as likely to own a home and only one-fifth as likely to have been arrested for repeat criminal offenses. All told, the program returned an estimated $7.16 for every dollar invested when the kids were toddlers.

• The Carolina Abecedarian Project, begun in 1972 with a group of babies from poor families as young as 6 weeks old, provided five years of year-round, full-day child care, along with biweekly visits from a home-school resource teacher. Children who completed the project proved only half as likely as their peers to require special education by grade 9; they were one-third more likely to graduate high school by age 19 and three times as likely to enroll in a four-year college by age 21. Participating mothers increased their own education during the project and were far more likely to hold good jobs.

• Houston Parent-Child Development Centers provided two years of support for Mexican American parents beginning when their children turned 1, offering home visits, parenting classes, and nursery school. When the participating children reached elementary school, they were placed in bilingual education less than half as often as a control group, and they proved far less likely to be held back.

These and other results led a National Academy of Sciences panel to conclude in 2000, "Programs that combine child-focused educational activities with explicit attention to parent-child interaction patterns and relationship building appear to have the greatest impacts."

To ITS CREDIT, THE HEAD START program has included much more parental involvement than most state-funded and private preschools. It requires two home visits and two parent-teacher meetings yearly, and supports parents in getting health insurance, medical care, education for themselves, and social services. Parents also play a key role in governing local programs. That said, Head Start's work with parents misses important opportunities. "We're still not looking at 'what do you want every Head Start parent doing for their own kid?'" says Heather Weiss of the Harvard Family Research Project. What's more, says Arthur Reynolds, a University of Wisconsin scholar, "There is no family-resource room in each Head Start facility, no place for parents to go within the particular center, and that limits what you can actually do with the parents."

For 20 years, Reynolds has been studying an alternative called Child-Parent Centers (CPC), which has operated in Chicago's neediest neighborhoods since 1967. The CPC model differs from Head Start in several ways, including a much greater investment in parental support. In addition to hiring a paraprofessional home visitor for each center, CPC sets aside a separate classroom for parents at every site and staffs the room full time with a trained parent-resource teacher. The results are striking. In data released three years ago, Reynolds found that children in the CPC program were 29 percent more likely than a comparison group to graduate from high school, had a 33 percent lower arrest rate, and were 40 percent less likely to be left back or placed in special education—far surpassing the results of any Head Start program ever evaluated. When Reynolds analyzed the data further, he found that parental involvement was one of three important factors linked to CPC children's success.

In Seattle, The Incredible Years program has also compounded Head Start's impact through greater investment in parental support. Working with children enrolled in Head Start, The Incredible Years combats behavioral problems with age-appropriate behavioral training for the children and parental training. In one project for children with behavioral problems, the combination of child and parent training returned 95 percent of the children to a normal range of behavior. The Incredible Years curriculum has also reduced problem behavior in a general population of Head Start children.

The most important window for engaging parents comes during the infant and toddler years—before children even reach preschool. Historically, Head Start paid almost no attention to children under 3, but in 1994, Congress and the Clinton administration enacted the Early Head Start program to begin filling that void. But as is detailed elsewhere in this special report, the program will consume just 10 percent of the total Head Start budget.

Likewise, whereas 46 states now operate pre-kindergarten programs and state funding for pre-K has skyrocketed from $700 million in the early 1990s to more than $2 billion today, only a few states have invested heavily in parent-focused services for 0- to 3-year-olds like Parents as Teachers, the Home Instructional Program for Preschool Youth, or the Parent-Child Home Program. Even including Early Head Start and projects funded by local governments and charities, parent-focused early-learning projects combined probably serve fewer than 150,000 children a year. That's a tiny fraction of the nearly 2 million children attending state-funded pre-K or traditional Head Start programs.

That gap is crippling, suggests Harvard's Heather Weiss. "Not only is a lot of your vocabulary and language set by age 3," she says, "but your notions of what you can learn ... are also set in those first three years of life." Parenting practices, she adds, "play a critical role." A 2002 evaluation showed that Early Head Start children had better cognitive and language development and showed better behavior than a control group. Early Head Start programs offering both center-based care and home visits for parents consistently yielded the best results.

"All of the research shows we have the capacity to change life trajectories," says Jack Shonkoff, dean of the Heller School of Social Policy and Management at

Brandeis University and co-editor of an influential National Academy of Sciences report on early-childhood development in 2000. "The strong science tells us that early-intervention programs that work with parents in addition to working with children themselves are more effective than programs that work only with the children." The question is, when will policy-makers start paying attention?

DICK MENDEL *is a freelance writer and editor based in Baltimore.*

The Case for Staying Home

Caught between the pressures of the workplace and the demands of being a mom, more women are sticking with the kids

By Claudia Wallis

It's 6:35 in the morning, and Cheryl Nevins, 34, dressed for work in a silky black maternity blouse and skirt, is busily tending to Ryan, 2 1/2, and Brendan, 11 months, at their home in the leafy Edgebrook neighborhood of Chicago. Both boys are sobbing because Reilly, the beefy family dog, knocked Ryan over. In a blur of calm, purposeful activity, Nevins, who is 8 months pregnant, shoves the dog out into the backyard, changes Ryan's diaper on the family-room rug, heats farina in the microwave and feeds Brendan cereal and sliced bananas while crooning *Open, Shut Them* to encourage the baby to chew. Her husband Joe, 35, normally out the door by 5:30 a.m. for his job as a finance manager for Kraft Foods, makes a rare appearance in the morning muddle. "I do want to go outside with you," he tells Ryan, who is clinging to his leg, "but Daddy has to work every day except Saturdays and Sundays. That stinks."

At 7:40, Vera Orozco, the nanny, arrives to begin her 10 1/2-hour shift at the Nevinses'. Cheryl, a labor lawyer for the Chicago board of education, hands over the baby and checks her e-mail from the kitchen table. "I almost feel apprehensive if I leave for work without logging on," she confesses. Between messages, she helps Ryan pull blue Play-Doh from a container, then briefs Orozco on the morning's events: "They woke up early. Ryan had his poop this morning, this guy has not." Throughout the day, Orozco will note every meal and activity on a tattered legal pad on the kitchen counter so Nevins can stay up to speed.

Suddenly it's 8:07, and the calm mom shifts from cruise control into hyperdrive. She must be out the door by 8:10 to make the 8:19 train. Once on the platform, she punches numbers into her cell phone, checks her voice mail and then leaves a message for a co-worker. On the train, she makes more calls and proofreads documents. "Right now, work is crazy," says Nevins, who has been responsible for negotiating and administering seven agreements between the board and labor unions.

Nevins is "truly passionate" about her job, but after seven years, she's about to leave it. When the baby arrives, she will take off at least

a year, maybe two, maybe five. "It's hard. I'm giving up a great job that pays well, and I have a lot of respect and authority," she says. The decision to stay home was a tough one, but most of her working-mom friends have made the same choice. She concludes, "I know it's the right thing."

TEN, 15 YEARS AGO, IT ALL SEEMED SO doable. Bring home the bacon, fry it up in a pan, split the second shift with some sensitive New Age man. But slowly the snappy, upbeat work-life rhythm has changed for women in high-powered posts like Nevins. The U.S. workweek still averages around 34 hours, thanks in part to a sluggish manufacturing sector. But for those in financial services, it's 55 hours; for top executives in big corporations, it's 60 to 70, says Catalyst, a research and consulting group that focuses on women in business. For dual-career couples with kids under 18, the combined work hours have grown from 81 a week in 1977 to 91 in 2002, according to the Families and Work Institute. E-mail, pagers and cell phones promised to allow execs to work from home. Who knew that would mean that home was no longer a sanctuary? Today BlackBerrys sprout on the sidelines of Little League games. Cell phones vibrate at the school play. And it's back to the e-mail after *Goodnight Moon.* "We are now the workaholism capital of the world, surpassing the Japanese," laments sociologist Arlie Hochschild, author of *The Time Bind: When Work Becomes Home and Home Becomes Work.*

Meanwhile, the pace has quickened on the home front, where a mother's job has expanded to include managing a packed schedule of child-enhancement activities. In their new book *The Mommy Myth,* Susan Douglas, a professor of communication studies at the University of Michigan, and Meredith Michaels, who teaches philosophy at Smith College, label the phenomenon the New Momism. Nowadays, they write, our culture insists that "to be a remotely decent mother, a woman has to devote her entire physical, psychological, emotional, and intellectual being, 24/7, to her children." It's a standard of success that's "impossible to meet," they argue. But that sure doesn't stop women from trying.

For most mothers—and fathers, for that matter—there is little choice but to persevere on both fronts to pay the bills. Indeed, 72% of mothers with children under 18 are in the work force—a figure that is up sharply from 47% in 1975 but has held steady since 1997. And thanks in part to a dodgy economy, there's growth in another category, working women whose husbands are unemployed, which has risen to 6.4% of all married couples.

But in the professional and managerial classes, where higher incomes permit more choices, a reluctant revolt is under way. Today's women execs are less willing to play the jug-

gler's game, especially in its current high-speed mode, and more willing to sacrifice paychecks and prestige for time with their family. Like Cheryl Nevins, most of these women are choosing not so much to drop out as to stop out, often with every intention of returning. Their mantra: You can have it all, just not all at the same time. Their behavior, contrary to some popular reports, is not a June Cleaver–ish embrace of old-fashioned motherhood but a new, nonlinear approach to building a career and an insistence on restoring some kind of sanity. "What this group is staying home from is the 80-hour-a-week job," says Hochschild. "They are committed to work, but many watched their mothers and fathers be ground up by very long hours, and they would like to give their own children more than they got. They want a work-family balance."

Because these women represent a small and privileged sector, the dimensions of the exodus are hard to measure. What some experts are zeroing in on is the first-ever drop-off in workplace participation by married mothers with a child less than 1 year old. That figure fell from 59% in 1997 to 53% in 2000. The drop may sound modest, but, says Howard Hayghe, an economist at the Bureau of Labor Statistics, "that's huge," and the figure was roughly the same in 2002. Significantly, the drop was mostly among women who were white, over 30 and well educated.

Census data reveal an uptick in stay-at-home moms who hold graduate or professional degrees—the very women who seemed destined to blast through the glass ceiling. Now 22% of them are home with their kids. A study by Catalyst found that 1 in 3 women with M.B.A.s are not working full-time (it's 1 in 20 for their male peers). Economist and author Sylvia Ann Hewlett, who

teaches at Columbia University, says she sees a brain drain throughout the top 10% of the female labor force (those earning more than $55,000). "What we have discovered in looking at this group over the last five years," she says, "is that many women who have any kind of choice are opting out."

Other experts say the drop-out rate isn't climbing but is merely more visible now that so many women are in high positions. In 1971 just 9% of medical degrees, 7% of law degrees and 4% of M.B.A.s were awarded to women; 30 years later, the respective figures were 43%, 47% and 41%.

■ THE GENERATION FACTOR

FOR AN OLDER GROUP OF FEMALE PROFESSIONALS who came of age listening to Helen Reddy roar, the exodus of younger women can seem disturbingly regressive. Fay Clayton, 58, a partner in a small Chicago law firm, watched in dismay as her 15-person firm lost three younger women who left after having kids, though one has since returned part time. "I fear there is a generational split and possibly a step backwards for younger women," she says.

Others take a more optimistic view. "Younger women have greater expectations about the work-life balance," says Joanne Brundage, 51, founder and executive director of Mothers & More, a mothers' support organization with 7,500 members and 180 chapters in the U.S. While boomer moms have been reluctant to talk about their children at work for fear that "people won't think you're a professional," she observes, younger women "feel more entitled to ask for changes and advocate for themselves." That sense of confidence is reflected in the evolution of

---

THE PROPORTION OF WORKING MARRIED MOTHERS WITH CHILDREN UNDER AGE 3 DROPPED FROM 61% IN 1997 TO 58% IN 2002

her organization's name. When Brundage founded it in Elmhurst, Ill., 17 years ago, it was sheepishly called FEMALE, for Formerly Employed Mothers at Loose Ends.

Brundage may be ignoring that young moms can afford to think flexibly about life and work while pioneering boomers first had to prove they could excel in high-powered jobs. But she's right about the generational difference. A 2001 survey by Catalyst of 1,263 men and women born from 1964 to 1975 found that Gen Xers "didn't want to have to make the kind of trade-offs the previous generation made. They're rejecting the stresses and sacrifices," says Catalyst's Paulette Gerkovich. "Both women and men rated personal and family goals higher than career goals."

A newer and larger survey, conducted late last year by the Boston-area marketing group Reach Advisors, provides more evidence of a shift in attitudes. Gen X (which it defined as those born from 1965 to 1979) moms and dads said they spent more time on child rearing and household tasks than did boomer parents (born from 1945 to 1964). Yet Gen Xers were much more likely than boomers to complain that they wanted more time. "At first we thought, Is this just a generation of whiners?" says Reach Advisors president James Chung. "But they really wish they had more time with their kids." In the highest household-income bracket ($120,000 and up), Reach Advisors found that 51% of Gen X moms were home full time, compared with 33% of boomer moms. But the younger stay-at-home moms were much more likely to say they intended to return to work: 46% of Gen Xers expressed that goal, compared with 34% of boomers.

Chung and others speculate that the attitude differences can be explained in part by forces that shaped each generation. While boomer women sought career opportunities that were unavailable to their mostly stay-at-home moms, Gen Xers were

the latchkey kids and the children of divorce. Also, their careers have bumped along in a roller-coaster, boom-bust economy that may have shaken their faith in finding reliable satisfaction at work.

Pam Pala, 35, of Salt Lake City, Utah, is in some ways typical. She spent years building a career in the heavily male construction industry, rising to the position of construction project engineer with a big firm. But after her daughter was born 11 months ago, she decided to stay home to give her child the attention Pala had missed as a kid. "I grew up in a divorced family. My mom couldn't take care of us because she had to work," she says. "We went to baby-sitters or stayed home alone and were scared and hid under the bathroom counter whenever the doorbell rang." Pala wants to return to work when her daughter is in school, and she desperately hopes she won't be penalized for her years at home. "I have a feeling that I'll have to start lower on the totem pole than where I left," she says. "It seems unfair."

■ MATERNAL DESIRE AND DOUBTS

DESPITE SUCH MISGIVINGS, MOST WOMEN who step out of their careers find expected delights on the home front, not to mention the enormous relief of no longer worrying about shortchanging their kids. Annik Miller, 32, of Minneapolis, Minn., decided not to return to her job as a business-systems consultant at Wells Fargo Bank after she checked out day-care options for her son Alex, now 11 months. "I had one woman look at me honestly and say she could promise that my son would get undivided attention eight times each day—four bottles and four diaper changes," says Miller. "I appreciated her honesty, but I knew I couldn't leave him."

Others appreciate a slower pace and being there when a child asks a tough question. In McLean, Va., Oakie Russell's son Dylan, 8, re-

cently inquired, out of the blue, "Mom, who is God's father?" Says Russell, 45, who gave up a dream job at PBS: "So, you're standing at the sink with your hands in the dishwater and you're thinking, 'Gee, that's really complicated. But I'm awfully glad I'm the one you're asking.'"

Psychologist Daphne de Marneffe speaks to these private joys in a new book, *Maternal Desire* (Little Brown). De Marneffe argues that feminists and American society at large have ignored the basic urge that most mothers feel to spend meaningful time with their children. She decries the rushed fragments of quality time doled out by working moms trying to do it all. She writes, "Anyone who has tried to 'fit everything in' can attest to how excruciating the five-minute wait at the supermarket checkout line becomes, let alone a child's slow-motion attempt to tie her own shoes when you're running late getting her to school." The book, which puts an idyllic gloss on staying home, could launch a thousand resignations.

What de Marneffe largely omits is the sense of pride and meaning that women often gain from their work. Women who step out of their careers can find the loss of identity even tougher than the loss of income. "I don't regret leaving, but a huge part of me is gone," says Bronwyn Towle, 41, who surrendered a demanding job as a Washington lobbyist to be with her two sons. Now when she joins her husband Raymond, who works at the U.S. Chamber of Commerce, at work-related dinners, she feels sidelined. "Everyone will be talking about what they're doing," says Towle, "and you say, 'I'm a stay-at-home mom.' It's conference-buzz kill."

Last year, after her youngest child went to kindergarten, Towle eased back into the world of work. She found a part-time job in a forward-thinking architectural firm but hopes to return to her field eventually. "I wish there was more part-time or job-sharing work," she says. It's a wish expressed by countless formerly working moms.

■ BUILDING ON-RAMPS

HUNTER COLLEGE SOCIOLOGIST Pamela Stone has spent the past few years interviewing 50 stay-at-home mothers in seven U.S. cities for a book on professional women who have dropped out. "Work is much more of a culprit in this than the more rosy view that it's all about discovering how great your kids are," says Stone. "Not that these mothers don't want to spend time with their kids. But many of the women I talked to have tried to work part time or put forth job-sharing plans, and they're shot down. Despite all the family-friendly rhetoric, the workplace for professionals is extremely, extremely inflexible."

That's what Ruth Marlin, 40, of New York City found even at the family-friendly International Planned Parenthood Federation. After giving birth to her second child, 15 months ago, she was allowed to ease back in part time. But Marlin, an attorney and a senior development officer, was turned down when she asked to make the part-time arrangement permanent. "With the job market contracted so much, the opportunities just aren't there anymore," says Marlin, who hates to see her $100,000 law education go to waste. "Back in the dotcom days, people just wanted employees to stay. There was more flexibility. Who knows? Maybe the market will change."

There are signs that in some corners it is changing. In industries that depend on human assets, serious work is being done to create more part-time and flexible positions. At PricewaterhouseCoopers, 10% of the firm's female partners are on a part-time schedule, according to the accounting firm's chief diversity officer, Toni Riccardi. And, she insists, it's not career suicide: "A three-day week might slow your progress, but it won't prohibit you" from climbing the career ladder. The company has also begun to address the e-mail ball and chain. In December PWC shut down for 11 days over the holidays for the first time ever. "We realize people do need to rejuvenate," says Riccardi. "They don't, if their eye is on the BlackBerry and their hand is on a keyboard."

PWC is hardly alone. Last month economist Hewlett convened a task force of leaders from 14 companies and four law firms, including Goldman Sachs and Pfizer, to discuss what she calls the hidden brain drain of women and minority professionals. "We are talking about how to create off-ramps and on-ramps, slow lanes and acceleration ramps" so that workers can more easily leave, slow down or re-enter the work force, she explains.

"This is a war for talent," says Carolyn Buck Luce, a partner at the accounting firm Ernst & Young, who co-chairs the task force. Over the past 20 years, half of new hires at Ernst & Young have been women, she notes, and the firm is eager not only to keep them but to draw back those who have left to tend their children. This spring Deloitte Touche Tohmatsu will launch a Personal Pursuits program, allowing above-average performers to take up to five years of unpaid leave for personal reasons. Though most benefits will be suspended, the firm will continue to cover professional licensing fees for those on leave and will pay to send them for weeklong annual training sessions to keep their skills in shape. Such efforts have spawned their own goofy jargon. Professionals who return to their ex-employers are known as boomerangs, and the effort to reel them back in is called alumni relations.

One reason businesses are getting serious about the brain drain is demographics. With boomers nearing retirement, a shortfall of perhaps 10 million workers appears likely by 2010. "The labor shortage has a lot to do with it," says Melinda Wolfe, managing director and head of Goldman Sachs' global leadership and diversity.

Will these programs work? Will part-time jobs really be part time, as opposed to full-time jobs paid on a partial basis? Will serious professionals who shift into a slow lane be able to pick up velocity when their kids are grown? More important, will corporate culture evolve to a point where employees feel genuinely encouraged to use these options? Anyone who remembers all the talk about flex time in the 1980s will be tempted to dismiss the latest ideas for making the workplace family-friendly. But this time, perhaps, the numbers may be on the side of working moms—along with many working dads who are looking for options.

On-ramps, slow lanes, flexible options and respect for all such pathways can't come soon enough for mothers eager to set examples and offer choices for the next generation. Terri Laughlin, 38, a stay-at-home mom and former psychology professor at the University of Nebraska at Lincoln, was alarmed a few weeks ago when her daughters Erin, 8, and Molly, 6, announced their intentions to marry men "with enough money so we can stay at home." Says Laughlin: "I want to make sure they realize that although it's wonderful staying at home, that's only one of many options. What I hope to show them is that at some point I can recreate myself and go back to work."

The Friendly Divorce

PARENTS MAY NOT WANT TO BE MARRIED ANYMORE,
BUT FOR THE SAKE OF THEIR KIDS, THEY SHOULD ALWAYS BE PARTNERS.

BY SARAH MAHONEY

When my husband and I finally agreed it was time to throw in the towel, I wasn't fooling myself: I knew that for Maggie, then 5, and Evan, then 3, our divorce would be a tragedy. The kids loved Jack; they loved me; they loved our family. Our divorce was going to rock their world.

But I didn't realize how much. The first three days after Jack moved out, Evan screamed himself awake; Maggie cried herself to sleep. Months later, I was bragging to my sister about how well the kids were doing, and she started flipping through a stack of Maggie's drawings. In almost every picture, a heart was flying out of a dog's chest with tiny red teardrops. "Look," my sister pointed out. "Bleeding hearts."

Seven years later, I'd like to say my kids have adjusted. Jack and I have a supportive, flexible arrangement. He sees them at least three times a week, usually more, and is a totally involved father. But as much as Jack and I would like to see our divorce as past tense, it's a permanent state to my kids. With each new developmental stage, they have new questions and worries.

That's because divorce plants a persistent fear in children, no matter how old they are: "If one parent can leave another, it's only natural for a child to wonder, 'How do I know they won't leave me?' " says Judith S. Wallerstein, Ph.D., a leading divorce researcher and coauthor of *What About the Kids? Raising Your Children Before, During, and After Divorce.*

However, there are experts who say that children of divorce can thrive if parents consciously focus on helping them feel secure. An increasing number of divorcing couples are determined to do what's best for their kids, and they're willing to make peace with one another to achieve that, says E. Mavis Hetherington, Ph.D., coauthor of *For Better or Worse: Divorce Reconsidered.*

Why the trend toward "friendly" divorces? First of all, divorce courts have undergone sweeping changes to em-phasize children's needs. Today, for example, in 28 states, divorcing parents must by law attend classes that explain how children are wounded by high-conflict divorces and that teach the importance of cooperative parenting.

In addition, the newest generation of parents is far more likely to have experienced divorce themselves as children, and they want to make it easier on their own kids. Young dads in particular are committed to staying involved in their children's lives, says therapist M. Gary Neuman, creator of the Sandcastles divorce therapy program used in many courts and author of *Helping Your Kids Cope With Divorce the Sandcastles Way.* That dad factor is priceless: Children who remain close to their fathers are less distressed by divorce, and dads who are connected to their kids are more likely to keep up their financial obligations.

In fact, friendlier divorces benefit mothers, fathers, and kids. "Everyone's realized that it's not so much the divorce that hurts children," says Claire Barnes, executive director of Kids' Turn, a program in San Francisco for parents and kids affected by divorce or separation. "It's the conflict that comes afterward."

Finding a Way to Get Along

The problem, of course, is that divorcing couples probably aren't feeling too friendly. The collapse of a marriage (even a lousy one) leaves most people feeling depressed, angry, vengeful, or betrayed, and prone to all kinds of out-of-character behavior. But no matter how bad couples feel, it's important for them to take the high road. While it's tough to be civil to an ex who's being difficult, research shows that the way parents interact and handle visitation during the initial separation will set the tone for the years ahead. Here are eight ways to make a divorce less traumatic for the children.

How Kids Adjust at Every Age

0 to 3 It may seem as if a baby is completely unaware of the divorce, but infants as young as 2 months react differently when they sense their parents become tense, angry, or depressed. Try to maintain a calm atmosphere, stick to normal routines, and make sure that wherever a child is, she has the toys and blankets that make her feel at home, says therapist M. Gary Neuman, author of *Helping Kids Cope With Divorce the Sandcastles Way.*

3 to 5 Preschoolers tend to suffer because they have few ways to comfort themselves. Crankiness, aggression, and other kinds of acting out are very common. Three- to 5-years-olds are the most likely to believe that they were responsible for the divorce, and they need repeated reassurance.

6 to 8 Children this age are more likely to keep their feelings from their parents. Increasingly concerned about fitting in, kids see divorce as a social problem as well as a personal loss and often hide what's happening from friends and teachers. Parents are likely to believe their kids are doing fine, but hidden sadness is a big problem, Neuman notes. It's helpful for a parent to tell her child that it's normal to feel upset and that she's there to talk whenever he wants to.

9 to 12 Older kids tend to react angrily to this huge change in their life, because the anger makes them feel more in control, Neuman says. They often take one parent's side against the other, in an effort to make sense of the situation. Preteens like acting older and may try to assume more of an adult role at home—but it's important for a single parent not to lean on her child for support and to let him continue to be a kid.

1. BREAK THE NEWS LOVINGLY. Children will remember this initial conversation for a long time, and it can have a major impact on how anxious—or safe—they'll feel. (They should be told at least a few days before someone moves out; a parent's vanishing without an explanation is just too frightening.) Ideally, a couple should talk to their kids together and let them know that they've both decided this is best for the family, Neuman notes. You might say that your marriage started with love and that you expected you would live together forever, but that you haven't been getting along, and you're making each other unhappy. You should acknowledge how upsetting the situation is so the kids will know it's okay to cry and show their feelings, Dr. Wallerstein says. It's important to make it clear that the separation is not your children's fault and to reiterate that both parents will always love them and be there for them even if the parents live in different homes.

2. KEEP IT TOGETHER IN THE EARLY DAYS. Try to maintain a calm and positive attitude in front of the children without being phony. It's okay to tell your kids that everyone will have to be brave together, Dr. Wallerstein says. "But the truth is that a successful divorce requires you to be stronger than you've ever been."

3. DON'T BAD-MOUTH YOUR EX. While most people realize it's harmful to put their children in the middle this way, it's often hard to grasp how much kids—even toddlers—can pick up on. If you need to call a friend to vent about what an SOB your ex is being, you need to remember that your child may be eavesdropping.

4. STICK TO A SCHEDULE. Children of divorce depend on routines in order to feel in control, Neuman explains. "The biggest effect the divorce has had on my son, Logan, is that he always wants to know what the plan is," Mark Fleener, of Nashville, says. "He has to know exactly who's picking him up, where, and at what time. He was 3 when we split up, and I got a calendar for him at my house so I could mark down which days he'd see me and how many days he'd spend away."

"Everyone's realized that it's not so much the divorce that hurts children. It's the conflict that comes afterward."

5. CREATE PEACEFUL TRANSITIONS. The moments when parents exchange their child are the most stressful for him. He's very aware of tension between the two people he loves most. This isn't the time to ask where that child-support check is or point out that french fries don't count as a vegetable. Save important conversations for a private phone call or e-mail. By simply saying, "Have a good time!" you're telling your child that you're happy he has a good relationship with his dad and that you want them to have fun.

6. JUST WORRY ABOUT YOUR OWN RULES. Many parents think that expectations and consequences need to be the same in both homes to avoid confusing their kids. But it's simply not possible to control what happens when the children are at one's ex's house, and unless it's a safety issue, it's probably not worth fighting over. "Even very young kids are capable of understanding that there are different rules in different places," Dr. Hetherington says.

7. REMEMBER, IT'S A BIG FAMILY. Another important step, if you're the parent with primary custody, experts say, is to make sure your ex's family knows you want them to stay involved in your child's life. Betsy Gallup, of Lenaxa, Kansas, has remarried and now has 1-year-old twins, but she's delighted that her son James, who was 3 when she and his father divorced, gets to see his dad's parents almost every weekend. "I've made it as easy as possible for them to have contact with him."

8. GO EASY IN NEW RELATIONSHIPS. While it may seem unthinkable at first, the odds are great that you and your ex will find new spouses, and in less time than you think: The average length of time between marriages is 3.6

years. But expect some bumps in the road. While step-families can be great for kids, a parents' remarriage creates a short-term disruption almost as intense as divorce, Dr. Hetherington says.

Finally, while it's smart to recognize that divorce puts children at higher risk for many problems, including learning difficulties and depression, with the right support, kids can beat the odds. And keep in mind that it's never too late to have a good divorce. Even if it takes you years to let go of the past and deal more maturely with each other, your kids will still benefit.

The Dynamics of Families Who Are Homeless

Implications for Early Childhood Educators

By Kevin J. Swick

Family homelessness has emerged as a serious global problem (Stronge, 2000). Over the past 25 years in the United States, the makeup of the homeless population has changed significantly. As De Angelis (1994) reports:

> The landscape of homelessness has changed since the early 1980s, when nearly all homeless people were men. Today, families—typically women with two children under age 5 make up 30 percent of the homeless population. (p. 1)

Some scholars (e.g., Bassuk, 1991) suggest that families may constitute 40 to 50 percent of the homeless.

Thus, the focus of this article is on articulating the various dynamics of families who are homeless, what this means for the early childhood education profession, and what strategies we can employ to effectively support homeless families with young children.

The Changing Concepts of Homelessness

Various government and private agencies have different concepts of homelessness. The U.S. federal government defines homeless individuals as:

those who lack a fixed, regular, and adequate nighttime residence; have a primary nighttime residence that is

- a supervised publicly or privately operated shelter designed to provide temporary living accommodations (including welfare hotels, congregate shelters, and transitional housing for the mentally ill);

- an institution that provides a temporary residence for individuals intended to be institutionalized; or

- a public or private place not designed for, or ordinarily used as, a regular sleeping accommodation for human beings. (cited in Heflin, 1991, p. 1)

Regarding children and youth, the McKinney-Vento Homeless Education Assistance Act, Section 725 (as cited in National Coalition for the Homeless, 1999) states,

"Homeless children and youths ..."

a) means individuals who lack a fixed, regular, and adequate nighttime residence (within the meaning of section 103(a)(1); and

b) includes—

(i) children and youths who are sharing the housing of other persons due to loss of housing, economic hardship, or a similar reason; are living in motels, hotels, trailer parks, or camping grounds due to the lack of alternative adequate accommodations; are living in emergency or transitional shelters; are abandoned in hospitals; or are awaiting foster care placement;

(ii) children and youths who have a primary nighttime residence that is a public or private place not designed for or ordinarily used as a regular sleeping accommodation for human beings (within the meaning of section 103(a)(2)(c);

(iii) children and youths who are living in cars, parks, public spaces, abandoned buildings, substandard housing, bus or train stations, or similar settings; and

(iv) migratory children (as such term is defined in section 1309 of the Elementary and Secondary Education Act of 1995) who qualify as homeless for the purposes of this subtitle because the children are living in circumstances described in clauses (i) through (iii). (p. 8)

The concept of homelessness continues to change, as many families that are not technically defined as homeless have all of the attributes of being homeless. For example, it is common among many families that are chronically poor to double- or triple-up with each other in order to survive, financially. In nations with high rates of poverty, it is common for three or more families to live in very small areas (Bellamy, 2003).

Women and children now represent up to one-half of the homeless population in many cities (National Coalition for the Homeless, 1999). When families with older children and adolescents are included in the count, over 50 percent of the homeless population is families (Shane, 1996). Vissing and Diament (1997) Indicate that the problem is likely to be more serious than the statistics indicate; many adolescents who are homeless avoid the label, fearing the stigma it may give them with their peers, and so may not be represented in the statistics. Furthermore, many children in foster care are "housing displaced"; that is, no longer able to live in their home of origin (Toth, 1997). Another dynamic in this complex situation is that a large number of working families live on the edge of homelessness, due to low-paying jobs and high expenses (Heyman, 2000).

Homelessness of children and youth is particularly tragic. Estimates indicate that 1 to 3 million children and adolescents in the United States are homeless (National Coalition for the Homeless, 1999). The impact of child and family homelessness on society is even greater when one considers the resultant problems being passed from one generation to the next. As Vissing (1996) notes, children learn what they observe, and when their most consistent experiences are within chronically poor, powerless, and homeless situations, they are bound to acquire many of the attitudes that go with being powerless.

Family homelessness is not necessarily a factor of socioeconomic status. Even middle- and upper-income mothers and children are not immune from homelessness. Physical, sexual, and psychological abuse destroys the family system of many economically advantaged women and children (Shane, 1996). Women may escape from an abusive home environment to protect themselves and/or their children, or they may be forcibly evicted by their spouse or friend (Peled, Jaffe, & Edleson, 1995).

Indeed, many people now become homeless because of abuse, natural disasters, and other trauma. The widening income gap between the poor and the rich and the increasing cost of raising children are also key factors (Coontz, 1995). Furthermore, war, famine, and disease have led to dramatic increases in family homelessness throughout the world (Bellamy, 2003).

Diverse and Unique Situations of Homeless Families

The situations that lead to homelessness for families and children/adolescents range from leaving an abusive relationship, eviction for failure to make rent payments, running away from parents, or being displaced because of unsafe housing (Bassuk, 1991; Heyman, 2000).

Families that are homeless are distinct from individuals who are homeless. For example, De Angelis (1994) and Bassuk, Browne, and Buckner (1996) report that homeless families typically have much lower levels of substance abuse and mental health problems than do homeless individuals. It is also noteworthy that homeless women with children are usually homeless for shorter periods and are more actively engaged in strategies to empower themselves (Morris, 1998). They are also more likely to be employed and less likely to engage in antisocial behavior (Edin & Lein, 1997).

Homeless mothers also have unique situations. Some homeless mothers have all their children with them; some have one child with them and have placed the others with a relative or friend (many shelters will not accept adolescents); in some cases, the children have been placed in the state's custody (Dail, 1990).

In yet other cases, the children may be in foster care (Shane, 1996; Toth, 1997) or in the state reform system (Ayers, 1997). Inclusion of these populations of "society's children" in homeless statistics would certainly increase the number of people classified as homeless. Also, "housed" children—who have a place to go home to, but who basically live on the streets without any adult supervision are often in worse condition than many homeless children (Berck, 1992).

Dail (1990) and Edin and Lein (1997) explicated the characteristics of women who are homeless, showing the diversity of these situations: 50 percent are between 17 and 25 years of age; a majority have never married, or are separated, divorced, or widowed; more than 50 percent have completed high school; and 75 percent have been employed at some point in their life (Buckner, Bassuk, & Zima, 1993).

As Dail (1990) suggests, the etiology of family homelessness is based in three areas of difficulty:

- A crisis, often of a violent nature, in a relationship with a male

- A prior crisis in the family of origin—sexual abuse, abandonment, parental death, or chronic neglect

- A consistent problem with mental illness and/or drug abuse.

While the situation of each homeless mother is unique, abuse, severe depression, chemical dependency, illiteracy, and chronic poverty are common contributing factors (Nunez, 1996).

The particular situation and complexities a homeless family faces will determine the type of services and assistance they need. For example, a middle class homeless mother who is seeking shelter from an abusive spouse may need a combination of short-term services with counseling for longer range needs. More intensive services are likely to be needed for the chronically poor and persistently homeless family (Wasson & Hill, 1998).

Early childhood educators can empower homeless mothers by building on their strengths. For example, homeless women with children appear to be more proactive than homeless women in general, and more so than chronically poor women who are not homeless (De Angelis, 1994). It appears that women who seek shelter and other support services for their children are more connected with sources of support in the community (Bassuk, 1991; Swick & Graves, 1993).

Success stories of homeless women and their children in attaining more self-sufficiency indicates that paying attention early on to homelessness in young families is crucial (Shane, 1996). In contrast, the prevalence of many poor "housed" families that live in violent and abusive environments indicates a pathology of isolation and neglect (Bassuk, Browne, & Buckner, 1996). Evidence suggests that homeless women with children "are the most likely to have finished high school and to have the lowest average of adult arrests" (De Angelis, 1994, p. 1). It also has been noted that homeless mothers are more likely to be gainfully employed than homeless women in general (Bassuk, Browne, & Buckner, 1996).

The observation that many housed but chronically poor women with children are more symptomatic of dysfunction than are classified homeless mothers (particularly those mothers with children in shelters or transitional housing) highlights the need for reconceptualizing "homelessness" within a broader context. The research suggests that American society has a large number of "hidden homeless families" that need the intensive services being provided for some homeless families (Swick, 1997).

Implications for Early Childhood Professionals: Relating and Responding to Family Homelessness

Early childhood professionals seeking to support homeless families should: 1) develop an ecological understanding of family homelessness; 2) develop responsive and supportive attitudes and behaviors; 3) create an inviting and validating center or school culture; 4) engage parents and families in all aspects of their children's learning and development; and 5) empower parents and families through adult education, job enhancement, and related family literacy (Nunez, 1996; Nunez & Collignon, 2000; Swick, 1997).

Develop an Ecological Understanding of Family Homelessness. The ecological framework theory emphasizes the influence of actions and events on people, and the transactive nature of the different "systems" in which people live (Bronfenbrenner, 1979). A basic construct of this perspective is that human development and learning are the result of dynamic interactions between people and their environment.

Three important elements can help early childhood professionals better understand the dynamic nature of family homelessness:

- The individual's system influences and is influenced by his or her interactive involvement in the various contexts of life. For example, comprehensive job support and training services, provided within a homeless shelter program, can improve mothers' job prospects (Nunez, 1996).

- Each system plays a role in the evolving life of human beings. As noted by Swick and Graves (1993), homeless families resolve their stressors most effectively when all systems are supportive and empowering.

- Whatever happens within and between systems influences people's functioning (Bronfenbrenner, 1979). For example, Powell (1998) indicates that quality child care affects parents' self-confidence and thus creates new possibilities for the family.

Develop Responsive and Supportive Attitudes and Behaviors. Swick and Graves (1993) emphasize that early childhood professionals need to first develop positive and supportive perspectives and behaviors toward families. They note four key elements of this process:

- Nurture and renew positive, supportive, and responsive attitudes and relationship patterns with parents and families.

- Seek to understand parent and family situations from the parental view first, so that you have the family's idea of what is important.

- Recognize and value the role of the parent and family.

- Model positive attitudes and behaviors to parents and families.

Create an Inviting and Validating Center or School Culture. "Homeless students and their parents develop their 'schema' of what schools are through direct experiences, including the messages they receive related to access and participation in social and educational activities" (Swick, 2000, p. 165).

Early childhood programs can foster an inviting atmosphere for homeless families by:

- Providing immediate and friendly access to basic human services

- Treating everyone in the center or school with respect, and making sure their ideas are represented in the fabric of the program

- Involving homeless families in shaping program goals and strategies, allowing them to take on ownership of the program

- Providing comprehensive services (such as adult education and family literacy practices), and being sure these services are family-friendly.

Engage Parents and Families in All Aspects of Their Children's Learning and Development. As Powell (1998) suggests, early childhood professionals need to develop and continually refine an "engagement, participatory" stance in relation to the involvement of homeless families. Quint (1994) notes that educators should begin this process during their initial contact with parents and families. Find out what parents believe is key to minimizing the stressors affecting them and their children. One school invites parents and children to list their top concerns about their lives and then integrates these issues into the plans for helping the families (Nunez, 1996).

Another important construct is that of engaging parents in positively relating to their children (Anooshian, 2000). Positive parent-child relations serve as a buffer to many stressors that otherwise can impede the learning and functioning of children and families (Stronge, 2000).

An extension of the parent-child relationship lies in the partnership between parents and teachers; in particular, home learning activities can empower the entire family (National Coalition for the Homeless, 1999). This partnership process can begin with early childhood educators providing critical home learning resources and community support in shelters and libraries.

It is also important that parents and families have regular opportunities to "educate" professionals about needed literacy and other support resources. Simple items like paper and pens, a quiet place to study, help for parents to understand the material being studied, and guidance on strategies parents can use to help their children are essential.

Empower Parents and Families Through Adult Education, Job Enhancement, and Related Family Literacy. The most empowering element in caring for homeless families is to strengthen parental competence and confidence. As Nunez and Collignon (2000) note, "The surest way to support homeless children's education is to sup-

port their parents" (p. 115). As parents complete GEDs, high school diploma programs, postsecondary education, and related job skills training, children receive additional emphasis and modeling of the value of education. Furthermore, parents' increased economic and educational skills can lead to an improved quality of life for the family (Swick, 1997). Of course, such services need to be secondary to assistance in meeting families' emergency needs.

Empowerment Strategies for Supporting Homeless Families

Empowerment interventions should focus on supporting homeless families in resolving issues and stressors they see as impeding their functioning (Nunez, 1996). Two examples will illustrate how this empowerment process helps many homeless families address the difficulties they face.

Quint (1994) tells how one school used an on-site family service scheme to help one mother attain permanent housing along with a job, providing stability for her family. The school counselor and a social worker guided the mother in her interactions with the job placement staff and helped her successfully negotiate the housing agency process. They also provided essential follow-up support so that the gains could be sustained and expanded.

Toth (1997) describes how the placement of a foster child who had been in four homes in one year with a stable family altered the child's attitudes toward life in a powerful way. The family eventually adopted the child, thus providing the security and continuity the child needed to gain a sense of competence. The child's school performance improved, and he also benefited from more positive peer relations and increased self-esteem.

Here are three further examples of how early childhood programs can nurture families toward more positive living:

- A preschool center for homeless children and their families ensures that all of the children have a special place at the center where they can develop their sense of security and love. Parents are also helped to feel valued and special.

- An early childhood program for families in abusive situations helps each parent to learn how to take pride in themselves and their children. Parents are encouraged to make and display collages of the things they value the most in their lives. Each parent also develops a plan to strengthen themselves to be more nurturing, positive, and supportive in their relations with their child.

- An elementary school uses a "buddy" program to match children who are new to the school with caring peer mentors. Many of the children in this particular school are homeless or at-risk, and several of them eventually become mentors themselves. The "buddy" activities focus on helping children feel secure, important, and connected to their new school. Teachers and staff also act as mentors, often in informal ways with the parents.

Two additional and very important strategy areas are 1) helping families develop trust in each other and in their relations in the community, and 2) helping homeless families form mutually supportive relationships (Pipher, 1996; Swick, 2000).

Promoting trust among families further strengthens their social and emotional skills (Swick, 1997). Early childhood educators can model trusting relations with parents and children, providing a supportive environment in which parents learn about having positive and trusting relations with their children. One parent who participated in a focus group for homeless mothers said, "This program has really helped me turn my trust issues toward the positive, helping me see the best in myself and, thus, in my child."

Families who are homeless also need to have mutually supportive and responsive relations with each other, thereby enabling them to view each other in positive ways (Swick, 2000). Early childhood educators can support families in this process by:

- Encouraging families to recognize and support each other's strengths

- Complimenting parents on their positive interactions with their children

- Including parent-child social learning activities in every aspect of the program

- Encouraging families to use appropriate conflict resolution strategies

- Nurturing in families the importance of open and continuing communication with each other.

Early childhood educators can positively affect the lives of children and families who are homeless or in other high-risk situations. By understanding the dynamics of what homeless families experience, we can be more responsive to the challenges impeding their functioning. For example, family literacy and adult education strategies have been successful in empowering parents, both educationally and economically. Providing basic services like child care and transportation can make a powerful difference in how families work and interact in the world. Educators need to realize just how powerful we can be in using the early years of the family's life as a time to strengthen them—thus preventing homelessness or other "housing-distressed" situations, or helping families gain the power to resolve their homeless situation.

References

Anooshian, L. (2000). Moving to educational success: Building positive relationships for homeless children. In J. Stronge & E. Reed-Victor (Eds.), *Educating homeless students: Promising practices.* Larchmont, NY: Eye on Education.

Ayers, W. (1997). *A kind and just parent: The children of juvenile court.* Boston: Beacon Press.

Bassuk, E. (1991). Homeless families. *Scientific American, 265,*66-74.

Bassuk, E., Browne, A., & Buckner, J. (1996). Single mothers and welfare. *Scientific American, 275*(4), 60-67.

Bellamy, C. (2003). *The state of the world's children 2002.* New York: United Nations Children's Fund.

Berck, J. (1992). *No place to be: Voices of homeless children.* Boston: Houghton Mifflin.

Buckner, J., Bassuk, E., & Zima, B. (1993). Mental health issues affecting homeless women: Implications for intervention. *Journal of Orthopsychiatry, 63*(3), 385-399.

Bronfeubrenner, U. (1979). *The ecology of human development and learning.* Cambridge, MA: Harvard University Press.

Coontz, S. (1995). The American family and the nostalgia trap. *Phi Delta Kappan, 76*(1), K-1-K-20.

Dail, P. (1990). The psychosocial context of homeless mothers with young children: Program and policy implications. *Child Welfare, 69*(4), 291-307.

De Angelis, T. (1994). Homeless families: Stark reality of the 90's. *American Psychological Association Monitor, 1,* 38.

Edin, K., & Lein, L. (1997). *Making ends meet: How single mothers survive welfare and low-wage work.* New York: Russell Sage Foundation.

Heflin, L. (1991). *Developing effective programs for special education students who are homeless.* Reston, VA: Council for Exceptional Children. (ERIC Document Reproduction Service No. ED 339 167)

Heyman, J. (2000). *The widening gap: Why America's working families are in jeopardy and what can be done about it.* New York: Basic Books.

Morris, J. (1998). Affiliation, gender, and parental status among homeless persons. *The Journal of Social Psychology, 138*(4), 241-271.

National Coalition for the Homeless. (1999). *Why are people homeless? NCH Fact Sheet #1.* Washington, DC: Author.

Nunez, R. (1996). *The new poverty: Homeless families in America* New York: Insight Books, Plenum Press.

Nunez, R., & Collignon, K. (2000). Supporting family learning: Building a community of learners. In J. Stronge & E. Reed-Victor (Eds.), *Educating homeless students: Promising practices* (pp. 115-134). Larehmont, NY: Eye on Education.

Peled, E., Jaffe, P., & Edleson, J. (Eds.). (1995). *Ending the cycle of violence: Community responses to children of battered women.* Thousand Oaks, CA: Sage.

Pipher, M. (1996). *The shelter of each other: Rebuilding our families.* New York: G.P. Putnam's Sons.

Powell, D. (1998). Reweaving parents into the fabric of early childhood programs. *Young Children, 53*(5), 60-67.

Quint, S. (1994). *Schooling homeless children.* New York: Teachers College Press.

Shane, P. (1996). *What about America's homeless children?* Thousand Oaks, CA: Sage.

Stronge, J. (2000). Educating homeless children and youth: An introduction. In J. Stronge & E. Reed-Victor (Eds.), *Educating homeless students: Promising practices* (pp. 1-20). Larchmont, NY: Eye on Education.

Swick, K. (1997). Strengthening homeless families and their young children. *Dimensions of Early Childhood, 25*(2), 29-34.

Swick, K. (2000). Building effective awareness programs for homeless students among staff, peers, and community members. In J. Stronge & E. Reed-Victor (Eds.), *Educating homeless students: Promising practices.* Larchmont, NY: Eye on Education.

Swick, K., & Graves, S. (1993). *Empowering at-risk families during the early childhood years.* Washington, DC: National Education Association.

Toth, J. (1997). *Orphans of the living: Stories of America's children in foster care.* New York: Simon & Schuster.

Vissing, Y. (1996). *Out of sight, out of mind: Homeless children and families in small-town America.* Lexington, KY: The University Press of Kentucky.

Vissing, Y., & Diament, J. (1997). Housing distress among high school students. *Social Work, 42*(1), 31-42.

Wasson, R., & Hill, R. (1998). The process of becoming homeless: An investigation of female-headed families living in poverty. *Journal of Consumer Affairs, 32*(2), 320-332.

Kevin J. Swick is Professor, Early Childhood Education, College of Education, University of South Carolina, Columbia.

independence
compassion
trust
creativity
self-control
perseverance
Skills for school readiness—and life

Quiz

Yes	No	
☐	☐	1. Children are ready for school when they know the letters of the alphabet and can sound out words.
☐	☐	2. Children entering kindergarten must know how to count to 20.
☐	☐	3. Children who are curious and creative will have lots of problems in school.
☐	☐	4. Children cannot be responsible for their own clothes, work, and lunch money in kindergarten.
☐	☐	5. Knowing how to make friends is less important in school success than knowing how to write your name.
☐	☐	6. Children cannot develop compassion until they reach high school.

If you answered yes to any of these questions, you may need to re-think your ideas about school readiness.

Too often early care and education teachers feel pushed to focus on academics. They may decide to drill letters and numbers. They may make flash cards and worksheets. They may order videos and computer programs that promise school readiness.

Let's take a step back and consider the skills children really need to succeed in school. Will 5-year-old Timmy succeed if he can count to 20 by rote on the first day of kindergarten? Or will he stand a better chance of success if he comes with a sense of self-confidence and trust? If he feels curious and creative? If he gets along well with others? If he has self-control and can finish what he starts? If he loves learning?

The truth is that if Timmy has the attitudes and behaviors that foster learning, he will likely learn what he needs to learn in every grade level. More than that, he will likely learn how to succeed in life.

The attitudes and behaviors children most need for school readiness are independence, compassion, trust, creativity, self-control, and perseverance. Our role as teachers is to create an environment where children can develop these traits.

Independence. Children begin learning independence as toddlers. They insist on doing things themselves one minute and wail in frustration the next. They say "no" and "mine" and resist taking a nap even when they can barely hold their eyes open.

Ideally by kindergarten, children are able to take some responsibility for their own success and failure. They discover that their actions have consequences and that they can influence those consequences by their actions. They learn to internalize motivation and don't

Readiness for life

Traits children need for school readiness extend throughout life.

Independence. We act independently when we make informed, competent decisions based on experience, information, and balanced judgment. We are willing to take reasonable risks, and look beyond "how we always do it" to improve a public or personal situation.

Compassion. Compassion enables us to recognize the humanity—and dignity—of all people. It is the characteristic that drives charity, volunteer work, tolerance, and mutual respect.

Trust. Trust allows us to accept our own worth, feel secure with friends, and have a positive, open outlook. We trust when we know the rules, want to abide by them, and expect consequences to certain behaviors.

Creativity. Creativity enables us to think through mental challenges and use negotiation techniques to solve social conflicts. It involves flexibility—not being locked into a routine for its own sake—and an eagerness to search for new answers and solutions.

Self-control. Self-control refers to the ability to think about a behavior and decide whether to act or not. Self-control enables us to be patient with ourselves and others.

Perseverance and resilience. We persevere by overcoming obstacles and solving problems. These qualities help us get to the bottom of the list—getting reports written, sweaters knit, cars manufactured, kitchens cleaned, and grass cut.

have to rely on rewards and praise to find success. They want to practice self-reliance—and show that they don't want or need the constant protection and supervision of adults. Encourage independence in the following ways:

- Give toddlers reasonable choices. "Do you want to read this book or that one?"
- Allow 18-month-old Jennie to use a spoon at mealtime but stand ready to help if she gets frustrated.
- Provide 3- and 4-year-olds with peanut butter, crackers, and plastic knives and let them prepare their own snack.
- Set up learning centers and let children choose activities within them. In the math center, for example, they might sort items by size, fit geometric shapes into a puzzle, or string beads in a pattern.

Compassion. Infants and toddlers regard themselves as the center of the universe. They are unable to understand the needs of others and can express only their own.

Ideally by kindergarten, children begin to empathize—to put themselves in another's place. Children begin to recognize the strengths and weaknesses of other people—and to share their sorrow or pride.

Encourage the development of compassion in the following ways:

- Talks about feelings. Give a name to pain, fear, anger, and joy, for example.
- Identify and encourage kindnesses, such as when Abby tries to console Abbot when he scrapes his knee.
- Make pet care more than routine by talking about feeling hungry, thirsty, or dirty.
- Encourage cooperative rather than competitive activities. Instead of challenging children to a foot race, plan an obstacle course that requires children to help each other squeeze through a cardboard box, for example.

Trust. When infants and toddlers have consistent, loving care they develop basic trust. They feel they are important members of the family or group and learn they can rely on adults for help in unfamiliar situations. Coupled with a desire for independence, trust enables children to feel the protection and support of adults as they explore, discover, and interpret the environment.

Ideally by kindergarten, children can understand the give-and-take of social situations. They are comfortable with the rules or "ways of doing" that keep them safe. They rely on our consistency to know what is expected of them and are eager to do things the right way.

Encourage the development of trust in the following ways:

- When a baby cries, respond as soon as possible.
- Follow daily routines for eating, play, and naps.
- Establish simple rules and enforce them consistently.
- Treat children fairly, with respect and consideration.
- Provide supervision to prevent biting, bullying, cruel teasing, and other violent behavior.

Creativity. Babies are born curious. They reach for objects and explore them with their mouths and hands. As toddlers, they get into everything and climb into interesting spaces.

Ideally by kindergarten, children are eager to work on and solve their own problems—in art and construction projects, computations, and social interactions. They approach ideas and tasks with initiative, playfulness, and inventive thinking. They ask lots of questions.

Encourage creativity in the following ways:

- Provide clay, paints, blocks, and other unstructured materials. Allow children time to explore the material without the need to make an object or paint a picture.
- Focus on the process, not the product. Avoid asking "What is it?" Rather say things like "Looks like you really enjoyed doing that" or "You worked hard on that."
- Ask open-ended questions. Instead of "Did you like the story?" ask "What did you like best about the story?"
- Notice and appreciate children's ideas. "Yes, Juan. We could take apart that old clock and see if we could make it work."
- Avoid rote learning and modeled projects that minimize individuality.

Self-control. Toddlers have little self-control. Ricky, for example, sees a truck and wants it. However, he does not have the intellectual or social skills to consider that Heddy is already playing with it and that he needs to wait for his turn.

Ideally by kindergarten, children understand and accept the need for rules—for their own sake and sake of others in community. They are learning the art of compromise and negotiation and can often see an event from someone else's point of view. Kindergarten children are usually able to identify their own property and respect the belongings of their peers. They are also able to take responsibility for simple tasks, have the self-control to stay focused, and follow through on a commitment.

Encourage self-control in the following ways:

- Model self-restraint. "I feel like eating a big bowl of ice cream right now, but I know I would feel too stuffed to move."
- Offer children choices.
- Consistently enforce simple rules.
- Offer to help children identify and deal with their frustrations. "Your face looks really angry,

Jacob. Shall we take some deep breaths before we talk about the problem?"
- Be clear about appropriate and inappropriate ways to express anger. "You can stamp your feet, Hannah, but I can't let you use your feet to kick Hank."

Perseverance and resilience. Toddlers learn to walk only after lots of trials and tumbles. Determination to succeed helps them ignore bumps and falls, and find success. When preschoolers dig canals in the sand, they learn cause and effect—what works and doesn't work.

Ideally by kindergarten, children have experience with problem-solving, brainstorming, and evaluating decisions. They can often use these skills to evaluate what went wrong with a project—and find the courage and determination to try again.

Encourage perseverance and resilience in the following ways:

- Encourage children to finish projects they begin—work a puzzle, build a structure, paint a picture, or play a game before quitting.
- Let children extend their projects over time—a block construction or multi-piece puzzle, for example, could take several days.
- Provide storage space for unfinished art projects.
- Avoid the temptation to do something for, rather than with, a child.
- Teach negotiation skills. "Cole and Bryan, how can you both play with the trike without fighting?"

Independence, compassion, trust, creativity, self-control, and perseverance—these attitudes are the real signs of school readiness. These are also the attitudes children need to grow into successful, competent adults. With these qualities, they will find satisfying jobs, form loving families, and be respected in society.

From *Texas Child Care*, Fall 2002, pp. 40-42. © 2002 by Texas Workforce Commission. Reprinted by permission.

The Role of Emotional Competence in the Development of the Young Child

BY RUTH WILSON, PH.D.

Jeremy and Maria are busy experimenting at the water table in Jodie Snell's preschool classroom. While Jeremy plays with funnels, cups, and an eyedropper, Maria floats small pieces of bark. Meredith walks over to join Jeremy and Maria, but she trips and falls as she approaches the table. Her arm hits the side of the water table and she begins to cry.

As Meredith gets up from her fall, Maria pushes her hard and almost knocks her down again. Then Maria yells at Meredith and tells her to go away. Jeremy, concerned about Meredith and the ensuing fight, calls Ms. Snell for help. He then tells Maria to stop hitting Meredith.

What Is Emotional Competence

There may be a number of reasons why Maria and Jeremy respond so differently to Meredith's "intrusion" at the water table. Some research, however, suggests that their reactions may be related to their different levels of emotional development and competence (Garner & Estep, 2001; Denham, 2001). Jeremy realizes that Meredith may have hurt herself during her fall and is concerned about her feelings. Maria, however,

doesn't even notice Meredith's distress and focuses only on protecting her own play space.

In terms of emotional development, Jeremy's response suggests competence in several related skills. He's aware of Meredith's feelings and expresses sensitivity to her plight. By calling to the teacher for help and telling Maria to stop hitting, he also actively intervenes to help Meredith in this stressful situation. In other words, Jeremy demonstrates skill in recognizing the feelings of others and responding appropriately to others in distress. In this way, he seems to be more emotionally competent than Maria. This article will discuss the four types of emotional competence, examine competence and behavior, and offer suggestions for guiding young children in the development of emotional competence.

Emotional Competence Versus Social-Emotional Development

While social-emotional development was at one time viewed as a single developmental domain, emotional competence is now being recognized as an area of development that is separate from, yet related to social competence (Garner & Estep, 2001). Emotional competence, as

an area of child development, "has long been underrated in both psychology and early childhood education, but no longer" (Denham, 2001, p. 6). New understandings about the impact of emotional competence to other areas of development are emerging. For example, we're learning that "when developmental milestones of emotional competence are not negotiated successfully, children are at risk, both at the time and later in life" (Denham, 2001, p. 5). Related areas of concern include behavioral difficulties, the development of a sense of well-being (Denham, 2001), and the ability to learn (Roffey & O'Reirdan, 2001). Emotionally competent children know how to vary their behavior to correspond with the thoughts, feelings, and situations of those around them. They are also less likely to be involved in angry disputes with peers and to use constructive strategies in response to potentially conflicting situations. We saw this in the case of Jeremy and Maria.

Types of Emotional Competence

Research on emotional competence suggests that there are four different types of emotional competence: situation knowledge, explanations of emotions, positivity of emotional expression, and emotional intensity (Garner & Estep, 2001). Situation knowledge and explanations of emotions represent children's knowledge of emotions, which can be defined as an awareness of one's own and others' emotions. Children who have developed knowledge of emotions can usually: 1) infer the thoughts and feelings of others, 2) justify their own behavior to peers, and 3) express sensitivity to the emotions of others. The other two types of emotional competence—positivity of emotional expression and emotional intensity—focus on children's expressivity. Expressivity refers to how emotions, both positive and negative, are expressed. Emotionally competent children are able to modulate emotional expressions and behavior (Garner & Estep, 2001), while children lacking such competence tend to be more explosive and demonstrative in expressing how they feel.

To help young children grow in emotional competence, early childhood educators should be aware of the four different areas of this developmental domain and have an understanding of related social implications. The following discussion provides a brief overview of each of these areas.

Situation Knowledge

Situaiton knowledge relates to children's understanding of contextual clues that can be used to infer the cause of an emotional display. Situation knowledge also relates to children's decisions about how to respond to emotionally charged situations. Children who are knowledgeable about emotions tend to have fewer negative exchanges with peers and, when disagreements do occur, they seem better able to use reasoned arguments to resolve conflicts than children who are not knowledgeable about emotions (Garner & Estep, 2001). Therefore, it is not surprising to find that children high in emotional knowledge experience a greater number of positive peer interactions than other children (Garner & Estep, 2001).

Explanations of Emotions

Children's ability to talk about the causes and consequences of others' emo-

tions falls under the explanations of emotions category. Such emotional discourse skills are often used to negotiate conflicts and misunderstandings with peers. Children's discussions about different emotions also provide a constructive way to convey their own feelings and to elicit feedback about those feelings. Research studies indicate that young children's ability to talk about emotions leads to greater peer-rated likeability and ease in initiating social contact and having others initiate contact with them (Denham, 2001).

Positivity of Emotional Expression

Positivity of emotional expression deals with emotion management skills. Such skills are used to initiate and maintain peer interactions, to offer comfort, and to minimize negative interactions. Related research indicates that children who have difficulty managing the expression of emotion are less likely to respond appropriately during highly charged negative interactions with peers than other children (Garner & Estep, 2001).

Emotional Intensity

The ability to control the expression of emotion describes the emotional intensity category. Examples of items on a questionnaire used by Garner and Estep (2001) to assess emotional intensity include: 1) "This child shows strong reactions to things, both positive and negative," and 2) "The child reacts strongly (cries or complains) to a disappointment or failure." In the case of Maria, we saw a strong reaction to a situation, suggesting a high level of emotional intensity on her part. Emotionally competent children tend to have greater control over the intensity of how they express their emotions.

Social and Other Developmental Implications

It seems obvious that children who are knowledgeable about their emotions and who can control the expression of emotion have a better chance of being successful in negotiating complex interpersonal exchanges with their peers

than children who are not as emotionally competent. Current research supports this hypothesis and found, for example, that emotional competence plays an important role in establishing and maintaining satisfying peer relationships (Garner & Estep, 2001). In the research, children who were adept at understanding expressive and situational cues of emotion were more popular with their peers than other children. Children who were deficient in emotional knowledge often misinterpreted social and emotional cues. Such misinterpretations interfered with their ability to initiate and maintain positive social interactions with peers.

Certain aspects of children's emotional competence, then, are considered to be prerequisites or "fundamental supports" for their growing social competence (Denham, 2001). The lack of emotional competence, on the other hand, tends to "promote spiraling difficulties" in children's ability to interact and form relationships with others (Denham, 2001, p. 6). A close connection between emotions and behavior also seems fairly obvious. Emotions tend to regulate both inter- and intrapersonal behaviors, and the literature on behavior disorders repeatedly addresses emotional factors (Denham, 2001).

As previously stated, there is also a connection between children's emotional competence and their ability to learn and be successful in a classroom setting. Research studies have shown that deficiencies in the area of emotional competence include disruptive behaviors and poor school performance (Roffey & O'Reirdan, 2001; Shields, Dickstein, Seifer, Giusti, Magee, & Spritz, 2001). Children who are unable to monitor and modulate their emotional arousal usually find it very difficult or impossible to maintain an optimal level of engagement within the school context (Shields, et al., 2001). They tend to have trouble adjusting to classroom structure, complying with rules and limits, and negotiating cooperative relationships with their peers. As a result, children who are able to control the expression of emotions in the classroom are more likely to perform better on cognitive tasks than other children (Garner & Estep, 2001).

Other research studies found that preschoolers' emotion regulation at the start of the school year was associated with school adjustment at year's end, whereas early emotional liability predicted poorer outcomes (Shields, et al., 2001). Such findings support school-based interventions, which will be discussed in detail below.

Helping Young Children Develop Emotional Competence

To appropriately guide young children in the development of emotional competence, teachers need to be aware of related expectations at different stages of development. A list of skills and abilities that can be expected of most preschool children who are developing emotionally at an optimum rate may be helpful. These skills and abilities, as developed by Roffey and O'Reirdan (2001), include:

- Being enthusiastic and motivated to learn
- Experiencing a wide range of feelings (but not necessarily able to identify them clearly)
- Being aware of feelings and able to relate these to wants
- Using a range of varied, complex and flexible ways of expressing emotions
- Using language for emotional control and expression
- Having increasing emotional control (but not able to hide feelings completely)
- Using play to work out emotional issues
- Demonstrating a growing sensitivity to the feelings of others
- Caring for and about pets and younger children
- Comforting distressed peers
- Identifying what is right and wrong in relation to family and cultural values
- Testing behavioral boundaries from time to time.

Recommended Children's Literature for Fostering Emotional Competence

Young children can feel overwhelmed by their emotions. At times, they may even be frightened by the power of their emotions. Carefully selected children's books can be used to help young children understand different emotions and ways of expressing their feelings in appropriate ways. The following list represents a small sample of the many books you can use to help children grow in emotional competence.

Anholt, C. and Anholt, L. (1994). *Makes Me Happy.* Cambridge, MA: Candlewick Press. A question and answer format is used to talk about different feelings (including being scared, sad, shy, excited, mad, proud, and jealous). While the answers as to what causes these different feelings vary from individual to individual, the book ends with a statement about what makes us all happy (such as playing in the sun, singing a song, and being together).

Anholt, C. and Anholt, L. (1991). *What I Like.* New York: Putnam's Sons. Different ideas about what individual children like and dislike are presented in this book. While one theme of the story is that we all have different tastes, another theme focuses on the idea that most of us feel the same about some things in life (such as friends).

Baker, L. (2001). *I Love You Because You're You.* New York: Scholastic. This book describes in rhyming text a mother's love for her child through all kinds of moods and behaviors. At different times, the child is sad, sleepy, frisky, silly, happy, and frightened—and through it all the mother's love remains constant.

Evans, L. (1999). *Sometimes I Feel Like a Storm Cloud.* Greenvale, NY: Mondo Publishing. *Sometimes I Feel Like a Storm Cloud* is about a child who describes how it feels to experience a variety of emotions. Different similes are used to describe the wide-ranging ups and downs of childhood: there's the rain cloud ready to burst into a shower of tears; a balloon that grows larger and larger with excitement and then becomes deflated as the air woooshes away; there's winter snow which is silent, cold, and alone; and there's a tornado that goes around bashing and smashing things to the ground.

Leonard, M. (1999). *Scared.* Lake Forest, IL: Forest House Publishing. *Scared* is an interactive book focusing on different things that scare some children, including the dark, thunder, bugs, strange dogs, and climbing up high. The text invites readers to identify some of the things that scare them. The text also offers some suggestions for dealing with fears, such as learning more about what scares you and talking to parents when you are scared. A special introductory page, written for adults, offers suggestions on how to encourage further discussion about things that children fear. It also presents several ideas for follow-up activities. *Scared* is one of four books in a "How I Feel" series published by Forest House Publishing Co. (P.O. Box 738, Lake Forest, IL 60045–0738. 1–800–394–READ). The other three titles in the series are *Angry, Happy,* and *Silly.*

Modesitt, J. (1992). *Sometimes I Feel Like a Mouse.* New York: Scholastic. Animal images are used to represent different feelings in this wonderful book. There's the shy mouse, the bold elephant, the happy canary, the scared rabbit, the excited squirrel, etc. The book ends with an important statement about feelings—that is, that everyone has feelings and that there is no such thing as a right or wrong feeling. The book encourages children to listen to their own feelings and to be comfortable with the idea that we have many different feelings.

As in other areas of development, intervention should start with prevention and a focus on building strengths. As Denham (2001) states, "We owe our children more than a mere lack of disorder, more than averting tragedy. We need to study not just weakness, but also strength, not just fixing what is broken, but nurturing what is best within our children" (p. 5). Preventive interventions are based on the premise that teachers can play a key role in fostering children's emotional competence (Denham, 2001). Examples of specific interventions include coaching students in areas such as recognizing emotions, coping with frustrating situations, understanding different situations, and developing perspective-taking skills (Shields, et al., 2001).

While "coaching" interventions (which tend to be somewhat didactic) have proven effective, studies examining teachers' naturally occurring influences indicate that preschoolers' secure emotional attachments to their teachers also impact children's display of emotions in school. Preschool children who develop secure attachments to their teachers are less likely to engage in unregulated anger and behavior problems. They are also more likely to exhibit positive emotions in the school setting (Shields, et al,

2001). A warm, close relationship between student and teacher, then, can positively influence young children's emerging emotional competence.

While theory strongly supports a "prevention-first" approach to fostering emotional competence, research indicates a lack of curricular attention to this area of development. "In the majority of preschool contexts ... emotion socialization does not have an easily defined place in the curriculum, and emotional issues are likely to receive sustained attention from school personnel only during crisis situations" (Shields et al., 2001, p. 90). For a more preventive approach, teachers should act as "emotion coaches" and models in even routine situations during an average school day (Shields et al., 2001). They recommend that teachers use the everyday situations in the classroom to help children identify emotions and develop effective coping skills.

There are many naturally-occurring opportunities for children to learn how to deal with the frustration of mastering a new academic skill, how to negotiate the complex behaviors involved in sharing and cooperative interactions with peers, and how to manage angry feelings when limits are placed on their behaviors. While teachers should certainly capital-

ize on these naturally-occurring situations, they should also consider the importance of establishing strong relationships with young children as a vehicle for fostering emotional competence.

Ruth Wilson, Ph.D., is a Professor Emeritus of Special Education at Bowling Green State University in Ohio. Dr. Wilson's expertise is early childhood special education, and much of her research has focused on early childhood environmental education. She retired from teaching and now devotes much of her time to writing.

References

Denham, S.A. (2001). Dealing with feelings: Foundations and consequences of young children's emotional competence. *Early Education and Development,* 12(1), 5–9.

Garner, P.W. & Estep, K.M. (2001). Emotional competence, emotion socialization, and young children's peer-related social competence. *Early Education & Development,* 12(1) 29–46.

Roffey, S.A. O'Reirdan, T. (2001). *Young children and classroom behavior.* London: David Fulton Publishers.

Shields, A.; Dickstein, S.; Seifer, R.; Giusti, L.; Magee, K.D.; & Spritz, B. (2001). Emotional competence and early school adjustment: a study of preschoolers at risk. *Early Education & Development,* 12(1), 73–90.

Childhood Obesity:
The Caregiver's Role

by Bernadette Haschke

Children are getting fatter. Newspaper reports describe young children with weights in excess of 100 pounds. Recent surveys (U.S. Department of Health and Human Services, 2002) indicate that 10 percent of children ages 2 to 5 and 15 percent of children ages 6 to 19 are overweight.

Obesity is becoming a serious concern. Excessive weight impedes normal physical and psychological development of young children. Obesity is a detrimental cycle that gets progressively worse. Being overweight leads to inactivity, and inactivity contributes to obesity.

The cause is apparent: obesity begins when a child eats more calories than are used. However, other interrelated causes that begin in childhood have long-term consequences for a lifetime battle with obesity and health issues. For young children dealing with obesity is primarily a parental responsibility, but medical professionals, caregivers, and teachers play important roles.

Causes of childhood obesity

Limited physical activity. Obesity is a behavioral issue for all age groups and a direct consequence of lifestyle, even for young children. Young children readily adopt the lifestyle of their parents.

Today's families are increasingly busy with many activities pulling members in different directions. Such busyness does not mean physical activity. Most often young children follow along, riding in a car seat as family members drive from dance lesson to grocery store. As a result, children have little time for play and self-selected activities.

In many neighborhoods, safety is a concern. Parents keep children inside so they can watch them at all times.

Increased sedentary activity. The nature of inside activities for children today is an important factor in obesity. The amount of time children spend with television, computers, and video games has increased and is often the major childhood activity.

Such activities may or may not be harmful in themselves, depending on the nature of programs and games. The major concern is that these activities have replaced physically active play. Not only are young children burning few calories, but watching TV and playing video games often go hand in hand with snacking on high-calorie fat foods.

Eating habits. Snacking by both adults and children most often involves foods that are high in calorie, high in fat, and low in fiber. Children who snack shortly before meals are less likely to be hungry at mealtime. Families increasingly order delivery meals such as pizza or bring home prepared meals from a restaurant or grocery.

Because of busy schedules, families are increasingly choosing to eat meals away from home. They are likely to choose high-fat and high-calorie foods from fast-food restaurants.

All of these factors contribute to a lifestyle that increases the risk for childhood obesity.

The caregiver's role

Caregivers have a unique opportunity to provide nutrition education on a continuing basis, not just a weekly nutrition unit once or twice during the year. Ongoing discussion of nutrition and daily activities with a food and nutrition emphasis are important for teaching basic concepts. Ideally nutrition is an ongoing part of the curriculum and used to teach other concepts.

Nutrition education during the early childhood years is especially important because it is during this period that lifetime eating habits are formed. The quality of nutrition for children ages 2 to 5 is especially important because it affects growth and development. It is easier to develop healthy eating habits during this time than it is to change eating habits in adulthood. Habits established during childhood will last a lifetime.

Caregivers need to provide healthy foods that meet the recommended dietary guidelines and to offer only those food options for children to select. Children do not automatically make healthy food decisions. Without nutrition education and guidance, they tend to choose foods high in sodium, salt, sugar, and fat or those foods familiar to them. The goal is that children learn to self-regulate the intake of food and to realize when they are full.

The quality of nutrition for children ages 2 to 5 is especially important because it affects growth and development.

Don't fall into the trap of encouraging, forcing, or bribing children to eat more than they actually need. They will not starve if they don't eat everything on their plates. The goal is to encourage children to make wise choices and assume responsibility for those choices.

The caregiver's responsibility is to teach children to recognize the link between nutrition and physical well-being. Children need knowledge of the nutrients in foods and their effect on physical growth and development—not just for now, but for their future health and well-being.

Learning nutrition concepts

Piaget concluded that children ages 2 to 7 learn by actively participating in their environment, not by passively listening to instruction (Swadener, 1994). According to Piagetian theory, nutrition education for this age group involves interaction with food. Abstract concepts and stylized pictures have no place in nutrition education for young children. Because nutrition is an abstract concept for preschoolers, caregivers will use examples of real foods that are meaningful for children.

Research by Birch (1987) has found that early experience with food and eating is crucial to the food acceptance patterns children develop. Everyday experiences with food and eating affect food acceptance and intake.

Babies are born with a preference for sweets, but all other food preferences are acquired (Birch, 1994). The natural tendency for children is to reject anything that tastes new and unfamiliar. One study by Birch (1987) shows that the children 2 to 6 years old are initially reluctant to taste new or unfamiliar foods. However, the preference for a food increases with many exposures, regardless of one's age.

Other studies (Birch, 1990) indicate that young children must be exposed to a new food up to 15 times before they accept it. It is not surprising that the best time to introduce children to new foods is during the toddler period before they reach the negative 2-year-old stage in which the first response is usually "no."

Tips for parents

- Avoid having prepared high-sugar or high-fat snacks in the home. Instead, have plenty of fresh fruits and vegetables to choose from.
- Provide foods high in fiber such as fruits, vegetables, and whole-grain breads and cereals.
- Know your child's food patterns and needs. Don't force a bottle or require that your child finish a meal. Instead serve small portions and leave the decision about being full to your child.
- Don't use food as reward or punishment for behavior.
- Avoid using dessert and candy as a reward for eating other foods.
- Provide whole milk until age 2. After that, use 2 percent or skim milk.
- Limit television and computer time.
- Provide opportunities for active, physical play.
- Participate with your child in activities such as walking, swimming, and sports.

From Morgan, R. "Evaluation and Treatment of Childhood Obesity," *American Family Physician*, Feb. 15, 1999.

Preparing and serving healthy foods

Those who prepare and serve meals and snacks to young children need to examine how their practices may contribute to obesity. In a recent nutrition education workshop, a cook at a child care center said she didn't fry any foods that were served to the children. When participants were asked later to list the favorite foods served to children in their centers, this same individual volunteered "steak fingers." When the workshop leader pointed out this was a fried food, she replied, "I didn't fry the meat. I just warmed it in the oven." She didn't realize that the prepared steak fingers had been previously fried.

Serving a prepared food may be faster and easier, but it may also add calories to the meal. Serving prepared foods is increasing, despite their higher cost, because child care staff do not have the time, energy, or expertise to fully prepare foods themselves. Extra calories contribute to potential obesity, and serving unhealthy food leads to lifelong preferences and habits.

The caregiver's responsibility is to teach children to recognize the link between nutrition and physical well-being.

Portion size is an important factor in obesity (Young, 2002). Americans now "super-size" everything and expect to be served mounds of food at every meal. Caregivers need to help children learn to regulate their food intake and recognize the sensation of feeling full. Serving recommended portion sizes to young children is essential.

Start with an appropriate amount and give seconds only if the child wants more. Many caregivers report that children are now requesting third, fourth, and fifth servings of specific foods. An appropriate rule is to provide only one additional serving of a specific food, unless the child has a diet restriction and cannot eat other foods that are served. When children request a second helping, don't make them eat all other foods on their plates.

Encourage children to eat slowly, because the fullness sensation develops over time. Involving children in conversation about foods and eating preferences during snacks and mealtime helps to slow the intake rate and also provides an opportunity to discuss nutrition and foods on a daily basis. By allowing children time to acquire the fullness sensation, you may reduce requests for additional servings.

Serve meals and snacks at specific times and remove food when mealtime is over. Some children are naturally slow eaters and may need a few extra minutes to finish the meal. Eating should not become a stand-off between caregiver and child. If a child chooses not to eat, then remove the food and ask the child to move on to the next activity. Explain that the child will have another chance to eat at the next snack or mealtime.

Eating is a social behavior that is strongly influenced by the culture and traditions of society. The eating behavior of other children can serve as a role model and a social pressure for influencing a child's food preferences. Seating a child who refuses to eat corn with other children who love corn will likely increase the child's willingness to eat corn.

Model what you teach. Don't have coffee, a donut, or a can of soda in the room if you expect children to eat healthy foods at regular times.

Encouraging physical activity

Many caregivers might be surprised to learn that experts recommend an increase in physical activity for preschool children. Most of us spend much of the day trying to calm children and lessen their activity.

However, young children need to develop and practice motor skills. By incorporating active play and activities in the daily routine, we encourage an active childhood and lay the foundation for an active and productive adulthood. Research (Gabbard, 1998) indicates that the "window of opportunity" for acquiring basic motor movements is from the prenatal

Health consequences for obese children

- Risk factor for heart disease, high cholesterol, and high blood pressure
- Increased risk for Type II diabetes
- 70 percent chance of becoming an overweight adult if overweight as a teen
- Social discrimination
- Poor self-esteem

From "The Surgeon General's Call to Action to Prevent and Decrease Overweight and Obesity—Fact Sheet," www.surgeongeneral.gov/topics/obesity/calltoaction/fact_consequences.html.

period to age 5. The development period for fine motor skills extends from infancy to around 9 years of age.

Childhood fitness and movement activity needs to be fun and appropriate for the age of the child. Remember that play is children's work and their way of exploring, learning, and exercising.

Children need early opportunities to climb, walk, run, kick, throw, and jump. They need to develop eye-hand coordination by participating in activities such as working puzzles, building blocks, and stringing beads. Development of eye-foot coordination depends on activities such as kicking large balls. Helping children acquire and practice these skills provides the foundation for physical abilities later in life.

What about children who are inactive and just sit on the playground? Consider a routine of rotating children through various areas such as swings, bikes, and sandbox to encourage more active participation. Encourage children to select or assign them to begin in a different area of the playground for the first few minutes each day before choosing their favorite play area. This encourages development of different types of motor play and helps children to develop proficiency and skills in many areas.

Working with parents

It's important to educate families about nutrition and preventing obesity. Here are suggestions for working with families and their children:

- Encourage parents to be involved in all areas of their child's life. Children need to know that parents love and care for them regardless of their physical qualities. Part of parents' love and care is encouraging a healthy diet and activities suitable for preschool children.

Some parents may need help in learning what is appropriate for children at a certain age. You can provide

What's an appropriate serving?

Grain group	1 slice of bread ½ cup cooked rice
Fruit group	1 piece of fruit ¾ cup of juice
Meat group	2–3 oz. cooked meat, fish, or poultry cup of cooked dry beans or pasta or 1 egg
Vegetable group	½ cup chopped raw or cooked vegetables 1 cup of raw leafy vegetables
Milk group	1 cup milk or yogurt 2 oz. cheese

Recommended for children ages 4 to 6. Offer 2- 3-year-olds less of all foods except milk.

Source: U.S. Department of Agriculture, Center for Nurtrition Policy, 1999.

information about your activities at the center and ways to follow up at home. Send home suggested activities for outside active play and for healthful snacks that children can help prepare.

Childhood fitness and movement activity needs to be fun and appropriate for the age of the child.

Nutrition information that reinforces food and cooking topics covered in the child's classroom is especially helpful. For example, "Chef Combo" nutrition materials distributed by the National Dairy Council (1998) include leaflets that you can copy and send home with parents.

- Be sensitive to the cultural backgrounds of parents. In some cultures a large child is considered healthy. Obese parents may feel an overweight child is not a problem. Be sensitive to such issues and approach obesity from the standpoint of long-term health and well-being. Emphasize the child's inability to participate in all activities and its effect on self-concept.

- Recommend a healthy diet to parents. Help parents to see the importance of healthy eating. Suggest healthy snacks children can eat on the way home at the end of the day. Recommend apples, carrots, and graham crackers instead of chips, fast foods and other high-fat foods that may seem more convenient to a hurried parent trying to get home with hungry children.

- Encourage parents to examine their own levels of activity and eating patterns as well as their need to set a healthy example. It is hard to keep children from eating while watching TV if the parents are having snacks. Parents may be unaware of how many calories they consume as they watch television.

Dealing with an obese child

These suggestions are primarily directed at preventing obesity in young children. What can you do about an obese child in the classroom.

Talk with parents in an effort to express concern and provide information. Describe how obesity is hampering the child's participation in activities and how that behavior is different from that of other children in the classroom. Discuss strategies for cutting back food consumption and for encouraging the child to become more active. Although most obesity is not caused by health-related problems, you might suggest that the parents contact their physician or public health staff in dealing with the problem.

Obesity has become a serious concern in this country. Preventing it in early childhood is much easier than trying to undo unhealthy eating habits and activity patterns in adulthood.

References

Birch, L. "Research Example 1: The Role of Experience in Children's Food Acceptance Patterns, " *Supplement to the Journal of the American Dietetic Association*, Vol. 87, No. 9, 1987, pp. S36–S40.

Birch, L.; L. McPhee; L. Steinberg; and S. Sullivan. "Conditioned Flavor Preferences in Young Children," *Physiology and Behavior*, Vol. 47, 1990.

Birch, L. "How Kids Choose Foods," research presented at International Conference of Gastronomy, Monterry, Calif., March 11, 1994.

Chef Combo's Fantastic Adventures in Tasting and Nutrition, National Dairy Council, Rosemont, Ill., 1998.

Gabbard, C. "Windows of Opportunity for Early Brain and Motor Development," *Journal of Health, Physical Education, Recreation and Dance*, Vol. 69, No. 8, 1998, pp. 54–30.

Morgan, R. "Evaluation and Treatment of Childhood Obesity," *American Family Physician*, Feb. 15, 1999.

The Surgeon General's Call to Action to Prevent and Decrease Overweight and Obesity—Fact Sheet. www.surgeongeneral.gov/topics/obesity/calltoaction/fact_consequences.html.

Swadener S. "Nutrition Education for Preschool Age Children: A Review of the Research," www.nal.usda.gov/fnic/usda/preschoolne.html.

U.S. Department of Agriculture, Center for Nutrition Policy and Promotion, 1999.

U.S. Department of Health and Human Services, "Obesity Still on the Rise, New Data Show," www.cdc.gov/nchs/releases/02news/obesityonrise/html.

Young, L. "The Contribution of Expanding Portion Sizes to the U.S. Obesity Epidemic," *American Journal of Public Health*, Vol. 92, No. 2, 2002, pp. 246, 49

About the author

Bernadette Haschke, PhD, is an associate professor in the Department of Family and Consumer Sciences at Baylor University in Waco, Texas. She has served as a teacher and director in early childhood programs. She is a trainer for the Texas Career Development System for Early Care and Education and conducts workshops on childhood obesity.

The Allergy Epidemic

We've conquered most childhood infections, but extreme
reactions to everyday substances pose a new threat

By Jerry Adler

THE FIRST INDICATION THAT something was not quite right with David Adams was subtle, a mild rash around his mouth after nursing. Luckily, the second clue, at the age of 3 months, was not so subtle: angry hives that erupted over his entire body during a plane trip. After the family returned home to Georgia, a specialist determined that David was among the 6 to 8 percent of children under the age of 3 with an allergy to food—in his case, peanuts. His sensitivity was so acute that the hives may have been caused by the residue of peanuts on his parents' fingers, and the rash by his mother's eating a peanut-butter sandwich and excreting tiny amounts of peanut protein in her breast milk. What made the episode lucky was this: on a day two years later, when David began vomiting and gasping after chomping an energy bar that had escaped his parents' anti-peanut scrutiny, his mother could inject him with epinephrine and save his life. Implausible as it seems, David's condition is at the cutting edge of modern pediatric medicine, right up there with hay fever.

If a popular magazine had run a children's health issue a hundred years ago, the first article might have been about diphtheria or cholera—external threats that the West has largely conquered by antibiotics and sanitation. Instead we are examining allergies, a self-generated danger, the result of an immune system out of sync with its surroundings. These are among the leading challenges of the next century, a threat that may in part be an unintended consequence of our triumph over the infectious scourges of the past.

Speaking of hay fever, or "seasonal allergic rhinitis," the incidence of this annoying sensitivity to tree, grass or ragweed pollen has increased remarkably just since 1996—from 6 percent of American children 18 and under to 9 percent, according to the National Center for Health Statistics. All allergies seem to be on the rise, in fact, but "it's not just that more kids have allergies," says Dr. Marc Rothenberg, director of allergy and immunology at Cincinnati Children's Hospital. "The severity of those allergies has also increased."

An allergy is an overreaction by the immune system to a foreign substance, which can enter the body through a variety of routes. It can be inhaled, like pollen or dander, the tiny flakes of skin shed by domestic animals. It can be injected, like insect venom or penicillin, or merely touch the skin, like the latex in medical gloves. Or it can be ingested. According to the Food Allergy & Anaphylaxis Network, almost any food can trigger an allergy, although eight categories account for 90 percent of all reactions: milk, eggs, peanuts (technically, a legume), tree nuts, fin fish, shellfish, soy and wheat. (Allergies have nothing to do with the condition known as food intolerance; people who lack an enzyme for digesting dairy products, for instance, may suffer intestinal problems, but they are not allergic to milk.)

For reasons not fully understood, in some people these otherwise harmless substances provoke the same reactions by which the body attempts to rid itself of dangerous pathogens. These may include sneezing, vomiting and the all-purpose localized immune-system arousal known as inflammation. The lungs may be affected; allergies are a leading trigger for asthma attacks. In extreme cases, the reaction involves virtually all organ systems and proceeds to anaphylaxis, a dramatic drop in blood pressure accompanied by extreme respiratory distress that may be fatal without prompt treatment. Which is why, to this day—and possibly for the rest of his life—David Adams never sets foot outside his home without an emergency supply of epinephrine.

What can underlie such a self-destructive reaction? An infant who grows violently ill in the presence of as little as one hundredth of a peanut almost surely has some sort of genetic predisposition. Indeed, there is a strong inherited component in allergies. If one parent has an allergy, chances are one in three that the child will be allergic, according to the Asthma and Allergy Foundation of America. If both parents have allergies, the odds rise to 70 percent. But *the children aren't necessarily allergic to the same things as the parents*— strongly suggesting that some other factor must be at work as

The Itchy Sneezies: Kids & Allergies

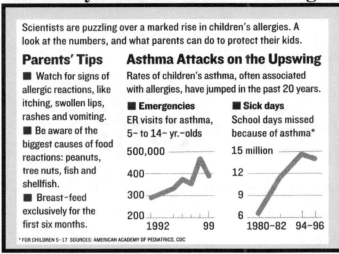

Scientists are puzzling over a marked rise in children's allergies. A look at the numbers, and what parents can do to protect their kids.

Parents' Tips
■ Watch for signs of allergic reactions, like itching, swollen lips, rashes and vomiting.
■ Be aware of the biggest causes of food reactions: peanuts, tree nuts, fish and shellfish.
■ Breast-feed exclusively for the first six months.

Asthma Attacks on the Upswing
Rates of children's asthma, often associated with allergies, have jumped in the past 20 years.

■ Emergencies
ER visits for asthma, 5- to 14- yr.-olds
500,000
400
300
200
1992   99

■ Sick days
School days missed because of asthma*
15 million
12
9
6
1980-82   94-96

* FOR CHILDREN 5-17 SOURCES: AMERICAN ACADEMY OF PEDIATRICS, CDC

well. And genetics cannot explain the rapid rise in allergies over the past few years or, for that matter, centuries. "The human race hasn't changed that much genetically in the last 200 years," since hay fever first came to the attention of doctors a single case at a time, says Dr. Andrew Saxon, chief of clinical immunology at UCLA.

So something must have changed in the environment—specifically, in the environment of developed nations, and especially their cities, where allergies are far more prevalent than in rural China and Africa. One obvious place to look is air pollution. Studies by Saxon and his colleague David Diaz-Sanchez have found a strong correlation between pollutants—diesel exhaust and cigarette smoke—and the development of allergies. Researchers don't believe pollution is the whole story, though; allergies have continued to climb even as smoking and air-pollution rates have fallen in recent decades. But industrialization has also brought about declines in infectious diseases and close exposure to farm animals. The "hygiene hypothesis" holds that it is precisely these (mostly desirable) trends that have contributed to the rise in allergies. The human immune system, which evolved in a natural environment teeming with hostile bacteria and parasites, finds itself uncomfortably idle in the antiseptic confines of the modern suburb, and, failing to mature properly, takes out its frustration on harmless peanuts and shrimp. Numerous studies have lent support to this general notion, notably one last year that showed a strong negative correlation between allergies and exposure to endotoxins, which are bacterial remains shed by farm animals. Research by Dr. Dennis Ownby of the Medical College of Georgia shows that children growing up with two or more pets, either cats or dogs, had a decreased risk of allergies—and not just to pet dander, but other unrelated allergens as well. But although many researchers accept the hygiene hypothesis in outline, the emerging picture is of "a complicated relationship, where dose and timing of exposure" play important but still uncertain roles, says Dr. Scott Weiss of Harvard.

So the hygiene hypothesis has yet to generate any concrete prescriptions (unless you count The New England Journal of Medicine's August 2000 editorial headlined PLEASE, SNEEZE ON MY CHILD). The eventual hope, says Ownby, is for a way to "artificially stimulate the immune system to reduce [allergy] risk without having all these diseases." Meanwhile, though, researchers are developing new drug therapies that go beyond epinephrine (for emergency treatment of anaphylaxis) and the growing array of over-the-counter antihistamines. (Histamine is a key substance in the cascade of biochemical events that constitute an allergic reaction.) Newer drugs, like Singulair and Xolair—just approved by the Food and Drug Administration in June for allergy-related asthma—block other chemicals in the chain. And even ordinary activated charcoal could be useful in blocking peanut allergies, according to a new study; if taken immediately it may neutralize the allergenic proteins in the stomach.

Pediatricians have also begun taking allergies more seriously. One key bit of advice to mothers is to breast-feed infants exclusively for six months. Delaying children's exposure to novel foods in this way is the "hallmark for food-allergy prevention," says the American Academy of Pediatrics. Nursing mothers should also be on the lookout for signs of a secondhand food reaction in their infants, including diarrhea, vomiting or itchy rashes (not counting diaper rash). If these rare reactions occur, the mother may want to avoid drinking milk, or eating eggs, fish, tree nuts and especially peanuts. Peanuts, in fact, are the one food the AAP recommends that a woman avoid, not only while nursing but also while pregnant, because of their allergic potential. For the same reason, the longer you can hold off feeding your child peanut butter, the better: the AAP suggests waiting until 3. Cow's milk, by contrast, is usually safe after the 1st birthday.

And once an allergy has been diagnosed, the only thing to do is what David Adams's parents did: draw a *cordon sanitaire* around the child. Again, this is especially important for peanut allergies. Unfortunately, peanuts and peanut butter are ubiquitous, found in many Asian and Mexican dishes, in baked goods—and in practically every other child's lunchbox. Peanut-free zones in school lunchrooms have become a vital amenity in many communities, but even so, parents with severely allergic children are constantly on alert—writing to food companies to double-check lists of ingredients, outlawing even innocuous bakery products (a spatula that came into contact with a peanut-butter cookie can transfer a dangerous dose of allergen to an oatmeal-raisin one) and equipping babysitters and teachers with dedicated cell phones and walkie-talkies for emergencies. Milk, another potentially potent allergen, is, if anything, even harder to avoid. "You're sitting at a [school] cafeteria table and someone across from you spills milk," says Denise Bunning, of suburban Chicago, describing her nightmare scenario; Bunning's two sons, Bryan, 9, and Daniel, 7, are both allergic to milk, along with several other foods. At the age of 4, Bryan went into anaphylaxis after eating a jelly worm from a dispenser that had previously held milk-chocolate candies.

Susan Leavitt of New York, whose 13-year-old son, David Parkinson, is allergic to milk products, eggs, fish, nuts and mustard, goes so far as to check out school art supplies; a fourth-grade teacher once mentioned adding eggs to tempera paint for a better texture. There's a lot he can't have—pizza, to start with—but a lot of it is stuff you wouldn't necessarily want your kid to have anyway. And thanks to her vigilance, her home-cooked and pre-frozen meals and New York's ubiquitous fruit and vegetable markets, David is a healthy, normal boy, an avid skier—and alive.

With Anne Underwood and Karen Springen

BIG SPENDERS

BY MARGARET MAGNARELLI

James Hansen, 5, can't read yet, but he has no problem identifying the logos of his favorite products. For a recent homework assignment, the kindergartner had to list all the words he knew by sight. As his mother, Barbara Brabec, of Studio City, California, held up food items and toy boxes, James began shouting out their names. In no time, they had filled a notebook page with brands he recognized, including Cheerios, Legos, Lunchables, and Skippy. At that moment Brabec realized just how much her son is influenced by marketers. "I was amazed by how many product names he knew," she says.

She shouldn't have been. Young children are bombarded by advertisements—on TV, on buses and billboards, in stores, and even at school. In fact, according to James U. McNeal, Ph.D., author of *The Kids Market: Myths and Realities,* the average child recognizes more than 200 logos by the time he enters first grade.

While preschoolers were once seen as having a limited effect on their parents' purchases, they are now widely viewed as little people with big buying influence. Companies spend an estimated $14.4 billion annually to advertise and promote their products to your kids, according to the U.S. Small Business Administration. And it's working. A 1999 study revealed that children become brand-conscious as early as age 3, and half ask for specific brands by age 5.

"They're not just grocery-store pants-pullers anymore," says Anne Sutherland, author of *Kid-fluence: The Marketer's Guide to Understanding and Reaching Generation Y—Kids, Tweens, and Teens.* "Young children today play an important part in making family decisions on everything from cars to vacations."

Kids are highly attractive to marketers for several reasons. First and foremost, they've got their hands in your pockets. Whether you call it the nag factor or the power of pestering, children sway parents' decisions to the tune of $290 billion annually. "McDonald's was one of the first companies to recognize that most family dining-out decisions are influenced by children," says Christie Nordhielm, Ph.D., an assistant professor of marketing at the Kellogg School of Management at Northwestern University, in Evanston, Illinois. That realization led to the introduction of Ronald McDonald and, later, the wildly successful (and imitated) Happy Meals.

Nor is it just your money your kids are spending. Children ages 4 to 12 shell out an estimated $35.6 billion of their own cash annually, more than four times what they did a decade ago. They may not have huge allowances, but what they do have is highly disposable.

KIDS AGES 4 TO 12 SPEND $35.6 BILLION OF THEIR OWN CASH ANNUALLY, FOUR TIMES MORE THAN A DECADE AGO.

And since many companies feel the brands kids connect with now will be the ones they'll stick with in the future, they're not just selling kid stuff. For instance, General Motors, in part because boys form impressions of cars at an early age, now sponsors a Test Track ride (including a display of future vehicle designs) at Walt Disney World's Epcot Center. And Home Depot offers a toy tool set designed to imprint its brand on youngsters.

"Marketing is teaching young children to be active consumers," says Linda Gulyn, Ph.D., an associate professor of psychology at Marymount University, in Arlington, Virginia. And that lesson is coming before they're capable of making informed decisions. "Until about age 6, a child doesn't recognize that an ad is intended to persuade him to want something," Dr. Gulyn says. "Preschoolers are very trusting of adults and other authorities. They believe what they hear and see is real and true."

Commercial Consequences

Television advertising is the most powerful way marketers reach kids. On average, a child spends four hours in front of the tube each day and views as many as 40,000 commercials per year.

Often, as Amy Kite, of Glencoe, Illinois, prepares dinner for her family of five, Benjamin, her 4-year-old son, will yell for her to come see an ad for a product he wants to buy. Lately, he's been fascinated by commercials for Hot Wheels cars and Lucky Charms cereal. (In the grocery store recently he asked, "Are these the ones with the new bigger marshmallows?")

MINIMIZE MARKETING

THE CENTER FOR A NEW AMERICAN DREAM OFFERS THESE TIPS FOR RAISING A CHILD IN TODAY'S COMMERCIAL CULTURE.

- **Consume responsibly.** Remember that you're a role model for your child. Speaking wistfully about things you wish you had will reinforce the idea that material goods make for a better life.
- **Educate him about ads.** By age 6, your child should be able to understand the manipulative purpose of a commercial. Explain the difference between want and need, and ask what he thinks he'll gain by having a product he desires.
- **Set limits.** If you feel a product is dangerous or wasteful, explain why to your child.
- **Cut back on television.** The fewer commercials your child watches, the less impact they'll have.
- **Talk to other parents.** Its easier to resist a child's lobbying efforts when you know how other parents handle similar situations.
- **Set an allowance.** Encourage your child to stash money in a piggy bank. Your child will appreciate a toy more once she buys it.
- **Focus on the nonmaterial.** Make time for simple activities that stimulate the imagination, like playing outside, reading, and drawing.
- **Take action.** Contact companies whose ads you think are inappropriate. Boycott products whose marketing you find offensive or exploitative. And log on to *www.commercialalert.org* to support the Parents' Bill of Rights.

Through focus groups and psychological research, companies are constantly studying how children think so they can maximize the impact of their messages. Using cartoon characters like Tony the Tiger and the Trix Rabbit has long been viewed as an effective selling and brand-building strategy. "Animated characters send a signal to children that this is their world, so they should listen," Sutherland says.

A more recent marketing twist: using characters from your kids' favorite programs—*Dora the Explorer, Blue's Clues*—to sell toothpaste, books, yogurt, macaroni and cheese, and more. Brands are also establishing product partnerships (think Kellogg's Disney Mickey's Magix cereal) that strengthen both brands.

The latest marketing escalation is McDonald's plan to introduce a licensed McKids line of clothing to be sold at Wal-Mart, as well as toys, educational videos, and books that both Target and Toys "R" Us will carry.

A growing number of companies are even marketing directly through schools. Toys "R" Us, Petco, and Sports Authority are among those participating in a cooperative called Field Trip Factory, which arranges to have kindergartners and grade-schoolers visit their stores. And then there is Channel One, which brings educational TV programming—along with paid commercials—to more than 8 million American students.

"There's almost no place where something isn't being sold to our children," says Diane Wood, executive director of the Center for a New American Dream, a Takoma Park, Maryland, advocacy group whose goal is to help Americans resist excessive consumerism.

And parents are concerned: A poll conducted by the center showed that almost 80 percent of respondents think marketing pressures kids to buy products that are unhealthy or too costly; seven out of ten say such advertising is bad for their kids' values; and almost two thirds of parents say that their children define their self-worth in terms of possessions and that the problem has worsened over time.

A Bad Rap?

While it's easy to see the downside of marketing to kids, critics tend to dismiss positive examples of the practice. A number of companies, for instance, use advertising money to support educational children's shows—like *Sesame Street* and *Clifford the Big Red Dog*.

"McDONALD'S WAS ONE OF THE FIRST COMPANIES TO RECOGNIZE THAT FAMILY DINING-OUT DECISIONS ARE INFLUENCED BY KIDS."

Strong brand association among preschoolers also has its pluses for parents. Amy Kite notes that Oral-B Stages Buzz Lightyear toothpaste and a Reach SpongeBob SquarePants toothbrush make her son, Benjamin, 4, excited to brush his teeth. And Dora the Explorer underpants and an Elmo potty seat made toilet-teaching her daughter, Emily, 2, a lot simpler. "It's as if I've got a whole team of characters on my side to get my kids to do things they might otherwise resist," she says.

Detractors argue that the way these characters are being used to sell products is exploitative. Advocacy groups are also up in arms about commercialized classrooms, saying children shouldn't have to sift through advertising messages to get to educational ones.

Gary Ruskin, executive director of Commercial Alert, a lobbying group cofounded by Ralph Nader, says commercials aimed at kids under 12 should be banned outright, as has been done in Norway and Sweden. That's just one provision of the Parents' Bill of Rights he's lobbying to Congress. Among the bill's other objectives: to prohibit marketers from tracking kids' purchases; to

eliminate all forms of school advertising; and to require that companies reveal all money paid to have their products appear in films and on TV shows.

"We're trying to prevent this commercial culture from subverting the values of our kids," Ruskin says.

Commercial Alert has already helped pass a law requiring parents to be notified about all market research being done at their kids' schools, and it has pushed individual school districts to remove junk-food vending machines. But while public support for the Parents' Bill of Rights is on the rise, the proposed legislation has yet to be introduced by Congress.

"WE'RE TRYING TO PREVENT THIS COMMERCIAL CULTURE FROM SUBVERTING THE VALUES OF OUR KIDS."

In the meantime, parents have an unlikely ally in their fight against inappropriate ads: the Children's Advertising Review Unit (CARU), which is funded by the marketers themselves as a means of self-regulation. CARU makes sure advertisements targeted at children don't make misleading claims or misrepresent a food product's nutritional value. The organization recently challenged a Sunny Delight spot that showed the bottle breaking through a concrete block, arguing that young kids might believe that the drink conveys great strength. The company promptly agreed to alter the content of the commercial.

CARU director Elizabeth Lascoutx says the watchdog group boasts a compliance rate of 95 percent. "No industry segment wants to get labeled as harming children, and that's partially what drives participation in our system," she says.

The Message Starts at Home

Despite such symbolic victories, kid-directed marketing remains a lucrative, powerful, and fast-growing business. The primary burden of regulating its impact remains with busy parents, who must find the time to teach children the difference between want and need, explain the manipulative role of commercials, and above all, stand up to their kids' constant demands for products.

Christina Kwik, a mother in San Diego, is doing her best to raise discerning consumers. She makes it a policy to stand firm about what to buy when she's in the supermarket, even if it means fending off tantrums from her children, Stephanie, 7, Monica, 5, and Kevin, 3. Kwik also tries to instill values by reading books such as *The Berenstain Bears Get the Gimmies* to her kids.

Moderating her children's wants, though, is an ongoing battle, as it is for every parent. It's a fundamental impulse to try to make your child happy whenever possible, and everyone caves from time to time.

"Sometimes when my 3-year-old son, Rob, says 'I want french fries at McDonald's,' I say okay, because I just don't have the energy to deal with it," says Lauren Monti, a mom from Chicopee, Massachusetts.

Giving in to commercial-driven desires on occasion is not such a bad thing, Dr. Gulyn concedes. However, she points out that making snap decisions out of convenience can make it a lot tougher to refuse a child's product requests in the future. "As a parent, it's critical to maintain your ability to say no to products that don't serve the best interests of your children."

UNIT 3
Educational Practices

Unit Selections

Key Points to Consider

- What are some of the pros and cons of retaining a child in the early grades?

- What are steps teachers can take to counteract negative aspects of some commercial toys and materials in the classroom?

- Make a brief listing of the components of developmentally appropriate practice that you believe are vital.

- What are some of the best design features of a preschool classroom where you have worked or observed?

- On a scale of 1 to 5 (1 is highest quality and 5 is lowest quality) how do you rate the playground of a preschool where you have observed or worked?

- Does your preschool have a policy for planning holiday celebrations? Why should a preschool have such a policy?

 **Links: www.dushkin.com/online/**
These sites are annotated in the World Wide Web pages.

Canada's Schoolnet Staff Room
  http://www.schoolnet.ca/home/e/
Classroom Connect
  http://www.classroom.com/login/home.jhtml
The Council for Exceptional Children
  http://www.cec.sped.org/index.html
National Resource Center for Health and Safety in Child Care
  http://nrc.uchsc.edu
Online Innovation Institute
  http://oii.org
Make your own Web page
  http://www.teacherweb.com

The passage of No Child Left Behind legislation by Congress in 2002 has many implications for early childhood care and educational practices. As academic assessment and accountability measures are implemented, the impact on children's play is becoming quite clear; preschool children are spending more and more time preparing for and taking tests and less time in developmental play. The lead article in this unit deals with how to reconcile appropriate practices and national standards. In "Achieving High Standards and Implementing Developmentally Appropriate Practice—Both ARE Possible," the author contends that the most effective way to achieve high learning standards is to use methods that are content rich but appropriate for young children.

Another implication of No Child Left Behind is an alarming increase in the number of children, particularly boys, who are retained in the early grades. The reasons most frequently cited for retention is to motivate failing students to try harder and raise their self-esteem. Yet research shows that retention has the opposite effect, achievement does not increase and self-esteem suffers. With schools under pressure to meet higher annual yearly progress goals, teachers are recommending more and more young children for retention. While retention is not proving to be an effective approach to low achievement or emotional problems, neither is social promotion. The issues involved in retaining young children are discussed in "Second Time Around."

Two of the articles in this unit address the need to protect children's right to play as an avenue of cognitive, emotional, and academic growth. Both articles also recognize that, to be beneficial to growth and development, play needs to be channeled and supported. In "Let's Just Play," the author emphasizes the importance of fostering cooperative, non-violent play. And in "The

Importance of Being Playful," teachers are encouraged to provide appropriate props and materials to foster the type of play that extends learning.

A hallmark of quality childcare is strong home-school partnerships, and parental involvement in a wide variety of activities is the way to develop partnerships. When parents are engaged in school activities, children are better able to learn and grow and their teachers gain respect and appreciation of family cultures. "Creating Home-School Partnerships" gives valuable strategies for understanding family diversity as the beginning point for working closely with parents.

Two articles in this unit deal with how to create a quality physical environment for young children. "Basic Premises of Classroom Design: The Teacher's Perspective" provides a thorough guide to planning a classroom for optimal learning. Instead of a simple checklist, the author urges teachers to think about environmental factors as a "balance of opposites." For example, in arranging materials, the teacher would consider independence versus dependence goals for children, and in planning the layout, the teacher would take into account pathways versus boundaries. Another area of the physical environment to consider is the playground. "How Safe Are Child Care Playgrounds?" summarizes an important national study of safety issues showing that many states have not made significant progress in playground safety. The authors describe four important aspects of playground design, supervision, and equipment that go into making a safe and appropriate outdoor play environment. They conclude with specific recommendations for early childhood educators to ensure that the playground meets children's physical, social, emotional, and intellectual development.

Achieving High Standards and Implementing Developmentally Appropriate Practice—Both ARE Possible

Harriet A. Egertson

Nearly two decades ago inappropriate influences from earlier educational reform movements coupled with the need to define best practice for the rapidly growing number of prekindergarten programs led to the development and dissemination of the construct of developmentally appropriate practice (Bredekamp & Copple, 1997) for the early childhood field and beyond. Now, nearly 20 years later, misunderstanding about the purposes of standards setting, arising from the most recent reform movement, is having similar negative influences on the early childhood settings of the early 21st century.

Continuing misunderstanding about the nature and purpose of developmentally appropriate practice has persisted, often resulting in early childhood settings that are "experientially rich" but "content poor." This is just as unacceptable as inappropriate application of learning standards in programs for young children.

The early learning years can provide rich experiences that

- offer high-quality content,
- are appropriate for the learning capabilities of the children,
- and lead children to achieve high standards.

High learning standards can be implemented and achieved at any level only through the application of teaching practices that are appropriate to the diverse learning needs of the children (Nebraska & Iowa Departments of Education, 2001).

The original documents defining and describing developmentally appropriate practice influenced the field far beyond what developers expected—many influences were positive and some were not. A large number of teachers, administrators, and teacher educators embraced the intent of the statements and re-examined and improved learning experiences for children across preschool and kindergarten/primary levels. As with any statement of public policy, however, some people ignored it and others misunderstood it (Kostelnik, 1992).

Similar misunderstandings have arisen within the current standards movement (Hatch, 2002). These misunderstandings can result in implementation of teaching practices that cause many children to fail or that do not sufficiently challenge children to reach their highest potential (Katz, 1987). Misunderstandings also result when teachers cling to familiar ways of

knowing and resist the opportunity to improve learning settings based on what the profession is coming to know about how children grow and learn.

Currently accepted best practices for working with young children are based on a newer synthesis of viewpoints about growth and learning. This synthesis transcends the maturationist view (children will only learn it when they are ready), the behaviorist/cultural transmission view (children will only learn it if we directly teach it), and/or a marriage of the two.

The unfortunate result of the marriage of readiness and behaviorist perspectives is that people adopt a "they can't learn it until they are ready" and "they won't learn it until I teach it" view of young children's capacity to learn and grow. This causes some educators and members of the public to think that setting high learning standards and then accepting children into programs only when they are "ready" to achieve in them is the way to elevate achievement.

Responsible teachers do not wait until the whole class is ready in order to create learning opportunities for individual children. Highly qualified teachers provide additional direct instructional support to those children who may not yet be clear about a particular skill or concept. They provide challenges to rapidly developing children and protect more slowly developing children from experiencing failure (the individual dimension). Teachers know, for example, that learning subtraction is an expectation for primary children in U.S. schools (the cultural context). This is the meaning of setting challenging, but achievable expectations for children (Bowman, Donovan, & Burns, 2000; NAEYC & NAECS/SDE, 1991).

Competent teachers approach the reach for high learning standards for all children by using both strategies. Standards must never be applied in ways that cause any young child to experience repeated failure. Failure is the antithesis of achieving high standards. Young primary-age children are especially vulnerable to negative long-term consequences when they experience repeated school failure.

Responsible practitioners ensure that expectations remain high, but that teaching practices are adapted to suit the range of capacities of young learners, so that repeated success leads each child toward higher and higher achievement. Appropriate practice is about <u>how</u> children learn and <u>how</u> highly qualified and competent teachers teach. Standards are the target. One does not abandon good practice to lead children toward the achievement of high standards. Doing so results in the opposite outcome.

> # Good teachers do not abandon good practice for high standards.

Persistent Misunderstandings and Ineffective Practices

In reaction to the adoption of preschool and early elementary learning standards by most states and many local school districts, some practitioners are returning to practices that were shown to be ineffective in the past. These practices, such as those described in this section, continue to be ineffective and continue to have unintended negative consequences. Reinstating them will do nothing to improve children's achievement (Meisels, 1992; NAECS/SDE. 2000).

Increasing Age of Entrance to Kindergarten

One response to concerns about children's capacity to be successful in kindergarten has been to tinker with the age of entrance. In states with early fall kindergarten-entry dates, concerns about children who are perceived to be unready are expressed in the same terms as those states that have late winter dates. During the past two decades a number of state legislatures have responded to pressures to raise the entrance age (i.e., cause children to be older when they are able to enter kindergarten). After experience with this practice in a few states, the date was moved back to the beginning of the summer. Others are now working to reinstate fall entry dates. Leaders in those states have discovered that variability was not reduced after all.

Research on age at kindergarten entrance does show a small benefit for older children in the age cohort. However, the advantage is very small and virtually disappears by the end of the primary grades. The differences within a class that can be ascribed to age are less pronounced than other naturally occurring differences among children (Wolf & Kessler, 1987). Given the need to establish a uniform and equitable entrance criterion, age continues to be the only non-discriminatory index. An effective way to reduce the range of age would be for each state to establish a compulsory attendance date that coincides with its kindergarten entrance date.

Teachers tend to aim instruction at the older, more able students in a class. Eventually this causes the curriculum to become even more accelerated and creates more risk of failure for the younger, less experienced children. The younger, less experienced children tend to be those from less advantaged backgrounds, so postponing school entry for the younger cohort of children stands to harm, rather than benefit, them. Schools continue to have the obligation to meet the learning needs of all children regardless of what they bring to the school (Kluth & Straut, 2001). *It does not help children achieve high learning standards to change the kindergarten entrance age*.

Delayed Entrance and Screening

A less formal manipulation of the entrance date is the trend of some parents (commonly more affluent parents) to delay entrance of some eligible children. The practice has now become very common, institutionalized by the use of screening and readiness testing in the 1970s and early 1980s. These tests came into use at that time because school personnel and parents were concerned about some children's capacity to be successful in the more skill-driven kindergartens of the day.

Unfortunately, the use of screening tests caused the exclusion of many children who would have been most likely to benefit by being in school. The reliability and validity of various forms of entrance tests continue to be of serious concern when they are used to make life-altering decisions affecting children (Shepard, 1994; Shepard & Smith, 1990).

Overall, school entrance testing tends to increase variability in kindergarten classes. It accelerates the curriculum even further by sorting out younger, less experienced children. *It does not help children achieve high learning standards to employ screening and/or readiness testing in connection with kindergarten entrance*.

Extra-Year Classes and Retention

Another common adaptation of the structure of kindergarten—a move intended to deal with the pressure of standards-escalating curriculum and the varied backgrounds, ages, and abilities of children—has been to use various forms of extra-year placements. Extra-year classes and retention are common practices. Holding a child out of kindergarten a year is a nonintervention form of extra-year placement. The effects for children are very closely related.

Extra-Year Class Placements. Some schools establish extra-year classes for those children perceived to be unsuited to the regular curriculum. When these programs come before kindergarten they are often called "readiness" or "developmental" kindergartens. When they follow kindergarten, they are commonly referred to as "pre-first" or "transition first." Studies have demonstrated that children who were recommended for a prekindergarten extra-year class, but whose parents declined, perform as well as those who participated in one (May & Welch, 1984; Meisels, 1992).

Extra-year programs are costly. A more effective use of resources is to provide preschool programs for 3- and 4-year old children, especially to those whose family income may limit their access to a high-quality early childhood program (Barnett, 1995). Well-designed and implemented preschool programs have been shown to have significant lasting benefits and are cost-effective.

To their credit, the curriculum and teaching practices teachers use in extra-year programs are usually more focused on the individual needs of children and are more consistent with recommended practices in early childhood education. But because extra-year classes are a form of ability grouping, children placed in them have less opportunity to benefit from interactions with children who are more developmentally advanced (Slavin, 1986).

This situation is particularly consequential for language development and is particularly worrisome when the practice is used to sort children who are learning English as a second language into segregated classes. In communities where extra-year classes have become common, the phenomenon of the upward creeping of the regular kindergarten curriculum is accelerated so each year more and more children are recommended for placement in the extra-year class.

Extra-year placements following kindergarten are made on the basis of performance, or lack thereof, in the kindergarten and therefore more closely resemble retention. Again, control group studies demonstrate that the performance of children who spend this extra year following kindergarten is not significantly different than similar children who move on to regular first grade with their age peers (Meisels, 1992). *It does not help children achieve high standards to reinstate extra-year programs*.

Retention. There is virtually no practice in education about which the research evidence is so clear: Retention in grade is not an effective strategy to assure that children will learn what is expected of them. It has serious negative consequences in both the short and long term for both academic and social/emotional development. School reform efforts resulting in increased demands for accountability and the use of grade-level standards and standardized testing in the lower grades appear to be increasing retention rates across the nation.

Most teachers who recommend children for retention in kindergarten do so out of genuine worry about children's capacity to benefit from the program of the first grade, especially in an excessively high standards environment. The decision to retain is frequency expressed as needing to "protect" children from first grade failure. Unfortunately, individual teachers are unable to predict the academic or social/emotional consequences of retention on any child. Despite compelling research evidence to the contrary, teachers and parents continue to believe that the practice has positive benefits.

When reliable studies with control groups are examined, the findings are consistent (CPRE, 1990; Shepard & Smith, 1990). Retention worsens academic achievement and has serious consequences for self-esteem. Other practices have been found to promote higher achievement. Such practices avoid the negative social/emotional consequences and allay public fears about social promotion. These include:

- availability of high-quality preschool
- full day, every day kindergarten
- promotion with remedial help targeted to the child's specific learning needs
- before- and after-school programs
- summer school
- paraprofessionals working with the child in the regular classroom
- cross-age tutoring

It does not help children achieve high standards to increase grade retention at the primary level.

Learning opportunities need to be promoted, not withheld from children based on an inadequate understanding of readiness. Nowhere has the concept of readiness been more misapplied than in the area of early reading and writing instruction. Recently, across the country there has been unprecedented interest in how children are taught and learn to read in the early elementary years.

Beneficial Practices That Lead to the Accomplishment of High Standards

Some widely accepted practices do improve the likelihood that children will accomplish the learning standards set for them.

Direct Interaction With Materials

Young children's learning is enhanced through direct interaction with materials, adults, and other children. Young children are naturally driven to make sense of the world and to become competent learners. This means that children in the early years benefit from direct first-hand experience with primary sources that permit them to actively explore materials and ideas.

Young children need opportunities to manipulate and to build, to experiment and to test, to question and to challenge. Constantly talking with them about what they are actively doing is me key to expanding their vocabulary and understanding. Language-rich practices assure mat children will have access to the challenging content at the heart of most standards.

> **Language-rich practices assure access to challenging content.**

Rich Verbal Interaction

Children show growth when classrooms are rich in verbal interaction with one another and with adults about … what they are doing, experiences with quality literature, and planned opportunities to write about their experiences. Children who have had early literacy experiences in their homes and early childhood settings rarely have difficulty in developing phonemic awareness and in learning the phonetic code.

Children who come from impoverished early settings often have difficulty in learning to read (Harr & Risley, 1995; Snow, Burns, & Griffin, 1998). Especially when children have not had the opportunity to experience high-quality preschool programs, the early years of elementary school must be spent in enriching children's background of language and experience.

Phonemic awareness develops through multiple daily experiences with conversation, stories, rhymes, poetry, singing, and pretend play. All children benefit from as many of these oral experiences as are possible within the school day, well into the middle school years.

Having mastery of the aural code (phonemic awareness) is prerequisite to formal instruction in the written code (phonics). From infancy on, young children need informal, continuous exposure to letters and words. Many will learn a good deal about the written code from exposure to print in their environment and through repeated exposure to books—by having books read to them every day.

Research in early literacy now favors a more systematic exposure to the phonic code by the end of first grade. How that instruction takes place is critically important. A systematic approach does NOT equate to the "drill and kill" of the past. Therefore, educators have a responsibility to become as informed as possible about new information on children's early literacy development and effective teaching approaches. Such practices include:

- Deliberately using rhyming, skipping, and word games to develop phonemic awareness;
- Providing daily opportunities to read, reread, and talk about stories to develop concepts about print, analytical skills, and vocabulary;
- Integrating writing into all areas of the curriculum; and
- Thoughtfully linking systematic code instruction with meaningful reading and writing activities (IRA/NAEYC, 1998; Snow, Burns, & Griffin, 1998; Yopp & Yopp, 2000).

Choices Among Learning Activities

Effective classrooms are arranged so that for much of the day children are able to make choices about what materials they will use and with whom they will work. These practices

- assure that children are more invested in their learning and it's evaluation and
- lead children to develop positive traits of initiative, perseverance, independence and responsibility.

When many levels of activities are made available, individualization of learning opportunities is possible to support high achievement across a wide range of abilities. When children initiate much of their own learning and are invested in it, disruptive behavior is greatly reduced and the overall climate of the classroom is more cooperative and productive.

Open-Ended Learning Materials

Broad curriculum goals are implemented through careful preparation of the physical environment. Teachers focus their energies on acquiring and preparing many learning materials that are largely open-ended and can be used over and over in different ways to challenge and meet the needs of individual children.

Learning experiences that are thoughtfully placed in the classroom, how they organized, and the strategies that are put into place to manage children's use of them form the basis of much of the daily program. The teacher's skill in selecting and organizing worthwhile materials becomes paramount. A high-quality environment is organized so that children can have optimum autonomy as they select activities or develop projects and carry them out either individually or with a group of classmates.

As much as possible, activities are self-correcting and provide direct feedback to children. Teachers assist children in

gathering and locating materials they need for projects. Work areas and the materials associated with them lead children to make normal connections among areas of inquiry (Katz & Chard, 2000; Drake, 2001).

> # Responsible teachers create learning opportunities for individual children.

Heterogeneous Groups

Children are assigned to heterogeneous groups which are preferably multiage and which have the same teacher for multiple years. Many young children today are required to adjust to multiple settings outside the home and the consequences of these experiences are not well understood. Effective early school programs promote stable relationships with limited numbers of adults and children. Although children may interact beneficially with several adults in school, the formation of a stable, secure relationship with one adult is critical for both the intellectual and social/emotional development of the child (Katz, Evangelou, & Hartman, 1990).

Experts widely believe that groupings should be flexible across as well as within the kindergarten/primary age range. Individual differences can be more sensitively accommodated if children are not moved automatically from one room/teacher to the next at the conclusion of each school year. Children may benefit from staying with the same teacher for more than one year in multiyear grouping patterns such as looping or multiage classes.

Grade-by-grade standards often do not accommodate naturally occurring variability in learning and development among younger children. Multiyear assignments enable teachers to see children's accomplishments over time, thus reducing some of the stress to reach discrete points of achievement every year.

Varied Instructional Approaches

Teachers regularly employ a variety of instructional approaches to assure that children learn both the skills they need and challenging, worthwhile content. Whole class, teacher-led activities continue to dominate classroom practice in the United States, even in settings where practitioners insist that they use varied approaches to meet diverse learning needs of their students.

Varying approaches support the accomplishment of learning standards and occasionally include whole-class lessons as well as the less structured strategies also described here. When direct instruction is used, it is carefully considered as the most effective teaching strategy for the skill or concept to be conveyed. Skilled teachers also know when it is appropriate to bring together a small group of children who need instruction on a particular skill. They know when individual or group projects are the best approach for the content under study.

Although teachers may initiate some class projects related to a particular curriculum standard, children are also encouraged to develop their own projects and to pursue them in some depth. Children of varying ages and abilities can effectively work together on a common project and learn from the endeavor as their levels of development enable them to do.

Overview of the Issues

A wide variety of organizational strategies and teaching approaches is more likely to assure that the learning levels and individual styles of young children are accommodated and that learning standards are addressed. Effective programs provide learning activities that extend well above and below the general expectations for children in that group's chronological age range and provide a range of options in terms of learning style.

Counterproductive approaches such as retention and extra-year classes as a means of accommodating ever-increasing variability among young children appear to result from efforts to preserve the year-by-year curriculum and uniform teaching strategies.

More effective schools and other early childhood programs employ careful observation and monitoring of children's current developmental levels and effective criterion assessment (Shepard, Kagan, & Wurtz, 1998). In these programs, children are encouraged to select and participate in ever more challenging learning explorations and intellectually stimulating projects. Indeed, the only way to assure that a group of children will achieve a common set of standards is to employ a wide range of instructional strategies.

References

Barnett, W.S. (1995). Long-term effects of early childhood programs on cognitive and school outcomes. *The Future of Children, 5*, 25–50.

Bowman, B., Donovan, M.S., & Burns, M.E. (Eds.). (2000). *Eager to learn: Educating our preschoolers*. Washington, DC: National Academy Press/National Research Council.

Bredekamp, S., & Copple, C. (Eds.). (1997). *Developmentally appropriate practice in early childhood programs*. (Rev. ed.) Washington, DC: National Association for the Education of Young Children.

Center for Policy Research in Education (CPRE), Rutgers University. (1990). *Repeating grades in school: Current practice and research evidence*. New Brunswick, NJ: Author.

Drake, S.M. (2001). Castles, kings … and standards. *Educational Leadership, 59*(1), 38–42.

Hart, B., & Risley, T.R. (1995). *Meaningful differences in the everyday experience of young American children*. Baltimore, MD: Brookes.

Hatch, J.A. (2002). Accountability shovedown: Resisting the standards movement in early childhood education. *Phi Delta Kappan, 83*, 457–462.

International Reading Association and the National Association for the Education of Young Children. (1998). Learning to read and write: Developmentally appropriate practices for young children. *Young Children, 53*(4), 30–46.

Katz, L.G. (1987). Early education: What should young children be doing? In S.L. Kagan & E.F. Zigler (Eds.). *Early schooling: The na-* tional debate (pp. 151–167). New Haven, CT: Yale University Press.

Katz, L.G., & Chard, S.C. (2000). *Engaging children's minds: The project approach* (2nd ed.). Stamford, CT: Ablex.

Katz, L.G., Evangelou, D., & Hartman, J.A. (1990). *The case for mixed-age grouping in early childhood education programs*. Washington, DC: National Association for the Education of Young Children.

Kluth, P., & Straut, D. (2001). Standards for diverse learners. *Educational Leadership, 59*(1), 43–49.

Kostelnik, M.J. (1992). Myths associated with developmentally appropriate programs. *Young Children, 47*(4), 17–23.

May, D.C., & Welch, E.L. (1984). The effects of developmental placement and early retention on children's later scores on standardized tests. *Psychology in the Schools*, 21, 381–385.

Meisels, S.J. (1992). Doing harm by doing good: Iatrogenic effects of early childhood enrollment and promotion policies. *Early Childhood Research Quarterly, 7*(2), 155–175.

National Association for the Education of Young Children & National Association of Early Childhood Specialists in State Departments of Education. (1991). Guidelines for appropriate curriculum and assessment in programs serving children ages 3 through 8. *Young Children, 46*(3), 21–38.

National Association of Early Childhood Specialists in State Departments of Education. (2000). *Still! Unacceptable trends in kindergarten entry and placement, A position statement*. Stares of Members: Author.

Nebraska and Iowa Departments of Education. (2001). *The primary program: Growing and learning in the heartland*. Lincoln, NE: Author.

Shepard, L.A. (1994). The challenges of assessing young children appropriately. *Phi Delta Kappan*, 76, 206–13.

Shepard, L.A., Kagan, S.L., & Wurtz, E. (Eds.). (1998). *Principles and recommendations for early childhood assessments*. Washington, DC: National Education Goals Panel.

Shepard, L.A., & Smith, M.L. (1990). Synthesis of research on grade retention. *Educational Leadership, 47*(8), 84–88.

Slavin, R.E. (1986). *Ability grouping and student achievement in elementary schools: A best-evidence synthesis*. Baltimore, MD: Center for Research on Elementary and Middle Schools, Johns Hopkins University.

Snow, C.E., Burns, M.S., & Griffin, P. (Eds.). (1998). *Preventing reading difficulties in young children*. National Research Council. Washington, DC: National Academy Press.

Wolf, J.M., & Kessler, A.L. (1987). *Entrance to kindergarten: What is the best age?* ERS Monograph. Arlington, VA: Educational Research Service.

Yopp, H.K., & Yopp, R.H. (2000). Supporting phonemic awareness development in the classroom. *The Reading Teacher, 54*(2), 130–143.

Harriet A. Egerston, Ph.D., is an independent consultant living in Temecula, California. She recently retired from leadership of the Early Childhood Office in the Nebraska Department of Education. This article is an elaboration of a position statement found in The Primary Program: Growing and Learning in the Heartland, a curriculum framework published jointly by the Departments of Education in Iowa and Nebraska (NE & IA, 2001). Correspondence concerning this article should be addressed to Harriet A. Egerston, 33163 Fox Road, Temecula, CA 92592. E-mail: haegertson@hotmail.com

From *Dimensions of Early Childhood*, Vol. 32, No. 1, Winter 2004, pp. 3-9. Copyright © 2004 by Southern Early Childhood Association (SECA). Reprinted by permission.

Second Time Around

If repeating a grade doesn't help kids, why do we make them do it?

By Susan Black

Making students repeat a grade hasn't worked for 100 years, so why is it still happening? And why do government officials, school leaders, and teachers persist in recommending retention as a remedy for low student achievement—even when researchers call it a failed intervention?

Linda Darling-Hammond, executive director of Columbia University's National Center for Restructuring Education, Schools, and Teaching, has a one-word answer: assumptions. Many schools, she says, operate on the assumption that failing students motivates them to try harder, gives them another chance to "get it right," and raises their self-esteem.

Those claims aren't true, Darling-Hammond maintains. The widespread trust in retention is uncritical and unwarranted, she says. It ignores several decades of research showing that, for most children, retention:

- Fails to improve low achievement in reading, math, and other subjects.
- Fails to inspire students to buckle down and behave better.
- Fails to develop students' social adjustment and self-concept.

Darling-Hammond concedes that grade retention might benefit some students in the short term, but in the long term, holding students back puts them at risk. More often than not, students who are retained never catch up academically. Many eventually drop out, and some end up in the juvenile justice system.

The belief that students, as well as their parents, are to blame for low achievement plays into most retention decisions. But teachers and principals seldom accept their share of blame for inept instruction, lackluster lessons, low expectations, and other school factors that contribute to students' academic disengagement and behavior problems, Darling-Hammond says.

As a result, most retained students are just recycled. But as Darling-Hammond points out, simply giving students more of what didn't work the first time around is an exercise in futility.

Teachers' power to retain

It's easy to see why teachers believe retention works. But it's less easy to understand why schools allow teachers to hold so much power over this practice.

Gwendolyn Malone, a fifth-grade teacher in Virginia and president of her local teachers union, writes in *NEA Today* that retention offers students the chance to "refresh, relearn, and acquire new skills," as well as to gain self-confidence and become good students. She urges schools to "nip problems in the bud by retaining students early in their school careers"—as early as kindergarten and first grade.

Malone believes the threat of retention is an incentive for students to study so they'll be promoted with their same-age classmates. Weak students who are promoted, she says, end up feeling ashamed, angry, and defensive about their so-called deficiencies.

In most schools, classroom teachers determine which students will pass or fail.

At the end of the 2003–04 school year, for instance, one New York City teacher identified 17 of her 28 third-graders for retention. The high numbers didn't trouble her—although she told a reporter that "there would be no fourth grade if all struggling children were held back."

Shane Jimerson of the University of California-Santa Barbara says teachers play a key role in deciding which students will be retained, even though most teachers are unfamiliar with research that casts a dubious light on this practice. School psychologists should study the research and present it to school staffs, Jimerson recommends, and they should head teams consisting of counselors, teachers, and administrators who will make pass/fail decisions.

But before they make those decisions, he says, team members should know these research findings:

- Retaining elementary-age students may provide an achievement "bounce," but gains tend to be slight and temporary; once the bounce tapers off, students either level off or again fall behind their classmates.
- Retaining kindergarten and first-grade students as a preventive intervention is no better for students than retaining them in upper grades.
- Retaining students without providing specific remedial strategies and attending to students' risk factors has little or no value.

Team decision making might help avoid a problem RMC Research Corporation's Beckie Anderson has identified.

She reports that teachers often retain students to avoid criticism from teachers in the next grade for promoting poorly prepared students. Many principals, it turns out, are quietly complicit in this practice by giving teachers complete authority over retention decisions.

A troubling process

Over the years I've watched a number of schools, both rural and urban, retain more students each year, especially in kindergarten, first grade, and ninth grade. Many of the schools I've studied now hold back 30 to 40 percent of their youngest students, but a handful of schools retain close to 50 percent.

And many of the teachers and principals I've interviewed think of retention as standard practice. A first-grade teacher told me, "By November, I know which half of my class will pass and which half will fail."

The retention ritual doesn't begin in earnest until April or May, however, when teachers submit a list of students for retention to their principals, who generally approve their recommendations.

Here's how one such decision played out a few weeks before the close of school in 2004. A third-grade teacher called in a 10-year-old boy's mother to discuss retention, and I sat in on the conversation. The teacher admitted that the boy—I'll call him Ryan—was "quite smart," especially in science and math. But, she insisted, Ryan, who is small for his age, needed another year to "grow into third grade."

The mother balked—Ryan had already repeated first grade for the same reason—but the teacher overruled her objection. The principal was nowhere to be seen, and neither were the school's counselor or psychologist.

At the end of the meeting the teacher brought a signed form to the office, and Ryan was officially retained. I thought of Lorrie Shepard and Mary Smith's 1989 book *Flunking Grades* in which they write that "teachers consistently underplay the extent of conflict with parents over the decision to retain and underestimate the degree of parents' active resistance or passive but unhappy compliance."

Teachers may believe retention does no harm, but Anderson says researchers' interviews with children who were held back in elementary school tell a different story. More than 25 percent of the children were too ashamed to admit that they had failed a grade. Almost without exception, the retained children said staying back made them feel "sad," "bad," and "upset," and they thought repeating a grade was "punishment."

When I met with Ryan over the summer, he told me, "I'll never be smart in school. I'm only smart at things we don't do in school—like inventing mazes and drawing." When I asked why he thought he had to repeat third grade he replied, without hesitation, "I got in lots of trouble for not walking on the red line." In this school, I learned, teachers drill students on walking silently and ramrod straight on a narrow red line that runs the length of the school's corridor.

Retention's long reach

According to best estimates, nearly 2.5 million students are retained each year in U.S. schools, with the highest rates found among boys—especially minorities, special education students, and those who come from low-income families and live in the inner city.

University of Wisconsin-Madison's Robert Hauser, who recorded national retention rates for the National Research Council, found that 25 percent of 6- to 8-year-olds and 30 percent of 9- to 11-year-olds have been retained at least once. By ages 15 to 17, retention rates for black and Hispanic students are 40 to 50 percent, compared with 35 percent for white students.

Retention rates in some metropolitan schools are even higher. In Baltimore, for instance, a nine-year study shows that 41 percent of white students and 56 percent of black students were retained by grade three, and up to a third of those students were retained again before entering middle school.

Schools often retain students on the basis of a shortsighted belief that repeating a grade will give kids a boost that will last through 12th grade. It's true that retention reaches far into students' futures, but often the long-term effects are

devastating. Jimerson's studies show that students who are retained once are 40 to 50 percent more likely to drop out than promoted students. Retaining students twice doubles their chances of dropping out, raising the risk to 90 percent.

Retention is a *predictor* of dropping out, not a *cause*, he says. Achievement, behavior, and home and school environments also factor into the equation. Still, retained students run a high risk of developing problems with self-esteem, social and emotional adjustment, peer relations, and school engagement—and such problems substantially increase the likelihood of giving up on school.

A better plan

But if retention isn't working, neither is promoting students who aren't learning. As Darling-Hammond puts it. "The negative effects of retention should not become an argument for social promotion."

The solution, say Richard Allington and Sean Walmsley, authors of *No Quick Fix*, requires whole-school reform, beginning with the school's "institutional ethos."

In schools with an adversarial climate (teachers against parents and students), Allington and Walmsley found that two out of three children were retained, assigned to transitional classes, or placed in special education. But schools with a respectful and professional climate retained only 1 or 2 percent of their students.

How can school leaders halt runaway retention? Darling-Hammond recommends four strategies:

1. Teach teachers how to instruct all students according to the ways they learn.
2. Redesign schools to give students more intensive learning opportunities through multiage classes, cross-grade grouping, and block scheduling.
3. Give struggling students support and services as soon as they're needed.
4. Use student assessments to monitor and adjust teaching content and strategies.

For his part, Jimerson suggests "constructive discussions" on prevention and intervention techniques that keep students from failing in the first place. In addition, he recommends:

1. Train school psychologists to be well-informed about retention research and serve as advocates for children as soon as they show problems learning.

2. Promote students' social competence as a counterpart to academic competence.

3. Establish protective factors, such as parent involvement programs and school-community partnerships that offer support to needy children.

4. Sponsor high-quality preschool programs that focus on child development.

These researchers layout a tough mission for schools. But perhaps the toughest job will be confronting and dismantling ungrounded assumptions about retention.

Selected references

Allington, Richard, and Sean Walmsley. *No Quick Fix*. New York: Teachers College Press/International Reading Association, 1995.

Anderson, Beckie. "Retention in the Early Grades: A Review of the Research." Learning Disabilities Online, Winter 1998; `www.ldonline.org/ld_indepth/legal_legislative/retention_in_early_grades.html`.

Darling-Hammond, Linda "Alternatives to Grade Retention." *The School Administrator Web Edition*, August 1998; `www.aasa.org/publications/sa/1998_08/Darling-Hammond.htm`.

Hauser, Robert, and others. "Race-Ethnicity, Social Background, and Grade Retention." Paper presented at the Laboratory for Student Success at Temple University, October 2000.

Jimerson, Shane. "A Synthesis of Grade Retention Research: Looking Backward and Moving Forward." *The California School Psychologist*, 2001; `www.education.ucsb.edu/jimerson/retention/CSP_RetentionSynthesis2001.pdf`.

Jimerson, Shane, and others. "Grade Retention: Achievement and Mental Health Outcomes." National Association of School Psychologists, July 2002; `www.nasponline.org/pdf/graderetention.pdf`.

Jimerson, Shane, and others. "Winning the Battle and Losing the War: Examining the Relation between Grade Retention and Dropping out of High School." *Psychology in the Schools*, 2002; `www.education.ucsb.edu/jimerson/retention/PITS_DropoutRetention2002.pdf`.

Malone, Gwendolyn, and Philip Bowser. "Debate: Can Retention Be Good for a Student" *NEA Today*, 1998. `www.nea.org/neatoday/9803/debatehtml`.

Shepard, Lorrie and Mary Smith. *Flunking Grades: Research and Policies on Retention*. London: Folmer Press, 1989.

Susan Black, an *ASBJ* contributing editor, is an education researcher in Hammondsport, N.Y.

LET'S JUST PLAY

Preserve a child's right to create and explore

BY JANET SCHMIDT

"[Participating countries] recognize the right of the child to rest and leisure, to engage in play and recreational activities appropriate to the age of the child and to participate freely in cultural life and the arts." ARTICLE 31, PART 1, OF THE UN CONVENTION ON THE RIGHTS OF THE CHILD

"I like the pink ranger!"

"My favorite is red."

"Mine, too!"

The *Mighty Morphin Power Rangers* captured the imaginations of the 3- and 4-year-olds in my suburban Boston public preschool class. For one little girl, whose language development was delayed, even the experience of naming her first few colors fell "captive" to the Rangers' original color scheme— pink, blue, red, yellow and black. Although I was pleased with the child's growing vocabulary, it disturbed me that her grasp of color concepts was connected to a violent TV show.

I should not have been surprised.

The plot of a typical *Power Rangers* episode features several fight scenes, complete with high kicks, powerful weapons, loud yells and grunts. Frequent commercial breaks promote other violent shows and toys. In the span of just one TV show, a child's vision is captivated and dominated by violence. And away from the screen, related action figures, lunch boxes, sheets, underwear and books ensure that Power Rangers images are ever present.

Children have a right to play. The idea is so simple it seems self-evident. But a stroll through any toy superstore, or any half-hour of so-called 'children's "programming on commercial TV, makes it clear that violence, not play, dominates what's being sold.

The problem got much worse in 1984, when the Federal Communications Commission deregulated children's television, paving the way for program-length commercials and massive marketing to children. In *Remote Control Childhood? Combating the Hazards of Media Culture* (1998), Diane Levin, professor of education at Wheelock College in Boston, writes that, within one year of deregulation, nine of the 10 best-selling toys were linked to TV shows and seven of these shows were violent.

Another study offers further proof.

The National Television Violence Study (*see Resources*) examined 10,000 hours of programming between 1994 and 1997 and found that 60 percent of all shows contained some kind of violence. The study also found that a preschool child watching two hours of cartoons each day will witness nearly 10,000 acts of violence each year.

Kathy Roberts, co-founder/director of the Dandelion School in Cambridge, Mass., from 1971 to 2002, has been following the evolution of children's play as a parent, grandparent and educator. In the 1970s, she and her colleagues observed that "children who watched little or no TV were more self-sufficient and creative in their play."

As the video culture boomed, however, violent TV and movie plots began to dominate the content of child's play, displacing the influence of children's imaginations and literature.

Roberts and her colleagues also observed an economic change. As marketing began to dominate children's entertainment, some families simply couldn't afford clothes and accessories tied to the latest media characters.

At the Dandelion School, Roberts and her colleagues worked against such influences. Parents and children alike understood that media-linked toys, clothes and backpacks stayed at home, and the school community could focus on topics from nature, children's own experiences and literature.

The policy got good reviews from parents.

As Roberts said, "When their children move on to public elementary school, they're bombarded with the media culture, and they feel like they have a grounding to deal with it."

CREATIVE PLAY, WITH DIRECTION

Teachers like Roberts and others promote creative play by providing a well-planned environment with engaging open-ended materials such as blocks, dolls, animal figures, paper, paint, glue, scissors, sand boxes and water tables. Children can create and explore, and teachers can be directly involved.

That direct involvement is especially important when children imitate what they've seen on TV and movie screens.

ACTIVITY

Making Shoe Box Gifts

Usually, for children, gift giving means buying manufactured toys at a store. Here is an alternative gift idea: Shoe Box Gifts are collections of small, familiar items that are organized around a play theme. They also show that expensive toys in fancy packages aren't necessarily the best.

Decorate an empty shoe box (or a larger box if needed) and gather items related to the chosen theme. Build dividers into the box or use small containers or zip-lock bags to keep things organized. Note that some suggested items might require adult supervision. Have fun!

Here are two suggestions to get you started:

Garden Box	Creating with Play Dough
• Plastic lining	• Buy some or make your own
• Potting soil	• Garlic press
• Seed packets	• Plastic knife
• Small watering can	• Popsicle sticks
• Popsicle sticks	• Plastic lids
• Garden tools	• Small tray/plate
• Gardening gloves	• Plastic animals

Adapted with permission from TRUCE (Teachers Resisting Unhealthy Children's Entertainment).

Tricia Windschitl and her colleagues at the Preucil Preschool in Iowa City, Iowa, take advantage of teachable moments that arise during play to interject ideas to make play more peaceful and respectful, while setting limits on pretend fighting. "Anything that makes someone feel uncomfortable or scared" is not allowed, Windschitl explains.

So if the boys are interested in Batman, Windschitl will encourage them to build a Batmobile, challenging their creativity and fostering cooperation.

"The focus goes away from the fighting and into more creative play," she says. "But if we completely ban superhero play, there is no opportunity to guide it."

Beyond preschool, recess becomes a testing ground for such play.

At first-grade teacher Sandra Rojas' school in Cambridge, Mass., students staked out part of the schoolyard as "Martian Land" in the 1980s. It has continued ever since, with boys and girls of various ages using rocks for money and setting up inventive trading-and-selling scenarios. "Real" toys are nowhere to be found.

"When there are no gadgets to play with," Rojas says, "they do really well coming together as a group."

Children's creativity in the absence of "store-bought play" is the core concept of WorldPlay, a grassroots project based in Atlanta that showcases toys made from found materials by children all over the world (*see Resources*). The group has also created Internet and videoconferencing opportunities that allow children to teach each other how to make such toys.

While adults can help by providing materials, suggesting safety guidelines and offering ideas, children have the right to bring their own ideas and experiences, even challenging ones, to life through play. Denise Jansen, a second-grade teacher in Madison, Wis., believes that denying children the opportunity to play is "taking away a right as necessary as eating or sleeping."

In support of that right, teachers and parents share responsibility to protect children from the onslaught of violent and scripted play ideas brought by TV, movies, video games and the vast collection of media-linked products.

CHOOSING GOOD TOYS

Choosing appropriate toys can go a long way toward improving play opportunities for children.

The Good Toy Group (*see Resources*), currently made up of more than 50 U.S. toy retailers, emerged at the 2000 American Specialty Toy Retailers Association convention. Colleen Pope, owner of The Dollhouse Shop in Montgomery, Ala., was part of the original group and contributes to the production of a catalogue that features toys chosen on the basis of creative play value, cultural sensitivity and nonviolence.

"We go to the annual Toy Fair and work in teams, looking for the best new stuff. Then we meet, compare notes and decide what to put in the catalogue," Pope explains.

TRUCE (Teachers Resisting Unhealthy Children's Entertainment), founded in 1995, also promotes creative and constructive play.

The group's Shoe Box Gifts (*see Activity*) provide an antidote for the aggressive marketing of media-linked toys. Parents and teachers can help children discover ways to channel their interests into creative dramatic play, using simple props and collective imagination.

The TRUCE *Media Violence Guide* (*see Resources*) provides suggestions for adults who seek to minimize the effects of media culture and violence on children.

SCREENING OUT VIOLENCE

According to The Lion and Lamb Project's short film *Video Games: The State of the "Art"*:

* 145 million Americans play video games;
* 65 million are under the age of 17;
* 20 million are 12 years old or younger;
* And 92 percent of 2- to 17-year-olds play video or computer games.

In addition, three different studies found that approximately 75 percent of youths between the ages of 13 and 16 who attempted to purchase M-rated (mature) video games were able to do so. Such M-rated games, including *Duke Nukem* and *Grand Theft Auto: Vice City*, depict graphic violence, complete with blood, vomit, sickening sounds and sexual images of women with exaggerated figures and scanty clothing. They include scenes of men beating prostitutes and encourages the player to shoot naked women who call out, "Kill me!"

While the First Amendment allows for the production of such violent material, adults are responsible for protecting children from exposure to it. Parents can't accomplish this alone; teachers, retailers and others need to monitor the video game world and take action to keep children safe from such images. Even E-rated (everybody) games include violent images, cautions Lion and Lamb's executive director Daphne White.

Also, be wary of videos and computer games with misleading terms such as "educational" and "interactive." Although such computer activities offer young users exciting choices and individualized responses to mouse clicks or screen touches, these are still no substitute for face-to-face interactions.

Children can learn to see the negative messages presented through entertainment and the manipulation involved in advertising. Teachers and parents can talk with children about what they see, and help them understand the realities that may conflict with the images on the screen.

Recently, for example, at the neighborhood video store, I heard a 5-year-old ask, "Dad, do all video games have violence?" Another 5-year-old, Morgan (*see In Focus*), persuaded his friends to play regular tag instead of Power Rangers tag at school.

'FIGHTING' BACK

Recently, Lion and Lamb's White, seeing the need for heightened awareness and powerful, nationwide collaboration in order to reduce the marketing of violence to children, has organized a working group of representatives from several organizations.

WEB EXCLUSIVE

Visit our Web site for a collection of resources about mass-marketed toys and creative play. Log onto www.teaching tolerance.org/magazine; click on "Let's Just Play."

Lion and Lamb also promotes community events such as Violent Toy Trade-Ins and Peaceable Play Days. Merle Forney, along with Jane and Dan Bucks, organized the first Trade-In in Columbia, Md., in 1995. Children who turned in a violent toy received a peacemaker certificate to use at a local specialty toy store. A team of sculptors helped attach the 300 collected toys to a serpent-shaped steel framework.

"A serpent sheds its skin, and the kids were also going through a transformation," recalls Forney, who now lives in Amesbury, Mass.

The first Trade-In took place on a Saturday, followed on Sunday by a "New Ways to Play Day," where parents and children participated together in a variety of creative, nonviolent play activities.

As Denise Janssen sees it, we have to find ways to work with children to build peaceful classrooms and to counteract the negative messages they get through TV and other media. Janssen and her teaching partner, Sue Harris find time in the busy school day to learn what their young students think and feel, through role-playing, reading and discussion of good literature, and talking about good role models from the past and present.

"When we talk about real people who have made a difference in the world, the children are fully involved and enthusiastic. These are the best discussions of the day," she says.

The challenge lies in channeling these positive images into their play.

"Kids don't know how to turn off the TV," Janssen says, "so they learn that most people who look good *are* good, that people who are not good-looking are bad, and that the good guys usually win."

While these simplistic associations permeate play, teachers can remind their students of the real, multidimensional people who captured their attention during classroom discussions. With adult guidance, children can think more critically about the images they see on TV and movie screens.

"Play," asserts Janssen, "represents not only the culture in which the children live, but also the process through which they develop the skills and behaviors needed to live as conscientious adult citizens within their communities."

Play is a child's right, and protecting it is everyone's responsibility.

RESOURCES

Two books by Diane Levin support teachers' efforts to promote peace and safety in children's lives. *Remote Control Childhood? Combating the Hazards of Media Culture* ($15) offers practical background information and concrete suggestions for working with parents and children to counteract negative aspects of toys, entertainment and advertising. The second edition of *Teaching Young*

Children in Violent Times ($24) is a guide to creating peaceful classrooms for children in preschool and Grades K-3.

National Association for the
Education of Young Children
(866) 424-2460
www.naeyc.org

TRUCE (Teachers Resisting Unhealthy Children's Entertainment) is a network of early childhood professionals that fosters adult collaboration to promote positive play and to resist negative effects of media culture on children's lives.

TRUCE
www.truceteachers.org

The Lion and Lamb Project works to reduce the marketing of violence to children through parent workshops, community events and outreach to government officials and leaders in the toy and entertainment industries. Resources include a *Parent Action Kit* ($15) and the manual *Toys for Peace: A How-to Guide for Organizing Violent Toy Trade-Ins* ($12).

The Lion and Lamb Project
(301) 654-3091
www.lionlamb.org

The Good Toy Group, made up of 58 independent toy retailers across the U.S., offers an online catalogue of high-quality, culturally-sensitive toys and a listing of nearly 90 stores.

The Good Toy Group
www.goodtoygroup.com

Through their Web site, traveling exhibits, how-to books, videos and CD-ROMs, WorldPlay introduces children from all over the world to each other's cultures through their handmade toys.

WorldPlay
www.worldplay.org

The National Television Violence Study, conducted between 1994 and 1997, is the largest ongoing study on the topic. Executive summaries and further information are available online.

The Center for Communication and Social Policy
University of California, Santa Barbara
www.ccsp.ucsb.edu/ntvs.htm

Janet Schmidt, an educator in Wellesley, Mass. and member of TRUCE, was the 2002-03 Teaching Tolerance Research Fellow.

From *Teaching Tolerance*, Fall 2003, pp.19-25. Southern Poverty Law Center, Montgomery, Ala. Reprinted by permission.

The Importance of Being Playful

With the right approach, a plain white hat and a plate full of yarn spaghetti can contribute to a young child's cognitive development.

Elena Bodrova and Deborah J. Leong

Educators have always considered play to be a staple in early childhood classrooms. But the growing demands for teacher accountability and measurable outcomes for prekindergarten and kindergarten programs are pushing play to the periphery of the curriculum. Some proponents of more academically rigorous programs for young children view play and learning as mutually exclusive, clearly favoring "serious" learning and wanting teachers to spend more time on specific academic content. But do play and learning have to compete? Research on early learning and development shows that when children are properly supported in their play, the play does not take away from learning but contributes to it (Bergen, 2002).

As researchers studying the ways to scaffold the development of foundational skills in young children, we have never met a teacher—preschool, Head Start, or kindergarten—who disagreed with the notion that young children learn through play. At the same time, many teachers worry that children's play is not valued outside of the early education community. These teachers must increasingly defend the use of play in their classrooms to principals, parents, and teachers of higher grades.

Early childhood teachers admit that the benefits of play are not as easy to understand and assess as, for example, children's ability to recognize letters or write their names. Teachers also tell us that they feel obligated to prove that play not only facilitates the development of social competencies but also promotes the learning of pre-academic skills and concepts. We believe that a certain kind of play has its place in early childhood classrooms and that the proponents of play and academic learning can find some much-needed common ground.

Effects of Play on Early Learning and Development

Play has been of great interest to scholars of child development and learning, psychologists, and educators alike. Jean Piaget (1962) and Lev Vygotsky (1978) were among the first to link play with cognitive development. In a comprehensive review of numerous studies on play, researchers found evidence that play contributes to advances in "verbalization, vocabulary, language comprehension, attention span, imagination, concentration, impulse control, curiosity, problem-solving strategies, cooperation, empathy, and group participation" (Smilansky & Shefatya, 1990). Recent research provides additional evidence of the strong connections between quality of play in preschool years and children's readiness for school instruction (Bowman, Donovan, & Burns, 2000; Ewing Marion Kauffman

Foundation, 2002; Shonkoff & Phillips, 2000). Further, research directly links play to children's ability to master such academic content as literacy and numeracy. For example, children's engagement in pretend play was found to be positively and significantly correlated with such competencies as text comprehension and metalinguistic awareness and with an understanding of the purpose of reading and writing (Roskos & Christie, 2000).

How Play Evolves

Make-believe play emerges gradually as the child moves from infancy to preschool. In the beginning, children are more focused on the actual objects that they use when they play. Later, they focus on the people who use the objects in social interaction. Whereas a toddler might simply enjoy the repetitive action of rocking a baby doll, an older child engaged in the same activity would call herself "Mommy" and add other mommy behaviors such as using baby talk when talking to the doll. These preschoolers depend heavily on props and may even refuse to play if they think that the props are not sufficiently realistic.

By the time most children turn 4, they begin to develop more complex play with multiple roles and symbolic uses of props. Many preschool- and even kindergarten-age children, however, still play at the toddler level. We define this kind of repetitive, unimaginative play as "immature play" to distinguish it from the "mature play" that is expected of older preschoolers and kindergartners. Mature play contributes to children's learning and development in many areas that immature play does not affect (Smilansky & Shefatya, 1990).

As children grow older, they tend to spend less time in pretend play and more time playing sports and board or computer games. In these activities, children have to follow the established rules and rarely have a chance to discuss, negotiate, or change those rules—an important skill that contributes to the development of social competence and self-regulation. When learning to play games takes its natural course (see Piaget, 1962; Vygotsky, 1978) and builds on the foundation of well-developed pretend play, children get an opportunity to both develop and apply their social and self-regulation skills. When pretend play is completely replaced by sports or other organized activities, however, these important foundational skills might not develop fully.

Characteristics of Mature Play

Teachers often disagree about what constitutes mature play. Some think that the play has to have more sophisticated content, such as playing archaeological dig or space station; others believe that children play in a mature way when they don't fight with one another. We, however, consider play to be mature only when it has the following characteristics, which we have extracted from research and best practices.

Imaginary situations. In mature play, children assign new meanings to the objects and people in a pretend situation. When children pretend, they focus on an object's abstract properties rather than its concrete attributes. They invent new uses for familiar toys and props when the play scenario calls for it. Sometimes children even describe the missing prop by using words and gestures. In doing so, they become aware of different symbolic systems that will serve them later when they start mastering letters and numbers.

Multiple roles. The roles associated with a theme in mature play are not stereotypical or limited; the play easily includes supporting characters. For example, playing "fire station" does not mean that the only roles are those of firefighters. Children can also pretend to be a fire truck driver or a phone dispatcher.

When children assume different roles in play scenarios, they learn about real social interactions that they might not have experienced (not just following commands but also issuing them; not only asking for help but also being the one that helps). In addition, they learn about their own actions and emotions by using them "on demand." (I am really OK, but I have to cry because I am playing a baby and the doctor just gave me a shot.) Understanding emotions and developing emotional self-control are crucial for children's social and emotional development.

Clearly defined rules. Mature play has clearly defined rules and roles. As children follow the rules in play, they learn to delay immediate fulfillment of their desires. A child playing "customer" cannot take an attractive toy if the toy—a scale or a cash register—is the prop for the role of the "checker." Thus, mature play helps young children develop self-regulation. To stay in the play, the child must follow the rules.

Flexible themes. Mature play usually spans a broad range of themes that are flexible enough to incorporate new roles and ideas previously associated with other themes. When children play at a more mature level, they negotiate their plans. For example, when playing "hospital" or "store," children can create a new play scenario in which a doctor goes to the grocery store to buy medicine for the hospital or a cashier in a grocery store gets sick and is taken to the hospital. By combining different themes, children learn to plan and solve problems.

Language development. A mature level of play implies an extensive use of language. Children use language to plan their play scenario, to negotiate and act out their roles, to explain their "pretend" behaviors to other participants, and to regulate compli-

ance with the rules. In doing so, they often need to modify their speech (its intonation, register, and even choice of words) according to the requirements of a particular role or as they switch from talking in a pretend way to talking for real. As the repertoire of roles grows, so do children's vocabulary, mastery of grammar and practical uses of language, and metalinguistic awareness.

Length of play. Mature play is not limited to one short session, but may last for many days as children pick up the theme where they left off and continue playing. Creating, reviewing, and revising the plans are essential parts of the play. Staying with the same play theme for a long time allows children to elaborate on the imaginary situation, integrate new roles, and discover new uses for play props.

How Teachers Can Support Imaginative Play

In the past, children learned how to play at a mature level simply by being part of an extended multi-age group within their own family or in their neighborhood. Unfortunately, with children spending more time in age-segregated groups, that is no longer the case. TV shows and computers, even with carefully selected educational content, cannot replace live play mentors. The teacher needs to take the primary role in helping children develop and maintain mature play.

Some teachers go overboard and become too involved so that the play loses its spontaneous, child-initiated character and changes into another adult-directed activity. Other teachers prefer to limit their interventions in play to the situations in which children get into fights or fail to communicate. They do not intervene when children's play remains stereotypical and unexciting day after day. Thus, children miss opportunities to expand the scope of their play. Teachers can maintain a balance between supporting mature play and keeping it truly child-initiated. To do so, they need to provide specific support for each of the key characteristics of mature play.

Create Imaginary Situations

A good way to guide children in the development of imaginary situations is to provide multipurpose props that can stand for many objects. For example, instead of placing specific dress-up costumes in the dramatic play area, stock it with bolts of differently colored and textured fabrics. Children can then use the same piece of lace to play Sleeping Beauty and Cinderella, wear the same white hat when playing a nurse or a chef, and drape themselves in a piece of fabric with an animal print when playing different animals. Instead of buying plastic food for a pretend restaurant, teachers might use generic paper plates and have children draw food on them or use other objects to represent food (for example, packing peanuts look like marshmallows, and pieces of yarn make great spaghetti).

Some children may not be ready to make their own props and will not play without realistic props. If many children are at this stage, teachers can combine multipurpose props with realistic ones to keep play going and then gradually provide more unstructured materials. At the same time, teachers can use additional strategies to help children create and maintain the imaginary situation. During small-group time, teachers can show the children different common objects and brainstorm how they can use them in different ways in play. For example, a pencil can be a magic wand, a thermometer, a space ship, a stirring spoon, or a conductor's baton. Teachers should always encourage children to use both gestures and words to describe how they are using the object in a pretend way.

Integrate Different Play Themes and Roles

Left to their own devices, children rarely come up with truly imaginative play scenarios because they lack knowledge about the roles and the language needed. As a result, play themes in most classrooms are limited to family, hospital, or store, with few roles to play.

Teachers should use field trips, literature, and videos to expand children's repertoire of play themes and roles. Children rarely incorporate the new themes into their play scenarios, however, if these resources are not used properly and the teacher focuses children's attention on the "things" part of the field trip or video—what is inside a fire station or what happens to the apples when they become apple cider. Instead, teachers should point out the "people" part of each new setting—the many different roles that people have and how the roles relate to one another. Learning about the new roles, language, and actions will help children reenact them later in their play.

Sustain Play

Teachers can support mature play by helping children plan play in advance. Planning helps children communicate about the roles and describe what the person in each role can and cannot do. Children benefit most from advance planning when they record their plans by drawing or writing them. By using these records later as reminders of their play ideas, they may be stimulated to create new developments in their play scenario.

TV shows and computers, even with carefully selected educational content, cannot replace live play mentors.

Children who put effort into planning their future play tend to stay longer with their chosen play theme and get less distracted by what is happening in other areas of the classroom. Teachers see fewer fights in the classrooms when children draw pictures of what they want to play first. For instance, when Monica wants to be the cashier in a pretend bakery, Isabella shows her the plan in which she drew herself at the cash register, so Monica agrees to choose a different role.

Positive Effects of Mature Play

As we worked with preschool and kindergarten teachers on scaffolding children's literacy development (Bodrova & Leong, 2001; Bodrova, Leong, Paynter, & Hensen, 2002; Bodrova, Leong, Paynter, & Hughes, 2002), we noticed that teachers achieved the best results when they focused on supporting mature play. Children in these classrooms not only mastered literacy skills and concepts at a higher rate but also developed better language and social skills and learned how to regulate their physical and cognitive behaviors (Bodrova, Leong, Norford, & Paynter, in press). By contrast, in the classrooms where play was on the back burner, teachers struggled with a variety of problems, including classroom management and children's lack of interest in reading and writing. These results confirm our belief that thoughtfully supported play is essential for young children's learning and development.

References

Bergen, D. (2002). The role of pretend play in children's cognitive development. *Early Childhood Research and Practice, 4*(1). [Online]. Available:http://ecrp.uiuc.edu/v4n1/bergen.html

Bodrova, E., & Leong, D. J. (2001). *The Tools of the Mind Project: A case study of implementing the Vygotskian approach in American early childhood and primary classrooms.* Geneva, Switzerland: International Bureau of Education, UNESCO.

Bodrova, E., Leong, D., Norford, J., & Paynter, D. (in press). It only looks like child's play. *Journal of Staff Development, 2*(24), 15-19.

Bodrova, E., Leong, D. J., Paynter, D. E., & Hensen, R. (2002). *Scaffolding literacy development in a preschool classroom.* Aurora, CO: Mid-continent Research for Education and Learning.

Bodrova, E., Leong, D. J., Paynter, D. E., & Hughes, C. (2002). *Scaffolding literacy development in a kindergarten classroom.* Aurora, CO: Mid-continent Research for Education and Learning.

Bowman, B., Donovan, M. S., & Burns, M. S. (2000). *Eager to learn: Educating our preschoolers.* Washington, DC: National Academies Press.

Ewing Marion Kauffman Foundation. (2002). *Set for success: Building a strong foundation for school readiness based on the social-emotional development of young children.* Kansas City, MO: Author.

Piaget, J. (1962). *Play, dreams, and imitation in childhood.* New York: Norton.

Roskos, K., & Christie, J. F. (Eds.). (2000). *Play and literacy in early childhood: Research from multiple perspectives.* Mahwah, NJ: Erlbaum.

Shonkoff, J. P., & Phillips, D. A. (Eds.). (2000). *From neurons to neighborhoods: The science of early childhood development.* Washington, DC: National Academies Press.

Smilansky, S., & Shefatya, L. (1990). *Facilitating play: A medium for promoting cognitive, socio-emotional, and academic development in young children.* Gaithersburg, MD: Psychological and Educational Publications.

Vygotsky, L. (1978). *Mind in society: The development of higher psychological processes.* Cambridge, MA: Harvard University Press.

Elena Bodrova is a senior consultant with Mid-continent Research for Education and Learning, 2550 S. Parker Rd., Ste. 500, Aurora, CO 80014, and a research fellow for the National Institute for Early Education Research; ebodrova@mcrel.org.

Deborah J. Leong is a professor of psychology at Metropolitan State College of Denver, P.O. Box 173362, Denver, CO 80217, and a research fellow for the National Institute for Early Education Research; leongd@mscd.edu.

From *Educational Leadership*, Vol. 60, No. 7, April 2003, pp. 50-53. Reprinted with permission of the Association for Supervision and Curriculum Development. © 2003 by ASCD. All rights reserved. The Association for Supervision and Curriculum Development is a worldwide community of educators advocating sound policies and sharing best practices to achieve the success of each learner. To learn more, visit ASCD at www.ascd.org

the ultimate guide to
preschool

Attending a good program gives your child a significant academic advantage.
But the number of options can be overwhelming.
We got answers to your most pressing questions.

By Beth Livermore and Ilisa Cohen

1 Is preschool really that important?

Your child may be at a disadvantage if he hasn't had any school experience before kindergarten. "In 1960, only 10 percent of 3- and 4-year-olds were enrolled in any type of classroom," says W. Steven Barnett, Ph.D., director of the National Institute for Early Education Research (NIEER), in New Brunswick, New Jersey. "But now nearly half of 3-year-olds and 70 percent of 4-year-olds are in some kind of program." Although this trend may reflect the rise in working moms, it's mostly due to the recognition that preschool provides a strong foundation for learning. That's not to say that a child from a loving home who has stimulation and social opportunities won't do well. But preschool teaches kids to be independent, to share, and to follow directions—crucial skills for kindergarten.

2 What are the choices?

You may be surprised by how many options there are—and how different they can be. For example, Montessori schools have mixed-age classes in which 3- to 5-year-olds play independently. Waldorf schools foster creativity, using activities such as baking, gardening, and pretend play. There are religious preschools, programs at private schools or daycare centers, and cooperatives run by parents. In addition, many states now provide free programs for low-income families. Some states, including Georgia and Oklahoma, offer public pre-K classes for all 4-year-olds. To find out what's available in your area, talk to your friends, neighbors, pediatrician, and employer; inquire at your place of worship, community center, and local school.

3. Is one type of program better than the others?

No. However, "studies show that children who are enrolled in programs with clear goals and carefully considered lesson plans are better prepared for school," says Suzanne Donovan, Ph.D., of the National Research Council. But avoid programs that limit spontaneity, individual differences, or special interests among kids, because children who are encouraged to make choices during the day have been found to have lower stress levels than those in very structured preschools. "They're less dependent on adult approval and more willing to try challenging tasks," says Diane Trister Dodge, author of *Preschool for Parents*.

4. When should I look for a preschool?

Most preschools hold open houses in October and November and take applications from November to February. Start investigating programs the September before you want your child to attend. For many parents, this is when their child is 2. But if yours will turn 3 between August and December, you may need to wait a year. Or look at programs for 2½-year-olds.

5. What are other hallmarks of high-quality programs?

Small class size and low child-teacher ratios are very important. "This allows teachers to meet children's individual needs," says *Parents* adviser Kathleen McCartney, Ph.D., a professor at Harvard Graduate School of Education, in Cambridge, Massachusetts. It also helps kids make friends more easily. The National Association for the Education of Young Children recommends classes of no more than 14 for 2½- to 3-year-olds and 20 for 3- to 5-year-olds. And there should be at least one adult looking after every seven 2½- to 3-year-olds or ten 3- to 5-year-olds. The classroom should also be well equipped with play materials that the children can reach easily. Of course, safety and cleanliness are crucial too. Make sure the staff is trained in first aid and that there are fenced outdoor play spaces. Ask how often toys and equipment are cleaned, and if kids are encouraged to wash their hands during the day.

6. What makes a good teacher?

Look for warm, enthusiastic teachers who are well trained and dedicated. The NIEER recommends that all preschool teachers have a bachelor's degree in early-childhood education. However, most states don't require teacher training for preschool accreditation, and only half of preschool teachers have a college degree. So you may have to consider experience and reputation too. Other good signs: programs that encourage teachers to seek ongoing professional training and have low teacher turnover.

7. Should academics be emphasized?

Good programs expose kids to academics through play, movement, and exploration. For example, teachers use storytime to build vocabulary and snacktime to practice counting. But this shouldn't be the sole focus, because preschoolers also need to hone social, emotional, and physical skills.

8. What's the best schedule?

Preschool schedules range from two half days to five full days (with structured activities in the morning and free play in the afternoon). What's best for your child depends primarily on his temperament and current schedule. Some children have an easier time adjusting when they attend five half days per week, because their schedule is consistent, Dr. McCartney notes. However, kids who are particularly shy or clingy may be better off in a two- or three-day-a-week program at first.

smart screening

Before you visit a preschool, call and ask these questions.

- What are the schedule options?
- What is the tuition?
- How old are children when they enter your school?
- What is the cutoff date for new students?
- Do you have openings for next September?
- How many children are in each class?
- How many adults supervise each class?
- What are the qualifications of the teachers?
- What training does the director have?
- Is the program licensed or accredited?

If a program meets your basic needs, ask about the enrollment process and schedule a time to visit. You should meet the director, take a tour, and spend an hour or two in a classroom. Try to revisit your top choices before making the final pick.

How can a classroom full of finger-paints and building blocks be educational?
Here's the real purpose behind the play.

block area

These traditional wooden toys teach basic math and science skills. Kids can count, compare sizes, measure, and plan patterns to build structures. Research has shown that playing with blocks improves spatial skills, which are key to success in subjects such as geometry and physics. Even at cleanup time, kids practice classification by putting the same blocks together on the shelf. Plus, blocks help kids develop hand strength, which is crucial for handwriting.

dramatic play corner

Whether this area is set up as a home, a hospital, or a post office, it gives children the chance to role-play, says Debbie LeeKeenan, director of the Eliot-Pearson Children's School at Tufts University, in Medford, Massachusetts. If they work through situations in their classroom, they'll be better prepared for real-life scenarios like going to the doctor. Through role-playing, kids not only express emotions but also exercise creativity and develop skills like cooperation and problem-solving.

sand/water tables

Kids love to experiment with different textures and forms—rough, smooth, liquid, or solid. "This is often the first place a child will go when he's dealing with separation from his parents," says preschool director Susan Isaacs Kohl, author of *The Best Things Parents Do*. "It's soothing to play with sand or water." The containers, pumps, tubes, and sieves prompt kids to explore cause and effect, measure volume, and learn concepts like squirting, sifting, floating, and sinking.

library

By reading aloud in the book nook, teachers show preschoolers how a story is told through words and pictures. Children discover that we read from left to right, and grasp the concepts of words and letters. In addition, the repetition and rhyme found in many children's books help kids gain familiarity with individual sounds, a vital step in learning how to read.

circle time

When everyone sits together, says good morning, and discusses the plan for the day, it gives children a sense of being part of a group. During circle time, kids practice many of the skills that will be key to elementary-school success: sitting patiently, listening, learning to take turns and to respect others, and speaking up in a group setting.

outdoor play

Climbing, running, jumping, skipping, and playing ball develop motor skills, strength, and coordination. Kids are constantly discovering what their bodies can do.

art area

Preschool teachers offer lots of supplies like construction paper, paints, and crayons so that children can experiment with their own creativity. But art appreciation is not the only aspect of development that blossoms through crafts. Holding a crayon, cutting with scissors, and folding paper help children master fine motor skills and hand-eye coordination, which are important for learning handwriting, Kohl says. Describing their work to other kids or to teaches also gives children practice with language and self-expression.

puzzle table

Puzzles, Legos, and beads improve a preschooler's concentration, focus, and hand-eye coordination. Children usually do puzzles on their own, so this activity helps them learn to solve problems independently.

science projects

Caring for class pets, such as guinea pigs or fish, and growing plants teaches preschoolers what living things need to survive. Magnets, scales, and magnifying glasses at this center help children master science skill like classifying, labeling, weighing, examining, and predicting.

From *Parents*, October 2004, pp. 124-127. Copyright © 2004 by Beth Livermore. Reprinted by permission of the author.

creating home-school partnerships

BY KERI PETERSON

"Home-school partnerships command a lot of attention these days. The federal government has issued documents to help schools organize parent participation programs. Major reform efforts and educational interventions list parental involvement as an important ingredient. Scholarly writing on the topic abounds, and various publications offer guidance to schools or describe exemplary programs" (Finn, 1998, p. 20). "Early interventionists have recognized for many years that the most powerful, efficient, and effective system for making a lasting difference in the life of a child has always been the family" (Gage and Workman, 1994, p. 74). Schools often recognize this, but teachers all too frequently get discouraged and don't spend the needed energy to establish and nurture partnerships with parents. This article will explain what home-school partnerships are, discuss the benefits that home-school partnerships create, present barriers for effective home-school partnerships and, finally, offer suggestions for improvement of home-school partnerships.

WHAT DO HOME-SCHOOL PARTNERSHIPS LOOK LIKE?

Parental involvement can simply be categorized in two ways: parental engagement in school activities and parental engagement at home. Traditionally, parental engagement in school activities "has encompassed a variety of activities such as volunteering in the classroom, participating in parent conferences and home visits, communications between parent and teacher via phone, and written means, assisting with fundraising and special events, and participating on advisory boards. Essentially, parents have been invited and welcomed to be involved in the established structure of a program for their child" (McBride, 1999, p. 62). Parents engaged at home may look differently from one family to another, but may include "actively organizing and monitoring the child's time, helping with homework, discussing school matters with the child, and reading to and being read to by their children" (Finn, 1998, p. 20).

WHO BENEFITS FROM HOME-SCHOOL PARTNERSHIPS?

All of those involved (teacher, child, and parent) in home-school partnerships stand to gain from the relationship that is created between the school and the family. In a study conducted of nine kindergarten children who seemed headed for reading difficulties in first grade, Goldenberg concluded that "the earlier in a child's school career his/her parents become involved, and that involvement is sustained, the bigger the payoff" (Eldridge, 2001, p. 65).

Parental involvement benefits children both academically and in their behaviors and feelings about school. "The benefits for young children begin with greater gains in reading for those children whose parents are encouraged by the teacher to help with reading activities at home" (Eldridge, 2001, p. 65). In an elementary school in Oakland, CA, four classrooms piloted a Home-School Connections project in their classrooms. "Activities included frequent information updates, via phone and mail, family homework projects that encouraged reading at home, and a series of family seminars on such topics as homework help and reading. Parents felt free to visit the classrooms and to communicate with the teacher by phone. Although it is difficult to assess the direct impact of this close family connection, students in the pilot classrooms had some of the highest reading scores in the school" (Cohn-Vargas and Grose, 1998, p. 45). "Extensive research reviews find that the home environment is among the most important influences on academic performance" (Finn, 1998, p. 20). Simply put, the amount of time parents spend monitoring their children's activities and assisting their children with homework has a dramatic effect on how successful their children are academically. "Additionally, children of parents who are involved have a more positive attitude about school, improved attendance, and show better homework habits than do children whose families are less involved" (Eldridge, 2001, p. 65).

Parents that become involved in their child's schooling can benefit significantly from the experience. "Parents involved with school in parent-related activities show increased self-confidence in parenting, more knowledge of child development, and an expanded understanding of the home as an environment for learning" (Eldridge, 2001, p. 66). Involved parents report that they feel they should help their child at home, that they understand more about what the child is being taught, that they know more about the school program, and that they support and encourage their child's school work (Eldridge, 2001, pp. 65–66). "Additionally, involved parents show an increased appreciation for a teacher's merits and abilities and are more likely to view positively a teacher's interpersonal skills" (Eldridge, 2001, p. 66).

Parental involvement also affects the teacher. "A teacher who involves parents in children's learning is more likely to report a greater understanding of families' cultures, an increased appreciation for parental interest in helping their children, and a deeper respect for parents' time and abilities" (Eldridge, 2001, p.

66). Teachers who are committed to parental involvement tend to reap significant positive benefits in terms of parental perceptions of their merits. When parents and teachers connect, both will see significant and lasting effects in their appreciation and understanding of each other's efforts (Eldridge, 2001, p. 66).

BARRIERS TO HOME-SCHOOL CONNECTIONS

There are several barriers that prevent effective home-school connections from happening in many schools across our nation. Most of these barriers involve the school and the parents. In my experience as a primary classroom teacher, children have always enjoyed their parents' involvement and have, in fact, shown much enthusiasm for it.

One barrier to home-school connections is the lack of knowledge and training teachers have regarding parental involvement. "Despite the strong evidence supporting the importance of home-school collaborations, prospective teachers receive little training, information, or experience working with parents. Surprisingly few in-service programs have been designed to support teachers in expanding or improving their parent involvement efforts" (Brand, 1996, p. 76). Many teachers feel uncomfortable and awkward around parents and have had little training on how to overcome their feelings, let alone truly support and encourage home-school partnerships.

Another barrier to home-school partnerships is that many parents do not fully understand how valuable and important their interactions with their children are. Parents also don't feel they have the ability to truly help their child academically. "Many parents express a belief that their assistance is not needed by the schools or teachers" (Eldridge, 2001, p. 66). "Well-designed school opportunities and incentives for parent involvement may have only limited success if they do not also address parents' ideas about their role in children's education and their self efficacy for helping their children succeed in school" (Powell, 1998, p. 64). Researchers have discovered that children succeed in school more often when the home is emotionally supportive, when parents provide reassurance when their

child encounters failure and when parents accept responsibility for assisting their children (Finn, 1998, p. 20). Barriers are created when homes and parents do not closely resemble these ideas.

"The reason some families don't become more involved in schools stems in part from parental perceptions of school. Menacker, Hurwitz, and Weldon (1988) reporting on home-school relations in inner-city schools, noted that most of the adults in these families had had unsuccessful or negative school experiences themselves, which contribute to their perception of the school as unresponsive" (Eldridge, 2001, p. 66).

Timing of home-school connections often creates a barrier for parents as well. "Time constraints and work schedules of parents have been found to be problems in involvement efforts" (Eldridge, 2001, p. 67). When schools do not offer programs that are flexible, such as evening events, participation levels decrease.

"Family circumstances also need to be addressed in attempts to remove barriers to participation in meetings" (Powell, 1998, p. 64). Schools that do not take into account child care arrangements and transportation barriers, for example, experience less parental involvement in home-school partnerships, especially with low-income families. In a recent study in 12 Baltimore schools, parental involvement increased by 10 percent when a high level of support (transportation to workshops, child care, meals, two meeting times) was offered to families. "It appeared that the additional 10 percent was a higher-risk group as measured by children's reading achievement and teacher ratings of the home educational environment" (Powell, 1998, p. 64). It is likely that there are many other barriers to effective home-school partnerships. It is important for schools to identify as many barriers as possible so that they may be eliminated in hopes of creating stronger partnerships with the families it serves.

SUGGESTIONS FOR IMPROVING HOME-SCHOOL PARTNERSHIPS

"Across all populations and programs, a major challenge is to develop ways of engaging parents that respond to a family's interests and life circumstances"

(Powell, 1998, p. 63). "Our understanding of parent involvement needs to be on a continuum that allows for parent participation on a variety of levels and through a wide variety of activities" (Gage and Workman, 1994, p. 77).

"First and foremost, a teacher should create a classroom climate that is open and accepting of parents and is based on a partnership approach. In this way the barriers of parental reluctance and awkwardness are lowered, and those parents who know the school to be unresponsive can begin to experience the classroom in another way" (Eldridge, 2001, p. 67). In order to do this, more universities and school districts need to be better training teachers on parental involvement concepts so that home-school partnerships are natural for teachers. "The currently weak attention to teachers' demonstrated skills in relating to parents must be strengthened in professional education and state certification requirements. It appears that, among the many competencies required for effective work with parents, special emphasis should be given to skills in learning and appreciating the perspectives of families" (Powell, 1998, p. 66).

One important thought to remember that may help improve home-school partnerships is the idea of what home-school partnerships "look like."

"Teachers pay more attention to students whose parents are involved in school" (Finn, 1998, p. 23). Often, educators dismiss the work that families do at home with their children—forgetting that the "home environment is among the most important influences on academic performance" (Finn, 1998, p. 20). One suggestion for improvement, then, would be for educators to recognize the work that families do at home. "The most powerful form of parent involvement has the parent actively involved with the child at home in all ways that relate to optimal learning and growing" (Gage and Workman, 1994, p. 77).

Research indicates that as educators we need to be telling parents about how important their job is and how much what they do with their children at home affects their achievement in the classroom. "Many parents feel they lack, or do lack, the skills to guide their children's reading or schoolwork" (Finn, 1998, p. 22). Sup-

BARRIERS TO POSITIVE FAMILY-TEACHER PARTNERSHIPS

BY AMY SUSSNA KLEIN, ED.D., AND MARIAN MILLER, M.ED.

There are a number of barriers that can prevent positive family-teacher relationships from forming. Some of these common obstacles include:

- **Differences in backgrounds.** The family and teacher come from different cultures, languages, and socio-economic statuses.
- **Stress.** There is stress for both families and teachers. For example, long hours and little flexibility at work reduce the time available for teachers to work on family communication and for parents/caregivers to relate to school.
- **Differing Values.** The family and teacher lack a mutual set of values.
- **Differences in viewing roles.** Differing views of the role of the school for the child between the teacher and the parent or caregiver.
- **Types of experiences.** Prior experiences with families/teachers have set up differing expectations.
- **Notions of openness.** Lack of openness to outsiders entering their territory (home or school).
- **Differences in experiences.** A parent's experience in school (positive or negative) sets up some expectations for their own interactions with school/teacher for their own child.

- **Communication abilities.** Teachers or families lack the ability to identify and communicate key experiences, ideas, or issues.
- **Communication discomfort.** Families or teachers are uncomfortable about communicating their needs, or do not have enough fluency in the language.
- **Need to feel valued.** Parents and teachers perceive that their perspective and opinions are not valued.
- **Differences in viewing child's needs.** The school views the child (her learning and development) differently than the family does. The school's philosophy differs from the family's view of appropriate child rearing. For example: The family equates teaching with telling, and the teacher equates learning with doing. Or, behavior issues are handled one way at home and another at school (spanking at home, explaining at school). When the school clearly explains philosophy, families get a better sense of the match between home/school expectations.

Amy Sussna Klein, Ed.D., is President of ASK Education Consulting. She can be reached by email at Askeducation@cs.com.

Marian Miller, M.Ed., is a faculty member at Lesley College

porting and encouraging parents in their role as their child's first teacher is vital to their child's success.

"To serve the needs of diverse children and families, teachers often must seek support for children and families beyond the traditional walls of the school" (Hurd, Lerner and Barton, 1999, p. 74). Schools need to continue to rely on community agencies to help in the effort of educating our children. "Dryfoos (1990) finds that when collaboration occurs between the school and the youth- and family-serving agencies and the community programs in which the school is embedded, an integrated and comprehensive community-wide system is established" (Hurd, Lerner and Barton, 1999, p. 74). Head Start is a well-known leader of an integrated services model.

CONCLUSION

"Teaching, nurturing, and caring for children is a community process. When most effective, many constituents—parents, teachers, extended family, neighborhoods, agencies, and community partners—are engaged. In the best of worlds, all parties work together to support children in the context of their families" (Hurd, Lerner and Barton, 1999, p. 74).

REFERENCES

Brand, S. (1996). Making parent involvement a reality: Helping teachers develop partnerships with parents. *Young Children,* 51(2), 76–80.

Cohn-Vargas and Grose, K. (1998). A partnership for literacy. *Educational Leadership,* 55(8), 45–48.

Eldridge, D. (2001). Parent involvement: It's worth the effort. *Young Children,* 56(4), 65–69.

Finn, J. (1998). Parental engagement that makes a difference. *Educational Leadership,* 55(8), 20–24.

Gage, J. and Workman, S. (1994). Creating family support systems: In head start and beyond. *Young Children,* 49(7), 74–77.

Hurd, T., Learner, R., and Barton, C. (1999). Integrated services: Expanding partnerships to meet the needs of today's children and families. *Young Children,* 54(2), 74–79.

McBride, S. (1999). Family centered practices. *Young Children,* 54(3), 62–68.

Powell, D. (1998). Reweaving parents into the fabric of early childhood programs. *Young Children,* 53(6), 60–67.

Keri Peterson is a teacher in the four-year-old program at Early Learning Center, Tiffany Creek Elementary School, in Boyceville, WI. She is currently enrolled in the M.S. program at the University of Wisconsin-Stout.

From *Earlychildhood News,* January/February 2002, pp. 39-45. © 2002 by Excelligence Learning Corporation. Reprinted by permission.

Basic Premises of Classroom Design

the teacher's perspective

BY TERRI JO SWIM, PH.D

It's that time of year—Fall. You and the children have settled into the daily routine. The curriculum is in full swing and learning is occurring all around the room. But is it optimal learning? What aspects of your work would you need to consider in addressing this question? Is it about the curricular experiences you have planned? Or is it about the physical layout of the classroom? Or could it be the types of materials you have provided the children? Or, still, could it be about the relationships you have developed with the children and their families?

Given the importance of the physical environment, this article will consider how the physical environment influences the children's learning and development. More specifically, the focus of this article is on answering the question: How do teachers create meaningful learning environments for themselves and the children? This article outlines some basic premises of designing classroom environments from the teacher's perspective and it is divided into several sections, each addressing a specific question. You should begin to answer each of these questions by reflecting on the age of children in your classroom, your program's philosophy, licensing and accreditation standards, and its guidelines for developmentally appropriate practice.

Within each section, you will be introduced to the concept of a "balance of opposites." This notion involves thinking about environmental factors that are in opposition to each other, such as messy/dry or pathways/boundaries. But first, a brief discussion about why teachers need to consider the physical environment will be presented.

The Importance of the Physical Environment

Taking the time to reflect on the physical environment is imperative as it is considered the "third" teacher in the classroom. In other words, the environment provides guidance to the children and adults about appropriate behavior. Consider for a moment how your behavior is influenced differently by being in a place of worship, a library, a shopping mall, or a family-dining restaurant. All of these environments send messages about appropriate behavior. Take, for example, the library with its special sections designated for quiet reading, small groups to gather and enjoy stories, computer work, and playing with puppets. The way the space and materials are arranged provides clues as to appropriate behavior. The adults responsible for managing the space seldom have to remind others of their expectations; the environment does it for them. Like the designer of the library environment, your careful planning can assist children with meeting your expectations for the use of the space.

Sketch of Room

Before we investigate how to prepare environments, you need to sketch the basic layout of your classroom including all attached spaces that you will use throughout the day such as a child bathroom or covered patio area. Also, indicate on your sketch the location of electrical outlets, partitions, and other permanent structures or furniture that cannot be moved (e.g., classroom sink with surrounding cabinets) as well as the type of floor covering. As you read this article, you will be prompted to add to your sketch.

Learning Centers

Given the importance of learning centers, it is assumed in this article that your classroom will be organized into them. When planning your learning environment, you will need to consider "how many and what learning centers you should have in your classroom?"

The number and type of learning centers available depends heavily on the size of the classroom and the age of the children. In general, to maximize choice and minimize conflict over possessions, a rule of thumb to follow is having one-third more work spaces than the number of children in your classroom. To illustrate, if you have 24 school-age children, you will need (24 x 1/3) + 24 or 32 spaces for working. This might mean including three spaces at the sensory table, two at the easel, four at the art table, four at the writing/homework center, six in blocks/construction, four in dramatic play, four at the discovery center, three in the listening/library area, and two private spots.

Real Objects Versus Open-ended Materials

Children need a balance of novel and familiar materials in the classroom to attract and maintain their attention (see next section for a more in-depth discussion). When children are engaged with materials and ideas, they have less opportunity to create mischief or misbehave; thus, altering teacher supervision from guidance of behavior to guidance of learning.

Throughout the early childhood period, young children are learning to use objects as tools for representing their thoughts and theories about how the world works. Therefore, providing a balance of real and open-ended materials promotes cognitive development. Making available real objects such as glass tumblers for drinks during meals, child-size shovels for digging in the garden, or Navajo pottery for storing paintbrushes, serves two purposes: 1) it demonstrates respect in the children's ability to care for objects, and 2) it connects home and school environments. The real objects, when introduced in response to the children's expressed interests, can facilitate thinking about a particular topic or concept.

Open-ended materials, on the other hand, can be used by the children to expand their understanding of concepts and demonstrate creative uses of materials. Open-ended materials include collected items such as fabric, cardboard, plastics, pebbles, shells, or egg cartons and commercially produced objects such as wooden blocks, animal and people figurines, or connecting manipulatives. Open-ended materials can spark, support, and enhance learning and development in any learning center of the classroom. Neatly arranging them in baskets or other containers and displaying them on a shelf at the children's height will make them easily accessible to the children. (Curtis & Carter, 2003; Isbell & Exelby, 2001).

the environment is often considered the third teacher in a classroom

Independence Versus Dependence

A primary goal for adults is that children become independent, self-regulated learners. In order for this to occur, teachers must carefully plan the physical environment with this in mind. As mentioned above, arranging open-ended materials neatly in baskets and displaying them on child-size shelves promotes cognitive development. This practice also promotes social and emotional development because the children can independently select the materials they need for their work and they can more easily clean up before they leave the learning area. Moreover, modifying the bathroom so that all necessary hand washing supplies can be reached independently facilitates the children's use of them.

Reflection Question: What learning centers are you considering or have you already selected for your particular group of children? How will you explain your choices to the children, families, and your colleagues? Make a list of the titles or labels for the centers on the back of your sketch.

Use of Space

An important question to begin your work is "how do I want the children to use this space?" Teachers create environments to promote learning in all of the content areas (e.g., mathematics, sciences, and social studies) and all areas of development. Therefore, a basic understanding of child development and learning theories will guide your thinking about how to use your classroom space (Herr & Swim, 2002; Swim, 2004).

Messy Versus Dry

Designing space for daily opportunities of exploring messy materials is a must. These experiences are particularly significant for young children because they build cognitive structures or schemas (i.e., tightly organized set of ideas about a specific object or situation) through sensorimotor and hands-on, minds-on experiences. Some typical messy centers include water and/or sensory tables, painting easel, and art. Water play, for example, provides opportunities for learning about quantity, building vocabulary, and negotiating the sharing of materials.

What does a teacher need to consider when managing messy experiences in a classroom setting? First, placing messy experiences over vinyl or linoleum flooring allows for ease of clean up when spills occur. Second, placing these experiences near a water source can simplify clean up as well as aid in refilling or adding a new element to an experience. For example, if a sensory table is filled with dry sand, children can transfer water from the source using pitchers thus transforming the properties of the sand. Third, if a material such as dirt is placed in the sensory table, placing a hand broom and dustpan nearby prompts children to maintain a safe environment.

If you do not have floor covering that is conducive to messy activities, you will need to be creative in order to provide such valuable learning experiences. Placing newspaper, towels, or a shower curtain under a sensory table or easel can resolve this issue. Another way to address this challenge is to plan daily experiences outside with messy materials.

Noisy Versus Quiet

Some classroom experiences seem to naturally be noisier than others. Cooperating and negotiating requires children to interact with one another and, sometimes, interactions can become heated. However, a teacher's goal should be to facilitate such interactions so that the children gain necessary perspective-taking and problem-solving skills, not to stop the interactions or prevent them in the first place (Marion, 2003).

To manage the environment and facilitate learning, teachers can place noisy areas close together. Some noisy centers include blocks and construction, dramatic play, music and movement, and project work space. Placing these centers adjacent to one another serves two purposes. First, the higher noise levels will be concentrated in a particular section of the room. This allows children to concentrate better in the quiet areas because there are fewer distractions close by. Second, placing areas together that need more teacher supervision and support (e.g., assisting children with problem solving) permits the adult to engage in these interactions without constantly being pulled between noisy centers that were placed in different parts of the room.

Quiet centers consist of the library and listening centers, and private spaces. For your and the children's mental health, you must provide areas for children to be alone. These private spaces allow the children to "regroup" and gather their thoughts before rejoining others (Honig, 2002). Play in other centers, such as manipulatives or science/discovery, fluctuate between quiet and noisy depending on the type of materials provided and the children's levels of engagement, thus, making them more difficult to classify. These areas can be used to transition between the noisy and quiet centers.

When deciding where to place learning centers, teachers also need to consider the needs of the different types of centers. To illustrate, the music and movement center needs an electrical outlet for a tape or CD player, shelves for musical instruments, baskets for scarves or strips of fabric, mirrors for observing motions, and space for creative movement and dance. Due to limited resources, teachers often need to maximize the use of equipment and materials that they do have. Locating the music and movement center near the dramatic play area is one way to do this because these centers can share the mirror and basket of fabric.

Reflection Question: How did you or will you arrange the learning centers you selected for your classroom? Write the names of the centers on your sketch in the location where you are placing them.

Calm, Safe Learning Environment

Another question that you will encounter in your work is "How can I create a calm, safe environment that provides stimulating learning experiences?" In this section, we will focus attention on the last part of this question: "stimulating learning experiences."

Novel Versus Familiar

Teachers and children deserve to be surrounded by beautiful objects and materials that are displayed in an aesthetically pleasing fashion. Some of these objects should be part of the environment on a regular basis while others can be included to spark interest. For example, hanging a framed print of Monet's sunflowers on the wall near the easel will create a beautiful environment for preschool children. However, surprising the children with a display of Pueblo Indian pottery will spark different interest in the easel.

Classroom space should be varied so that children have the opportunity to explore different perspectives. To illustrate, having the ability to change one's physical location by climbing up the stairs to a loft and looking down on a teacher provides a child with a new view of the world. Another way that teachers can vary the space and provoke thinking is through providing a new display or object to explore and discuss. When the flooring of the room has two or more variations, this provides a natural occurrence of hard versus soft and warm versus cold. Sitting an infant on the vinyl or linoleum flooring on a hot summer day will feel cool to the

touch, thus providing them an opportunity to experience their environment in a new or different manner.

Another way to conceptualize the familiar is to create spaces that parallel those found in home environments. Placing a couch, rocking chair, and end table with a light, for example, in the entryway mimics a living room in a home. Doing this not only adds warmth and comfort to the learning environment but it also helps to create a sense of security at school: our home away from home. (Honig, 2002; Bergen, Reid, & Torelli, 2001).

Pathways Versus Boundaries

As you are planning your classroom layout, you need to consider how you will designate your learning centers. Having visible boundaries for learning centers provides children with a clear message for the use of materials in a particular area. For ease of supervision, use a variety of dividers such as short shelving units, bookcases, transparent fabrics, and sheets of decorated acrylic.

Transparency, or the ability to see between centers in the classroom, also facilitates children's play because they can make connections between materials in different centers around the room. Thus, even though we are designing clear learning centers, we should be flexible in allowing the children to move materials that they need from one center to another. When planning the boundaries for a learning center, you must carefully consider how much space to devote to this area. The noisier areas described above often require more space than quieter areas (also described above). This is due to the fact that these areas tend to elicit more associate and cooperative play, which require two or more children at a time. A teacher also needs to consider how to utilize open space. Because we need gathering spaces that can easily accommodate all of the children and adults in the room at one time, we often set aside this space. However, when the entire group is not using the space, it can be perceived by children as a place for "rough and tumble" play. Sharing this location with the music and movement area is logical given the space needs of each center.

Pathways into and out of the room as well as between centers need to be carefully considered. When children arrive for the day, they should be able to gradually enter the classroom and transition from home to school. Having to walk to the opposite side of the classroom to store their belongings in their cubby can be stressful, especially if they must pass by noisy centers. When considering movement between centers, walking through one center to get to another can cause children to be distracted. Do you, for example, want the children to walk through the block/construction area to get to the music center? It would quickly become evident from the children's behavior that such an arrangement does not work.

"How do I plan the environment to meet the basic needs of the children?"

Reflection Question: Add to your sketch boundaries for your learning centers. What types of structures will you use or are you using to physically divide the space? Mark also the pathways of how the children might move between them.

Basic Needs

As you are considering the educational needs of the children, you must also dedicate space for meeting the children's basic needs. The question becomes, "How do I plan the environment to meet the basic needs of the children?"

Eating Versus Toileting

Some infant and toddler classrooms separate the changing table and food preparation counter with a small sink. Although this may optimize the use of counter space on built-in cabinets, it could jeopardize both the adults' and the children's health. For hygienic purposes, then, it is imperative that the eating and toileting areas are separated. Although this is relatively simple in a preschool, kindergarten, or school-age classroom, it may be more difficult for an infant and toddler classroom because the typical restroom just does not have enough space for toilets, sinks, and a changing table.

The need to continually supervise the children is an issue facing infant and toddler teachers. Diapering requires a significant amount of teacher time during a day. Thus, for ease of supervision, changing tables are often placed in the classroom. Where in the class should they be located? Placing the changing table next to a water source promotes good hand washing practices. You should also position it away from a wall so that your back is not to the rest of the children when you are changing a diaper.

The food area can require a number of small appliances such as a mini-refrigerator or microwave (per licensing regulations); therefore, cabinet space near electrical outlets is very important. For toddlers and older children, space for eating can be shared with other areas of the classroom. For example, the tables that are used for art can be cleaned and sanitized when it is snack or mealtime. For teachers of infants, other issues must be addressed when planning the environment. Depending upon your state regulations, you may or may not need a separate high chair for each infant. Moreover, finding storage space when it is not meal time must be given careful consideration.

Sleep and Comfort Versus Play

Children and adults need locations to store special items and belongings from home. This not only reaffirms the importance of both environments but it also facilitates learning to respect your and others' belongings. Switching between environments can be stressful for people of all ages. Therefore, plan for comfortable places for children to make the transition from home to school, snuggle, relax, and enjoy reunions with family members. Couches and rocking chairs, for example, located in a variety of classroom areas provide an excellent avenue for this.

All children need time throughout the day to rest and rejuvenate. The environment should be managed to create a calm relaxing environment during nap or rest time. Closing blinds on the windows, plugging in a night light, playing soft instrumental music, and providing comfort items for each child (e.g., blankets, favorite stuffed animals) might assist with shifting from play to sleep. You should also organize the environment to address the needs of children who require less sleep during the day. For example, creating baskets with books, paper and pencils, and other quiet toys that can be used by a child lying on a cot or sitting at a table can meet these children's need.

Reflection Question: How have I included on my sketch ample space for meeting the basic needs of the children? Where will I store necessary equipment (e.g., cots or high chairs) when they are not in use?

On-going Reflection of Physical Environment

How often do you consider the primary question of this article, "How do teachers create meaningful learning environments for themselves and the children?" If you cannot recall the last time you reflected on this question, then you may be thinking about your environment in a static or fixed manner. In other words, you may not be thinking about all the ways that physical environment impacts the children's learning and vice versa. Early childhood professionals should regularly revisit this question because the answer is constantly evolving.

Teachers must continually assess and respond to the changing developmental needs and interests of the young children. For example, with a group of young infants, a teacher will provide safe areas for exploring toys and manipulatives. As the children acquire gross motor skills, areas and structures for creeping, crawling, and cruising should be made available. Moreover, when the preschool children are investigating railroads, centers and materials will reflect this interest. As this interest evolves into traveling, the number and types of centers available as well as the materials available in the classroom will need to be altered.

Conclusion

This article was designed to help you plan a classroom environment that meets the social, emotional, physical, and cognitive needs of developing children. If you are new to the profession, I hope that you have a deeper understanding of the impact physical environments have on behavior and learning. If you are a "seasoned pro," I hope that this article prompted you to reflect on your existing classroom environment. If you are considering making changes to your classroom for an already-established group of children, please think about how people typically respond to changes in the physical environment. Changes seem to be more tolerable for everyone when they are made a little at a time. Thus, as you reflect on your physical environment, you will want to ponder which changes to make first, second, and so on.

In conclusion, if you want the children to run across the room, then placing your centers around the perimeter of the classroom leaving a large open space in the middle tells children that this is acceptable. If you prefer that children wander in and out of learning centers without becoming engaged, then provide undefined spaces for each learning center and/or unclear pathways between them. If, on the other hand, you desire the children to work cooperatively on block constructions, then offer a raised platform for building in a space that easily accommodates small groups of children.

References

Bergen, D., Reid, R., & Torelli, L. (2001). *Educating and caring for very young children: The infant/toddler curriculum.* NY: Teachers College Press.

Curtis, D., & Carter, M. (2003). *Designs for living and learning: Transforming early childhood environments.* St. Paul, MN: Redleaf Press.

Edwards, C., Gandini, L., & Forman, G. (1998). The hundred languages of children: The Reggio Emilia approach—advanced reflections (2nd ed.). Westport, CT: Ablex Publishing.

Herr, J., & Swim, T.J. (2002). *Creative resources for infants and toddlers* (2nd ed.). NY: Delmar Learning.

Isbell, R., & Exelby, B. (2001). *Early learning environments that work.* Beltsville, MD: Gryphon House.

Marion, M. (2003). *Guidance of young children* (6th ed.). Upper Saddle River, NJ: Merrill Prentice Hall.

Swim, T.J. (2003). Respecting infants and toddlers: Strategies for best practice. *Earlychildhood NEWS,* 15 (3), 16-23.

Swim, T.J. (2004). Theories of child development: Building blocks of developmentally appropriate practices. *Earlychildhood NEWS,* 16 (2), 36-45.

Terri Jo Swim, Ph.D., is an Assistant Professor of early childhood education and child development at Indiana University Purdue University Fort Wayne (IPFW) in Fort Wayne, IN. She is also the co-author with Judy Herr of the award-winning books *Creative Resources for Infant & Toddlers* from Thomson Delmar Learning (www.delmarlearning.com). She teaches in undergraduate and graduate programs. Her research interests include infant-toddler and preschool curriculum, Reggio Emilia, and teacher education.

How Safe are Child Care Playgrounds?

A PROGRESS REPORT

BY DONNA THOMPSON, PH.D.,
SUSAN D. HUDSON, PH.D.,
AND HEATHER M. OLSEN, M.A.

A major portion of a child's day is spent in play. Children develop, physically, emotionally, socially, and intellectually through play. To help facilitate these play experiences, whether indoors or outdoors, the play environment will contain playground equipment. Children explore themselves and the environment through this equipment. In recent years, however, a fundamental question has arisen: "How safe are the playgrounds in which children play?"

In the public arenas of child care centers and schools, playground injuries are the leading cause of injury (Briss, Sacks, Addiss & O'Neill, 1994; U.S. Congress, Office of Technology Assessment, 1995). Because playgrounds are one of the major educational and recreational environments that all children are exposed to during their developmental years, it is critical that adults create SAFE playgrounds. Considering that every year over 200,000 children receive emergency department care for playground-related injuries, with nearly one-third classified as severe (Mack, Hudson & Thompson, 1997) and that the American Association of Orthopedic Surgeons indicates that the number of playground injuries may be as high as 500,000, it's clear that America's playgrounds are not safe enough.

The Report Card

In April 2000, The National Program for Playground Safety (NPPS) released the results of the largest nationwide survey of child care, school, and park playgrounds ever. Of the 3052 playgrounds assessed, 1163 (38%) were child care playgrounds. (Hudson, Mack, & Thompson, 2000). Of the 3052 playgrounds assessed, 1163 (38%) were child care program playgrounds.

NPPS sought to replicate this study in the spring of 2003 by revisiting the sites identified in the 2000 report.

Table 1.	
Grade Comparison by Year	
2000	**2004**
A's = 0	A's = 2
B's = 23	B's = 25
C's = 22	C's = 20
D's = 5	D's = 3

Again all 50 states were visited and 38 percent were child care centers. Overall, many states significantly increased their safety rating as the nation improved its grade by moving from a C to a C+. However, in the child care sector, the grade C+ remained the same from the earlier survey. Table 1 shows the results of the grade comparison from the 2000 and 2004 studies.

While the data indicates slight improvement, it is clear that more progress needs to be made in improving playground safety. Maintaining C+ playgrounds is not good enough. All children deserve to be playing on Grade A playgrounds. How can this be achieved? Perhaps by looking at the different components that contribute to a SAFE playground, a better picture of what needs to be done can emerge.

What is SAFE?

The National Program for Playground Safety believes that there are four areas that encompass the safety of children on a playground. First, the playground must have adequate supervision. Within this concept are two observable components. First, the playground must be designed so that a supervisor can observe children on the equipment and second, there must be supervisors on the playground when children are present.

Age-appropriate design is the second element of the SAFE model. This means that the equipment must be designed for the ages of the children who will use it. Presently, equipment is designed for children 2-5 or 5-12 years of age.

The third area of consideration is fall surfacing. Since 70 percent of injuries that occur on playgrounds are related to falls to the surface, it is critical that suitable fall surfacing materials be present. In addition, it is important that loose fill materials such as sand, pea gravel, rubber, and wood products be at the adequate depth to maintain cushioning characteristics.

Finally, it is important that the equipment and the surfacing be regularly maintained. For example, the equipment must be repaired so spaces that can entangle, string or entrap heads are not allowed to develop. How did the child care playgrounds measure up regarding Supervision, Age appropriateness, Fall surfacing and Equipment and surfacing maintenance? Let's look at each of those areas individually.

S = Supervision

Supervision of children on the playground is extremely important since it is estimated that over 40 percent of the injuries that children sustain on playgrounds are related to a lack of or inappropriate supervision. Table 2 presents the grade for child care centers concerning supervision.

It appears from looking at Table 2 that work needs to be done in terms of observation and design of playgrounds for supervision.

Of the 121 playgrounds observed in the 2004 survey where children were playing on the playground, 84 percent of those playgrounds had adult supervisors present. That is very good. However, room for improvement remains since it is important that children be supervised all of the time. While the number of children present at each playground was not recorded, the number of supervisors present was reported. Half of the time there were two adults present while 29 percent of the time there was one supervisor watching the children. Most of the time, there appears to be adequate supervision on the child care playgrounds. NPPS recommends that two supervisors always be present. If a child is injured or some other crisis occurs, one supervisor can maintain control of the children while the other attends to the emergency situation.

The survey also attempted to determine whether or not the adults appeared to be actively supervising the children. Of those observed, most (86%) appeared to be watching the children carefully, whereas some (30%) seemed as though they were not paying attention as carefully as they should be. The latter group of individuals may have been putting children at risk.

Another concern was whether or not the children could be easily viewed on the playground. Was the equipment designed in a fashion so that the children could be easily monitored? It was not easy to view the children in only 11

Table 2.

Report Card on Supervision on Child Care Playgrounds

Overall Grade

2000 = B-   2004 = C

Supervision Component			
2000 %	2004 %	2000 Grade	2004 Grade
Adults present when children are present on the playground			
93	84	A-	B-
Children are easily viewed on equipment			
96	89	A	B+
Children can be easily viewed in crawl spaces			
89	72	B+	C-
Supervision rules are posted			
6	3	F	F

percent of the playgrounds. This suggests that the design of the equipment is facilitating supervision.

If the design caused a supervision problem, what precluded observation of the children? There were two items that drew our attention. One concern was blind spots and the other was enclosed spaces that had openings. Interestingly enough, 100 percent of the playgrounds where children were not easily viewed had blind spots. This would suggest that in order to make playgrounds more supervisable, the design must not have blind spots and must have enclosed spaces such as tube slides that have some type of opening so that it can be seen if children are inside of them. Finally, few child care centers did have signage indicating the age of children for whom the equipment was designed. In some respects this is not as necessary as at parks unless the playground is accessible to the community when the center is not functioning. However, when the standard for play equipment for children under two is published, this consideration will be crucial to placing children in the proper outdoor learning environment.

All in all, the supervision of the playgrounds at child care centers is adequate but needs improvement. Child care specialists have a reputation for providing good supervision and especially caring for their clients. Hopefully, that aspect can receive more attention in the future to improve the safety of the children in the outdoor environment.

A = Age-Appropriate Design

The next component of safety examined was age-appropriate design (Table 3). Most playground equipment areas at child care programs were designed for children from 2-5. Some centers provided equipment for children

Table 3.

Report Card on Age-Appropriate Design on Child Care Playgrounds

Overall Grade

2000 = C   2004 = C

Age Appropriate Design Components

2000 %	2004 %	2000 Grade	2004 Grade
Separate play areas present			
49%	26%	F	F
Signage for age group provided			
6%	5%	F	F
Platforms provide for change of directions			
92%	87%	A-	B+
Guardrails are present on elevated platforms higher than 3 feet.			
92%	87%	A-	B+
Equipment pieces are designed to prevent children from climbing outside of structures.			
74%	80%	C	B-
Equipment pieces are designed to discourage children from climbing on supporting structures.			
79%	80%	C+	B-

ages 5-12. However, there was no clear separation of play areas in 74 percent of the playground equipment provided for children ages 2-12. This is a discouraging increase (51%) from 2000. When playground equipment for differing age groups isn't distinctly separated, younger children are likely to play on equipment that is too big for them, which may result in injuries. This is a problem that should be immediately corrected.

Child care providers need to purchase equipment that is appropriate for the development of their children. At this point in time, there is equipment manufactured for children ages 2-5 and 5-12. No, this overlap is not a mistake. Children go to child care centers and to elementary school at age five. In addition, it is important for early childhood educators to take preschool children to equipment designed for children ages 2-5 in park settings, as well.

Signage regarding the age appropriateness of playground equipment is still problematic. While signage would clarify the differences in design for children ages 2-5 and 5-12, it would also indicate that the equipment is inappropriate for children under two. Again, it should be noted that the current playground equipment is not appropriate for that age level, a fact particularly important to owners' of public centers or centers available to other constituents after hours.   .

While the grade for the provision of change of direction on platforms is above average, it did decrease. That

suggests that the equipment may be older or that care in observing that feature when purchasing new equipment is not being noticed.

The grade for the provision of guardrails also declined. Although the decrease was not great, the point is that guardrails do prevent children from falling to the surface. Since falls to the surface are responsible for a great number of injuries that children sustain on playgrounds, it would be good that caregivers attended to this situation promptly.

On the positive side, the assessors did observe that more equipment at child care programs is being provided that prevents children from climbing on the outside of it. As such, it suggests that children are less likely to climb on equipment in a manner in which it is not designed. The result should be that children are being prevented from falling from inappropriate places. It also indicates that child care personnel are being more careful in the selection of equipment.

Lastly, the equipment being selected is that which discourages children from climbing on support structures. The grade for that item increased from C+ to B-. Although the change was small, it is important to provide equipment that is less likely to cause children to be injured by inappropriate use.

While the overall grade did not change, we would challenge early childhood educators to increase their attention to age appropriateness so that children are provided with equipment that meets their physical, emotional, social, and intellectual development.

F = Fall Surfacing

As mentioned above, inappropriate fall surfacing or the lack of appropriate surfacing is seen as being responsible for 70 percent of the injuries that children sustain on playgrounds. When preschool children fall, they tend to sustain head injuries. That is why it is important that caregivers never allow asphalt, cement, dirt, or grass under or around playground equipment. Suitable surfaces that may be used include loose-fill products such as sand, gravel, wood products, rubber products, or non-organic products such as rubber tiles or poured-in-place products. The following table provides the report card for fall surfacing.

Proper surfacing under and around playground equipment is determined by four factors: 1) suitable surfacing materials, 2) height of the equipment, 3) depth of loose-fill surface materials, and 4) placement of suitable materials at the adequate depth in the playground use zone.

In relation to the first factor, suitable materials provided, child care programs are about the same in the provision of suitable surfacing under and around playground equipment. Since surfacing is such an important factor, it is critical that major attention be paid to this situation. Suitable surfacing is available and its provision will not only prevent an injury, but a lawsuit that may follow if this situation is ignored. Better than 95 percent of the child care programs used loose-fill surfacing materials sand, pea gravel, wood chips, or wood fiber and unitary surfaces of the rubber mats or poured in place materials. However, regardless of whether it is loose-fill or unitary, suitable surfaces need to be used 100 percent of the time.

What is the height of equipment on child care playgrounds? Child care programs received an A in this section, but please note the caution that follows. Since some programs care for children ages 2-12, it is noted that 99.7 percent have equipment that is eight feet high or less. On the other hand, 85 percent have equipment that is six feet high or less. We recommend that equipment for children ages 2-5 be six feet or less since children are twice as likely to be injured from a fall over six feet in height.

What about the depth? Even though, child care programs are providing suitable materials, they are not providing enough depth of those materials. In fact, in the report card, that area has worsened. It is imperative to the safety of children that greater attention be focused on this element. Lack of adequate depth means that the cushioning characteristic of the suitable materials is non-existent. The depth of the surfacing should be proportionate to the height of the equipment. As a matter of fact, eight percent of the playgrounds surveyed had no surfacing at all.

Last, but not least, the suitable material at the appropriate depth needs to be in the proper place under and around the equipment. This placement is known as the use zone. Child care programs have worsened in this category (Table 4) and the lack of attention here is truly placing children at risk. Not only is the surfacing not thick enough, it is not in the place where children are likely to fall. Forty six percent of the time surfacing was not in the use zone for stationary equipment, 49 percent of the time surfacing was not in the use zone for slides, and 66 percent of the time surfacing was not in the use zone for swings. Considering that children see surfacing and assume that the area is safe, child care programs are giving children a false sense of security.

On the bright side, child care programs are doing an excellent job of covering concrete footings so that children cannot fall on them. However, the study showed that far too many of these play areas were littered with foreign objects, which created potential hazards.

E = Equipment and Surfacing Maintenance

The last component of the report card dealt with equipment maintenance. Unfortunately, this was another area that child care programs seem to be doing a worse job than in 2000 (Table 5).

Without routine inspection and repair, any equipment will fall into disrepair and pose a hazard to children using the equipment. It appears that maintenance of metal and wooden equipment is insufficient in comparison to plastic equipment. Part of this problem lies in the fact that wood and metal equipment tend to be older than plastic. Proportionately, metal equipment installed prior to 1991 had more rust present than equipment installed after 1991. A similar finding was seen with wooden equip-

Table 4.

Report Card on Fall Surfacing on Child Care Programs

Overall Grade

2000 = C	2004 = C+		

Fall Surfacing Component

2000 %	2004 %	2000 Grade	2004 Grade
Suitable materials provided			
71%	73%	C-	C-
Height of equipment 8 feet			
NA	99%	NA	A
Appropriate depth of loose fill			
44%	9%	F	F
Six Foot Use Zone has appropriate surfacing material			
62%	53%	D-	F
Concrete footings are covered			
89%	95%	B+	A
Surface is free of foreign objects			
89%	81%	B+	B-

Table 5.

Report Card on Equipment Maintenance on Child Care Playgrounds

Overall Grade

2000 = B-	2004 = C+		

Equipment Maintenance Components

2000 %	2004 %	2000 Grade	2004 Grade
Equipment is free of broken parts			
85%	86%	B	B
Equipment is free of missing parts			
85%	90%	B	A-
Equipment is free of protruding bolts			
83%	83%	B-	B-
Equipment is free of noticeable gaps			
75%	65%	C	D
Equipment is free of head entrapments			
81%	71%	B-	C-
Equipment is free of rust			
79%	74%	C+	C
Equipment is free of splinters			
80%	71%	B-	C-
Equipment is free of cracks/holes			
95%	96%	A	A

ment. More plastic equipment has been installed since 1994 than before that time.

Having said that, it is good to see that most of the equipment is free from broken parts and free from protruding bolts. Both can pose a problem in relation to injuries to eyes and cuts. However, room for improvement continues to exist. When broken parts or missing parts were observed, owners failed to rope off the area to prevent children from being injured over 90 percent of the time.

Grades also declined from 2000 in regards to the appearance of noticeable gaps and spaces in the equipment where children's heads could be potentially trapped due to inappropriate installation or aging equipment. The older the equipment, the more gaps are liable to be present. This is an area that deserves immediate attention as both of those situations have the potential to cause death and severe disability. In addition, the frequency of rust and splinters on playground equipment also rose in the last four years. Again, the older the equipment, the more likely these conditions are to exist.

Child care program equipment did, however, manage to receive an A in terms of being free of cracks and holes. That is probably because there is more new equipment in child care centers that is composed of plastic. Nevertheless, on the whole, the grade for the section has decreased from a B- to a C+. That suggests that equipment and surfacing maintenance needs attention.

Recommendations Based on the Report Card

Based on the findings from this report card, the National Program for Playground Safety makes the following recommendations:

Supervision

The results of this section suggest that manufacturers need to pay attention to sight lines especially in relation to crawl spaces and blind spots when they develop playground equipment and composite structures.

Further, owners/operators of playground areas should provide signage indicating the importance of supervision and other behaviors that the wish to encourage on playgrounds.

Age-Appropriate Design

All new playground areas designed for children ages 2-12 should have two distinct areas: one for ages 2-5 and the other for ages 5-12. In addition, composite structures that provide for mixed aged use (ages 2-12) should not be purchased. All playgrounds should have signage or labels directing adults to equipment designed for the appropriateness of the development of the children.

Fall Surfacing

Suitable surfacing materials need to be purchased and maintained at the appropriate depth proportionate to that height of the equipment.

Surfacing materials must be in the appropriate use zone so that the falls of children can be absorbed by the appropriate thickness of suitable surfacing.

Equipment and Surfacing Maintenance

Child care personnel need to form a maintenance policy and place a person in charge of dealing with maintenance on a regular basis.

Areas that need special attention in relation to maintenance include noticeable gaps and spaces that may be head entrapments.

In conclusion, while the child care playgrounds grade was maintained at a C+, we contend that all children deserve an "A" playground for the sake of safety. In addition, children should be able to assume that the play area in which they play is safe so that children can go out and to what they do best and that is play.

Actions for Early Childhood Educators

Now, what can early childhood educators do to improve the playground environment for children? There are four areas in which teachers can influence the safety of the playground: Supervision, Age-Appropriate Design, Fall Surfacing and Equipment and Surfacing Maintenance.

First, child care educators can develop a supervision plan that includes training their teachers to supervise on the playground. Encourage them to move around the playground and observe the movements of the children. Supervision is more than watching; it is paying attention to the way children play and only intervening when needed.

Second, be sure that children are allowed to play on play equipment appropriately designed for their age group. At this point, equipment is manufactured for preschool children ages 2-5. Do not allow children younger than two to play on equipment designed for older children.

Third, it is critical that child care directors place suitable surfacing under and around playground equipment. In addition, consider placing unitary surfacing in shaded areas where children, ages 0-2, are playing. It does not make sense to have those children trying to learn to walk out the door onto cement. A more forgiving surface such as rubber mats or poured-in-place materials would be more appropriate.

Fourth, child care directors need to make maintenance plans and assign individuals to check both the equipment and surfacing on a regular basis. That timeline is determined on the frequency and numbers of children who use the area.

Finally, plan ahead by using a planning process to decide on the purpose of the play area and then decide what equipment to purchase based on curricular needs. Make the area an outdoor learning environment, even though it may be also be used for free play. NPPS has pamphlets and other products such as a planning video and a supervision kit to help with the process.

By following those suggestions, early childhood educators can be proactive in making the play environment safe for children. In addition, the playground can be transformed into an outdoor learning environment. Thus, it can become safe and satisfying for the children.

Donna Thompson, Ph.D., Director; **Susan D. Hudson, Ph.D.,** Education Director; and **Heather M. Olsen, M.A.,** Project Coordinator. All are from The National Program for Playground Safety, University of Northern Iowa, School of HPELS, Cedar Falls, IA 50614-0618. For further information, please visit www.playgroundsafety.org or call 800-554-PLAY(7529).

References

American Academy of Orthopaedic Surgeons (1999). Play it safe background information. Rosemont, IL: AAOS.

Briss, P.A., Sacks, J.J., Addiss, D.G., & O'Neill, J. (1995). Injuries from falls on playgrounds: Effects of day care center regulation and enforcement. *Archives of Pediatric Adolescent Medicine,* 149, 906-911.

Hudson, S., Mack, M., & Thompson, D. (2000). *How safe are America's playgrounds? A national profile of child care, school and park playgrounds.* Cedar Falls, IA: National Program for Playground Safety.

Hudson, S., Olsen, H. & Thompson, D. (2004). *How safe are America's playgrounds. A progress report.* Cedar Falls, IA.: National Program for Playground Safety.

Mack, M., Hudson, S., & Thompson. D. (December, 1997). An analysis of playground surface injuries. *Research Quarterly for Exercise and Sport.* 68 (4) 368-372.

U.S. Congress, Office of Technology Assessment (1995). *Risks to children in school.* Washington, DC: U.S. Government Printing Office.

U.S. Consumer Product Safety Commission. (1997). *Handbook for Public Playground Safety,* Washington, DC: U.S. Government Printing Office.

Planning holiday celebrations: An ethical approach to developing policy and practices

by Katie Campbell, Mary Jamsek, and P.D. Jolley

"I really want to change how I plan for holidays in my classroom. What I'm doing now doesn't feel right, but the parents aren't going to like it and my coworkers think I'm crazy."

"What is happening to my child? He's never behaved like this before!"

"Why don't you have your skeletons out? We have them up at our house."

Comments like these can arise in the struggle to incorporate cultural, religious, and individual beliefs into early childhood programs. One person's real and sincere holiday "spirit" offends another. Children's emotions may range from wild enthusiasm to increased stress, even depression. And celebrations and decorations associated with "traditional" holidays are so pervasive that we may not recognize that there are alternatives.

In this article, we propose that programs develop a policy for celebrating holidays based on core values and ethical principles.

A holiday policy can lead to teaching practices that enhance our understanding of, and respect for, the different cultures and beliefs of children, families, staff, and community.

Re-thinking dominant-culture holidays

Many teachers use holiday-theme activity books to plan their school-year curriculum. Some examples of holiday-based monthly themes include Halloween in October, Thanksgiving in November, and Christmas in December—and maybe Kwanzaa or Hanukkah in a nod toward multiculturalism.

The themes mentioned above represent holidays of the dominant culture. For the purposes of this article, we define *dominant culture* as the "ruling or prevailing culture exercising authority or influence" (York 1991). Dominant-culture holidays, then, are the holidays celebrated most widely by a large segment of a population.

In the United States, the holidays most commonly celebrated in both elementary schools and early childhood programs are religious in origin. The celebrations themselves, however, are generally secular in nature. While a great number of people celebrate the dominant-culture holidays—Halloween, Thanksgiving, Christmas, Valentine's Day and Easter—many do not. Of those people who do, not all celebrate in the commercialized manner popular in our society.

While getting trikes from the shed during the week of Halloween, Chad asked his teacher, "Where are your skeletons?" You need to put them up. We have them up at our house. The teacher replied, "So, you celebrate Halloween by putting up skeletons at your house." Chad said, "Yeah, and we should have them here too!"

Some early childhood programs have begun moving away from dominant-culture holidays in an effort to respect the diversity of their children, families, and communities. Results range from celebrating no holidays to celebrating every holiday on the calendar. Other options include celebrating the major American holidays, celebrating unique program or classroom celebrations, and celebrating only those holidays observed by the families and staff in the program.

Regardless of which holidays you choose to celebrate, the key is to make a conscious choice. We propose that programs write a holiday policy, using a process of careful planning that involves teachers and parents.

At a recent meeting of educators and parents, the topic turned to creating a holiday policy. "What's a holiday policy?" someone asked. A teacher responded by describing how the current practice of celebrating dominant-culture holidays had left children and teachers feeling overwhelmed and out of control the previous year. "We need a written policy that spells out which holidays we celebrate, if any, and why." Others in the meeting began offering suggestions about what they wanted to see happen at their program over the next year. Finally, several teachers and one parent expressed interest in forming a committee to write a holiday policy. Though hesitant to bring up the issue at first, they felt relieved that the topic was out in the open and action on it had begun.

A holiday policy, like other program policies, requires a basis in knowledge and ethics. One source of this knowledge and ethics is the National Association for the Education of Young Children. In particular, we can look to NAEYC's standards of developmentally appropriate practice. These standards describe interactions, curricula, and environments that reflect knowledge about how children develop and learn both individually and in groups as well as the social and cultural contexts of that learning (Bredekamp and Copple 1997). In other words, we propose that the needs of children be the most important curricular consideration—not the calendar.

In addition, we can look for guidance to NAEYC's Code of Ethical Conduct and the principles behind an anti-bias curriculum.

A holiday policy can lead to teaching practices that enhance our understanding of, and respect for, the different cultures and beliefs of children, families, staff, and community.

For the purposes of this article, we have identified several sections of the ethics code that can be used to evaluate and inform particular aspects of typical holiday celebrations. You may choose other sections that more closely fit your program's goals and vision.

Identify core values
The NAEYC Code of Ethical Conduct describes standards of ethical behavior based on core values deeply rooted in the history of our field. We have committed ourselves to these principles and values.
- We appreciate childhood as a unique and valuable stage of the human life cycle.
- We base our work with children on knowledge of child development.
- We appreciate and support the close ties between the child and family.
- We recognize that children are best understood and supported in the context of family, culture, community, and society.
- We respect the dignity, worth, and uniqueness of each individual (child, family member, and colleague).

Definitions

Developmentally appropriate practice describes professional decision-making that applies child development knowledge to
- making thoughtful and informed predictions about safe, healthy, interesting, and achievable activities, materials, interactions, and experiences for children within a particular age range;
- using what is known about the strengths, interests, and needs of a particular child for planning; and
- responding to social and cultural contexts to ensure meaningful, relevant, and respectful learning experiences for children and their families (Bredekamp and Copple 1997).

Anti-bias curriculum describes a deliberate, activist approach to challenging prejudice, stereotype, and bias in early care and education programs (Derman-Sparks 1989).

- We help children and adults achieve their full potential in the context of relationships that are based on trust, respect, and positive regard.

These ethical considerations are the basis of all program policies. We use them to examine all aspects of our interactions with children and adults, health and safety practices, environments, curriculum, and other services, including holiday celebrations.

You can thoughtfully approach the development of a holiday policy from many directions. Make sure, however, that any policy resects your ethical principles.

Ethical responsibilities to children
Ideal 1.1: To be familiar with the knowledge base of early childhood care and education and to keep current through continuing education and in-service training.
Ideal 1.2: To base program practices upon current knowledge in the field of child development and related disciplines and upon particular knowledge of each child.

In December Mari approached the teacher with concerns about her 4-year-old son. "He's not himself," she said. The more they talked about the family's December schedule, it became clear that her family had overdosed on all the shopping, cooking, singing, cleaning, and decorating of the season. After the winter break, Mari arrived at school the first morning with news that her son was back to normal. He was back to his regular routine and his behavior reflected this at home.

One reason teachers and directors often dread the holiday season is the disruption it brings. In many settings where traditional fall holidays are celebrated, disruptions in routines occur non-stop from October until January. This pace is exhausting for teachers and even more so for children. The continuous disruption in routine can cause children to feel unsure of their environment. When children are off balance, they tend to react erratically. This unpredictable behavior can frustrate teachers, and an unhealthy cycle begins.

The holiday pace can be stressful for young children, particularly since similar changes may also be happening at home.

The holiday pace can be stressful for young children, particularly since similar changes may also be happening at home. Family members that children rarely see come to stay at their home and may take over their own beds and bedrooms. Stores, streets and homes are decorated profusely with Santas, greenery, and toys. Well-meaning friends and relatives ask: "Have you told Santa what you want?" and "Are you being good?"

Parents stressed by extra shopping, cooking, and gift wrapping often act tired and irritable.

All of this can overwhelm young children, as well as confuse them about a holiday's true intent. Often the very things that we are doing for children are the things that are contributing to their stress. Regardless of which holiday is being celebrated, the activities pull children out of their routine.

Steps for creating an anti-bias holiday policy

If you are developing a holiday policy, we strongly recommend Julie Bisson's book *Celebrate! An Anti-bias Guide to Enjoying Holidays in Early Childhood Programs* as a starting point. Bisson offers these recommendations:

- Include everyone who wants to be included.
- Choose a model of collaboration—facilitator or committee.
- Set ground rules.
- Review your past holiday practices.
- Develop agreed-upon goals to guide you in changing or improving practices.
- Determine the process you will use to decide which holidays to celebrate.
- Allow time to work out implementation issues.

Holiday activities often involve the creation of decorations and gifts. These craft activities are often product—rather than process—oriented. When children make teacher-directed holiday crafts, they lose valuable time that could be devoted to more open-ended, creative art activities. In assessing the appropriateness of holiday activities, consider what we know about young children's motor skills and their need to explore and experiment with materials.

Another area to evaluate is children's holiday performances for parents. These performances pressure children to memorize spoken lines, move on cue, and perform before a crowd of family members and strangers. These activities do not take into account the children's stage of memory development, level of social-emotional development, and individual differences in temperament.

All holiday activities need to be re-examined for bias or historical inaccuracy. Consider the inappropriateness of dressing African-American, Hispanic and Asian-American children in paper-bag vests and construction-paper feathers and teaching them about "our forefathers" and the first Thanksgiving. Reviewed from a developmental perspective, these common Thanksgiving activities are incompatible with preoperational children's inability to understand history. These practices negate the children's (and their families.) own rich and varied cultural histories.

Ethical responsibilities to families

Ideal 2.3: To respect the dignity of each family and its culture, language, customs, and beliefs.

Ideal 2.4: To respect families. childrearing values and their right to make decisions for their children.

As Abraham dropped his daughter off at school, he reminded her, "We don't have a tree. We don't celebrate Christmas, and I don't want you to make an ornament at school." After he leaves, the teacher tells her, "Oh, you can make one anyway." Later Abraham complained to the director. The director, in turn, confronted the teacher. Her explanation: "He's just trying to spoil everyone's Christmas fun!"

A respectful way to include families in our programs is to have a policy that is inclusive of their customs and cultures. Parents are often invited to provide food, decorations, and activities for holiday celebrations. This does involve families in school life, but it can have a drawback. Providing food or activities can be a financial hardship and potentially an additional burden on top of holiday preparations at home. Some parents feel embarrassed to let anyone know this, so they may remove their child from school on the day of the party.

A respectful way to include families in our programs is to have a policy that is inclusive of their customs and cultures.

So if it isn't the sugar...what is it?

"The results have consistently shown that sugar intake does not negatively affect behavior in a majority of children. In reality, these studies suggested that sugars tend to calm both children and adults, but this effect could go unnoticed due to other influences. Examples of this include the excitement of a birthday party or Halloween trick or treating. These events could override the calming effects of sugar."

The Recurring Myth of Sugar and Hyperactivity

Making gifts or cards for Father's Day and Mother's Day assumes that children have a father or mother at home. A well-meaning teacher may suggest that a child make a card for another family member instead. This suggestion can make the child feel singled out.

Some families' religious or cultural beliefs preclude celebration of dominant-culture holidays. There are a few solutions to this dilemma that do not single out particular children and make them feel less a part of the classroom. One solution is to invite parents to share their family celebrations and traditions—with classmates in the role of guests. In this way, children are exposed to a wider view in a manner appropriate to their developmental level.

Through reflection and experience, we have learned to respect each and every family's traditions and beliefs. We believe program personnel have no right to impose personal holiday customs and traditions, religious or otherwise, on children and families. Common classroom situations include the following:

- children who are Jehovah's Witnesses and are unable to celebrate any holidays at school,
- children whose allergies disallow wheat or dairy foods (common ingredients in holiday treats),
- children whose parents do not support the promulgation of myths such as the Easter Bunny and Tooth Fairy.

When evaluating program policy, engage parents in respectful negotiation. In the give-and-take, a policy may emerge that both honors the ethical foundation as well as the families. beliefs. The resulting policy can be truly satisfying to both parents and staff.

Our ethical standards also guide us to respect and support the well-being and positive self-esteem of our peers.

Ethical responsibilities to colleagues

Ideal 3A.1: To establish and maintain relationships of respect, trust, and cooperation with co-workers.

Ideal 3C.1: To promote policies and working conditions that foster mutual respect, competence, well-being, and positive self-esteem in staff members.

A teacher struggled with her decision whether to attend the annual holiday party. The party would include a gift exchange, mainstream holiday food, caroling, and festive holiday attire. At the next staff meeting, the teacher informed her director and colleagues that she would not attend.

Some caregivers love holidays and want to share their excitement with the children by providing holiday experiences. They may do this by bringing in decorations, preparing traditional holiday foods, planning parties, or exchanging gifts. Caregivers may plan activities, particularly crafts, around the current holiday. Every day it may feel as though the new and different is replacing the comforting and familiar in the classroom.

Teachers are a part of the classroom community, and their interests should play a part in forming policy. But as ethical professionals, we need to consider the backgrounds, experiences, and developmental levels of children in our classrooms before adding, or changing, any activities and experiences.

Our ethical standards also guide us to respect and support the well-being and positive self-esteem of our peers. Teachers working in settings that appear similar to the culture in which they grew up may assume that the children and families will celebrate the same holidays in the same ways. A way to explore the backgrounds and traditions of both the individual classroom and the larger program community is to conduct a family and staff survey. Ask whether the holidays being celebrated reflect the lives of all children and families. Ask whether families celebrate different holidays and if parents would be willing to share those with the classroom.

While a holiday policy ideally incorporates the views of all stakeholders—children, families, and staff—it does not guarantee that everyone will participate. As in all conflicts, listen to what the parent or teacher wants, and ask why this is important to them. Refer to the values the program has adopted and try to help the parent or teacher figure out a way to celebrate within the framework of the policy.

For parents who do not wish to follow school policies, consider planning a party outside of school. Your role could include attending as a guest or facilitating communication between families. Private, off-campus celebrations are not subject to school policies.

Ethical responsibilities to community and society

Ideal 4.1: To provide the community with high-quality (age and individually appropriate, and culturally and socially sensitive) education/care programs and services.

In a recent workshop on developing an anti-bias curriculum, a participant from Mexico shared the cultural differences she experienced upon moving to Texas. She said that in her community and family Christmas celebrations, children received only one gift. When she moved here, after marrying a man from Texas, she was surprised to see the huge number of gifts bought and exchanged. She noted that it felt much more commercialized and more "about the presents" here than it did in her country, where the celebration had more of a religious and family focus.

As with everything else that happens in the classroom, values are being transmitted through all that we do and say.

As with everything else that happens in the classroom, values are being transmitted through all that we do and say. As we develop holiday policies, we need to consider what values will be passed on to the children during holiday activities and celebrations.

The United States as a capitalist country is based on commercial enterprise. The celebration of dominant-culture holidays reflects this. When we buy and exchange gifts, we may be passing on the value of generosity along with an emphasis on things. When we accumulate decorations and trinkets associated with holidays, we may be passing on the values of creativity and beauty as well as consumerism. We need to think about which values we want to emphasize.

Positive values that typically accompany holiday celebrations are togetherness, family, sharing, friendship, giving to others, and tradition. Negative values include consumerism, greed, competition, and commercialism. Many holiday activities have been done for so long that we're not really sure why we do them anymore. We get so caught up in the planning and decorating that we can't defend the message our celebrations give children.

The tradition and continuity of holiday celebrations are important. In writing a holiday policy, state how you will evaluate it. A yearly examination of holiday activities can ensure that the values you want to send are the messages actually being sent.

Religious celebrations in public institutions

Beyond the ethical considerations of holiday celebrations, you need to be aware of First Amendment rights under the U.S. Constitution if you are teaching in a public school or a publicly funded program, such as Head Start.

Religious holiday observances, if held under public school auspices, violate the First Amendment's mandate for separation of church and state.

Joint celebrations (Christmas-Hanukkah, for example) do not solve the problem, because they only serve to introduce religious observances into the schools. They also tend to put holidays in competition with each other and distort the significance of each.

Look carefully at traditional icons used for holiday crafts and be certain that they are not religious symbols. Recognizing a diverse group of holidays—Easter and Passover in March; and Christmas, Hanukkah, and Kwanzaa in December—might validate the beliefs of children and their families. But bringing religious observances into a public setting is not appropriate.

Plan carefully before using religious symbols such as a cross, menorah, crescent, Star of David, crèche, Native-American talismans, the Buddha, and other symbols that form part of a religious tradition. Use of such symbols is permitted as a teaching aid, provided they are displayed only as an educational example of the culture and religious heritage of the holiday, and are temporary in nature. It's inappropriate to use these symbols as decorations. Consider the religious symbols you have seen displayed in early childhood programs. To guide your use of religious symbols, consider the following questions:

- How were the symbols handled?
- Were they discussed or merely displayed?
- How do you feel about displaying religious symbols in your classroom?
- Would you display different symbols for different age groups?
- How would you explain the display of religious symbols to a non-religious parent?

Tips for ethical holiday practices

Celebration is important to a well-rounded life. One way to transmit this value is to encourage children in a class or in all classes to create their own reasons to celebrate. Some classroom ideas that have been successful in other programs include beach day, snow day, pajama day, stuffed animal picnic, fall festival, starry night, and first spring leaf celebrations.

When children, families and staff develop and plan celebrations, we take into account family and cultural considerations and develop a celebration that includes everyone. Use these suggestions.

- Provide holiday activities as a free-choice activity, rather than as all-class activities.
- Think of providing opportunities for children to give back to the community rather than the children or program "taking from" or being passive recipients of the community's goodwill.
- Instead of observing Mother's Day and Father's Day, create a separate holiday at a different calendar time. Encourage all children to choose either a family member to celebrate and appreciate—a favorite brother, sister, grandparent, aunt, uncle, or godparent.

- Focus on seasonal changes instead of dominant-culture holidays.
- Move from holiday-theme-based curriculum planning to emergent planning based on children's needs and interests.
- Plan inclusive celebrations. For example, substitute a family spring picnic for an Easter egg hunt.

In *Reflecting Children's Lives* (Carter and Curtis, 1996) two October curriculum plans are compared and contrasted. One "centers around the traditional practice of using commercialized, European-American holidays as the focus for planning." The other "reflects the concrete and sensory aspects of children's daily experiences" and provides "ways for them to explore and learn more about what they can see, hear, and smell all around them." The first contradicts and the second supports the tenets of developmentally appropriate practice and conforms to clear, ethical standards and program policy.

By developing and using a holiday policy, you will have a guide for choosing, implementing, and evaluating holiday activities (Bisson 1997).

Remember, there is no universal model for celebrating holidays. Make your program's holiday policy vital—not static. Revisit it every year and make sure it reflects the diversity of your program's families and staff.

A dynamic holiday policy is an opportunity to share perspectives and bond with all partners in the care and education of children.

When the world slips into a classroom

As we know from other areas of early childhood care and education, the world outside our door slips easily into our classrooms. Children will be exposed to a nearly non-stop onslaught of holiday hype for much of the fall and winter with one holiday being introduced before the previous one has even occurred.

The media will focus heavily on the few well-known, dominant-culture holidays. Acknowledge the children's awareness of, and experiences with, the saturation of holiday hoopla.

In developing your holiday policy, decide what the focus will be in your program and how to counter-balance or integrate the wider media world into it.

Sometimes segments of the community, in an attempt to be helpful, will provide materials like packets of green and red construction paper that do not support your policy. How do you encourage participation in your program in a way that's true to the policy without rejecting community interest and support. When community organizations offer their involvement, welcome the help and thank them for it. Share your holiday policy and the phi-

losophy behind it. Then together determine an effort that will meet both your needs.

A *teacher in an established center said, "Thirteen years ago I started to implement an anti-bias approach in my classroom and I am still not finished. I know it will be different every year because each year brings a new group of children and families, and I keep learning more."*

Change is rarely easy. Often when changes need to be made, the implicit message is that what was being done before was wrong all along, or worse, harmful. It may be helpful to remember that prior to the change, the staff or parents were doing the best they could with the information at hand. Now there is new information, so new decisions can be made. This cycle is continuous: new information will become available, new decisions will be made based on the most current information, and then change will happen again.

Respectfully listening to differing viewpoints is part of the process. But it may or may not guarantee full participation by everyone. Not all adults will fully buy in to every modification of policy and philosophy. Authentic change cannot be forced, so the process usually takes time.

A dynamic holiday policy is an opportunity to share perspectives and bond with all partners in the care and education of children. A written policy ensures that staff and teachers can explain why they celebrate the holidays they do. While nothing is guaranteed, creating a holiday policy will lessen the possibility of children and families being left out of celebrations. The construction of a holiday policy can help an early childhood setting examine values and beliefs and perhaps form a stronger community relationship.

Resources and references

Bisson, J. 1997. Celebrate! *An Anti-bias Guide to Enjoying Holidays in Early Childhood Programs.* St. Paul, Minn.: Redleaf Press.

Bredekamp, S. and C. Copple, eds. 1997. *Developmentally Appropriate Practice in Early Childhood Programs, revised edition.* Washington, D.C.: National Association for the Education of Young Children.

Copple, Carol, ed. 2003. *A World of Difference.* Washington, D.C.: National Association for the Education of Young Children.

Derman-Sparks, L., and the A.B.C. Task Force. 1989. *Anti-bias Curriculum: Tools for Empowering Young Children.* Washington, D.C.: National Association for the Education of Young Children.

Feeney, Stephanie and Nancy Freeman. 1999. *Ethics and the Early Childhood Educator: Using the NAEYC Code.* Washington, D.C.: National Association for the Education of Young Children.

The Brown School. *Holiday Policy.* http://thebrown-school.com/AboutBrown/holiday_policy.htm.

Mountain Brook Schools. *Holiday Policy.* www.mtn-brook.k12.al.us/Policies/k7.htm.

Mayesky, Mary. *Online Companion: Creative Activities for Young Children, 7th Edition* "Think about it—constitutional concerns and celebrations." www.delmarlearning.com/com-panions/content/0766825213/critical/concerns_ch07.asp.

National Association for the Education of Young Children. *Position Statement—Code of Ethical Conduct*. www.naeyc.org/re-sources/position_statements/pseth98.htm.

National Association for the Education of Young Children. *Position Statement—Developmentally Appropriate Practice in Early*

Childhood Programs Serving Children from Birth through Age 8. www.naeyc.org/resources/position_statements/dap-toc.htm.

Pistone, Roy. *The Recurring Myth of Sugar and Hyperactivity*. www.palmbeach.k12.fl.us/sfs/articles/sugarmyth.pdf.

York, Stacy. 1991. *Roots and Wings: Affirming Culture in Early Childhood Programs*. St. Paul, Minn.: Redleaf Press.

Re-thinking holiday celebrations

When I went to the grocery store yesterday, I saw pumpkins in the produce section, displays of frozen turkey in meats, and tinsel and toys in the seasonal aisle," Ms. Jones said to her child's teacher. "Is it me, or do the holidays all run together?"

"I know what you mean," replied the teacher, "and it's so confusing and stressful to the children. We've decided to re-think our holiday celebrations. Would you like to help? We'll talk about it at tomorrow's parent meeting."

Some child care facilities and schools have begun moving away from traditional patterns of celebration in order to reduce the stress it creates for everyone. Simple, more authentic celebrations also respect the diversity of children, families, and communities.

Has your child's facility changed its policy on celebrating holidays? Does it have a holiday policy at all? As a partner in your child's education, you have a say in shaping policies. Think about the following activities:

- **crafts such as holiday decorations and gifts.** When all children make a Christmas ornament according to the teacher's directions, they lose an opportunity to use their own creativity. And certain crafts are not consistent with some families' beliefs.
- **holiday performances.** Preschool children often cannot memorize spoken lines or songs. They generally have not developed the social-emotional skills needed for performing as a group. Some don't have the temperament to perform before a crowd of family members and strangers.
- **historical re-creations.** Dressing children in paper-bag vests and construction-paper feathers to teach them about the first Thanksgiving ignores the inability of preschoolers to understand and separate factual and fanciful interpretations of U.S. history. These efforts also can be demeaning to African-American, Hispanic, Native-American, and Asian-American children who have their own rich cultural histories.
- **parties.** Parents are often invited to provide food, decorations, and activities for holiday celebrations. For some families, this can be a financial hardship and an added source of stress. Some children have allergies to wheat or dairy foods, which are common ingredients in holiday treats. Some families

have religious beliefs that forbid any holiday celebrations at school. Other parents simply want to avoid myths such as Santa Claus, the Easter Bunny, and the Tooth Fairy, and focus instead on simple, uncommercial rituals.

Creating a holiday policy

Parents and teachers can work together to celebrate holidays in ways that are agreeable to everyone. Consider the following:

- Conduct a survey of parents and staff. Ask about attitudes toward current holiday celebrations. Would anyone like to celebrate different holidays? Would they be willing to share those with the classroom?
- Plan a party outside of school. Private, off-site celebrations are not subject to school policies.
- Invite a speaker to talk at a parent meeting about how values are being transmitted through all that we do and say. Positive values that typically accompany holiday celebrations are togetherness family, sharing, friendship, giving to others, and tradition. Negative values include consumerism, greed, competition, and commercialism.
- Introduce holidays as part of learning activities. In December, for example, different families could share their traditions surrounding Christmas, Hanukkah, and Kwanzaa. Or holiday activities could be offered as a free-choice option rather than as all-class participation. If your child's facility receives public funding (Head Start or a public school, for example), make sure the activity is not a religious observance. That would violate First Amendment rights under the U.S. Constitution.

Celebration is important to a well-rounded life. When families and staff work together thoughtfully to plan celebrations, we have an opportunity to reduce stress, respect family and cultural diversity, and make celebrations more meaningful.

Adapted from an article written by P.D. Jolley, Katie Bennett, and Mary Jamsek in the fall 2004 issue of *Texas Child Care*.

About the authors

Katie Campbell has been employed in the field of child development and early childhood education since 1984. She has been a center director in programs serving culturally and economically diverse groups, and a training specialist since 1991. She is currently an adjunct faculty member in the Child Care and Development Department at Austin Community College, teaching CDA classes.

Mary Jamsek has taught young children in a variety of settings including private and for-profit preschool, public school, and laboratory school classrooms since 1988. She is also an adjunct faculty member at Austin Community College in the Child Care and Development Department, as well as a trainer and consultant in early childhood care and education.

P.D. Jolley has been teaching young children since 1985 and college classes since 1988. Currently she is a master teacher working with 4- and 5-year-olds at the University of Texas Priscilla Pond Flawn Child and Family Laboratory and an adjunct faculty member in Child Care and Development at Austin Community College. She conducted her first antibias training in 1992.

UNIT 4

Guiding and Supporting Young Children

Unit Selections

Key Points to Consider

- What are some of the differences between the ways boys and girls learn in the preschool years?

- What role should preschool children have in making classroom rules?

- How can a teacher build positive relationships with children?

- Make a list of some of the school-related stresses primary-grade children may experience.

- What are three things you know about autism?

- What are some of the typical symptoms of attention deficit hyperactivity?

 **Links: www.dushkin.com/online/**
These sites are annotated in the World Wide Web pages.

Child Welfare League of America (CWLA)
http://www.cwla.org
You Can Handle Them All
http://www.disciplinehelp.com
Tips for Teachers
http://www.counselorandteachertips.com

Early childhood teaching is all about problem-solving. Just as children work to solve problems, so do their teachers. Every day, teachers make decisions about how to guide children socially and emotionally. In attempting to determine what could be causing a child's emotional distress, teachers must take into account a myriad of factors. They consider physical, social, environmental, and emotional factors, in addition to the surface behavior of a child. Whether it is an individual child's behavior or interpersonal relationships, the pressing problem involves complex issues that require careful reflection and analysis. Even the most mature teachers spend many hours thinking and talking about the best ways to guide young children's behavior: What should I do about the child who is out of bounds? What do I say to parents who want their child punished? Are the needs of boys and girls handled equally well in my classroom? How do I guide a child who has been diagnosed as ADHD?

The first article in this unit begins with a discussion of provocative research showing significant differences in characteristics of girls' and boys' brains. Based on this information, the authors of "With Boys and Girls in Mind" describe how the nature-based classroom would function to meet gender-specific needs of children. Although science has made amazing advances to give us the data on the brains of boys and girls, the authors contend that our teaching methods need to evolve to be more effective.

Teachers and caregivers who find that boys have a more difficult time adjusting to classroom life than girls may find helpful suggestions in "Building an Encouraging Classroom with Boys in Mind." The author gives a number of recommendations for expanding children's opportunities for physical movement and exploratory play. In general, the article encourages teachers to make the learning environment more active, to support the needs of children who need to explore and experiment.

The authors of "When Children Make Rules" provide a useful approach to classroom functioning and daily operations. By using a constructivist approach, teachers engage children in forming classroom rules, discussing problems, and finding solutions. The organizational benefit is that children take more ownership of the process and ultimately follow the rules they have helped form. The developmental benefit is that children exercise autonomy.

The themes in children's play tell a lot about what they watch on TV, the kind of games they play, and the type of toys their parents give them. Violence has always been a theme of children's play, and many experts say that children need to express the pressures of life. But instead of simply declaring war and superhero play off limits, teachers can use specific approaches to promote creative play. "Beyond Banning War and Superhero Play" includes suggestions for guiding children to positive themes and open-ended toys.

Two articles in this unit deal with new information that teachers need to help children who are autistic and ADHD. According to the author of "Six Facts You Need to Know About Autism Now!" autism is on the rise, striking more boys than girls. Because of increased attention and research, autism is being diagnosed earlier, making it very important for teachers to understand the behavior signals. With early treatment and a wholistic approach to development, autistic children can accomplish so much more than we have expected in the past. The same is true for children with attention disorders. Those children who have not been diagnosed with ADHD early often struggle in school and experience low self-esteem. In "The Latest News on ADHD," the author discusses startling evidence from brain scans about the relationship between ADHD and brain size. This is must-read information for teachers in understanding the complexity of ADHD and how medication and therapy are used to treat symptoms.

Determining strategies of guidance and discipline is important work for an early childhood teacher. Because the teacher-child relationship is foundational for emotional well-being and social competence, guidance is more than applying a single set of discipline techniques. Instead of one solitary model of classroom discipline strictly enforced, a broad range of techniques is more appropriate. It is only through careful analysis and reflection that teachers can look at children individually, assessing not only the child but the impact of family cultures as well, and determine what is appropriate and effective guidance.

With Boys and Girls in Mind

Research on gender and education reveals a disconnect between teaching practice and the needs of male and female brains.

By Michael Gurian and Kathy Stevens

Something is awry in the way our culture handles the education needs of boys and girls. A smart 11-year-old boy gets low grades in school, fidgets and drifts off in class, and doesn't do his homework. A girl in middle school only uses the computer to instant-message her friends; when it comes to mastering more essential computer skills, she defers to the boys in the class.

Is contemporary education maliciously set against either males or females? We don't think so. But structurally and functionally, our schools fail to recognize and fulfill gender-specific needs. As one teacher wrote,

> For years I sensed that the girls and boys in my classrooms learn in gender-specific ways, but I didn't know enough to help each student reach full potential. I was trained in the idea that each student is an individual. But when I saw the PET scans of boys' and girls' brains, I saw how differently those brains are set up to learn. This gave me the missing component. I trained in male/female brain differences and was able to teach each individual child. Now, looking back, I'm amazed that teachers were never taught the differences between how girls and boys learn.

New positron emission tomography (PET) and MRI technologies enable us to look inside the brains of boys and girls, where we find structural and functional differences that profoundly affect human learning. These gender differences in the brain are corroborated in males and females throughout the world and do not differ significantly across cultures.

It's true that culture affects gender role, gender costume, and gender nuances—in Italy, for example, men cry more than they do in England—but role, costume, and nuance only affect some aspects of the learning brain of a child. New brain imaging technologies confirm that genetically templated brain patterning by gender plays a far larger role than we realized. Research into gender and education reveals a mismatch between many of our boys' and girls' learning brains and the institutions empowered to teach our children.

We will briefly explore some of the differences, because recognizing these differences can help us find solutions to many of the challenges that we experience in the classroom. Of course, generalized gender differences may not apply in every case.

The Minds of Girls

The following are some of the characteristics of girls' brains:

- A girl's corpus callosum (the connecting bundle of tissues between hemispheres) is, on average, larger than a boy's—up to 25 percent larger by adolescence. This enables more "cross talk" between hemispheres in the female brain.
- Girls have, in general, stronger neural connectors in their temporal lobes than boys have. These connectors lead to more sensually detailed memory storage, better listening skills, and better discrimination among the various tones of voice. This leads, among other things, to greater use of detail in writing assignments.
- The hippocampus (another memory storage area in the brain) is larger in girls than in boys, increasing girls' learning advantage, especially in the language arts.
- Girls' prefrontal cortex is generally more active than boys' and develops at earlier ages. For this reason, girls tend to make fewer impulsive decisions than boys do. Further, girls have more serotonin in the bloodstream and the brain, which makes them biochemically less impulsive.
- Girls generally use more cortical areas of their brains for verbal and emotive functioning. Boys tend to use more cortical areas of the brain for spatial and mechanical functioning (Moir & Jessel, 1989; Rich, 2000).

These "girl" brain qualities are the tip of the iceberg, yet they can immediately help teachers and parents understand why girls generally outperform boys in reading and writing from early childhood throughout life (Conlin, 2003). With more cortical areas devoted to verbal functioning, sensual memory, sitting still, listening, tonality, and mental cross talk, the complexities of reading and writing come easier, on the whole, to the female brain. In addition, the female brain experiences approximately 15 percent more blood flow, with this flow located in more centers of the brain at any given time (Marano, 2003). The female brain tends to drive itself toward stimulants—like reading and writing—that involve complex texture, tonality, and mental activity.

> **Girls tend to multitask better than boys, with fewer attention span problems.**

On the other hand, because so many cortical areas are used for verbal-emotive functioning, the female brain does not activate as many cortical areas as the male's does for abstract and physical-spatial functions, such as watching and manipulating objects that move through physical space and understanding abstract mechanical concepts (Moir & Jessel, 1989; Rich, 2000). This is one reason for many girls' discomfort with deep computer design language. Although some girls excel in these areas, more males than females gravitate toward physics, industrial engineering, and architecture. Children naturally gravitate toward activities that their brains experience as pleasurable—"pleasure" meaning in neural terms the richest personal stimulation. Girls and boys, within each neural web, tend to experience the richest personal stimulation somewhat differently.

The biological tendency toward female verbal-emotive functioning does not mean that girls or women should be left out of classes or careers that use spatial-mechanical skills. On the contrary: We raise these issues to call on our civilization to realize the differing natures of girls and boys and to teach each subject according to how the child's brain needs to learn it. On average, educators will need to provide girls with extra encouragement and gender-specific strategies to successfully engage them in spatial abstracts, including computer design.

The Minds of Boys

What, then, are some of the qualities that are generally more characteristic of boys' brains?

- Because boys' brains have more cortical areas dedicated to spatial-mechanical functioning, males use, on average, half the brain space that females use for verbal-emotive functioning. The cortical trend toward spatial-mechanical functioning makes many boys want to move objects through space, like balls, model airplanes, or just their arms and legs. Most boys, although not all of them, will experience words and feelings differently than girls do (Blum, 1997; Moir & Jessel, 1989).
- Boys not only have less serotonin than girls have, but they also have less oxytocin, the primary human bonding chemical. This makes it more likely that they will be physically impulsive and less likely that they will neurally combat their natural impulsiveness to sit still and empathically chat with a friend (Moir & Jessel, 1989; Taylor, 2002).
- Boys lateralize brain activity. Their brains not only operate with less blood flow than girls' brains, but they are also structured to compartmentalize learning. Thus, girls tend to

multitask better than boys do, with fewer attention span problems and greater ability to make quick transitions between lessons (Havers, 1995).

- The male brain is set to renew, recharge, and reorient itself by entering what neurologists call a *rest state*. The boy in the back of the classroom whose eyes are drifting toward sleep has entered a neural rest state. It is predominantly boys who drift off without completing assignments, who stop taking notes and fall asleep during a lecture, or who tap pencils or otherwise fidget in hopes of keeping themselves awake and learning. Females tend to recharge and reorient neural focus without rest states. Thus, a girl can be bored with a lesson, but she will nonetheless keep her eyes open, take notes, and perform relatively well. This is especially true when the teacher uses more words to teach a lesson instead of being spatial and diagrammatic. The more words a teacher uses, the more likely boys are to "zone out," or go into rest state. The male brain is better suited for symbols, abstractions, diagrams, pictures, and objects moving through space than for the monotony of words (Gurian, 2001).

These typical "boy" qualities in the brain help illustrate why boys generally learn higher math and physics more easily than most girls do when those subjects are taught abstractly on the chalkboard; why more boys than girls play video games that involve physical movement and even physical destruction; and why more boys than girls tend to get in trouble for impulsiveness, shows of boredom, and fidgeting as well as for their more generalized inability to listen, fulfill assignments, and learn in the verbal-emotive world of the contemporary classroom.

Who's Failing?

For a number of decades, most of our cultural sensitivity to issues of gender and learning came from advocacy groups that pointed out ways in which girls struggled in school. When David and Myra Sadker teamed with the American Association of University Women in the early 1990s, they found that girls were not called on as much as boys were, especially in middle school; that girls generally lagged in math/science testing; that boys dominated athletics; and that girls suffered drops in self-esteem as they entered middle and high school (AAUW, 1992). In large part because of this advocacy, our culture is attending to the issues that girls face in education.

At the same time, most teachers, parents, and other professionals involved in education know that it is mainly our boys who underperform in school. Since 1981, when the U.S. Department of Education began keeping complete statistics, we have seen that boys lag behind girls in most categories. The 2000 National Assessment of Educational Progress finds boys one and one-half years behind girls in reading/writing (National Center for Education Statistics, 2000). Girls are now only negligibly behind boys in math and science, areas in which boys have historically outperformed girls (Conlin, 2003).

Our boys are now losing frightening ground in school, and we must come to terms with it—not in a way that robs girls, but in a way that sustains our civilization and is as powerful as the lobby we have created to help girls. The following statistics for the United States illustrate these concerns:

- Boys earn 70 percent of *D*s and *F*s and fewer than half of the *A*s.
- Boys account for two-thirds of learning disability diagnoses.
- Boys represent 90 percent of discipline referrals.
- Boys dominate such brain-related learning disorders as ADD/ADHD, with millions now medicated in schools.
- 80 percent of high school dropouts are male.
- Males make up fewer than 40 percent of college students (Gurian, 2001).

These statistics hold true around the world. The Organisation for Economic Co-operation and Development (OECD) recently released its three-year study of knowledge and skills of males and females in 35 industrialized countries (including the United States, Canada, the European countries, Australia, and Japan). Girls outperformed boys in every country. The statistics that brought the male scores down most significantly were their reading/writing scores.

We have nearly closed the math/ science gender gap in education for girls by using more verbal functioning—reading and written analysis—to teach such spatial-mechanical subjects as math, science, and computer science (Rubin, 2004; Sommers, 2000). We now need a new movement to alter classrooms to better suit boys' learning patterns if we are to deal with the gaps in grades, discipline, and reading/writing that threaten to close many boys out of college and out of success in life.

The Nature-Based Approach

In 1996, the Gurian Institute, an organization that administers training in child development, education, and male/female brain differences, coined the phrase *nature-based approach* to call attention to the importance of basing human attachment and education strategies on research-driven biological understanding of human learning. We argued that to broadly base education and other social processes on anything other than human nature was to set up both girls and boys for unnecessary failure. The institute became especially interested in nature-based approaches to education when PET scans and MRIs of boys and girls revealed brains that were trying to learn similar lessons but in widely different ways and with varying success depending on the teaching method used. It became apparent that if teachers were trained in the differences in learning styles between boys and girls, they could profoundly improve education for all students.

Between 1998 and 2000, a pilot program at the University of Missouri–Kansas City involving gender training in six school districts elicited significant results. One school involved in the training, Edison Elementary, had previously tested at the bottom of 18 district elementary schools. Following gender training, it tested in the top five slots, sometimes coming in first or second. Statewide, Edison outscored schools in every subject area, sometimes doubling and tripling the number of students in top achievement levels. Instead of the usual large number of students at the bottom end of achievement testing, Edison now had only two students requiring state-mandated retesting. The school also experienced a drastic reduction in discipline problems.

Statewide training in Alabama has resulted in improved performance for boys in both academic and behavioral areas. Beaumont Middle School in Lexington, Kentucky, trains its teachers in male/female brain differences and teaches reading/writing, math, and science in separate-sex classrooms. After one year of this gender-specific experiment, girls' math and science scores and boys' Scholastic Reading Inventory (SRI) scores rose significantly.

The Nature-Based Classroom

Ultimately, teacher training in how the brain learns and how boys and girls tend to learn differently creates the will and intuition in teachers and schools to create nature-based classrooms (see "Teaching Boys, Teaching Girls" for specific strategies). In an elementary classroom designed to help boys learn, tables and chairs are arranged to provide ample space for each child to spread out and claim learning space. Boys tend to need more physical learning space than girls do. At a table, a boy's materials will be less organized and more widely dispersed. Best practice would suggest having a variety of seating options—some desks, some tables, an easy chair, and a rug area for sitting or lying on the floor. Such a classroom would allow for more movement and noise than a traditional classroom would. Even small amounts of movement can help some boys stay focused.

The teacher can use the blocks area to help boys expand their verbal skills. As the boys are building, a teacher might ask them to describe their buildings. Because of greater blood flow in the cerebellum—the "doing" center of the human brain—boys more easily verbalize what they are doing than what they are feeling. Their language will be richer in vocabulary and more expansive when they are engaged in a task.

An elementary classroom designed to help girls learn will provide lots of opportunities for girls to manipulate objects, build, design, and calculate, thus preparing them for the more rigorous spatial challenges that they will face in higher-level math and science courses. These classrooms will set up spatial lessons in groups that encourage discussion among learners.

Boys and Feelings

An assistant principal at a Tampa, Florida, elementary school shared a story of a boy she called "the bolter." The little boy would regularly blow up in class, then bolt out of the room and out of the school. The assistant principal would chase him and get him back into the building. The boy lacked the verbal-emotive abilities to help him cope with his feelings.

> **Boys' language will be richer in vocabulary and more expansive when they are engaged in a task.**

After attending male/female brain difference training, the assistant principal decided to try a new tactic. The next time the boy bolted, she took a ball with her when she went after him.

Teaching Boys, Teaching Girls

For Elementary Boys

- Use beadwork and other manipulatives to promote fine motor development. Boys are behind girls in this area when they start school.
- Place books on shelves all around the room so boys get used to their omnipresence.
- Make lessons experiential and kinesthetic.
- Keep verbal instructions to no more than one minute.
- Personalize the student's desk, coat rack, and cubby to increase his sense of attachment.
- Use male mentors and role models, such as fathers, grandfathers, or other male volunteers.
- Let boys nurture one another through healthy aggression and direct empathy.

For Elementary Girls

- Play physical games to promote gross motor skills. Girls are behind boys in this area when they start school.
- Have portable/digital cameras around and take pictures of girls being successful at tasks.
- Use water and sand tables to promote science in a spatial venue.
- Use lots of puzzles to foster perceptual learning.
- Form working groups and teams to promote leadership roles and negotiation skills.
- Use manipulatives to teach math.
- Verbally encourage the hidden high energy of the quieter girls.

When she found the boy outside, she asked him to bounce the ball back and forth with her. Reluctant at first, the boy started bouncing the ball. Before long, he was talking, then sharing the anger and frustration that he was experiencing at school and at home. He calmed down and went back to class. Within a week, the boy was able to self-regulate his behavior enough to tell his teacher that he needed to go to the office, where he and the assistant principal would do their "ball routine" and talk. Because he was doing something spatial-mechanical, the boy was more able to access hidden feelings.

Girls and Computers

The InterCept program in Colorado Springs, Colorado, is a female-specific teen mentor-training program that works with girls in grades 8–12 who have been identified as at risk for school failure, juvenile delinquency, and teen pregnancy. InterCept staff members use their knowledge of female brain functioning to implement program curriculum. Brittany, 17, came to the InterCept program with a multitude of issues, many of them involving at-risk behavior and school failure.

One of the key components of InterCept is showing teenage girls the importance of becoming "tech-savvy." Girls use a computer-based program to consider future occupations: They can choose a career, determine a salary, decide how much education or training their chosen career will require, and even use income projections to design their future lifestyles. Brittany quite literally found a future: She is entering a career in computer technology.

The Task Ahead

As educators, we've been somewhat intimidated in recent years by the complex nature of gender. Fortunately, we now have the PET and MRI technologies to view the brains of boys and girls. We now have the science to prove our intuition that tells us that boys and girls do indeed learn differently. And, even more powerful, we have a number of years of successful data that can help us effectively teach both boys and girls.

The task before us is to more deeply understand the gendered brains of our children. Then comes the practical application, with its sense of purpose and productivity, as we help each child learn from within his or her own mind.

References

American Association of University Women. (1992). *AAUW Report: How schools shortchange girls*. American Association of University Women Foundation.

Baron-Cohen, S. (2003). *The essential difference: The truth about the male and female brain*. New York: BasicBooks.

Blum, D. (1997). *Sex on the brain: The biological differences between men and women*. New York: Viking.

Conlin, M. (2003, May 26). The new gender gap. *BusinessWeek Online*. Available: www.businessweek.com/magazine/content/03_5f21/b3834001_5fm2001.htm

Gurian, M., Henley, P., & Trueman, T. (2001). *Boys and girls learn differently! A guide for teachers and parents*. San Francisco: Jossey-Bass/John Wiley.

Havers, F. (1995). Rhyming tasks male and female brains differently. *The Yale Herald, Inc*. New Haven, CT: Yale University.

Marano, H. E. (2003, July/August). The new sex scorecard. *Psychology Today*, 38–50.

Moir, A., & Jessel, D. (1989). *Brain sex: The real difference between men and women*. New York: Dell Publishing.

National Center for Education Statistics. (2000). *National Assessment of Educational Progress: The nation's report card*. Washington, DC: U.S. Department of Education.

Organisation for Economic Co-operation and Development. (2003). *The PISA 2003 assessment framework*. Author.

Rich, B. (Ed.). (2000). *The Dana brain daybook*. New York: The Charles A. Dana Foundation.

Rubin, R. (2004, Aug. 23). How to survive the new SAT. *Newsweek*, p. 52.

Sommers, C. (2000). *The war against boys*. Simon and Schuster.

Taylor, S. (2002). *The tending instinct*. Times Books.

Michael Gurian is Cofounder of the Gurian Institute, which trains education professionals in gender difference and brain-based learning. He is the author of *The Wonder of Boys* (Tarcher/Putnam, 1997) and *The Wonder of Girls* (Atria, 2003) and coauthor of *Boys and Girls Learn Differently!* (Jossey-Bass/John Wiley, 2001). **Kathy Stevens** is Director of the Gurian Institute Training Division and the Women's Resource Agency, both located in Colorado Springs, Colorado. She coordinates the InterCept Teen Mentoring Program for Girls. The authors may be contacted at www.gurianinstitute.com.

From *Educational Leadership*, Vol. 62, No. 3, November 2004, pp. 21-26. Copyright © 2004 by Association for Supervision and Curriculum Development. Reprinted by permission. The Association for Supervision and Curriculum Development is a worldwide community of educators advocating sound policies and sharing best practices to achieve the success of each learner. To learn more, visit ASCD at www.ascd.org

Building an Encouraging Classroom with Boys in Mind

Margaret King with Dan Gartrell

For reasons of development and temperament, a lot of boys have difficulty fitting the traditional classroom expectations of many teachers. *Active, aggressive, challenging,* and *noncompliant* are words teachers often use to describe young boys. Even the most competent teachers are sometimes challenged by the behavior of some boys, and many find it difficult to distinguish problem behavior from typical "boy behavior." Educators frequently describe boys as socially immature or developmentally young. In a recent study (Pastor & Reuben 2002) researchers found that boys too frequently are labeled as having ADD (attention deficit disorder) or ADHD (attention deficit hyperactivity disorder).

In fact, many boys do need more physical activity and may be developmentally younger by 6 to 18 months than girls.

Teachers tend to view boys who are energetic and active as difficult to manage. In fact, many boys do need more physical activity and may be developmentally younger by 6 to 18 months than girls (Soderman et al. 1999). Active, energetic children, notably boys, seem to spend a lot of time engaged in off-task behavior, looking for and finding mischief. The following example describes such a situation.

In a well-organized preschool classroom with well-defined areas and activities based on children's developmental levels and interests, a group of boys are causing their teacher to question her skills. They dump containers of small Legos or Unifix cubes on the floor when she isn't looking. They wrestle with each other during group time—with horseplay sometimes escalating into serious conflicts. When asked the reasons for their behavior, they say, "It's fun!" and then giggle.

The adults are not amused, but the boys seem to enjoy their mischief. The overall pattern of behavior is persistent and disrupts the flow of the day's routines and activities. The teacher worries about the effects of the frequent conflicts on the boys themselves, the rest of the children, her assistant and herself. She wonders, "Is the problem the boys? Is it the way I teach them? How can I create a classroom that is more responsive to the children—especially the boys?"

Rethinking environments and activities

After observing the children's interactions in different parts of the environment and at different times of the day, the teacher reflected on what she had seen and heard. She realized that the boys were off task because they were not interested in many of the activities the teaching team provided. She decided to make changes in the learning environment to address the boys' development, interests, and activity levels.

Some of the ideas on these pages worked for this teacher, and they could help other teachers plan for and respond to young boys. Making an environment more encouraging for boys is likely to empower girls to become more active, independent, and creative as well.

Conclusion

You can expect that the changes you make will modify the classroom culture. Previously bored and uninvolved boys will become more engaged, significantly reducing program-influenced mistaken behavior. As a result, the other children, less upset by frequent conflicts, may seem more relaxed and comfortable. They too are likely to enjoy new areas, such as those for large muscle activities and woodworking. Addressing the needs of boys can make the program more developmentally responsive for all the children in the class.

Large Motor and Whole Body Experiences

Physical activity is necessary for all children, but it is especially important for young boys who enjoy running, jumping, and moving their bodies. There are many ways to foster opportunities for large muscle activity and whole body experiences in the indoor and outdoor classroom environments. Here are some suggestions:

Extend classroom learning to the outdoors. At center time plan at least one adult-led, small group, outdoor activity. The outdoor activity might be as simple as taking a nature walk or conducting a scavenger hunt, or as complex as creating a water system using pipes and joints. When the weather allows, spend lots of time outside. Respect this period as an opportunity for children to learn what their bodies can do (to develop their "physical intelligence" [Gardner 1993]). Remember that children tend to get more lower body exercise than upper. Climbing, building with various materials, and gardening develop the arms, shoulders, and trunk muscles. Use teachable moments to make outdoor time educational.

Plan activities to occur during regular outdoor playtime. Have at least one outdoor teacher-planned and -led play activity each day. Present several options—let the children choose whether to build and then negotiate an obstacle course, wave huge bubble wands and chase the bubbles, or play a climbing game.

P hysical activity is especially important for young boys who enjoy running, jumping, and moving their bodies.

Create an indoor large motor environment outside the classroom. For example, transform a large storage area into an indoors large-muscle activity room. Place safety floor mats, balls, and climbing equipment in the room, and use it for rough-and-tumble play, dancing and movement, and climbing. (See "The Inside Information about Safety Surfacing," *Young Children,* March 2003, pp. 108-11, for guidelines on safe indoor surfacing material.)

Create a large-motor/physical fitness center in the classroom. Besides the all-important climber and safety surfacing, include beanbags for throwing, carpet squares for jumping, boards for walking and balancing, and music for dancing. Construct a classroom physical fitness center featuring a homemade weight table (for weights, fill plastic bottles with sand and attach them to a sawed-off broom handle) and a floor mat for calisthenics. With a little creativity, you can devise a mini-exercise-bike. Make the fitness center as permanent a part of your room as the housekeeping area.

Integrate whole body movements into activities. Offer tools such as feather dusters or paintbrushes to use indoors with tempera or diluted finger paint on large pieces of Plexiglas or cardboard or outdoors with water on the walls. Include large hollow blocks or cardboard blocks in the block area. Lead daily music and movement activities.

Building and Construction

Boys tend to spend a significant amount of time playing with blocks, Legos, and other construction materials. Teachers need to help children plan their building and construction ideas as well as remind them how to use blocks appropriately. The ideas that follow can enhance the block area and offer new ways to build and construct.

Focus on the block area. Enlarge the block area to provide plenty of space for children to carry out their construction plans. Change block accessories to fit current themes and interests and include pads of paper and pencils so children can make plans and notes about their constructions. Some children prefer to draw before building; others plan by talking about what they will do. Use digital photographs and video recordings to document the building process. Share and discuss the documentation with children to help them reflect on what they did and plan new constructions.

Create a woodworking area. Many art activities are two-dimensional and of little interest to boys. Boys will, however, enjoy a woodworking area where they can use a variety of carpentry tools and materials to experiment, practice, and make three-dimensional constructions. Be sure to provide plenty of safety goggles. Invite parents and local carpenters to help plan and create developmentally appropriate woodworking projects.

Boys tend to spend a significant amount of time playing with construction materials.

Offer variety in art and writing. Add construction and building materials to the art area, thus allowing more choices for whole hand manipulation of materials as well as fine motor manipulation. Offer a variety of wide and narrow writing and drawing tools so children have a choice. Staple along the left edge of a stack of several sheets of paper to create blank booklets that children can turn into their own action picture books about their imaginary experiences.

Assess and update manipulatives. Although many boys like to build, some have difficulty using Legos. Large manipulatives such as Duplos are better for creative work, while Legos continue to be useful for fine motor skill development.

Offer variety and new experiences. Less dramatic changes to the environment can also be effective in engaging the attention of boys. From time to time reorganize and outfit the housekeeping area to become a dramatic play setting for camping, gardening, fishing, or restaurant play. Active and educational computer activities and games of strategy require boys—and girls—to work in cooperative groups. At group story times, teachers can vary the books read aloud by alternating information books on topics of interest to boys with favorite picture books.

Sensory Exploration and Experimentation

Boys frequently enjoy exploring and experimenting—for example, digging in sandboxes or taking block constructions apart (Grossman & Grossman 1993). Offer these activities to encourage children to engage in spontaneous scientific exploration:

Exploring and experimenting. Create daily opportunities for exploration and experimentation such as an activity that allows children to answer the question, "What happens if ...?" ("What happens if you mix water with sand or cornstarch?")

Sensory play. Include standard materials—sand and water, playdough, clay—and create new ones such as glurch (a mixture of powdered starch and water) and a homemade version of Silly Putty (using fabric softener and white glue). Many boys are especially interested in combining and mixing substances as well as pouring and filling containers with solids and liquids. Invite children to help make the putty, playdough, and glurch.

Cooking. Cooking and food preparation create opportunities for children to experiment and explore, make predictions, and observe what happens. Plan a simple cooking activity weekly or more often, if possible. Fruit salads, raw vegetables, puddings, mashed potatoes, bread, and pancakes are just a few of the foods children can prepare. Have cooks—men and women—visit the class.

Boys frequently enjoy exploring and experimenting.

References

Gardner, H. 1993. *Multiple intelligences: The theory in practice.* New York: Basic.

Grossman, H., & S. Grossman. 1993. *Gender issues in education.* Boston: Allyn & Bacon.

Pastor, P.N., & C.A. Reuben. 2002. Attention deficit disorder and learning disability: United States, 1997-98. National Center for Health Statistics, Vital Health Stat, Series 10, No. 206, May 2002.

Soderman, A.K., S. Chikara, C. Hsiu-Ching, & E. Kuo. 1999. Gender differences that affect emerging literacy in first grade children: The U.S., India, and Taiwan. *International Journal of Early Childhood* 31 (2): 9-16.

Margaret King, Ed.D., is professor of early childhood teacher education in the School of Human and Consumer Sciences at Ohio University in Athens. Margaret has worked in the field of early childhood education for more than 30 years as a teacher, administrator, and teacher educator. Her current research focuses on boys. She is a former NAEYC Governing Board member and officer.

Dan Gartrell, Ed.D., is professor of early childhood and elementary education and director of the Child Development Training Program at Bemidji State University in Minnesota. A former Head Start and elementary teacher, Dan is the author of *A Guidance Approach for the Encouraging Classroom* (Delmar Learning) and *What the Kids Said Today: Using Classroom Conversations to Become a Better Teacher* (Redleaf).

This article is adapted, by permission of the publisher, from Margaret King with Dan Gartrell, "Guidance with Boys," in Dan Gartrell's *The Power of Guidance: Teaching Social-Emotional Skills in Early Childhood Classrooms* (Albany, NY: Thomson/Delmar Learning, in press). The book will be distributed as an NAEYC Comprehensive Membership benefit.

Building Positive Teacher-Child Relationships

M.M. Ostrosky • E.Y. Jung

While busy greeting children and preparing for the day, the teachers heard Alan, a 4-year boy, crying in the hallway. Every morning, Alan cried very loudly and refused to come into the classroom from the bus. Mrs. Hannon, the lead teacher, found herself becoming very frustrated with Alan, and she told him to come to the classroom without asking why he was upset. During circle time, Alan repeatedly kicked his feet on the carpet and did not pay attention as Mrs. Hannon read a story to the group. Mrs. Hannon told Alan to stop kicking, but he continued kicking his feet in the air. Exasperated, Mrs. Hannon snapped at Alan, "Stop kicking, I have had enough. You are going to leave circle time. Go over there and sit on the chair. I am going to tell your mom about this." As Alan moved to the thinking chair, he began to cry. He was very mad at Mrs. Hannon and wished someone would "snuggle him" instead of yell at him.

What Are Positive Teacher-Child Relationships?

In early childhood settings, each moment that teachers and children interact with one another is an opportunity to develop positive relationships. Teachers can use a variety of strategies to build positive relationships with children. Teacher behaviors such as listening to children, making eye contact with them, and engaging in many one-to-one, face-to-face interactions with young children promote secure teacher-child relationships. Talking to children using pleasant, calm voices and simple language, and greeting children warmly when they arrive in the classroom with their parents or from the buses help establish secure relationships between teachers and children.

In early childhood settings, each moment that teachers and children interact with one another is an opportunity to develop positive relationships.

It is important for teachers to use developmentally and individually appropriate strategies that take into consideration children's differing needs, interests, styles, and abilities. For example, with infants and toddlers, teachers respond to their cries or other signs of distress. Teachers let children know they care about them through warm, responsive, physical contact such as giving pats on the back, hugging, and holding young children in their laps. For preschool children, teachers encourage mutual respect between children and adults by waiting until children finish asking questions before answering them, and by encouraging children to listen when others speak. In addition, teachers' use of positive guidance techniques (e.g., modeling and encouraging appropriate behavior, redirecting children to more acceptable activities, setting clear limits) helps children develop trusting relationships with their teachers.

It is important for teachers to use developmentally and individually appropriate strategies that take into consideration children's differing needs, interests, styles, and abilities.

In developing positive teacher-child relationships, it is important to remember to:

- Engage in one-to-one interactions with children
- Get on the child's level for face-to-face interactions
- Use a pleasant, calm voice and simple language
- Provide warm, responsive physical contact
- Follow the child's lead and interest during play
- Help children understand classroom expectations
- Redirect children when they engage in challenging behavior
- Listen to children and encourage them to listen to others
- Acknowledge children for their accomplishments and effort

Given the above information, if we "revisit" our hypothetical early childhood classroom, we might observe the following scenario:

During center time, Mrs. Hannon heard Alan crying, while she was helping another child with an art project. Mrs. Hannon, realizing that she was again feeling very frustrated with Alan, decided that she needed to develop some new strategies when interacting with him. The next day, when Mrs. Hannon heard Alan coming to-ward the classroom, she went out into the hallway and bent down to his level, greeting him warmly and smil-ing at him. As Alan entered the classroom holding Mrs. Hannon's hand, he did not cry; he even smiled. During circle time, Alan listened to Mrs. Hannon read The Very Quiet Cricket, *and he responded when she had the class rub "their wings together" by flapping their arms up and down in response to the book's re-peated phrase "Nothing happened, not a sound." At the end of the day as she considered all that had hap-pened, Mrs. Hannon was pleased with how well the day went for Alan. She decided to look for resources on developing positive relationships with young chil-dren. She found that affectionate behaviors (such as smiles, pats, and hugs), a calm voice, and truly listen-ing to young children help build positive relationships between teachers and children. She realized that she was often so busy managing the group of children that she missed the individual interactions with them. The next day, when Mrs. Hannon saw her students coming down the hall to enter her classroom, she stopped talk-ing with her assistant teacher so she could greet each child with a warm smile and welcome. During circle time, instead of giving attention to children who were not listening, Mrs. Hannon praised children who were listening and engaged in story time. Also, when Ms. Gloria, the teaching assistant, did some finger plays with the children, Mrs. Hannon sat next to Alan. After the finger plays, Mrs. Hannon gave Alan a high five and told him what a great job he did following along with the finger plays. The tone in the classroom felt more positive, and Mrs. Hannon felt she was using her energy to help children become engaged in classroom activities and enjoy their time in the classroom rather than using her energy to constantly nag and attend to challenging behaviors.*

Why Are Positive Teacher-Child Relationships Important?

Research has suggested that teacher-child relationships play a significant role in influencing young children's social and emo-tional development. In studies of teacher-child relationships, children who had a secure relationship with their preschool and kindergarten teachers demonstrated good peer interactions and positive relationships with teachers and peers in elementary school. On the other hand, children who had insecure relation-ships with teachers had more difficulty interacting with peers and engaged in more conflict with their teachers. In addition, re-search has shown that teachers' interaction styles with children help children build positive and emotionally secure relation-ships with adults. For instance, teachers' smiling behaviors, af-fectionate words, and appropriate physical contact help promote children's positive responses toward teachers. Also,

children whose teachers showed warmth and respect toward them (e.g., teachers who listened when children talked to them, made eye contact, treated children fairly) developed positive and competent peer relationships. Moreover, children who had secure relationships with their teachers demonstrated lower levels of challenging behaviors and higher levels of competence in school.

Research has suggested that teacher-child relationships play a significant role in influencing young children's social and emotional development.

Who Are the Children Who Have Participated in Research on Teacher-Child Relationships?

Research on teacher-child relationships has been conducted with children from culturally diverse families in child care set-tings, university preschools, family child care settings, Head Start programs, and kindergarten classrooms. Participants have included children from European American, African American, Hispanic, and Asian American families. However, no studies indicated whether children with disabilities were included. When developing relationships with young children, teachers should pay attention to the cultural, linguistic, and individual needs of the children. The importance of adapting strategies to meet the unique needs of the children and families in a teacher's care cannot be overstated.

Where Do I Find More Information on Implementing This Practice?

Practical information on teacher-child relationship can be found in journals such as *Young Children*. See the following articles and books for examples of how to develop positive teacher-child relationships:

Bredekamp, S., & Copple, C. (Eds.). (1997). *Developmentally appro-priate practice in early childhood programs* (Rev ed.). Washington, DC: National Association for the Education of Young Children.

Center on the Social and Emotional Foundations for Early Learning. (2003). *Promoting the social-emotional competence of children. Training modules* [Online]. Champaign, IL: Author. Available: http://csefel.uiuc.edu/modules/facilitatorguide/facilitators-guide1. pdf [2003, August 12].

Elicker, J., & Fortner-Wood, C. (1995). Adult-child relationships in early childhood programs. *Young Children, 51*(1), 69-78.

Kontos, S., Howes, C., Shinn, M., & Galinsky, E. (1995). *Quality in family child care and relative care.* New York: Teachers College Press.

Kontos, S., & Wilcox-Herzog, A. (1997). Teachers' interactions with children: Why are they so important? *Young Children, 52*(2), 4-12.

Spodek, B., & Saracho, O. N. (1994). *Right from the start: Teaching children ages three to eight.* Needham Heights, MA: Allyn & Bacon.

What Is the Scientific Basis for This Practice?

For those wishing to explore this topic further, the following researchers have studied teacher-child relationships in early childhood settings:

Birch, S. H., & Ladd, G. W. (1998). Children's interpersonal behaviors and the teacher-child relationship. *Developmental Psychology, 34*(5), 934-946.

Howes, C., & Hamilton, C. E. (1993). The changing experience of child care: Changes in teachers and in teacher-child relationships and children's social competence with peers. *Early Childhood Research Quarterly, 8*(1), 15-32.

Howes, C., Philips, D. A., & Whitebook, M. (1992). Thresholds of quality: Implications for the social development of children in center-based child care. *Child Development, 63*(2), 449-460.

Kontos, S. (1999). Preschool teachers' talk, roles, and activity settings during free play. *Early Childhood Research Quarterly, 14*(3), 363-383.

Pianta, R. C., Steinberg, M. S., & Rollins, K. B. (1995). The first two years of school: Teacher-child relationships and deflections in children's classroom adjustment. *Development and Psychopathology, 7*(2), 295-312.

Webster-Stratton, D., Reid, M. J., & Hammond, M. (2001). Preventing conduct problems, promoting social competence: A parent and teacher training partnership in Head Start. *Journal of Clinical Child Psychology, 30*(3), 238-302.

Zanolli, K. M., Saudargas, R. A., & Twardosz, S. (1997). The development of toddlers' responses to affectionate teacher behavior. *Early Childhood Research Quarterly, 12*(1), 99-116.

This *What Works Brief was developed by the Center on the Social and Emotional Foundations for Early Learning. Contributors to this Brief were M. M. Ostrosky and E. Y. Jung.*

When Children Make Rules

In constructivist classrooms, young children's participation in rule making promotes their moral development.

Rheta DeVries and Betty Zan

Sherice Hetrick-Ortman's kindergartners were passionate about block building. These children at the Freeburg Early Childhood Program in Waterloo, Iowa, lavished care on their complex structures and felt justly proud of their creations. Some of the children were concerned, however, about problems in the block area. They discussed the matter at group time and came up with some new rules to post in the block-building area:

- Keep hands off other people's structures.
- No knocking people's structures down.
- Four friends in the block area at one time.

When children care about a classroom problem such as this one and take part in solving it, they are more likely to view the resulting rules as fair. Having *made* the rules, they are more likely to observe them. Just as important, participating in the process of rule making supports children's growth as moral, self-regulating human beings.

Rules in schools have traditionally been made by teachers and given to children. Today, many teachers see the benefits of allowing children to have a voice in developing classroom rules. But if we are not careful, this involvement can be superficial and meaningless. How can we best involve children in making classroom rules?

Morality and Adult-Child Relationships

We speak from a constructivist point of view, inspired by the research and theory of Jean Piaget. In constructivist education, rule making is part of the general atmo-sphere of mutual respect, and the goal is children's moral and intellectual development (DeVries & Zan, 1994).

Piaget (19832/1965) identified two types of morality that parallel two types of adult-child relationships: one that promotes optimal moral and intellectual development, and one that retards it. *Heteronomous* morality consists of conformity to external rules without question. Overly coercive relationships with adults foster this type of morality and can impede children's development of self-regulation. *Autonomous* morality, by contrast, derives from an internal need to relate to other people in moral ways. Cooperative relationships with adults foster this type of morality and help children develop high levels of self-regulation.

Obviously, children and adults are not equals. However, when the adult respects the child as a person with a right to exercise his or her will, their relationship has a certain psychological equality that promotes autonomy.

Piaget, of course, did not advocate complete freedom, and neither do we. Although constructivist teachers minimize the exercise of adult authority or coercion in relation to children, *minimize* does not mean *eliminate* (DeVries, 1999; DeVries & Edmiaston, 1999; DeVries & Kohlberg, 1987/1990). Rather, we strive for a balance that steadily builds the child's regulation of his or her own behavior.

Norms and Rules in Constructivist Classrooms

To investigate how constructivist teachers use external control and how they develop classroom norms and rules, we inter-viewed the teachers at the Freeburg Early Childhood Program, a laboratory school serving children ages 3–7 in a predominantly low-income neighborhood. The school's aim is to demonstrate constructivist practices.

Norms Established by Teachers

We define *norms* as specific expectations that teachers establish for children's behavior—ways of behaving that everyone takes for granted as part of the culture of the classroom. A norm is usually unwritten and sometimes unspoken until someone violates it and the teacher takes corrective action. The Freeburg teachers' reflections revealed three kinds of norms that existed in their classrooms:

- *Safety and health norms* ensure children's well-being. Our teachers articulated these as non-negotiables. Examples include "No hurting others," "Lie down at rest time," "Keep shoes on outside," "No crashing trikes or other vehicles," and "Don't throw sand."
- *Moral norms* pertain to respect for people and animals. They often relate to fair treatment or distribution of goods. Examples of these are "Take fair turns," "Talk through a conflict until there is a resolution," "If you bring a live animal into the classroom, try to make it comfortable," and "No hurting animals."
- *Discretionary norms* consist of routines and procedures to make the classroom run smoothly and make learning possible. Kathy Morris, the teacher in the 3-year-olds' class, pointed out that

young children do not like chaos, and they need adults to figure out routines that work so that events run smoothly. Discretionary norms also include societal norms for politeness and individual responsibility that children need to know. Examples include "Sit with the group at group time," "Wait until all are seated at lunch before eating," and "Clean up your place after lunch."

All teachers must sometimes exert external control.

All teachers have safety and health norms, moral norms, and discretionary norms. These norms are acceptable and necessary uses of external authority in a constructivist classroom. But constructivist teachers carefully evaluate their reasons for norms and attempt to minimize the use of external control as much as possible.

Rules Made by Children

We define rules as formal agreements among teachers and children. Constructivist teachers often conduct discussions of problems that relate to their norms and engage children in making classroom rules that arise from these norms.

When teachers first suggest that children make rules, children often parrot such adult admonitions as "Never talk to strangers" or "Raise your hand and wait to be called on." This occurs especially when children are unaccustomed to a sociomoral atmosphere in which they feel free to express their honest opinions. Children may view rule making as another exercise in trying to figure out the right answer or say what they think the teacher wants to hear. The rules that they suggest may not reflect a real understanding of the need to treat others in moral ways. When children only mindlessly restate adults' rules, they have not engaged in true rule making.

Children who engage in true rule making sometimes reinvent rules that elaborate on already established norms. Although these elaborations are not entirely original, they still give the children feelings of autonomy in their power to create rules. For example, Gwen Harmon's 4-year-olds, working within the classroom norm "Don't hurt animals," developed the following practical and concrete rules regarding the chicks that they hatched in the classroom:

- Pick them up safely.
- Don't push them.

- Don't squeeze them.
- Don't put things in their box.
- Don't punch them.
- Don't put them on the light bulb.
- Don't drop them.
- Don't throw them.
- Don't pick them up by their wings.
- Don't color on them.
- Don't pull their heads off.

Reinvented rules demonstrate children's understanding of the moral norm because they translate the norm into children's own words and provide elaborations that make sense to them. Sometimes the elaborations are novel, dealing with situations that the teacher had not considered discussing. For example, in Beth Van Meeteren's 1st grade classroom, where the norm is to treat others with respect, children made the rule, "When people pass gas, do not laugh, or they will be upset or embarrassed."

Sometimes children develop entirely original rules. Unlike reinvented rules, invented rules reflect children's power to make decisions in the classroom. For example, Dora Chen's class of 4-year-olds invented a new rule in response to a problem they saw during one of their classroom routines. One day during clean-up, a child saw another child finishing a snack and felt that no one should eat snacks during clean-up time. He told the teacher, who raised the issue at group time. She asked, "What should our rule be?" After a 17-minute discussion in which the children suggested various possibilities, the teacher clarified the choice between "No snack during clean-up: throw it away" or "Finish snack before going outdoors." The children voted to throw away their unfinished snacks when clean-up started.

The new rule, driven by children's interest and concern, went beyond the teacher's concerns. Although the teacher preferred giving the children more time to finish their snacks, she believed that the children's solution was fair given the one-hour activity time in which to eat snacks.

Guidelines for Exerting External Control

Some people have the misconception that constructivist teachers are permissive and that external control never occurs in constructivist classrooms. In fact, all teachers must exert external control sometimes. From our discussions with teachers and our understanding of research and theory,

we have derived four general guidelines for the use of external control.

Provide a general and pervasive context of warmth, cooperation, and community. We draw inspiration for this guideline from the work of Jean Piaget, especially from *The Moral Judgment of the Child* (1932/1965). Many others, however, have come to this same conclusion starting from different theoretical perspectives (Nelson, 1996; Watson, 2003). In fact, almost all of the recent classroom management programs on the market, with the exception of Assertive Discipline, stress the importance of cooperation and community (Charles, 2002).

Act with the goal of students' self-regulation. A developmental perspective leads us to focus on the long term. We want to contribute to the development of autonomous, self-regulating human beings who can make decisions based on the perspectives of all involved. Therefore, compliance is not our primary goal. Of course, we all wish sometimes that children would be more compliant. But we constantly remind ourselves and one another that developing self-regulation takes time, and we celebrate significant events, such as when an aggressive child actually uses words for the first time to tell another child what he wants instead of slugging him.

Minimize unnecessary external control as much as is possible and practical. Constructivist teachers do use external control; in fact, they use it quite a bit. As Piaget states, "However delicately one may put the matter, there have to be commands and therefore duties" (1932/1965, p. 180). Teachers in constructivist classrooms, however, use external control of children consciously and deliberately, not impulsively or automatically. The teachers with whom we work constantly ask themselves whether the external regulation is absolutely necessary.

Through discussions with teachers Gwen Harmon, Shari McGhee, and Christie Sales, we have identified several situations that can lead to unnecessary control of children. Avoidable control-inducing situations occur when

- The classroom arrangement invites rowdy behavior.
- Children do not know the classroom routine.
- Too many transitions lead to too much waiting time.
- Crowding in a part of the classroom leads to conflicts.

- Group time goes on for too long; children become restless, and some act out.
- Activities are not sufficiently engaging to appeal to children's purposes, and children become aimless.
- The classroom does not contain enough materials, and children compete for what is available.
- Clean-up is poorly organized, and children resist cleaning up after activity time.
- A mismatch exists between the teacher's expectations and the children's competencies.
- The teacher attributes a character flaw to a child who misbehaves.

When external control is necessary, use the least amount necessary to secure compliance. Ideally, the constructivist teacher uses external control judiciously to make sure that the child's experience overall is a mixture increasingly in favor of the child's self-regulation. When external regulation becomes necessary, the teacher must preserve the child's dignity and autonomy—for example, by giving the child a choice and thus returning a degree of autonomy as soon as possible.

Meaningful Rule Making

For many years, we have advocated allowing young children to make classroom rules, arguing that such opportunities are part and parcel of a constructivist, democratic classroom. By encouraging children to make classroom rules, the teacher minimizes unnecessary external control and promotes the development of children's moral and intellectual autonomy.

To genuinely think for themselves and exercise autonomy, children must be given the power to make rules and decisions that both elaborate on classroom norms and break new ground. By actively seeking out appropriate opportunities and recognizing them when they arise in the daily life of the classroom, teachers can create classrooms that are fair and democratic.

References

Charles, C. (2002). *Building classroom discipline* (7th ed.). Boston: Allyn and Bacon.

DeVries, R. (1999). Implications of Piaget's constructivist theory for character education. In M. Williams & E. Schaps (Eds.), *Character education.* Washington, DC: Character Education Partnership.

DeVries, R., & Edmiaston, R. (1999). Misconceptions about constructivist education. *The Constructivist, 13*(3), 12–19.

DeVries, R., & Kohlberg, L. (1987/1990). *Constructivist early education.* Washington, DC: National Association for the Education of Young Children.

DeVries, R., & Zan, B. (1994). *Moral classrooms, moral children: Creating a constructivist atmosphere in early education.* New York: Teachers College Press.

Nelson, J. (1996). *Positive discipline.* New York: Ballantine Books.

Piaget, J. (1932/1965). *The moral judgment of the child.* London: Free Press.

Watson, M. (2003). *Learning to trust.* San Francisco: Jossey-Bass.

Rheta DeVries is a professor and Director of the Regents' Center for Early Developmental Education, University of Northern Iowa, 107 Schindler Education Center, Cedar Falls, IA 50701; (391) 273–2101; rheta.devries@uni.edu. **Betty Zan** is an assistant professor and Research Fellow at the Regents' Center for Early Developmental Education; (319) 273–2101; betty.zan@uni.edu.

GUIDANCE & DISCIPLINE STRATEGIES FOR YOUNG CHILDREN:
TIME OUT IS OUT

BY KATHY PREUESSE

In a typical early childhood classroom, children engage in a variety of behaviors—some appropriate and some inappropriate. Early childhood teachers need to deal with all behaviors, but of course it is the inappropriate ones that are the subject of so much study! And even more than the inappropriate behaviors themselves, our response to the behaviors is weighed, measured, and quantified by a wide range of early childhood experts. The question remains: how do teachers react to children's behavior, and how does that reaction impact the child in later incidents? Through the years, styles of discipline have changed. "Spare the rod and spoil the child"—the in vogue punishment over perhaps a hundred years—gave way to time out sometime in the late 1970s. And now time out, the "strategy of choice" for 20 years or so, seems to be falling out of favor. What is time out, why has it been so popular, and what strategy will replace it if indeed it is on the way out?

What Is Time Out?

Sheppard and Willoughby (1975) define time out as the "removal of an individual from a situation which contains minimal opportunity for positive reinforcement." According to Schreiber (1999) the intent of time out is to "control and extinguish undesirable behaviors." When you say time out to a classroom teacher, many

times the image evoked is that of a chair in the corner of the classroom where a child is put when she has "misbehaved." The length of time that child needs to "think about what she has done wrong" is many times determined by the child's age. The rule of thumb generally has been one minute per year.

The Use of Time Out as a Discipline Strategy

Time out was originally used in institutional settings with people who had a variety of mental or emotional disorders (Marion, 2001). In that setting, time out might have been used to ensure the safety of other residents by removing a dangerous or disruptive resident from a setting. It might also have been used as a consequence, when a resident refused to comply with requests of the staff. In such a setting, time out was considered a legitimate guidance strategy.

At some point during the 1970s, time out made its way into schools as a discipline technique. As corporal punishment declined, time out arose to fill the void with what seemed as a more caring, humane, and non-violent method. In an early childhood classroom, time out has seemingly been used as a discipline strategy to control and extinguish undesirable behaviors. Well-meaning teachers might use it to cope with non-compliance in young children, or to give a con-

sequence for unsafe behavior. In some situations time out may be viewed as a logical consequence to inappropriate behavior or the loss of self-control (Gartrell, 2001).

How effective is time out in the typical early childhood environment? *Two-and-half-year-old Ben runs over to giggling two-year-old Jack and pushes him. The teacher says, "Ben! I told you not to push Jack! Use your words!" Ben tries again to push Jack. The teacher shouts, "Ben! That is not okay! You need to sit in the time-out chair!" She leads Ben to the chair and sits him down. In the time-out chair, Ben might be thinking, "I'm sitting in the chair... What is that noise?... I'm sitting in the chair... I want my mommy... I'm sitting in the chair." Ben is probably not thinking, "Wow! I guess I'll never push Jack again! I'm really sorry I did that!" Jack might be thinking: "What happened? I was giggling and then I was pushed down!"* (Schreiber, 1999, p. 22).

Should the Use of Time Out be Questioned?

Although many teachers view this technique as discipline, the lost opportunities and deprivation of positive interactions move this technique into the punishment category. The NAEYC Code of Ethical Conduct, P-1.1, states, "Above all, we shall not harm children. We shall not participate in practices that are disrespectful, degrading, dangerous, exploitative, intimidating, psychologically damaging, or physically harmful to children. This principle has precedence over all other in this code." Marion and Swim (2001) point out that "punishment has great potential for doing harm to children because it often serves as a model of negative, hurtful and aggressive measures."

Teachers may view time out as discipline rather than punishment, but children view these strategies as painful. When two-, three- and four-year-old children were asked in a study about time out, they expressed sadness and fear, as well as feeling alone, feeling disliked by the teacher and feeling ignored by peers (Readdick and Chapman, 2000).

Many early childhood experts agree with Readdick and Chapman. For example, Montessori (1964) sees these external controls that reward and punish as an opportunity lost to teach children how to self-regulate (Gartrell, 2001). The removal period can be confusing to the child because he lacks the cognitive ability to understand the process (Katz, 1984; Gartrell, 2001). Schreiber (1999) calls the practice of using time outs "undesirable" for five reasons: 1) external controls overshadow the need to develop internal controls; 2) adult needs are met at the expense of the child's needs; 3) a negative effect can be seen in the child's self-worth and self-confidence; 4) confusion arises over the connection between the action and the consequence; and 5) the lost opportunity for learning. These "undesirable" aspects of time out, along with the others mentioned above, make this strategy developmentally inappropriate. The needs of the child are not met, thus, causing harm to the child.

Guiding Children's Behavior

Time out needs to be revisited under the broader umbrella of guidance. Guidance can be defined as "Everything adults deliberately do and say, either directly or indirectly, to influence children's behavior, with the goal of helping them become well-adjusted, self-directed, productive adults" (Hildebrand and Hearron, p. 4, 1999). Using this definition, it is obvious that teachers have a re-

sponsibility to guide interactions towards a meaningful end. It is through positive actions or techniques that learning takes place. Today many positive techniques are available to early childhood teachers. Let's look at three areas: 1) managing the environment, 2) demonstrating developmentally appropriate practices, and 3) fostering the development of self-regulation in children.

Managing the Environment

Managing the environment must start with safety as the first priority. Consider the child who seems to be always running in the classroom. The teacher says, "*John, stop running before you hurt yourself. I've told you many times that if you run you will have to sit on a chair and slow down.*" A positive alternative to this would be to take a look at the environment. Is there sufficient space for large muscle or active play? Instead of changing the child's behavior with negative consequences, add a tunnel for crawling through, steps for walking up and down or change your schedule to provide outdoor play earlier in your morning routine. Schreiber (1999) lists several ways to minimize conflicts such as keeping group sizes small so each child gets more attention and minimize crowding of play spaces to minimize disruptions. Classrooms need personal spaces and social spaces. Personal space refers to an area where children put belongings or spend time when privacy is needed. Social space refers to an area around the child that the child feels is his such as a seat at the art table, or a section of the sand box (Hildebrand & Hearron, 1999). Teachers need to provide enough social spaces in their classrooms so children feel comfortable while playing. Take a look around your room. Is there adequate play space? Consider having 50 percent more play spaces than the number of children present.

Developmentally Appropriate Practices

Developmentally appropriate practices and positive guidance strategies go hand in hand. As teachers, we must make sure

our expectations are in line with the developmental levels of the children.

Giving children choices is one of Eaton's (1997) suggestions for positive guidance techniques. For example, *if a two-year-old is having difficulty coming to the snack table, the teacher can say, "It is time to sit down for snack now Jody. You may sit on the red chair or this blue chair."* Choices allow the child to have control over her environment within the boundaries set by the teacher.

Teaching expected behavior is another positive guidance strategy (Marion & Muza, 1998). As teachers we model behavior continuously. As a toddler teacher, I find myself modeling appropriate behaviors in the house area in my room especially at the beginning of the year. The children love to set the table and serve food. They also love to put everything in their mouths as they play and pretend to eat. In order to keep the toys clean (and out of the sanitizing container), I need to model how to hold the food inches from my mouth and move my lips as if I was eating. I tell them what I am doing and why. I label it by saying, "I'm pretending to eat the spaghetti." They love to watch and then repeat the modeled behavior.

Redirecting behavior takes on many forms—diverting, distracting, substituting (Marion, 1999). Consider having two of some items in your room so that substituting can easily happen such as in this example: *Sydney is playing with a doll when Michael tries to take it away. The teacher redirects by substitution when he hands Michael the second doll and replies, "Michael you may use this doll. Sydney is feeding that doll now."*

Setting limits in a preschool classroom provides boundaries for the children and teacher. Limits are set to assure the safety of children, adults, and materials. They also provide a framework in which trust, respect, equality, and accepting responsibility can flourish. Routines and transition times are ideal opportunities to apply positive guidance strategies. Use phrases such as, "It's time to (wash hands, go outside, rest quietly,)" "It's important to (use soap to remove germs, stay where a teacher can see you)," and "I need you to (wait for me before you go outside, pick up those two blocks)." (Reynolds, 2001).

Using action statements to guide behavior in young children. Telling children what to do, such as "we walk inside," takes the guesswork out of the situation. The child knows exactly what is expected of him. Hildebrand and Hearron (1999) point out that putting the action part of the statement at the beginning of the sentence is an effective method. For example, saying, "Hold on to the railing" is better than, "You might fall off the slide, so be sure to hold on." This allows the important part to be stated before it's too late or the child loses interest in your comments.

Demeo (2001) suggests when using positive guidance strategies a teacher must also take into account the variables that affect compliance. When advocating for behavior change in young children we should:

- Use statements
- Give the child time to respond
- Use a quiet voice, don't give multiple requests
- Describe the behavior we want to see
- Demonstrate and model
- Make more start requests than stop requests (do vs. don't)
- Be at the child's eye level and optimal listening distance of three feet.

Fostering the Development of Self-Regulation in Children

Self-regulation allows children to control their actions. They must develop the ability to know when to act, when to control their impulses and when to search for alternative solutions. This is a learned, ongoing process that can be fostered by teachers who use an integrated approach that considers the whole child and the developmental level of that child. "To support developing impulse control [in toddlers], caregivers can use responsive guidance techniques that emphasize individual control over behavior, provide

simple cause-and-effect reasons for desired behaviors, use suggestions rather than commands, and use language to assist self-control" Bronson (2000, p. 35). When we teach problem-solving skills, we help children take responsibility for their actions, see a situation from another point of view, and develop decision-making skills (Miller, 1984). These internal processes help children think of alternative solutions and possible outcomes. As teachers we can start the thought process by asking children, "How can you...?" or "What could we do to...?" As children develop these skills they will soon generate their own solutions and gain control of their actions.

Conclusion

Time out is out! As early childhood professionals, we must abide by the code of Ethical Conduct laid out by NAEYC, which states that "Above all we shall not harm children." The use of time out as a discipline strategy can harm children and must not be used in our classrooms. It is our responsibility to help "children and adults achieve their full potential in the context of relationships that are based on trust, respect, and positive regard" (NAEYC, 1990). As teachers we influence children daily. We can choose to affect children in positive ways by managing the environment, using developmentally appropriate practices, and fostering self-regulation. An effective teacher uses a mix of several techniques. One strategy may work one day while another may be best another day. It takes forethought and reflection. Positive guidance strategies help children develop into caring, respectful human beings.

References

Bronson, M. (2000). Recognizing and supporting the development of self-regulation in young children. *Young Children,* 55 (2), 33–37.

Demeo, W. (2001). Time-out is out: Developing appropriate alternatives for helping difficult young children develop self-control. Presentation at NAEYC Conference, Anaheim, CA.

Eaton, M. (1997). Positive discipline: Fostering the self-esteem of young children. *Young Children,* 52 (6), 43–46.

Gartrell, D. (2001). Replacing time-out: Part one—using guidance to build an encouraging classroom. *Young Children,* 56 (6), 8–16.

Hildebrand V. & Hearron P. (199). *Guiding young children.* Upper Saddle River, NJ: Prentice-Hall, Inc.

Katz, L. (1984). The professional early childhood teacher. *Young Children,* 39 (5), 3–10.

Marion, M. (1999). *Guidance of young children.* Upper Saddle River, NJ: Prentice-Hall, Inc.

Marion, M. & Muza, R. (1998). Positive discipline: Six strategies for guiding behavior. *Texas Child Care,* 22, (2), 6–11.

Marion, M. & Swim, T. (2001). First of all, do no harm: Relationship between early childhood teacher beliefs about punitive discipline practices and reported use of time out. Manuscript, under review.

Marion, M. (2001). Discussion information.

Miller C. (1984). Building self-control: Discipline for young children. *Young Children,* 39 (6), 15–19.

Montessori, M. (1964). *The Montessori method.* New York: Shocken Books.

NAEYC Code of Ethical Conduct and Statement of Commitment (1990).

Readdick & Chapman, P. (2000). Young children's perceptions of time out. *Journal of Research in Childhood Education,* 15 (1).

Reynolds, E. (2001). *Guiding young children: A problem-solving approach.* Mountain View, CA: Mayfield Publishing Company.

Schreiber, M. (1999). Time-outs for toddlers: Is our goal punishment or education? *Young Children,* 54 (4), 22–25.

Sheppard, W. & Willoughby, R. (1975). *Child behavior: Learning and development.* Chicago: Rand McNally College Publishing Company.

Kathy Preuesse is currently a lab school teacher in the two-year-old toddler class at the Child and Family Study Center at the University of Wisconsin-Stout in Menomonie, WI.

From *Earlychildhood News,* March/April 2002, pp. 12-16. © 2002 by Excellence Learning Corporation. Reprinted by permission.

Beyond Banning War and Superhero Play

Meeting Children's Needs in Violent Times

Diane E. Levin

Four-year-old Jules is particularly obsessed. Telling him no guns or pretend fighting just doesn't work. When he's a good guy, like a Power Ranger, he thinks it's okay to use whatever force is needed to suppress the bad guy "because that's what a superhero does!" And then someone ends up getting hurt. When we try to enforce a ban, the children say it's not superhero play, it's some other kind of play. Many children don't seem to know more positive ways to play or play the same thing over and over without having any ideas of their own. I need some new ideas.

THIS EXPERIENCED TEACHER'S ACCOUNT captures the kinds of concerns I often hear from teachers worried about how to respond to war play in their classrooms (Levin 2003). These expressions of concern about play with violence tend to increase when violent world events, like 9/11 and the war against Iraq, dominate the news.

Play, viewed for decades as an essential part of the early childhood years, has become a problem in many classrooms, something even to avoid. Teachers ask why is play deemed as being so important to children's development when it is so focused on fighting. Some are led to plan other activities that are easier to manage and appear at first glance to be more productive. Reducing playtime may seem to reduce problems in the short term, but this approach does not address the wide-ranging needs children address through play.

Why Are Children Fascinated with War Play?

There are many reasons why children bring violent content and themes into their play. They are related to the role of play in development and learning as well as to the nature of the society in which war play occurs (Cantor 1998; Carlsson-Paige & Levin 1987, 1990; Katch 2001; Levin 1998a & b, & 2003).

Exposure to violence.

From both therapeutic and cognitive perspectives, children use play to work out an understanding of experience, including the violence to which they are exposed. Young children may see violence in their homes and communities as well as entertainment and news violence on the screen. We should not be surprised when children are intent on bringing it to their play. Children's play often focuses on the most salient and graphic, confusing or scary, and most aggressive aspects of violence. It is this content they struggle to work out and understand. Typically, the children who seem most obsessed with war play have been exposed to the most violence and have the greatest need to work it out.

Need to feel powerful.

Most young children look for ways to feel powerful and strong. Play can be a safe way to achieve a sense of power. From a child's point of view, play with violence, especially when connected to the power and invincibility of entertainment, is very seductive. Children who use war play to help them feel powerful and safe are also the children who feel the most powerless and vulnerable.

Open-ended toys, like blocks, stuffed animals, and generic dinosaurs, can be used in many ways that the child control.

Influence of violent, media-linked toys.

Children's toys give powerful messages about what and how to play. Open-ended toys, like blocks, stuffed animals, and generic dinosaurs can be used in many ways that the child controls. Highly structured toys such as play dough kits with molds to make movie characters and action figures that talk tend to have built-in features that show children how and what to play. Many of today's best selling toys are of the highly structured variety and are linked to violent media. Such toys are appealing because they promise dramatic power and excitement and then they channel children into replicating the violent stories they see on screen. Some children, like Jules, get "stuck" imitating media-linked violence instead of developing creative, imaginative, and beneficial play.

Why Are Teachers Concerned about Today's War Play?

There are many reasons why teachers are concerned about war play and why they seek help figuring out how to deal with it.

Lack of safety in the classroom.
Play with violence tends to end up with children out of control, scared, and hurt. Managing the play and keeping everyone safe can feel like a never-ending struggle and a major diversion from the positive lessons we want children to learn.

Old approaches not working.
Many veteran teachers say that the bans they used to impose on war play no longer work. Children have a hard time accepting limits or controlling their intense desire or need to engage in the play. And children find ways to circumvent the ban—they deny the play is really war play (i.e., learning to lie) or sneak around conducting guerilla wars the teacher does not detect (i.e., learning to deceive).

Worries about the limited nature of the play.
Like Jules, some children engage in the same play with violence day after day and bring in few new or creative ideas of their own. Piaget called this kind of behavior "imitation," not "play" (Carlsson-Paige & Levin 1987). Such children are less likely to work out their needs regarding the violence they bring to their play or benefit from more sustained and elaborated play.

Concerns about lessons learned from the play.
When children pretend to hurt others, it is the opposite of what we hope they will learn about how to treat each other and solve problems. Children *learn* as they play— and what they play affects what they learn. When children are exposed to large amounts of violence, they learn harmful lessons about violence whether they are allowed to play it in the classroom or not.

> *When children are exposed to large amounts of violence, they learn harmful lessons about violence, whether they are allowed to play it in the classroom or not.*

At the same time, children do not think about the violence they bring into their play the same way adults do. Jules focuses on one thing at a time—the bad boy is one dimensional and bad, without thinking about what makes him bad. He thinks good guys can do whatever hurtful things they want because they are "good." Except when he gets carried away and hurts another child, Jules probably does know that at some level his play is different from the real violence he is imitating.

Approaches to Working with Children's Violent Play

- **Address children's needs while trying to reduce play with violence.** Banning play rarely works and it denies children the opportunity to work out violence issues through play or to feel that their interests and concerns are important. Trying to ban media-controlled imitative play, or even just to contain it, can be an appropriate stopgap measure when problems become overwhelming. However, a total ban on this kind of play may leave children to work things out on their own without the guidance of adults.
- **Ensure the safety of all children.** Involve children in developing rules for indoor and outdoor play that ensure safety. Help children understand the safety issue and what they can do to prevent injuries (physical and psychological) to themselves and others. Encourage children to paint, tell stories, and write (as they get older) to deal with issues of violence in ways that are safe and easier to control than play.
- **Promote development of imaginative and creative play (rather than imitative play).** To work through deep issues and needs in a meaningful way, most children require direct help from adults. How you help depends on the nature of children's play (Levin 1998b). Take time to observe the play and learn what children are working on and how. Use this information to help children move beyond narrowly scripted play that is focused on violent actions. Help children gain skills to work out the violent content they bring to their play, learn the lessons you aim to teach, and move on to new issues.

Approaches to Working Outside Violent Play

- **Encourage children to talk with adults about media violence.** As children struggle to feel safe and make sense of violence—regardless of the source—they need to know that we are there to help them with this process (Levin 2003). Start by trying to learn what they know, the unique meanings they have made, and what confuses and scares them.

  When a child raises an issue it is helpful to start by using an open-ended question like "What have you heard about that?" Respond based on what you learn about their ideas, questions, and needs. Keep in mind that children do not understand violence in or out of play as adults do. Try to correct misconceptions ("The planes that go over our school do not carry bombs"), help sort out fantasy and reality ("In real life people can't change back and forth like the Power Rangers do"), and provide reassurance about safety ("I can't let you play like that because it's my job to make sure everyone is safe").

- **Try to reduce the impact of antisocial lessons that children learn both in and out of play.** It can be helpful to encourage children to move from imitative to creative play so they can transform violence into positive behavior. Then talk with them about what has happened in their play ("I see Spiderman did a lot of fighting today. What was the problem?"). Help children to connect their own firsthand positive experiences about how people treat each other to the violence they have seen ("I'm glad that in real life you could solve your problem with Mary by..."). These connections can help diffuse some of the harmful lessons children learn about violence.

  Talking with children about violence is rarely easy, but it is one of our most powerful tools. It is hard to predict the directions in which children might take the conversations and teachers will often find it challenging to show respect for the differing ways families try to deal with these issues.

- **Work closely with families.** Reducing children's exposure to violence is one essential way to reduce their need to bring violence into their play. Most of young children's exposure occurs in the home, so family involvement is vital. Through parent workshops and family newsletters that include resource materials such as those listed below, teachers can help families learn more about how to protect children from violence, help children deal with the violence that still gets in, and promote play with open-ended toys and non-violent play themes (Levin 1998a, 2003). In addition, families can learn about how to resist the advertising for toys linked to violence in ways that keep the peace in the family (Levin 1998; Levin & Linn in press).

Reconcile Children's Needs and Adults' Concerns

In our society children are exposed to huge amounts of pretend and real violence. There are no simple or perfect solutions that simultaneously address children's needs and adults' concerns (Carlsson-Paige & Levin 1987). However, there is much teachers can do working with and outside of the play to make it better for everyone (see "Approaches to Working with Violent Play" and "Approaches to Working Outside Violent Play").

More Important Now Than Ever

There is no perfect approach for dealing with children's play with violence in these times. The best strategy is to vastly reduce the amount of violence children see. this would require adults to create a more peasceful world and limit children's exposure to media violence and toys marketed with media violence.

Given the state of the world, including the war against Iraq, children now more than ever need to find ways to work out the violence they see. For many, play helps them do so. We have a vital role in helping meet their nneds through play. We must create an approach that addresses the unique needs of children growing up in the midst of violence as well as concerns of adults about how play with violence contributes to the harmful lessons children learn.

References

Cantor, J. 1998. *"Mommy, I'm scared!" How TV and movies frighten children and what we can do to protect them.* NY: Harcourt Brace.

Carlsson-Paige, N. & Levin, D.E. 1987. *The war play dilemma: Balancing needs and values in the early childhood classroom.* NY: Teachers College Press.

Carlsson-Paige, N. & Levin, D.E. 1990. *Who's calling the shots? How to respond effectively to children's fascination with war play and war toys.* Gabriola Island, BC, CAN: New Society.

Katch, J. 2001. *Under dead man's skin: Discovering the meaning of children's violent play.* Boston: Beacon Press.

Levin, D.E. 1998a. *Remote control childhood? Combating the hazards of media culture.* Washington, DC: NAEYC.

Levin, D.E. 1998b. Play with violence. In *Play from birth to twelve: Contexts, perspectives, and meanings*, eds. D. Fromberg & D. Bergin. New York: Garland.

Levin, D.E. 2003. *Teaching young children in violent times: Building a peaceable classroom.* 2d ed. Cambridge, MA: Educators for Social Responsibility & Washington, DC: NAEYC.

Levin, D.E. & Linn, S. In press. The commercialization of childhood. In *Psychology and the consumer culture*, eds. T. Kasser & A. Kanner. Washington, DC: American Psychological Association.

Classroom Problems That Don't Go Away

Laverne Warner and Sharon Lynch

W*ade runs "combat-style" beneath the windows of his school as he makes his getaway from his 1st-grade classroom. It is still early in the school year, but this is the third time Wade has tried to escape. Previously, his teacher has managed to catch him before he left the building. Today, however, his escape is easier, because Mrs. Archie is participating with the children in a game of "Squirrel and Trees" and Wade is behind her when he leaves the playground area. She sees him round the corner of the school, and speedily gives chase. When she reaches the front parking lot of their building, however, she cannot find him. Wade is gone!*

Experienced and inexperienced teachers alike, in all grade levels, express concern about difficult classroom problems—those problems that don't ever seem to go away, no matter what management techniques are used. Wade's story and similar ones are echoed time and again in classrooms around the world as adults struggle to find a balance between correcting children's behavior and instructing them about self-management strategies.

Educators emphasize an understanding of appropriate guidance strategies, and teachers learn about acceptable center and school district policies. An abundance of books, videotapes, and other teacher resources are available to classroom practitioners to enhance their understanding of appropriate guidance strategies. Professional organizations such as the Association for Childhood Education International define standards of good practice. Textbooks for childhood educators define well-managed classrooms and appropriate management techniques (e.g., Marion, 2003; Morrison, 2001; Reynolds, 2003; Seefeldt & Barbour, 1998; Wolfgang, 2001).

Despite this preparation, educators daily face problems with guiding or disciplining children in their classrooms. Understanding the developmental needs of children and meeting their physical needs are two ingredients to happy classroom management. It is also important to look at the larger problems involved when children's misbehaviors are chronic to the point that youngsters are labeled as "difficult." Are these children receiving enough attention from the teacher? Are they developing social skills that will help them through interactions and negotiations with other children in the classroom?

Mrs. Archie's guidance philosophy is founded on principles that she believes are effective for young children. Taking time at the end of the day to reflect on Wade's disappearance, Mrs. Archie concluded that she had done what she could, as always, to develop a healthy classroom climate.

She strives to build a classroom community of learners and act with understanding in response to antisocial behavior in the classroom, and she knows that the vast majority of children will respond positively. Mrs. Archie's classroom layout promotes orderly activity throughout the day and is well-stocked with enough materials and supplies to keep children interested and actively engaged in their learning activities. Although the activities she provides are challenging, many simple experiences also are available to prevent children from being overwhelmed by classroom choices.

Furthermore, Mrs. Archie's attitude is positive about children, like Wade, who come from families that use punitive discipline techniques at home. Her discussions with Wade's mother prior to his escape had been instructive, and she thought that progress was being made with the family. Indeed, when Wade arrived at home the day he ran off, his mother returned him to school immediately.

So what is the teacher to do about children, like Wade, with chronic and intense behavioral difficulties? If serious behavior problems are not addressed before age 8, the child is likely to have long-lasting conduct problems throughout school, often leading to suspension, or dropping out (Katz & McClellan, 1997; Walker et al., 1996). Since the window of opportunity to intervene with behavior problems is narrow, childhood educators must understand the nature of the behavior problem and design an educative plan to teach the child alternative approaches.

The ABC's of the Problem

The first step in analyzing the behavior problem is to determine the "pay-off" for the child. Challenging behaviors usually fall into one of the following categories: 1) behavior that gets the child attention, either positive or negative; 2) behavior that removes the child from something unpleasant, like work or a task; 3) behavior that results in the child getting something she or he wants, like candy or a toy; and 4) behavior that provides some type of sensory stimulation, such as spinning around until the child feels dizzy and euphoric.

To understand the pay-off for the child, it is important to examine the ABC's of the behavior: the antecedents, behaviors, and consequences associated with the problem. The *antecedent* requires a record, which describes what was happening just prior to the incident. The actual *behavior* then can be described in observable, measurable terms: instead of saying that the misbehaving child had a tantrum, detail that he threw himself to the floor, screamed, and pounded his fists on the floor for four minutes. Finally, we examine the pay-off (*consequences*) for the behavior.

Did the behavior result in close physical contact as the child was carried into the adjoining room and the caregiver attempted to soothe him? Did the behavior result in his being given juice so that he could calm down? Did the behavior result in scolding by the teacher, providing the kind of intense individual attention that some youngsters crave because it is the only demonstration of love and caring they have experienced? When teachers and caregivers examine the ABC's of the behavior, they are better able to understand the child's motivation, establish preventive strategies, and teach alternative social skills the child can use to meet his or her needs.

Prevention Strategies

Mrs. Archie knows that she needs to learn specific strategies that will help her work with "difficult" behaviors, like those of Wade, because these problems certainly don't seem to go away on their own. The following intervention methods are designed to preempt anti-social behaviors and often are referred to as prevention strategies. It is always better to prevent the behavior as much as possible.

Accentuate the Positive For the child who demonstrates inappropriate behavior to gain attention, the teacher should find every opportunity to give the child positive attention when he or she is behaving appropriately. Often, these opportunities to "catch the child being good" occur relatively early in the day. When children receive plenty of positive attention early in the day and the teacher continues to find opportunities for praise and attention as the day goes on, the child is not as likely to misbehave for attention as his need is already being met (Hanley, Piazza, & Fisher, 1997). This intervention is based on the principle of deprivation states. If the child is deprived of attention and is "hungry" for adult interaction, he will do anything to gain the attention of others, even negative attention.

Player's Choice When educators see a negative pattern of behavior, they can anticipate that the child is likely to refuse adult requests. This is often referred to as "oppositional behavior." A teacher may remark, "It doesn't matter what I ask her to do, she is going to refuse to do it." One successful strategy for dealing with this type of oppositional behavior is to provide the child with choices (Knowlton, 1995). This approach not only gives the child power and control, but also affords the child valuable opportunities for decision making. Example of choices include, "Do you want to carry out the trash basket or erase the chalkboard?," "Do you want to sit in the red chair or the blue chair?," or "Do you want to pick up the yellow blocks or the green blocks?"

The teacher must be cautious about the number of choices provided, however. Many children have difficulty making up their minds if too many choices are presented—often, two choices are plenty. Also, adults need to monitor their own attitude as they present choices. If choices are presented using a drill sergeant tone of voice, the oppositional child is going to resist the suggestions.

On a Roll When adults anticipate that a child is going to refuse a request, teachers can embed this request within a series of other simple requests. This intervention is based on the research-based principles of high-probability request sequences (Ardoin, Martens, & Wolfe, 1999). The first step in this procedure is to observe the child to determine which requests she consistently performs. Before asking the child to perform the non-preferred request, ask her to do several other things that she does consistently. For example, 8-year-old Morgan consistently resists cleaning up the dollhouse area. While she is playing with the dollhouse, her teacher could ask her to "Give the dolls a kiss," "Show me the doll's furniture," and "Put the dolls in their bedrooms." After she has complied with these three requests, she is much more likely to comply with the request to "Put the dolls away now" or "Give them to me."

Grandma's Rule This strategy often is referred to as the Premack Principle (Premack, 1959). When asking a child to perform an action, specifying what he or she will receive after completing it more often ensures its completion. Examples here include: "When you have finished your math problems, then we will go outside," "When you have eaten your peas, you can have some pudding," and "After you have rested awhile, we will go to the library."

A Spoonful of Sugar Helps the Medicine Go Down This principle involves pairing preferred and non-preferred activities. One particular task that is difficult for preschoolers, and many adults, is waiting. Most of us do not wait well. When asking a child to complete a non-preferred activity such as waiting in line, pairing a preferred activity with the waiting will make it more tolerable.

Businesses and amusement parks use the principle of pairing when they provide music or exhibits for customers as they wait in line. Similarly, with young children, teachers can provide enjoyable activities as children wait. Suggested activities that can be used during waiting periods include singing, looking at books, reading a story, or holding something special such as a banner, sign, or toy.

Another difficult activity for many young children is remaining seated. If the child is given a small object to hold during the time she must remain seated, she may be willing to continue sitting for a longer period. The principle of pairing preferred and non-preferred activities also gives the child increasing responsibility for her own behavior, instead of relying on teacher discipline.

Just One More This particular intervention is most effective when a child behaves inappropriately in order to escape a low-preference task. The purpose of the intervention is to improve work habits and increase time on task. The first step is to identify how long a particular child will work at a specific task before exhibiting inappropriate behavior. Once the teacher has determined how long a child will work on a task, the teacher can give the child a delay cue to head off misbehavior. Examples of delay cues are "Just one more and then you're finished," "Just two minutes and then you're finished," or "Do this and then you're finished."

In this intervention, a teacher sets aside preconceived ideas about how long children *should* work on a task and instead focuses on improving the child's ability to complete tasks in reference to his current abilities. As the children's challenging behaviors decrease, the adult gradually can increase the time on task, and the amount of work completed, before giving them the delay cue and releasing them from the task.

The More We Get Together Another way to improve task completion is by making the job a collaborative effort. If a child finds it difficult to complete non-preferred activities, then the instructor can complete part of the task with the student. For example, when organizing the bookshelf, the adult completes a portion of the task, such as picking up the big books as the student picks up the little books. She prefaces that activity by stating, "I'll pick up the big books, and you pick up the little books." As the child becomes more willing to complete her part of the task, the caregiver gradually increases the work expectations for the child while decreasing the amount of assistance.

Communication Development

In addition to preventing inappropriate behavior, another tactic is replacing the problem behavior by teaching the child alternative behaviors. The key to this process is "functional equivalence." Teachers must determine the *function* or pay-off for the inappropriate behavior and then teach an alternative *equivalent* action that will service the same purpose as the negative behavior. This often is referred to as the "fair pair" rule (White & Haring, 1976). Rather than punishing the behavior, teaching children a better way to behave assists in meeting their needs.

Bids for Attention The first step in addressing attention-seeking negative behaviors is to reduce their occurrence by providing plenty of attention for the child's appropriate behaviors. The next step is to teach the child appropriate ways to gain attention from others. Most children learn appropriate social skills incidentally from their family and teachers; some children, however, have learned negative ways to gain social attention. Some of the social skills that may need to be taught include calling others by name, tapping friends on the shoulder for attention, knowing how to join others in play, and raising one's

hand to gain the teacher's attention. Numerous other social skills may require direct instruction. Any time a behavior is considered inappropriate, adults need to teach the child a better way to have his needs met.

When teaching social skills to chldren, break the skill into a maximum of three steps. Then model the steps and have the child demonstrate the skill. Provide positive and negative examples of the step and have the children label the demonstration as correct or incorrect. Use class discussion time to role-play and talk about when this particular social skill is appropriate. Throughout the day, set up situations that allow practice of the social skill and encourage the child to use the new skill. Finally, promote carry-over of the skill by communicating with the family about the social skills instruction in order for the child to practice the social skills outside of the classroom—on the playground, in the lunch room, and at home.

Ask for Something Else If we know that the child has disruptive behaviors when presented with tasks that are disliked, then the teacher can present the child with an alternative task or materials, something she likes, *before* the problem behavior occurs. Then the child can be taught to ask for the alternative activity or object. When the child requests the alternative, provide it and preempt the negative behavior. In this way, children can learn to communicate their needs and prevent the challenging behavior from occurring.

Ask for Help Many children behave disruptively because they are frustrated with a task. Teachers usually can determine when the child is becoming frustrated by observing and reading nonverbal communication signals. Possible signs of frustration might be sighing, fidgeting, reddening of the face, or negative facial expressions. Noticing these signs helps the teacher know that it is time to intervene. Rather than offering help when the child needs it, the teacher says, "It looks like you need some help. When you need help, you need to tell me. Now you say, 'I need help.'" After the child has responded by saying, "I need help," the teacher provides assistance. This strategy is much more effective if the group already has role-played "asking for help."

Ask for a Break This strategy is similar to the two listed above; in this case, educators teach the child to ask for a break during a difficult and frustrating task. Prior to presenting the task, the teacher can explain that she knows that the activity can be difficult, but that the child can have a break after spending some time working hard at it. Then, the child can be taught to request a break while other students are engaged in various tasks.

Although teachers would like to think that instruction and activities are always fun for children and that learning should be child-directed, certain important activities must be mastered if children are to become successful in school. Especially as children progress into the primary grades, teachers expect them to work independently on pencil-and-paper tasks. Teaching youngsters communication skills that will help them handle frustration and low-preference activities will improve their outcomes as learners in school and in life.

Reviewing Options

Mrs. Archie, in reviewing her options for working with Wade, is gaining confidence in her ability to work more carefully with the family and with Wade to ensure his successful re-entry to her classroom. Her resolve is to continue developing a "community of learners" (Bredekamp & Copple, 1997) by helping Wade become a functioning member of her group. She intends to teach him how to enter a play setting, negotiate for what he wants in the classroom, and learn how to make compromises, while nurturing him as she would any child. These are goals that she believes will help turn around Wade's negative behavior.

Mrs. Archie also knows that her administrator is a caring woman, and, if necessary, Wade could be placed in another classroom so that he could have a "fresh start" with his entry into school. Her hope is that this will be a last-resort strategy, because she understands how much Wade needs a caring adult who understands him and his needs. Her phone call to Wade's mother at the end of the day will be friendly and supportive, with many recommendations for how the school can assist the family.

A Long-Term Plan

Most children with chronic difficult behaviors did not learn them overnight. Many of these children experience serious ongoing problems in their families. As teachers, we cannot change home dynamics or family problems. Sometimes a parent conference or parent education groups can be helpful, as the family learns to support a difficult child at home. With others, we do well to teach the child socially appropriate behavior in the classroom. As a child learns socially appropriate behavior in school, she learns that the behavior is useful in other settings. Often, the school is the only place where the child has the opportunity to learn prosocial behaviors. Children's negative behaviors may have, in a sense, "worked" for them in numerous situations for a substantial period of time. When we work to teach the child a better way to get his or her needs met, we must recognize that this process takes time and effort. When we as educators invest this time and effort with children during childhood, we are pro-

viding them with the tools that can make the difference in their school careers and in their lives.

References

Ardoin, S. P., Martens, B. K., & Wolfe, L. A. (1999). Using high-probability instruction sequences with fading to increase student compliance during transitions. *Journal of Applied Behavior Analysis, 32*(3), 339–351.

Bredekamp, S., & Copple, C. (Eds.). (1997). *Developmentally appropriate practice in early childhood programs* (Rev. ed.). Washington, DC: National Association for the Education of Young Children.

Hanley, G. P., Piazza, C. C., & Fisher, W. W. (1997). Noncontingent presentation of attention and alternative stimuli in the treatment of attention-maintained destructive behavior. *Journal of Applied Behavior Analysis, 30*(2), 229–237.

Katz, L., & McClellan, D. (1997). *Fostering children's social competence: The teacher's role.* Washington, DC: National Association for the Education of Young Children.

Knowlton, D. (1995). Managing children with oppositional defiant behavior. *Beyond Behavior, 6*(3), 5–10.

Marion, M. (2003). *Guidance of young children* (3rd ed.). Englewood Cliffs, NJ: Prentice Hall.

Morrison, G. (2001). *Early childhood education today* (8th ed.). Englewood Cliffs, NJ: Prentice Hall.

Premack, D. (1959). Toward empirical behavior laws: I. Positive reinforcement. *Psychological Review, 66,* 219–233.

Reynolds, E. (2003). *Guiding young children* (2nd ed.). Mountain View, CA: Mayfield.

Seefeldt, C., & Barbour, N. (1998). *Early childhood education: An introduction* (4th ed.). Columbus, OH: Merrill.

Walker, H. M., Horner, R. H., Sugai, G., Bullis, M., Sprague, J. R., Bricker, D., & Kaufman, M. J. (1996). Integrated approaches to preventing anti-social behavior among school-age children and youth. *Journal of Emotional and Behavioral Disorders, 4*(4), 194–209.

White, O. R., & Haring, N. G. (1976). *Exceptional teaching.* Upper Saddle River, NJ: Merrill/Prentice Hall.

Wolfgang, C. H. (2001). *Solving discipline and classroom management problems* (5th ed.). New York: John Wiley and Sons.

Laverne Warner is Professor, Early Childhood Education, and Sharon Lynch is Associate Professor of Special Education, Department of Language, Literacy, and Special Populations, Sam Houston State University, Huntsville, Texas.

6 FACTS You Need to Know About AUTISM NOW!

There are lots of frightening rumors about what causes this mysterious brain disorder in children. We asked leading experts across the country for the very latest news.

By Jan Sheehan

Nancy Wiseman had a feeling early on that something wasn't quite right with her daughter. When Sarah was 6 months old, she stopped babbling, and by 10 months, she was silent. By 18 months, the increasingly aloof toddler no longer responded to her name, and she resisted being held, kissed, or touched. "I felt that I was losing my child a little more each day," says Wiseman, of Merrimac, Massachusetts. When Sarah wasn't saying any words or even making sounds that resembled words by 20 months, her grandmother, a school psychologist, suspected that the girl might actually be deaf. Instead, Wiseman was devastated to learn that her daughter had autism. "The diagnosis really knocked the wind out of me," she recalls, "but I was relieved to finally know what was wrong."

Although the severity of autism can vary widely, many children with the neurological disorder—which typically appears in the first three years of life—have problems speaking, interacting with others, sharing affection, and learning. Thanks to the tireless efforts of parents and advocates, public awareness of autism has grown tremendously since it was first identified in 1943, but it is gaining even more attention today than ever before. Congress has held hearings on the condition. Public-health agencies are spending millions to study it. Researchers at countless universities are racing to find the causes and best treatments.

"There are many unanswered questions," says Alice Kau, Ph.D., an autism expert at the National Institutes of Health, which funded more than $74 million in autism research in 2002, as compared with only $22 million in 1997. Still, researchers are beginning to make progress in unraveling this baffling disorder, and the number of resources available for families is increasing. Here, six facts about autism that every parent should know.

1. RATES ARE ON THE RISE

Autism is ten times more common today than it was in the 1980s, according to the Centers for Disease Control and Prevention. More than three in 1,000 children in this country have autism to some degree. In California, the number of kids with autism in the state's social-services program nearly doubled between 1998 and 2002, surpassing cases of childhood cancer, juvenile diabetes, and Down syndrome. Nationwide, autism strikes three to four times more boys than girls; the rates are about the same for kids of all races.

Although there seems to be an autism epidemic, most experts attribute the increasing prevalence to improved diagnosis and reporting. The definition of autism has been expanded in the past decade to include a wider spectrum of problems with communication and social interaction. "Ten years ago, many children with mild autism were simply not diagnosed," says Adrian Sandler, M.D., a developmental-behavioral pediatrician at Mission Children's Hospital, in Asheville, North Carolina, and chair of the American Academy of Pediatrics' committee on children with disabilities. Plus, there are more state and federal programs for autistic kids, giving doctors an incentive to diagnose and refer them. However, there may be additional, unknown reasons for the spike in autism rates, and researchers are investigating everything from environmental toxins to viruses to food allergies.

2. KIDS ARE GETTING DIAGNOSED SOONER

There's no laboratory or medical test for detecting autism, so doctors must rely on behavioral signs. In the past, many were reluctant to label a child as autistic until symptoms became obvious. "The average age for diagnosis had been about 3 1/2, with many children diagnosed much later," says Amy Wetherby, Ph.D., director of the Center for Autism and Related Disabilities at Florida State University, in Tallahassee. But that's changing.

One reason is that pediatricians are becoming more aware of autism. At the same time, autism specialists are better at identifying early telltale signs such as a lack of babbling or pointing. "Most children with autism will show some signs of developmental disruption by their first birthday," says Rebecca Landa, Ph.D., an autism researcher at Baltimore's Kennedy Krieger Institute.

And while no one is yet diagnosing autism in children that young, doctors can now make a reliable assessment by 24 months—when a child's brain is still rapidly developing. "If we can intervene while a child's brain is very immature, it will be much easier to help change her behavior," Dr. Wetherby says.

3. AUTISM IS A GENETIC DISORDER

Although autism was once believed to be the result of improper parenting, researchers now believe that genes—not psychological factors—are to blame. If a couple has one autistic child, there is a 5 to 10 percent chance that siblings will have some sort of autistic disorder. With identical twins, the likelihood is 60 percent. Even though profoundly autistic people rarely have children, researchers often find that a relative has mild autistic symptoms or a high-functioning autistic-spectrum disorder known as Asperger's syndrome.

Experts believe that autism is the result of multiple genes—anywhere from three to 20—interacting with each other. This may explain why the symptoms and severity of the disorder vary greatly. These genes may cause a baby's brain to develop abnormally in utero or make him more susceptible to unknown triggers. "There is probably a combination of genetic and environmental influences," says Catherine Lord, Ph.D., director of the Center for Autism and Communication Disorders at the University of Michigan, in Ann Arbor. Although the genes linked to autism have not yet been pinpointed, intense research is under way.

4. THERE IS NO KNOWN SCIENTIFIC LINK BETWEEN VACCINES AND AUTISM

There's been widespread controversy about a possible connection between vaccines and the soaring autism rates. Some parents of children whose autistic symptoms first appeared shortly after their measles-mumps-rubella (MMR) immunization are convinced the shot was the cause, but repeated studies have failed to find scientific evidence. Although one small, heavily publicized British study published in 1998 suggested a link, ten of the 13 authors publicly retracted the findings this March, saying they were unreliable. (The lead researcher reportedly had a conflict of interest because he was also working with lawyers filing a suit against vaccine manufacturers.)

Because the MMR vaccine is routinely given at 12 to 15 months—when the first symptoms of autism often become noticeable—the apparent association is a coincidence, says *Parents* adviser Neal Halsey, M.D., director of the Institute for Vaccine Safety at Johns Hopkins University, in Baltimore. Up to 40 percent of children with autism typically experience regression at 12 to 18 months; they start developing normally but then suddenly lose communication and social skills.

Even so, some pediatricians have been offering the option of delaying the vaccine until 21 to 24 months of age to ease parents' worries. By then, toddlers are typically talking, so autism can be ruled out. But Dr. Halsey warns that this trend could be more harmful than helpful, because it leaves children unprotected from potentially fatal illnesses.

The possibility that mercury poisoning might cause autism has also been in the news. Since the 1930s, a preservative called thimerosal, which contains small amounts of mercury, had been used in some childhood vaccines (not MMR). Although mercury is known to be harmful to the brains of infants and young children, most vaccine experts say the amounts used in the preservative were too tiny to cause neurological damage. Nevertheless, manufacturers voluntarily began removing thimerosal in 1999, and by the end of 2001, none of the routine vaccines given in early childhood contained the preservative. The preservative is now used only in flu shots and some vaccines given to adults and adolescents.

5. LARGE HEAD SIZE IS A RED FLAG

Recent findings published in the *Journal of the American Medical Association* suggest that the brains of children with autism develop differently from an early age. Researchers discovered that most infants who were later diagnosed with autism had small head circumferences at birth but had heads—and brains—much larger than normal by 6 to 14 months. "Some of them went all the way up to the 90th percentile in just a few months," says study co-author Natacha Akshoomoff, Ph.D., an assistant professor of psychiatry at the University of California, San Diego. Those who ended up with the most severe form of autism were found to have the most dramatic acceleration of brain growth during infancy.

Pediatricians don't always measure head circumference at well-baby visits, so it's wise to request it. However, don't panic if your baby's head size is above the norm. Some babies just have big heads. "Rapid head growth is not a way to diagnose autism," Dr. Akshoomoff points out, "but it means that a child should be watched closely to be sure that she meets speech and behavioral milestones."

6. EARLY TREATMENT IS CRUCIAL

There is no known cure for autism, but intensive therapy helps a child learn a wide range of skills—from making eye contact to hugging to having a conversation. And the sooner a child begins, the better. A panel of experts convened by the National Academy of Sciences in 2001 recommended that children should have 25 hours of therapy per week as soon as autism is suspected. Because children with autism have very different behaviors and abilities, the most effective approach takes into account a child's unique challenges and encourages healthy development through play, rather than just trying to change specific symptoms. "Intervention can take many forms, from going to a regular preschool to a parent's working with her child over the course of a normal day to direct therapies from well-trained teachers and professionals—all depending on the child," Dr. Lord says.

Thanks to early intervention, some children—like Nancy Wiseman's daughter, Sarah—make remarkable progress. "At the very least, we're able to lessen the severity of symptoms," says Dr. Lord, who chaired the expert panel. "The latest studies show that almost 80 percent of kids with autism now have some speech by age 9, whereas only 50 percent of these kids were talking 20 years ago." And though past research suggests that most autistic children have below-average cognitive abilities, a recent study found that early treatment raised children's IQ scores by about 20 points, to almost normal levels. Those who started therapy as toddlers were also more likely to attend regular kindergarten.

AUTISM ALERT

Have your child evaluated as soon as possible if he:
- Does not babble or coo by 12 months.
- Does not gesture (point, wave, grasp) by 12 months.
- Does not say single words by 16 months.
- Does not say two-word phrases on his own (rather than repeating someone else) by 24 months.
- Has any loss of language or social skill at any age.

SOURCE: National Institute of Child Health and Human Development.

One of the biggest remaining challenges is the shortage of trained therapists and spots in special-education programs and schools for children with autism. To address this problem, the federal government recently announced a ten-year plan to provide adequate services.

While there's still much about autism that remains a mystery, research scientists are making new discoveries every day. In fact, they say, it may be possible to cure autism one day—perhaps through gene therapy even before a child is born. But for now, early diagnosis and therapy offer the best hope. "There's no doubt that today's generation of autistic kids will be better off than previous generations, because they're getting help sooner," Dr. Wetherby says.

The Latest News on ADHD

Doctors are learning more and more about attention disorders, which affect as many as 12 percent of school-age kids. Here's what parents need to know now.

By Debra Gordon

Energetic. Fearless. Impulsive. That's how Patti Flesher, of Waukegan, Illinois, used to describe her son, Liam, when he was a preschooler. If there was a tree, he'd climb it; a street, he'd cross it. He was prone to minor accidents and usually ended up in the emergency room several times a year. "His body was always moving faster than his mind," she says.

When Liam was 4, his preschool teachers suggested testing: They thought he might have attention deficit hyperactivity disorder, or ADHD. "My first reaction was that they were making a mountain out of a molehill, that he was just an active little boy," his mom says. But after a year of escalating problems at school and at home, the Fleshers finally took Liam to a pediatric neurologist, who officially diagnosed him with ADHD and prescribed medication. "We started noticing improvements almost immediately," Flesher says.

Attention disorders still carry enough stigma that many parents are reluctant to seek help for a child's problems. In large part, that's because there's a lot of misunderstanding and confusion surrounding ADHD. Here are seven important facts every parent should know.

1. IT OFTEN GOES UNTREATED. There's a perception that every child who can't sit still or who interrupts the teacher gets a diagnosis of ADHD—along with a prescription for Ritalin. But the reality is far different, says Stephen V. Faraone, Ph.D., a clinical professor of psychiatry at Harvard Medical School.

The latest studies show that between 8 and 12 percent of school-age kids have been diagnosed with ADHD—a marked increase over the past several decades. Still, many doctors believe the disorder is still widely *under*diagnosed. A landmark study by the National Institute of Mental Health (NIMH) found that as many as half of kids with ADHD had either not been diagnosed or were not being treated properly.

Failure to identify attention disorders can exacerbate the problem, research shows. Children who struggle through school untreated often have significant academic problems. What's more, their peers ostracize them and their self-esteem plummets. A 2001 survey of 507 parents of kids with ADHD, conducted by the New York University Child Study Center, found that they were nearly three times more likely to report that their child had difficulty getting along with other kids and more than twice as likely to say that their child got picked on by peers, compared with parents of children without ADHD. Other research has found that as untreated kids who have ADHD move into adolescence, they are at increased risk for substance abuse, antisocial behavior, depression, and anxiety disorders.

2. DIAGNOSIS CAN BE DIFFICULT. There are no laboratory tests to definitively identify ADHD. And the typical symptoms—disorganization, distractibility, forgetfulness, and impulsivity—read like a list of everyday childhood behaviors.

"The difference is that kids with ADHD exhibit the extreme of these behaviors, and their symptoms seriously interfere with their ability to function," says Andrew Adesman, M.D., director of Developmental and Behavioral Pediatrics at Schneider Children's Hospital, in New Hyde Park, New York.

Most doctors won't diagnose ADHD in a child under age 5, because all preschoolers have the symptoms to some degree. Even among older kids, though, detection can be tough. Doctors rely on parents and teachers to evaluate a child's symptoms—and their observations may differ: A kid with ADHD might be able to focus on a video game for hours at home, yet may be unable to stay seated for a ten-minute spelling test at school. What's more, there are three different subtypes of ADHD: hyperactive-impulsive, inattentive, and a combination of the two. Some kids with the disorder never exhibit any kind of hyperactivity at all.

If you think your child may have attention problems, it's best to consult with a psychologist, psychiatrist, neurologist, or pediatrician who is specially trained in ADHD and can spot the subtler forms of the condition and differentiate it from other mental disorders.

3. IT'S A TRUE BRAIN DISORDER. New scanning technology has allowed scientists to better understand the biological roots of ADHD. In the late 1990s, detailed brain imaging found that kids with the disorder have less electrical activity and are less reactive to stimulation in certain areas. A more recently published study showed that the brains of children with ADHD are about 4 percent smaller than those of kids without the disorder. "This suggests that physical differences in the brain are producing the symptoms," Dr. Faraone says.

Other research has found that children with ADHD may have difficulty regulating dopamine and norepinephrine, brain chemicals that play a significant role in our ability to focus on a task and control impulses.

Certain behaviors may also have an impact. A recent study from Children's Hospital & Regional Medical Center, in Seattle, found a link between early television exposure and ADHD. The study showed that each hour of television watched daily by a child between ages 1 and 3 increases the risk of attention problems by almost 10 percent by the time a child reaches age 7.

4. IT AFFECTS BOTH GENDERS. Conventional wisdom used to hold that ADHD primarily affected boys, with some studies suggesting that boys are seven times more likely than girls to have it. But more recent research has found the ratio is actually about three to one, says Robert J. Resnick, Ph.D., a psychology professor at Randolph-Macon College, in Ashland, Virginia.

It is not that more girls are suddenly developing the disorder. Rather, psychiatrists are starting to understand the subtle differences in how ADHD manifests itself in the genders. For example, girls tend to be less disruptive and may spend more time either daydreaming or chatting. They are also somewhat more likely to fall into the inattentive rather than the impulsive-hyperactive category, says Stephen P. Hinshaw, Ph.D., chair of the psychology department at the University of California at Berkeley.

5. MEDICATION HAS A GOOD TRACK RECORD. The most commonly prescribed medications for ADHD are methylphenidate hydrochloride (Ritalin or Concerta) and dextroamphetamine sulfate (Dexedrine or Adderall). It's not known precisely how these drugs alleviate ADHD, but researchers believe that they regulate levels of dopamine and noreprinephrine, the neurotransmitters involved in a child's ability to focus. And although they're technically stimulants, they don't cause children

IS IT ADHD?

THESE ARE SOME OF THE SYMPTOMS OF ATTENTION DISORDERS IN SCHOOL-AGE KIDS. ALL CHILDREN EXHIBIT THEM TO SOME DEGREE; IT'S ONLY A PROBLEM WHEN THE BEHAVIOR IS PERSISTENT AND EXTREME.

A CHILD SHOWS SYMPTOMS OF INATTENTION IF SHE:
- Fails to pay attention to details or makes careless mistakes in schoolwork or other activities.
- Has difficulty sustaining interest in tasks or play activities.
- Does not seem to listen when spoken to directly.
- Doesn't follow instructions and fails to finish schoolwork or chores.
- Has difficulty organizing tasks and activities.
- Is reluctant to engage in tasks that require sustained mental effort, such as schoolwork or homework.
- Often loses toys, books, or other important items.
- Is easily distracted or forgetful.

A CHILD SHOWS SYMPTOMS OF HYPERACTIVITY IF HE:
- Figets with his hands or feet or squirms in his seat.
- Leaves his seat in the classroom or in other situations in which he is expected to remain seated.
- Runs about or climbs excessively in inappropriate situations.
- Has difficulty playing quietly.
- Talks excessively and is often "on the go."

A CHILD SHOWS SYMPTOMS OF IMPULSIVITY IF SHE:
- Blurts out answers before questions are completed.
- Has difficulty waiting for her turn.
- Butts into conversations or games.

Criteria summarized from the American Psychiatric Association.

to be more active; rather, they help manage impulsivity so children can better control their own behavior. A newer drug called atomoxetine—known by the brand name Strattera—was introduced last year as the first FDA-approved nonstimulant treatment for ADHD. It works by targeting specific neurotransmitters in the brain.

None of these medications are entirely benign. The potential side effects of stimulants range from loss of appetite and temporarily slowed growth to tics and sleeping problems. Nevertheless, most experts feel the benefits far outweigh the risks. Many point to an NIMH study that followed nearly 600 children with ADHD, who were divided into groups: One group was treated with stimulant medication, another received intensive therapy, a third got a combination of medication and therapy, and a fourth was given routine care from doctors. When results were compared after 14 months of treatment, scientists found that the kids who had taken medication fared far better than those who had not.

Of the children given drugs plus intensive therapy, 68 percent were identified as "normal" (that is, they were indistinguishable from kids without ADHD) after treatment; in the medication-only group, 56 percent were rated as such. About a third of kids who had gotten only therapy and a quarter of those who had just been treated by a physician were identified as normal.

6. THERAPY IS OFTEN NEEDED TOO. Many psychologists say that medication alone won't erase a child's problem entirely: A kid with ADHD who has had trouble forming friendships may benefit from social-skills training or therapy to overcome low self-esteem. A child who hasn't developed strong organizational skills may need therapy too. "Medication increases children's attention, but once you've got their attention, you have to teach them how to behave," Dr. Resnick says. Behavioral techniques include various forms of therapy, counseling, and behavior modification. Because ADHD can affect the entire family, therapists usually work with parents and other family members as well as with the affected child.

7. ADHD MAY BE A LIFELONG PROBLEM. Doctors used to think that attention disorders disappeared by the time a child reached high school. But it now appears that ADHD may persist far beyond childhood. Research shows that between 40 and 80 percent of children with ADHD continue to have symptoms into adolescence, and more than 50 percent continue to have the disorder well into their adulthood.

Of course, the disorder looks different as a child ages. A 20-year-old may not seem as restless, but he may still have a hard time focusing during long classes or at a tedious desk job. Overall, it seems that hyperactivity diminishes—or can be channeled into acceptable behavior such as exercise or sports—while inattention increases as the years pass. Further evidence of both the longevity of the disorder and the genetic connection: A recent study found that parents of children with ADHD are 24 times more likely to have the condition than parents of non-ADHD kids.

As research into the disorder continues, scientists will no doubt learn more about the causes and cures. But for now, what's most important is that parents seek help for any child who may be suffering from ADHD.

Patti Flesher says she's glad she got help for Liam, who is now a well-adjusted fourth-grader. Thanks to his treatment, he can now patiently wait his turn for the slide, raise his hand instead of shouting out an answer, and stay focused on homework long enough to complete his assignments. "Getting treatment for him has made a world of difference for our whole family," she says.

UNIT 5
Curricular Issues

Unit Selections

Key Points to Consider

- What role do standards play in early education? Why must teachers be aware of state and national standards when planning learning experiences for young children?
- Describe the critical role teachers play in developing appropriate curricula for young children.
- What are some of the important components of education in Reggio Emilia classrooms?
- How can teachers provide an environment that is appropriate for all kindergarten age children to learn?
- What information should teachers be sending to parents about their children's early literacy experiences?
- What are some of the key essentials of early literacy instruction?
- Why is the role of movement so valuable in learning for young children?

 **Links: www.dushkin.com/online/**
These sites are annotated in the World Wide Web pages.

Association for Childhood Education International (ACEI)
http://www.acei.org/

Early Childhood Education Online
http://www.umaine.edu/eceol/

International Reading Association
http://www.reading.org

PE Central
http://www.pecentral.org

Phi Delta Kappa
http://www.pdkintl.org

Reggio Emilia
http://www.ericdigests.org/2001-3/reggio.htm

Teacher Quick Source
http://www.teacherquicksource.com

Teachers Helping Teachers
http://www.pacificnet.net/~mandel/

Tech Learning
http://www.techlearning.com

Awesome Library for Teachers
http://www.neat-schoolhouse.org/teacher.html

Future of Children
http://www.futureofchildren.org

Prospects: The Congressionally Mandated Study of Educational Growth and Opportunity
http://www.ed.gov/pubs/Prospects/index.html

Busy Teacher's Cafe
http://www.busyteacherscafe.com

The Educators' Network
http://www.theeducatorsnetwork.com

Technology Help
http://www.apples4theteacher.com

Grade Level Reading Lists
http://www.gradelevelreadinglists.org

In developing curriculum for young children, teachers and administrators are interested in various strategies and techniques that can further positive educational experiences. The lead article, "Beyond the Basics: Using the Project Approach in Standards-Based Classrooms" by Judy Harris Helm, helps teachers evaluate the steps they take in planning challenging yet appropriate curriculum for preschool age children. This article is part of the trend found in articles addressing the growing interest in standards in the early childhood classroom. Increasingly, preschool teachers are becoming aware of the tremendous responsibility to plan learning experiences which are aligned with standards to allow children to develop a lifelong love of learning along with the necessary skills they will need to be successful.

Programs following the philosophy of the Reggio Emilia schools of north central Italy are gaining more and more attention in their second decade of popularity with American Educators. In "Reggio Emilia: New Ways to Think About Schooling," Rebecca New presents an excellent overview of Reggio classrooms for those not familiar with the approach. The total focus on the interests of the children help to guide Reggio teachers to provide an environment where investigation and exploration are central to the curriculum. The analogy of children in a Reggio Emilia preschool enjoying a leisurely learning journey vs. children in a typical U.S. preschool program participating in a race

to see who can get to the end first works well when thinking about the two approaches.

Again this year the ongoing focus on kindergarten readiness is evident in "Emergent Curriculum and Kindergarten Readiness." Schools that offer a pre-kindergarten or developmental kindergarten class are missing the whole point of the kindergarten. Teachers in preschool and kindergarten, more than at any other level, are responsible for differentiating the curriculum and planning activities to meet the needs of all children. When the kindergarten is a place where all children who are age eligible to attend are welcomed into a classroom well equipped to meet their needs and interest we will have made great strides. Until then, we keep moving ahead at a slow pace.

As discussed in the preface for this edition, one of the key trends the editors noted while reading the hundreds of articles to make the selections for this edition is the focus on early literacy, beginning at birth. The well respected journal *Zero to Three* is the source for "Early Literacy and Very Young Children." Author Rebecca Parlakian examines strategies to introduce young children to reading. Educating parents and teachers of infants and toddlers about the role they play in introducing children to the many aspects of learning to read is critical for future school success. Children who enter kindergarten having an understanding of the reading process have a distinct advantage over children who are not aware of the meanings of little black squiggles on the page. This article is followed by "The Essentials of Early Literacy Instruction" which includes suggestions for shared book experiences, emergent writing, and conversations with children in a variety of settings.

This unit ends with four new articles each addressing an important issue for teachers of young children. Healthy discussion can take place about each of the articles and the role technology, movement, education, and creativity play in early education. The last article, "Building Culturally and Linguistically Competent Services" includes lists of appropriate anti-bias materials as well as a checklist for teachers to ensure their classroom provides the appropriate multicultural materials.

A number of the articles in unit 5 provide opportunities for the reader to reflect on the authentic learning experiences available for children. How can they investigate, explore, and create while studying a particular area of interest? Make children work for their learning. This unit is full of articles addressing different curriculum areas. Active child involvement leads to enhanced learning. Suggestions for project-based activities in literacy, movement, and technology are also included. Again, the theme runs deep. Hands-on equals Minds on!

Professional organizations, researchers, and educators are reaching out to teachers of young children with a clear message that what they do in classrooms with young children is extremely important for the children's future development and learning capabilities. Of course the early childhood community will continue to support a hands-on experiential based learning environment, but teachers must be clear in their objectives and have standards that will lead to future school success firmly in mind. Only when we are able to effectively communicate to others the importance of what we do and receive proper recognition and support for our work, will the education of young children be held in high regard. We are working toward that goal, but need adults who care for and educate young children to view their job as building a strong foundation for children's future learning. Think of early childhood education as the extremely strong and stable foundation for a building that is expected to provide many decades of active service to thousands of people. If we view our profession in that light we can see the importance of our jobs. Bring passion and energy to what you do with young children and their families and you will be rewarded ten times over. Enjoy your work.

Beyond the Basics:
Using the Project Approach
in Standards-Based Classrooms

What is the project approach? How can teachers use this way of teaching to engage children, explore topics in depth, integrate the curriculum, and address learning standards? Explore the possibilities!

Judy Harris Helm

When standards or required curriculum goals are introduced in an early childhood program, teachers sometimes think that this means that they can no longer use integrated, meaningful curriculum approaches. They fear that the time required to "cover standards" will prohibit the use of rich, complex investigations such as those that occur in the project approach. However, project work can be a vehicle for meaningful introduction and practice of academic knowledge and skills.

A good example is the Salt Truck Project which occurred in Rebecca Wilson's bilingual pre-kindergarten program in West Liberty, Iowa, in a program that has required outcomes.

This is what happened:

> One day during journals, Misael drew a truck and told me it was the kind that "puts salt on the road." This prompted a big discussion among the children about why the salt goes on roads and how the truck puts it there. I contacted our city service garage and arranged a visit from our city snowplow.

> Both the Spanish speakers and the English speakers in the prekindergarten program were wide-eyed and attentive as the city workers drove a backhoe and a plow-truck into the school parking lot. They jumped up and down with excitement as the backhoe loader picked up snow and put it in the truck.

> After watching the demonstrations, the children sketched the snowplow and backhoe loader. Books about trucks, plows, and snow removal were brought into the classroom. A web was made about what they knew about backhoe loaders and trucks. A word list was posted of words they might want to copy. They also represented their learning through painting.

> Later, after much discussion and planning, the children created a play structure of a snowplow truck. When the snowplow was complete, the children made a list of whom they wanted to invite to see their project. The students created their own invitations, an we ended with a snowplow open house to share their learning with parents, other children in the school, and the community.

Ms. Wilson used the project approach as one way for children to develop the knowledge and skills required by the standards for her program. The Salt Truck Project is a good example of how children become engaged in project work and how in-depth exploration of a topic extends into all areas of the curriculum, providing children with meaningful learning opportunities that address required curriculum standards.

What Is the Project Approach?

The project approach is an indepth investigation of a topic that is worth studying (Katz & Chard, 1989). It provides a structure for *approaching* the curriculum. For many early childhood educators, the word *projects* brings to mind learning experiences that they have seen documented in the schools of Reggio Emilia, Italy (Cadwell, 1997; Edwards, Gandini, & Forman, 1998; Katz & Cesarone, 1994). However the project approach in a standards-based classroom or in a school where there are required curriculum goals is significantly different. In both approaches to project work, the projects are indepth. Children's interests and questions guide the process. Children are deeply engaged and their work is documented.

Project topics are likely to be concrete.

In other ways, the project approach is different from projects in Reggio Emilia. In the project approach-as it is implemented in standards-based classrooms-project topics are more likely to be concrete (rather than abstract) and relate to the child's immediate world. Curriculum goals are integrated into project work. Projects usually involve considerable utilization of literacy and math skills during the investigation process. Often these projects focus on topics that are part of the required curriculum, such as living things (a project on worms) or places where people work (restaurants, stores, auto repairs).

Through projects like these, children learn concepts required in the science or social studies curriculum. Children represent what they are learning; they draw, paint, build, and create in many ways. This provides many experiences in problem solving, working with others, and representation.

The project approach, however, is not a curriculum. It is instead another way to meet curriculum goals. Projects coexist in classrooms where teachers do direct teaching, units, themes, and teacher-directed inquiry (Helm & Katz, 2001). Project work is an effective way for children to learn a significant amount of knowledge and to develop skills identified in standards or required curriculum goals. In addition, the documentation of the project provides evidence of the children's achievement of these standards.

Ways That Direct Teaching Can be Part of Project Work

Usually in classrooms that are standards based, project work is not the only kind of learning experience. There are also times when teachers are directly teaching children concepts or skills within the context of a project. The term *direct teaching* as used in this article refers to the teacher directly teaching a concept to the children, providing meaningful opportunities to practice, and then observing and assessing children's mastery of the skill. Direct teaching can happen at many different times while doing project work.

Preparing for Projects. During a year in which Ms. Wilson taught kindergarten, her class did a Combine Project. When she discovered that the children were interested in the number of parts on the harvester combine, she thought that this would be a good time to teach one-to-

Christian's combine. Christian was curious about how many pieces were on the front part of the combine. He counted the corn headers and wrote down the numerals, demonstrating the use of mathematical concepts and skills in the context of project work.

one correspondence and tallying. During another part of the day, she taught the children how to tally and demonstrated the process. Then they practiced tallying by looking at pictures of farm equipment.

Before the children went to visit a combine, she developed recording sheets on which children could tally the number of wheels, windows, steering wheels, and seats. She introduced the sheets to the children and taught them how to use them. Children practiced completing the tally sheets. Then on the field site visit, they tallied the parts of the real combine. This is an example of direct teaching that occurred in preparation for project work.

Within the Project's Context. Sometimes direct teaching occurs within the context of a project, while the children are investigating or representing what they are learning. For example, in the Salt Truck Project, the teacher taught the children the letter T. She showed them how to make the letter and where it was in the truck books that they were using. If teachers note how letters are introduced, they can be sure to introduce all the letters and their sounds throughout the year, at a time when learning each letter is most meaningful to the children. Letters that are not introduced within the context of a project can be directly taught.

Ms. Wilson also encouraged the children to sketch the salt truck and the backhoe loader and gave them word cards so that they could copy the words on their drawings

Kathy's project. *During the Combine Project, Kathy became very interested in watching the teacher write down dictation of captions for photos telling the story of the project. She then did her own writing about the pictures. She wrote, "We were watching," and "There are 8 bolts in the wheel."*

and sketches. She helped them make a book of trucks in which they dictated words to go with the pictures. She added truck signs to the block area. As she was doing this she explained to the children what the signs were for and how to use them. During this time, she read big books about transportation using a guided reading approach. Even though these experiences occurred during the children's project work, they are considered to be direct teaching because they are goal-directed instructional experiences provided by the teacher.

During Responsive Instruction. Another time that direct teaching occurs in project work is during responsive instruction. The teacher observes children's work, listens to their conversations, and then supports and extends the child-initiated learning.

For example, during the Salt Truck Project two girls were driving vehicles in the dramatic play area. They said they needed a map to know where to go. The teacher went out to her car, brought in her road map, and showed it to the children. She explained where the roads were and pointed out rivers and names of towns. Then she stepped back. The children studied the map carefully and eventu-

ally tacked it to the bulletin board for quick use. A number of children in the room used it.

Within a few days, children were creating their own maps, copying names of places, and writing numbers of miles and roads. Although the teacher was using direct teaching, she was doing it in response to child-initiated learning, so the strategy strengthened the children's dispositions to satisfy their curiosity, to figure our how something works, and to use the academic skills they were developing.

When to Teach and When to Follow?

One way that teachers in standards-based classrooms decide when to teach directly and when to follow the children's lead is through the use of anticipatory planning (Helm & Beneke, 2003). Teachers make an anticipatory web of concepts that children might learn, write in standards that these concepts address, and list strategies they intend to use as final assessment plans. In this way teachers can teach many skills to children that they will then use in the project. At the same time, teachers can incorporate IEP goals for individual children. Teachers can modify the web, and their teaching, as they discover what children are and are not learning.

Responsive teaching is more likely to happen when teachers anticipate what might occur in project work. For example, anticipating that children would want to write the word *truck*, Ms. Wilson prepared to introduce the letter T and show children how to write the word truck. During a morning group time after children began doing sketches and finding pictures of trucks in books, she. talked about the sound a T makes, how it begins the word *truck*, and what other words begin with T.

Children's interest in the topic is integrated into responsive teaching, so they are motivated to not only learn the skill but also to see the value of learning it. The teacher provided instruction because she knew that children would find learning about the letter T meaningful at that time. The letter T was introduced in a meaningful, integrated way when children were eager to write it.

Direct Teaching and Direct Instruction: What's the Difference?

Direct teaching, however, does not replace the mini-adventures that occur as part of project work when children follow their own interests in investigation. Teachers probe and support children as they learn to hypothesize, estimate, and synthesize their thoughts about a topic. It is also necessary that children be provided time for play, because play is so extremely important for young children. Play about project topics enables children to practice vocabulary and skills learned through their project work.

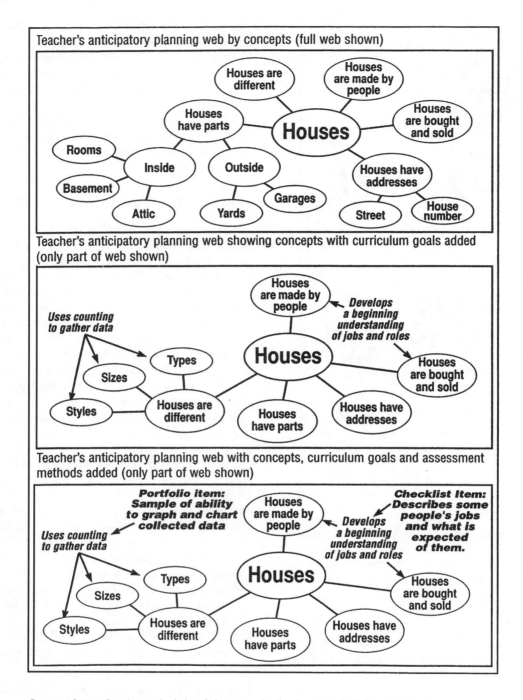

Teacher's anticipatory planning web by concepts (full web shown)

Teacher's anticipatory planning web showing concepts with curriculum goals added (only part of web shown)

Teacher's anticipatory planning web with concepts, curriculum goals and assessment methods added (only part of web shown)

One way that teachers in standards-based classrooms decide when to teach directly and when to follow children's lead is through the use of anticipatory planning.

These child-initiated and child-determined learning experiences are often intertwined in many project approach experiences in classrooms that are standards based.

In direct teaching, teachers

- provide instruction in knowledge and skills

- integrate instruction in knowledge and skills into projects

- create an environment that motivates children to explore and practice the knowledge and skills

Children are self-motivated to use their skills repeatedly.

Direct teaching, however, is not to be confused with direct instruction, which refers to a highly scripted method for teaching that is fast-paced and provides constant interaction between students and the teacher (Adams & Engelmann, 1996). In *direct instruction* there is predetermined content that is introduced in a required sequence. Children practice this isolated content. Direct instruction disregards the importance of child initiation and interest in the learning process. Although direct instruction is not likely to occur in the project process, it might occur during other parts of the school day and coexist in the same classroom. Project work does not provide all learning experiences children need and teachers will often use other instructional methods.

Benefits of Project Work in Meeting Standards

What projects can provide—that direct instruction cannot provide— is a context in which children can see the meaningfulness of academic skills such as listening, reading, writing, and using numbers. Many approaches, such as direct instruction, can teach children to perform skills or to repeat information. Project work, however, introduces children to the pleasures of

- satisfying their curiosity
- communicating what they want to communicate
- learning information they want to know from others
- finding answers to questions that they want to answer

Because children see these academic skills as useful, they are motivated to learn them. Perhaps even more importantly, children are motivated to use their new skills repeatedly and outside of school.

Most academic skills (such as reading, writing, and using mathematical principles in problem solving) are very complex and require practice in many different contexts. There is seldom a point at which an individual ceases to learn and perfect these skills. People continue to develop and refine reading skills throughout their lives. Although sound-symbol relationships and the ability to decode words are important beginning reading skills, many comprehension strategies are required for people to be efficient readers as adults, such as to read complex business plans. These strategies develop the more they are used and the more the individual is challenged to use them.

It may be helpful to think of these complex academic skills as *amplitude skills* with a range of performance that increases in magnitude the more people practice them in different situations. The concept is similar to adjusting the volume on the radio. It is possible to turn on the radio, but then the listener must adjust the volume by continuing to turn the dial. In reading, children must learn the basic rules, but it is continual, purposeful reading that enables them to become good readers. Meaningful, self-

motivated practice provides continuity of development of these skills. Even adults are still learning how to read. Think about the process of en-countering new material such as brain research reports or stock folios.

Understanding the alphabetic principle alone is simply not enough for young children to be able to learn to read. There must also be many opportunities where children are highly self-motivated to figure out a word, to try to remember how to write a word, or to write a phrase. This provides practice in reading skills at the same time that the skill becomes refined with an ever-increasing number of strategies.

In project work, many children are highly motivated to copy a word such as *salt truck.* They will then notice the differences between words for different kinds of trucks such as *pickup truck* and *fire truck.*

Likewise, in math, it is not enough for children to learn the skill of counting and adding. They also need opportunities to figure out when they should add, or subtract, or multiply in real-life situations. This kind of learning requires that children put forth mental effort and that they engage their minds in problem solving and creative thinking. This type of effort requires self-motivation. In project work, strengthening children's dispositions is important (Katz, 1995). If children develop positive dispositions toward reading and writing, they will read and write more, thus becoming better readers and writers.

Why Documentation Is Important

Documentation is an important aspect of project work and is especially important in classrooms that are standards based. As teachers plan learning experiences, they also plan for assessment and collection of documentation. If the teacher plans, to introduce the letter T responsively during project work, or teach it directly at a time other than during project work, she or he will also want to determine which children do, and do not, know the letter.

One way teachers do this is to devise a simple chart for use on a clipboard. Teachers can list children's names down the side and each alphabet letter across the top. They can put a circle in the column when they introduce the letter to a child, mark a minus the first time they observe or collect evidence that a child has learned the name of the letter, then change the minus to a plus sign when a child repeatedly shows that he or she knows the letter.

A similar tracking system can also be used for letter sounds, numeral recognition, or any other standard that teachers must monitor. By collecting information on a regular basis, teachers can then decide when to provide direct teaching for children or to offer more practice at a time that it is most beneficial to improving instruction.

Documentation also enables teachers to see whether or not the class as a whole is achieving the standards and what kinds of large-group experiences or additional materials might be brought to the room. Evidence of achievement of standards can also be recorded on a developmental checklist, such as the Work Sampling Checklist (Dichtelmiller, Jablon, Dorfman, Marsden, & Meisels, 1997).

If accountability statistics on standards are to be reported, it is important that the checklist be reliable and valid so that the data is meaningful. One common technique is to display a list of standards with documentation of project work. Others use a blank developmental checklist with standards that were achieved in the project highlighted with a marker.

Project work also provides wonderful samples for assessment portfolios. Because children are meaningfully involved in their project work, photographs and samples of their drawing and writings tend to capture children's best work and higher-level thinking.

> # Documentation is an important aspect of project work.

In Conclusion

The project approach can be used effectively in a standards-based classroom. The approach provides a structure which enables teachers to integrate standards into meaningful learning experiences in which children are highly motivated to learn and use knowledge and skills. Required curriculum skills may be learned through direct teaching before the children need the skill, in response to children's interests, or embedded in the project process.

Anticipatory planning enables teachers to anticipate what might need to be taught directly and what can be learned through the project experience. The project approach can also provide opportunities for children to practice skills they learn in other parts of the day, such as during large-group or small-group times. Documentation, such as checklists and portfolios, is a natural part of the project process and can be used as evidence of success. Most importantly, the project approach can provide children with engaging experiences that motivate them to learn much of the knowledge and skills listed in standards.

References

Adams, G., & Engelmann, S. (1996). *Research on direct instruction: 20 years beyond DISTAR.* Seattle WA: Educational Achievement Systems.

Cadwell, L.B. (1997). *Bringing Reggio Emilia home.* New York: Teachers College Press.

Dichtelmiller, M.L., Jablon, J.R., Dorfman, A.B., Marsden, D.B., & Meisels, S.J. (1997). *Work sampling in the classroom: A teacher's manual.* Rebus, Inc., Suite 6, P.O. Box 4479, Ann Arbor, MI 48106-4479.

Edwards, C., & Gandini, L., & Forman, G. (1998). *The hundred languages of children: The Reggio Emilia approach, advanced reflections.* Norwood NJ: Ablex.

Helm, J.H., & Beneke, S. (Eds.). (2003). *The power of projects: Meeting contemporary challenges in early childhood classrooms.* New York: Teachers College Press

Helm, J.H., & Katz, L.G. (2001). *Young investigators: The project approach in the early years.* New York: Teachers College Press.

Katz, L.G. (1995). *Talks with teachers of young children: A collection.* Norwood, NJ: Ablex.

Katz, L.G., & Cesarone, B. (1994). *Reflections on the Reggio Emilia approach.* Perspectives from ERIC/EECE: Monograph series no. 6. Urbana, IL: ERIC Clearinghouse on Elementary and Early Childhood Education.

Katz, L.G., & Chard, S.C. (1989). *Engaging children's minds: The project approach.* Greenwich, CT: Ablex.

Judy Harris Helm, Ed.D., is President of Best Practices, Inc., an educational consultation and training company located in Brimfield, Illinois.

Understanding Curriculum: An Umbrella View

By Judith Colbert, Ph.D.

What is curriculum? Chances are, the first response that comes to mind is that curriculum is a written document outlining topics to be covered or activities that will take place at a given time. Its format may range from a short-term plan, to a large book or e-document that sets out a step-by-step learning process that may take months to complete. But is there more to curriculum? If learning occurs all of the time, shouldn't curriculum have a wider meaning, something closer to "everything that happens"? Within that definition, wouldn't curriculum include both what is planned and what is unplanned?

A Double Perspective

Truth is, it is important to think of curriculum in both ways. Try to imagine curriculum as something that grows along a line that starts with a narrow, very specific view and extends to a wider, all-encompassing view. Another way of looking at curriculum is to picture it as a giant umbrella. This umbrella shelters a rich mixture of experiences that include not only the planned and unplanned events that occur in the child care setting, but also what occurs in the world beyond that may have an impact on what children learn. It is important to think of curriculum from this double perspective for two reasons.

1. **Having a specific plan matters.** The authors of *Eager to Learn* (2000), a report of the National Academy of Sciences, say that, although they cannot identify a "single curriculum or pedagogical approach," children who attend "well-planned, high quality early childhood programs in which curriculum aims are specified and integrated across domains" are "better prepared" for formal schooling (Bowman, Donovan, & Burns, 2000, p.6). In short, teachers in all settings need to have a plan for daily activities that meets specific goals.

2. **The big umbrella view also matters.** Everything that happens to each of us, teaches us something. What happens in the wider world influences what happens in the classroom. The character of curriculum is achieved from being embedded in "contexts of the larger society" that "interact with teachers, learners, other curriculum developers, and the culture of classroom life all at once—each interacting with and influencing the others" (Schubert, 1986, p. 9).

What Are the Responsibilities of Teachers?

Unlike children, adults have the ability to analyze their experiences, learn from what seems valuable, and reject what is inappropriate or appears to be of no benefit. Adults interacting with children have to recognize that children watch and learn from the adults in their midst, and are vulnerable to the effects of what is happening around them at all times, not just in formal teaching moments. If teachers do not wash their hands, the observant child is likely to ask, "Why should I?" As a result, teachers have additional responsibilities to 1) Model appropriate behavior; 2) Respond to unexpected events and integrate them into existing activity plans; 3) Filter external events; and 4) Provide a context for learning.

A Traditional Role

In carrying out these responsibilities, teachers fill a traditional role described by Joseph Schwab, an important researcher in the education field. Schwab (1973) described curriculum in relation to interactions among four elements: learner, teacher, subject matter, and environment, or milieu, as he called it. He saw curriculum as the product of a dynamic process, captured by a fifth element, a curriculum-developer who is sensitive to the nature of the individuals involved, the topics being considered, and the setting where learning is to occur.

All of this may sound familiar to teachers in early childhood settings who in most cases also fill a role, both formally and informally, that could best be described as a "curriculum developer." You focus on the learner when you try to "match" what happens to the "varying needs of the children" (Crosser, 1996) and to achieve what NAEYC calls "developmentally appropriate practice" (Bredekamp & Copple, 1997). You make decisions about how you interact with the children. For example, you decide whether you will be directive and instruct the children or whether you will permit what happens to emerge by standing aside and allowing the children to make choices. In either case, your decision is likely based on both what is appropriate to the child and situation, and your own preferred style. In addition, you search out and respond to subject matter and, finally, consider details of the setting as a member of a profession that has long understood that the arrangement and content of the environment influences what is learned (Colbert, 1997a).

Questions to Answer

In describing the process of curriculum development, Schwab was building on the work of an even earlier pioneer, Ralph Tyler. In 1980, Tyler's *Basic Principles of Curriculum and Instruction* (1949) was rated, with John Dewey's *Democracy and Education,* one of the two most influential books on curriculum thought and practice (Harold Shane, cited by Schubert, 1986, p. 171). In this influential work, Tyler proposed that curriculum-developers answer four basic questions related to:

- **Purpose -** What educational purposes should the school/child care program seek to attain?
- **Learning Experiences -** How can learning experiences be selected which are likely to be useful in attaining your learning objectives?
- **Organization -** How can learning experiences be organized for effective instruction?
- **Evaluation -** How can the effectiveness of learning experiences be evaluated? (See Schubert, p.171).

More than 50 years after they were formulated, Tyler's (1949) questions continue to be of value. They provide a framework for developing planned curriculum and helping teachers integrate unplanned events occurring both inside and outside the child care setting. As these questions are considered in more detail below, it is important to remember that each is related to the one that precedes it. In sequence, they create a cycle that moves from purpose to evaluation and generates yet another cycle, as the results of evaluation lead to the establishment of yet another purpose.

Purpose

The very first question teachers should ask is, "What is the purpose of what we are doing?" The purpose of any learning activity should be described clearly so that it is objective, measurable, and specific. For example, if you say that your purpose is to help children understand "bad weather," you are likely to have difficulty evaluating the results of your efforts. "Bad" is a subjective word. A rainstorm that spoils a picnic is "bad weather" but one that ends a drought is "good." "Weather" is also a very general word. It applies to a whole range of conditions. If you are not sure what "bad weather is" it is very difficult to evaluate whether your curriculum successfully helped children to understand the concept. On the other hand, if you say that your purpose is to help children understand a specific aspect of weather, such as rain, wind, or snow, you can find out from their drawings and discussions if they understand those specific conditions. It is also important to be clear at the very beginning about the purpose of what is happening in relation to both the "big picture" and the specific children who will experience the curriculum.

Linking Your Purpose to the Big Picture

Purposes that focus on the big picture illustrate how what happens relates to program philosophy. For example, consider how a sudden rainstorm might affect a planned program of activities in three early childhood settings, with different program philosophies, whose characteristics are revealed in distinctive responses to the question, "What is the purpose of what you are doing?" In each case, the teacher has an opportunity to integrate this unplanned event into existing curriculum plans:

- **Teacher #1:** We are providing a safe place for children. It is likely that this program is providing basic custodial care with minimum focus on curriculum. The teacher monitors the class to ensure that the children are safe, but pays little or no attention to what the children might learn. For example, if a rainstorm arises, they will bring the children indoors where they are warm and dry, but will make little attempt to discuss what is happening outside.
- **Teacher #2:** We are providing a safe place where children can develop emotionally, socially, cogni-

tively, and physically. The children in this program are likely to be exposed to a wide variety of experiences. In programs that focus on child development and where teachers are responsive to change, a rainstorm might lead to rapid revision of the planned curriculum. The teacher is likely to encourage spontaneous discussion topics such as what is rain, where does lightening come from, or what it means to be afraid of loud noises.

- **Teacher #3:** We are providing a safe place where children can develop emotionally, socially, cognitively, physically and gain respect for the world around them. In addition to focusing on child development, this program includes concern for the environment. In such a program, the teacher might respond as described in the second example, however, the discussion might also focus on the importance of rain as a source of water for all living things and a necessary ingredient in the production of food.

In every case, broad, "big picture" curriculum decisions are linked to ideas about the program's purpose or goals that are embedded in program philosophy. A clear understanding of the link between program philosophy and what happens in the child care setting helps determine answers to curriculum questions for the children in your care.

Learning Experiences

Answers to questions about your purpose provide a context for curriculum development, but do not give you enough information for creating learning experiences for specific children. For that information, it is helpful to consider what Schwab's four curriculum elements—the learner, the teacher, the subject matter and the environment—contribute to individual learning experiences.

The Learner

Decisions about what to put in a curriculum plan, or how to integrate spontaneous events into an existing plan must be made with knowledge of the specific children involved. That knowledge comes from at least two sources: what

---

Curriculum Development in Action

Purpose: To reduce conflict in the child care setting and help a specific child, Zack, participate more effectively in group activities.

Situation: Ellen has been a preschool teacher for several years. She knows that the character of the room changes from time to time and that the behavior of one child can make a difference. Recently she has noticed an increase in the amount of conflict among the children. Every time there is an outbreak, it seems that Zack is somehow involved.

Analysis of Behavior: Zack plays well when he is alone or in a small group and seems to prefer being in a quiet corner with a few playthings. However, he is always at the center of a dispute when he is with a large group of children. On the one hand, she thinks that Zack has difficulty socializing with others, but he functions well in small groups so simply relating to others may not be his problem. Given that the group size seems to be related to the problem, she is wondering about the level of stimulation. After all, he is usually fine when he has just a few playthings in a quiet corner.

Solution: Ellen decides to tailor the curriculum for Zack by including activities that would permit her to relate differently to him, depending on the situation. When he is alone or in small groups, she gives him freedom to choose his activities, but when he is involved in more complex situations, she takes a more directive approach and intervenes before trouble develops. Over time, she structures learning experiences that foster success in increasingly complex situations. She tries to ensure that he does not have to confront an overwhelming number of toys, and gradually increases the number over time. She creates a classroom environment with clear pathways and quiet areas where only a few children can gather, and provides ample "cool down" time by alternating periods of high activity throughout the day. As time passes, she records her observations of Zack's behavior and discusses her findings with his parents to determine whether her interventions are resulting in less conflict in the classroom and helping Zack to participate more effectively in group activities.

---

the teacher has learned about child development, and what the teacher has observed about the behavior of the specific children for whom the curriculum is being designed.

From the outset, curriculum developers consider the age and abilities of individual learners. Training and experience will give them a general idea of what is appropriate for children of a specific age. Only careful observation of individual children, however, will tell them what is important for a specific child to learn, and what is the best approach for helping that child to grow and develop. Teachers, therefore, need to make notes describing behaviors that are either positive or negative and take time later to reflect on how what they have observed might influence the activities they plan.

The Teacher

When planning curriculum, it is also important to think about the role the teacher will play in fulfilling its purpose. On the one hand, the teacher may be directive and require the children to be passive recipients of specific facts and skills. On the other, the teacher may be reactive, remaining in the background while the children largely determine what happens. In such cases, what results is often called an "emergent curriculum."

Allowing children to appear to take the lead in curriculum development does not mean teachers are idle. Teachers are busy observing, organizing, and responding. Wien, Stacy, Keating, Rowlings, and Cameron (2002) provide an excellent description of an emergent curriculum project that illustrates aspects of the teacher's role. Most of the teachers in the project were unfamiliar with emergent curriculum, however, the authors saw this lack of experience as an advantage: "It allowed them to take each step slowly and to observe children's responses carefully. Gradually, they created new possibilities for curriculum." In this project, each of the children received a handmade cloth doll with no features. After some discussion, the children set about to correct this deficiency in a variety of ways. As they did so, one teacher reports struggling "trying not to control" where the children put eyes on their dolls" (Wien et al., 2002, p. 34). Wien et al. acknowledges the difficulty of the process: "It wasn't easy. With planning that is responsive rather than programmed, teachers don't know what comes next until they collaborate on devising the best plan to suit the children's responses and interests" (pp. 36-37).

For some, the teacher's role in emergent curriculum is too passive. For example, researchers at Project Spectrum,

a 10-year research project established to test Howard Gardner's theory of multiple intelligences, regard learning as a complex interaction between the learner, the teacher, and the environment. In their view, the teacher is actively involved and provides support through what they call "scaffolding and bridging" (Chen, Krechevsky, Viens, & Isberg, 1998, p. 63). In contrast to the emergent curriculum study, Spectrum researchers believe that "teachers need to act as coaches and facilitators to guide and challenge students' learning and thinking. We encouraged the teachers to ask children thought-provoking questions and to pose problems, suggest different hypotheses, and urge children to test these hypotheses in a variety of ways." (Chen et al., 1998, p. 63; cited Colbert, 2000, p. 8-9).

From time to time, depending on circumstances, teachers are likely to adopt all three roles—directive, reactive, and interactive. As they do, it is important to recognize that the role they play helps shape what happens and, as a result, what the children learn.

Subject Matter

In planning curriculum, teachers can choose from a wide range of topics. As Tyler (1949) suggests, it is important that the subject matter supports the curriculum purpose. The purpose of the curriculum mentioned above is to teach children about weather. Clearly the subject matter for the learning experience should relate to weather. On the other hand, the curriculum may be designed to fulfill a much more fundamental purpose and weather-related topics may be only vehicles for encouraging the development of more basic skills and abilities. For example, on a rainy day, the children might exercise their mathematical skills by collecting and measuring how much rain has fallen. They might develop their artistic ability by drawing a variety of cloud formations or by using cotton balls to create a 3-D tactile version of the clouds in the sky. They might also write a poem about rain or learn some of the scientific thinking about the causes of thunder and lightening. They might talk about how they feel when there is a storm and whether it helps to be with friends.

Many readers will recognize these as activities that support Howard Gardner's multiple intelligences (Gardner, 1993; Colbert, 1997a). Whether they concentrate on Gardner's intelligences or some other learning theory, teachers who establish curriculum goals that focus on the individual child, rather than on a specific topic, have a foundation for flexibility. Although they might have planned to discuss bugs, body parts or some other topic, they can shift easily to rain if a sudden storm should arise and still accomplish their curriculum goals.

The Environment

Finally, the nature and organization of the environment contributes to the learning experience. As long as concerns about the safety of the children have been addressed, curriculum developers can shape the children's learning experience through the decisions they make about the physical environment. One obvious question to consider is whether an activity is more appropriate for indoors or outdoors. More complex questions relate to the organization of the space, which is closely related to both teacher roles and educational philosophy (Colbert, 1997a). For example, space that includes open pathways to activity areas promote children's independence and free teachers to work with individual children. In contrast, space encourages

wandering and conflict when it includes pathways that interrupt existing activities or that lead to dead ends or activities which do not hold the children's attention. Teachers in such settings spend much of their time sorting out conflicts and directing group behavior, at the expense of attention to individual children.

Organization

Having explored the learning experience from a number of perspectives, it is important to consider how those experiences are going to be organized to fulfill the purpose of the curriculum. When thinking about organizing a curriculum plan that will unfold over time, it is important to start with basic information or foundation skills and build toward more complex subject matter and abilities. When organizing a plan for daily activities, teachers must consider routines (diaper changing, washroom visits, lunch) and transitions (the times between activities such as line-ups) as well as learning activities. When organizing learning activities, it is important to consider a blend of quiet and strenuous activities, and ensure that major events are not planned for times when the children are tired or hungry. Teachers can solve many behavior management problems by scheduling events at times of the day when children are most able to participate. Once again, careful observation of the children's behavior provides clues to the ways in which the organization of activities can make positive contributions to the achievement of curriculum goals.

Evaluation

Finally, Tyler's fourth question requires that some means be in place to evaluate whether curriculum purposes are being fulfilled. Answering that question requires closing the circle, returning to the beginning of the cycle, and considering once again, "What is the purpose?" Evaluation will only be effective if the purpose has been clearly stated and if observations along the way provide evidence that either supports the achievement of a specific purpose or indicates that it has not been met. In either case, the results of the evaluation set the stage for the next curriculum cycle—findings from one cycle lead to the formulation of

new purposes in the next. If the evaluation suggests that learning has occurred, it is time to move on to new challenges. If it suggests that there is more to learn, the lesson can be repeated, with adjustments based on what has been observed.

Conclusion

Clearly, what happens in classrooms is based on observation and careful planning. No matter how careful the preparation, however, what happens is also beyond the control of any individual and cannot be fitted into any one theory of curriculum development. Children, like adults, learn from everything that happens. Curriculum is, in fact, a giant umbrella that shelters a myriad of events. A solid grounding in curriculum theory and a good idea of who participates and what questions to ask can help teachers and caregivers establish and achieve appropriate curriculum goals, and respond more effectively to everything that happens inside and outside the child care setting.

Judith Colbert, Ph.D., is a consultant who specializes in early care and education. She is the author of several articles on curriculum and a major study on the relationship between brain research and curriculum.

References

Bowman, B., Donovan, M.S. & Burns, M. S. (Eds.) (2000). *Eager to learn: Educating our preschoolers.* Executive Summary, Report of the Committee on Early Childhood Pedagogy established by the National Research Council. Washington, DC: National Academy Press. [Full report published 2001.]

Bredekamp, S. & Copple, C. (Eds.) (1997). *Developmentally appropriate practice in early childhood programs serving children from birth to age 8.* Revised Edition. Washington, DC: NAEYC.

Chen, J., Krechevsky, M., & Viens, J. with Isberg, E. (1998). *Building on children's strengths: The experience of Project Spectrum.* Project Zero Frameworks for Early Childhood Education, Vol. 1, Ed. Gardner, H., Feldman, D. & Krechevsky, M. NY: Teacher's College Press.

Colbert, J. (1997a, May-June). Classroom design and how it influences behavior. *Earlychildhood NEWS,* IX (3).

Colbert, J. (2000). *Brain research and curriculm: Perspectives on intelligence and learning.* Waterloo, Canada: author.

Crosser, S. (1996, September-October). The butterfly garden: Developmentally appropriate practice defined. *Early Childhood News,* VIII (5).

Gardner, H. (1993). *Frames of mind: The theory of multiple intelligences.* 10th Anniversary Edition. NY: Basic Books.

Shane, H. (1980). Significant writings that have influenced the curriculum: 1906-1981. *Phi Delta Kappan,* 62(5), 311-314 [cited by Schubert].

Schubert, W. (1986). *Curriculum: Perspective, paradigm, and possibility.* NY: Macmillan Publishing Company.

Schwab, J.J. (1973). The practical 3: Transition into curriculum. *School Review,* 508-509.

Tyler, R. (1949). *Basic principles of curriculum and instruction.* Chicago, IL: University of Chicago Press.

Wien, C., Stacey, S., Keating, B., Rowlings, J. & Cameron, H. (2002). Handmade dolls as a framework for emergent curriculum. *Young Children,* 57(1), 33-38.

Reggio Emilia:
New Ways to Think About Schooling

The Reggio Emilia approach offers educators a catalyst for change and for developing new kinds of collaboration in teaching and learning.

Rebecca S. New

How can parents ensure that young children are ready for school? How should teachers prepare for the children who arrive? Which assessment strategies can enhance students' learning, inform teacher practice, and engage parents in their children's education experiences?

These questions continue to plague educators despite dramatic new insights into children's early brain development and vastly improved theoretical understandings of how children learn (Bransford, Brown, & Cocking, 2000). Faced with expanding curriculum mandates amid draconian budget cuts, U.S. public schools have become the target of political rhetoric and tough-love reform initiatives. Opinion surveys convey little improvement in public satisfaction with U.S. schools; worse still, students often describe school as "boring, irrelevant, and mindless" (Carpenter, 2000, pp. 383-384). What's a teacher to do?

Go to Italy! Over the past decade, a small but growing number of elementary educators across the United States have joined their early childhood colleagues in finding new ideas and inspiration from the early care and education pro-

gram of the city of Reggio Emilia in northern Italy. Reggio Emilia is also increasingly a source of new ideas for educators in more than 40 countries, from Brazil to Tanzania to the Philippines.

How Did It Begin?

The town of Reggio Emilia lies in a prosperous area of northern Italy known for its civic engagement. Following World War II, a small group of parents began Reggio Emilia's municipal early childhood program, which thrived under the leadership of early childhood educator Loris Malaguzzi and the hard work of hundreds of parents and teachers. After decades of innovation and experimentation, city leaders sent traveling exhibitions throughout Europe and to the United States to share the Reggio Emilia approach. As news of Reggio Emilia spread, educators, parents, and policymakers began to take note.

What Is the Reggio Emilia Approach?

Embedded in the Reggio Emilia approach to education is an image of children, families, and teachers working together to make schools dynamic and democratic learning environments. Reggio Emilia has attracted educators interested in

- The role of the classroom environment in children's learning;

- Long-term curriculum projects that promote inquiry among teachers and children;

- Partnerships with parents that include collaboration in the learning process;

- Documentation for observation, research, and assessment; and

- "The hundred languages of children"—children's multiple means of expression and understanding (Edwards, Gandini, & Forman, 1993, 1998).

A visitor to a Reggio Emilia classroom finds an inviting environment, with adult- and child-sized furnishings, plants and natural light, large panels documenting the children's ideas, and very few commercially produced materials. The children are deeply immersed in their own dramatic or constructive play, or perhaps they are in small groups with a teacher, exploring how best to design the highways around a block city, construct a functioning water fountain for the birds, or draw a life-size dinosaur to scale. Later on, the teachers, armed with tape recorders and their own drawings, discuss the children's ideas as they plan for the next day.

A return visit in the evening might find groups of parents poring over the teachers' photos and notes and discussing how best to help their children express their mathematical ideas about distance and speed, or their quandaries about the meanings of love, or their fears of the dark, or, more recently, of pending war. On another evening, parents work in the kitchen with the cook, sharing recipes and making friends as they debate current events. Imbued in these activities are a deep respect for children's intelligence and a commitment to adult engagement.

Reggio Emilia's education philosophy resonates with key ideas in contemporary education, including Howard Gardner's theory of multiple intelligences, Lev Vygotsky's notions of the role of symbolic languages in cognition, James Comer's ideas about parental involvement, and Nel Nodding's challenge to create caring schools. Many educators note Reggio Emilia's similarities to John Dewey's education philosophy and to the play-based learning of British Infant Schools in the early 1970s. These key ideas run counter to a subject-centered, outcomes-based view of education and have challenged educators to rethink the purpose and scope of what they do.

Reggio Emilia and Early Childhood Educators

Historically, such challenges to the utilitarian approach to education have been more popular among early childhood educators than among elementary school educators. Partly because of the relatively autonomous status of early education outside mainstream public education in the United States, its educators have often felt freer to consider alternative approaches to learning (New, 2002). Nearly a century ago, the ideas of Germany's Friedrich Froebel influenced the establishment of the U.S. kindergarten as a place for children to learn in a nurturing and carefully planned environment. Italy's Maria Montessori furthered the development of environments and materials designed specifically for young children. British Infant Schools and the project approach are more recent international influences on early childhood education.

Reggio Emilia's ideas did not, however, always resonate with early childhood educators. When the approach first came to the attention of U.S. educators in the 1980s, early childhood educators had translated Piaget's interpretations of children's cognitive development into an emphasis on individual children learning in isolation from classmates. They viewed play as central to children's learning and teacher-directed activity as unnecessary or even counterproductive. Reggio Emilia served as a powerful catalyst in reexamining these beliefs and their associated theories (New, 1997) and revealed some of the biases embedded within the field's traditional views (Bredekamp, 2002). The guidelines for developmentally appropriate practice developed in 1987 by the National Association for the Education of Young Children (Bredekamp, 1987) had paid scant attention to these ideas, but the 1997 guidelines frequently cite examples from Reggio Emilia to illustrate principles of social cognition, scaffolding, and the role of symbolic languages in knowledge construction (Bredekamp & Copple, 1997).

Reggio Emilia's Appeal for Elementary Educators

The academic goals of elementary education have often been at odds with the developmental approach of early childhood education. Many parents and teachers continue to raise concerns about children arriving in structured and academically focused elementary classrooms for which their previous child-centered classrooms have failed to prepare them.

Elementary educators find that Reggio Emilia offers new perspectives on many current issues, including notions of readiness and transitions from home to school, ways of promoting family engagement in children's learning, the benefits of looping and multi-age grouping for using children's relationships to promote academic achievement, and the importance of staffing practices, such as teams of teachers, to promote professional development. The greatest attraction, however, is the way in which Reggio Emilia stimulates a rethinking of what schools do.

Embedded in the Reggio Emilia approach to education is an image of children, families, and teachers working together to make schools dynamic and democratic learning environments.

Reggio Emilia has helped bridge the divide between early and elementary educators in three ways: by revealing new ways for promoting children's academic learning in the realm of big ideas; by offering documentation as a tool for studying, sharing, and planning children's education experiences; and by provoking a new way to think about the role of the teacher.

New Possibilities for Children's Learning

Reggio Emilia's optimistic and respectful image of the child has influenced educators' views of what and how children learn. Conflicts between academic goals and child-initiated activities have lost their punch as teachers have experienced the benefits of hypothesis-generating projects rich and varied enough to provide authentic learning experiences for both adults and children. As children work together—for example, to create the rules for an athletic event—teachers notice how far they stretch their mathematical skills of measurement, estimation, and computation. Signs and invitations for such events serve as forms of authentic assessment when they reveal emerging skills and future learning goals. As teachers provide materials and purposeful questioning, they relish the ease with which children become deeply engaged in their projects.

Many of the values and practices associated with Reggio Emilia's interpretation of curriculum appeal to U.S. educators who have tired of standardized interpretations of effective teaching and children's learning. Thus, an elementary special education teacher in New Hampshire was inspired by Reggio Emilia to use collaborative projects to address individual education plan goals, taking her students with special needs into the community to explore their curiosities about plumbing and public transportation. An intern in a 1st grade class in a small Massachusetts fishing town drew on state-mandated curriculum goals while responding to children's anxieties about the impact of changing fishing regulations on their families' lives. The resulting community-based project included interviews with parents, tours of

fishing plants, and the creation of a board game based on new federal regulations.

Documentation for Discussion and Discovery

When U.S. educators first began to adopt the Reggio Emilia approach, they often confused Reggio Emilia's concepts of documentation with traditional child-centered observations. As teachers began to share and discuss the meanings of their photos, tape recordings, and samples of children's work with other colleagues and children's families, however, they learned how to "make learning visible"—their own and that of the children they teach. Project Zero's uses of documentation strategies to capture children's individual learning within the context of group experiences has also helped U.S. educators to see the value of the pedagogical strategy of long-term projects (Project Zero & Reggio Children, 2001). In groups and as individuals, U.S. teachers are now sharing their ideas, experiences, frustrations, and inspirations through national and statewide conferences, an e-mail forum, and a Reggio Emilia Web site (http:// ericeece.org/reggio.html).

The Role of the Teacher

What attracts educators most to Reggio Emilia's approach is how it changes their understandings of themselves—as teachers, as citizens, and as learners. U.S. teachers have reached the limits of their tolerance for the go-it-alone approach to teaching. More than half of the teachers responding to a 1990 Carnegie Foundation survey noted the limited time for meeting with colleagues, and less than 10 percent were satisfied with the opportunities available for them to establish collegial relationships (Darling-Hammond & Sclan, 1996).

The role of the teacher inherent in Reggio Emilia's approach offers new hope for lonely educators and corresponds with recent research on teacher collaboration (Cochran-Smith & Lytle, 1993; Fu, Stremmel, & Hill, 2002). Teams of teachers, such as those at the Crow Island School in Winnetka, Illinois, now travel together to workshops and conferences, bringing back new ideas to discuss with the whole faculty. School-based groups in Ohio participate in monthly statewide Reggio study groups. Massachusetts teachers meet regularly to share their documentation of children's learning in gatherings sponsored by Project Zero at Harvard University. Collaboration also involves parents: Two teachers in Ohio, frustrated by the problem of birthday parties in an economically and religiously diverse classroom, turned the issue over to the parents, setting the stage for more active partnerships with children's families throughout the year. All of these experiences have transformed the teacher's role from single expert to collaborative participant in an adult learning community (New, 2000).

Challenges and Possibilities

The reasons for Reggio Emilia *not* having much impact on U.S. elementary education are numerous. International education research has a poor track record for influencing changes in U.S. education practice in grades 1-12. Skeptics of Reggio Emilia's relevance to U.S. classrooms cite cultural challenges associated with Italy's philosophical roots, including the cultural support for close relationships between teachers and parents. Reggio Emilia's goals also stand in sharp contrast to a growing emphasis in the United States on high-stakes testing, a view of teachers as tools rather than decision makers, and a focus on individual learning in a competitive environment.

Others point to the practical challenges of building sustained relationships in an increasingly fragmented and hurried society; of planning curriculum that will be responsive to the diverse needs of children and families; and of finding the time, resources, and support necessary for what is surely more rewarding work—but also more work. Still others join me in cautioning against the idea that any one city, program, or set of guidelines can adequately determine what and how children are educated.

And yet there are many reasons to be optimistic about Reggio Emilia's usefulness in helping U.S. educators rethink their approach to public education. Of all of its features, Reggio Emilia's reconceptualization of the working environment of teachers may have the most to offer. The respect for children and parents is central, but the international success of Reggio Emilia's example is surely due to the respect given to teachers—as capable of asking good questions, willing to debate with one another, and committed to consultation with children's families. Even middle school teachers are beginning to think about how to adapt the Reggio Emilia approach to their instruction (Hill, 2002).

Of all its features, Reggio Emilia's reconceptualization of the working environment of teachers may have the most to offer U.S. educators.

Anderson (2000) notes that new ideas in education often weave in and out of public awareness for years, waiting for the right time and place for implementation. He argues that new common ground serves as a foundation for current reform initiatives, including the convergence of a shared understanding that

the rigid graded structure of schools must be overhauled; self-containment in any professional role is less than desirable.... classrooms must become busy, active, even noisy ... curriculum shouldn't be strictly compartmental-

ized; high expectations are good; participation of all players is essential and workable. (p. 403)

Reggio Emilia has much to contribute to helping to make these changes more desirable and, therefore, more likely. Such changes would go a long way toward contributing to a more dynamic culture of education as envisioned by Bruner (1996) and living up to John Dewey's faith in schools as catalysts for societal change. There has never been a better time to give it a try.

References

Anderson, R. H. (2000). Rediscovering lost chords. *Phi Delta Kappan, 81*(5), 402-404.

Bransford, J., Brown, A., & Cocking, R. R. (Eds.) & Committee on Developments in the Science of Learning, National Research Council. (2000). *How people learn: Brain, mind, experience, and school* (Expanded ed.). Washington, DC: National Academies Press.

Bredekamp, S. (1987). *Developmentally appropriate practice in early childhood programs serving children from birth through age 8.* Washington, DC: National Association for the Education of Young Children.

Bredekamp, S. (2002). Developmentally appropriate practice meets Reggio Emilia: A story of collaboration in all its meanings. *Innovations, 9*(1), 11-15.

Bredekamp, S., & Copple, C. (Eds.). (1997). *Developmentally appropriate practice in early childhood programs* (Rev. ed.). Washington, DC: National Association for the Education of Young Children.

Bruner, J. (1996). *The culture of education.* Cambridge, MA: Harvard University Press.

Carpenter, W. A. (2000). Ten years of silver bullets: Dissenting thoughts on education reform. *Phi Delta Kappan, 81*(5), 383-389.

Cochran-Smith, M., & Lytle, S. L. (Eds.). (1993). *Inside/outside: Teacher research and knowledge.* New York: Teachers College Press.

Darling-Hammond, L., & Sclan, E. M. (1996). Who teaches and why. In J. Sikula (Ed.), *Handbook of research on teacher education* (2nd. ed., pp. 67-101). New York: Macmillan Library Reference.

Edwards, C. P., Gandini, L., & Forman, G. (1993). *The hundred languages of children: The Reggio Emilia approach to early childhood education.* Norwood, NJ: Ablex.

Edwards, C. P., Gandini, L., & Forman, G. (1998). *The hundred languages of children: The Reggio Emilia approach—advanced reflections* (2nd ed.). Greenwich, CT: Ablex.

Fu, V. R., Stremmel, A. J., & Hill, L. T. (Eds.). (2002). *Teaching and learning: Collaborative exploration of the Reggio Emilia approach.* Upper Saddle River, NJ: Merrill/Prentice-Hall.

Hill, L. T. (2002). A journey to recast the Reggio Emilia approach for a middle-school. In V. Fu, A. Stremmel, & L. Hill (Eds.), *Teaching and learning: A collaborative exploration of the Reggio Emilia approach* (pp. 83-108). Upper Saddle, NJ: Merrill/Prentice-Hall.

New, R. (1997). Reggio Emilia: An approach or an attitude? In J. Roopnarine & J. Johnson (Eds.), *Approaches to early childhood education* (Rev. 3rd ed.). Columbus, OH: Merrill.

New, R. (2000). *Reggio Emilia: Catalyst for change and conversation.* (EDO-PS-00-15). Champaign, IL: ERIC/EECE Clearinghouse on Elementary and Early Childhood Education.

New, R. (2002). Culture, child development, and early childhood education:Rethinking the Relationship. In R. Lerner, F. Jacobs, & D. Wertleib (Eds.), *Promoting positive child, adolescent, and family development.* Thousand Oaks, CA: Sage.

Project Zero & Reggio Children. (2001). *Making learning visible: Children as individual and group learners.* Reggio Emilia, Italy: Reggio Children.

Rebecca S. New is an associate professor in the Eliot-Pearson Department of Child Development, Tufts University, 105 College Ave., Medford, MA 02155, becky.new@tufts.edu.

From *Educational Leadership*, Vol. 60, No. 7, April 2003, pp. 34-38. Reprinted with permission of the Association for Supervision and Curriculum Development. © 2003 by ASCD. All rights reserved. The Association for Supervision and Curriculum Development is a worldwide community of educators advocating sound policies and sharing best practices to achieve the success of each learner. To learn more, visit ASCD at www.ascd.org

Emergent Curriculum and Kindergarten Readiness

Deborah J. Cassidy, Sharon Mims, Lia Rucker, and Sheresa Boone

Recently, the focus on "readiness" in early childhood education in the United States has increased dramatically in the face of growing concerns about the number of failing students and failing schools. The National Education Goals Panel (Shore, 1998) endorses an approach to school readiness that focuses on five domains of children's development and learning: physical health and motor development, social and emotional development, approaches toward learning, language development, and cognition and general knowledge. Both the National Education Goals Panel, Goal 1 Ready Schools Resource Group and the National Association of State Boards of Education emphasize the following important points about school readiness: 1) all children are to be ready to benefit from school, 2) readiness constitutes much more than knowing the ABC's and numbers, and 3) as the backgrounds of children vary, it is not appropriate to expect all children to have a common set of skills as they enter school (North Carolina School Improvement Goal Panel Ready for School Goal Team, 2000).

It is important to note, however, that the concept of "readiness" cannot be addressed by focusing only on the children. We must scrutinize the environment into which they are entering. The following four "Cornerstones of Ready Schools" are identified in *School Readiness in North Carolina* (2000) as the requisite components of school settings that allow children to be successful:

- Knowledge of growth and development of typically and atypically developing children
- Knowledge of the strengths, interests, and needs of each individual child
- Knowledge of the social and cultural contexts in which each child and family lives
- The ability to translate developmental knowledge into developmentally appropriate practices.

The concept of "ready schools" implies the need for flexibility to address individual differences in the physical environment, in the curriculum, and in the teaching strategies employed. The degree to which the professionals in our schools possess an in-depth knowledge of child development, and their ability to use this knowledge when making decisions about individual chil-dren, is a fundamental determinant of children's success, regardless of their individual "readiness."

In spite of the promising language regarding "ready schools" and developmental readiness of *individual* children in recent documents on school readiness, the pervasive sentiment still seems to be that many young children are inadequately prepared for the rigors of an often inflexible public school curriculum. The response of many preschools, child care programs, and public schools to the barrage of information indicating that young children arrive at kindergarten unprepared has been a rapid retreat "back to the basics." This usually means a more academic and highly structured approach to early childhood education.

> *The concept of "readiness"
> cannot be addressed by
> focusing only on the children.
> We must scrutinize the
> environment into which they
> are entering.*

The available research on child-centered, developmentally appropriate curriculum models indicates, however, that such a retreat is unwarranted. High-quality, developmentally appropriate curricula have been shown to result in positive cognitive and social outcomes for young children (Cost, Quality, & Child Outcomes Study Team, 1995; Marcon, 1999; Schweinhart & Weikart, 1998). It is essential, however, for programs that espouse more child-centered and developmentally appropriate curriculum approaches to articulate the many cognitive, social, emotional, and physical developmental accomplishments of their curricula. Only then can they answer those parents, kindergarten teachers, and public school administrators who question how a play-based approach to educating young children can serve as preparation for kindergarten.

This article describes the curriculum activities in one child-centered, developmentally appropriate child care facility preschool classroom. In particular, it explains how activities are selected according to children's needs, interests, and abilities, and how the activities address the core competencies mandated by the public school system in kindergarten. This emergent or "grassroots" curriculum (Cassidy & Lancaster, 1993; Cassidy & Myers, 1987) is based on specific observations made of individual and small groups of preschool children. Teachers in this classroom of 3- to 5-year-olds use daily planning to respond to observed behaviors, and then facilitate learning and development for each individual child. Since this child care facility is located in the state of North Carolina, the authors delineate which competencies from the North Carolina Standard Course of Study for Kindergarten (North Carolina State Department of Public Instruction) are addressed through the activities.

> *When planning an activity, the teachers first considered the child's (or group of children's) interest and how they could extend the interest to increase understanding and learning.*

The various activities described here address competencies at or beyond the competency levels required in kindergarten. In the science area, for example, preschool children were involved in higher level skills of exploration and use of the scientific method—skills not included in the state Standard Course of Study until the 1st, 2nd, or even the 3rd grade. The Kindergarten Standard Course of Study for science requires competencies in areas such as identifying animal appearance and measuring growth and changes. The classroom pets provided an ongoing opportunity to learn such concepts, while also providing opportunities to learn about pet care. Another focus of the kindergarten science curriculum is to understand weather concepts. Each day, classroom conversations focused on daily and seasonal changes in weather and temperature. The lists of competencies in each activity description are not exhaustive. Indeed, they capture only a small number of the learning objectives met through the activities.

The Preschool Classroom

During the 6-month period of time described in the following curriculum strands, there were 15 children in this classroom, ranging in age from 3 to 5. Planning in this particular classroom is observation-based. When planning an activity, the teachers first considered the child's (or group of children's) interest and how they could extend the interest to increase understanding and learning. Then they shaped the activity to accommodate specific skills. If children demonstrated interest, or if similar play was observed in other areas, then the activities were further extended. Children also could request specific activities. The same activity could be repeated or altered to increase a child's experience/involvement and to target specific skills. Such

repetition was an important part of this classroom and allowed children to experience mastery and develop feelings of self-competence. Strands of interest (represented by child play) and planned activities extended from day to day, sometimes lasting for months.

Treasure Hunts

TREASURE HUNT

Social Studies Curriculum　　　　*Grade: Kindergarten*
Competency Goal 8:

8.2. Construct simple maps, models, and drawings of home, classroom, and school settings.

Science Curriculum　　　　　　　　　*Grade: One*

Competency Goal 2: The learner will build an understanding of solid earth materials.

2.02. Classify rocks and other earth materials according to their properties: size, shape, color, and texture.

Competency Goal 3: The learner will build an understanding of the properties and relationships of objects.

3.01. Determine the many ways in which objects can be grouped or classified.

Treasure hunting was a tremendous source of interest and the basis for many classroom activities from September to March. This strand was completely child-initiated; original activities began as a result of child requests and ideas. Related play often continued outside of planned activities, and lasted the entire school year, despite gaps of several weeks between the planned activities. The children began in September by hiding classroom treasures and creating their own treasure chests. In planned extensions, the children made their own treasure, complete with foil, glitter, glue, and cellophane. The children also conducted treasure hunts, which involved marking the spot where the treasure was hidden with an "X." For subsequent hunts, the children asked teachers to draw maps of the classroom and playground, putting an "X" to mark the spot of the treasure. These activities ignited the children's imagination, and laid the groundwork for role-playing and developing their sense of visual representation through creating and using maps.

The teachers continued the activities with more maps and hidden eggs. At snack time one day, the children used graham crackers, peanut butter, and raisins to create edible treasure maps. Several children began to design their own more traditional maps. The purchase of a related computer game further reinforced and enhanced the interest in this topic.

One of the teachers visited a gem mine in the mountains of North Carolina and brought back buckets of dirt and sand in which the children could search for treasure. As they found the gems/"treasure," the children discovered the properties of the stones, and determined how they were alike and different, and why. The children then classified the gems, expanding their knowledge about solid materials in the earth. The children eventually put the gems to use again as hidden treasure.

The children used their literacy skills daily to plan and create increasingly detailed treasure maps. One day a parent brought in a box of household materials for the classroom. One of the items was a jewelry box that reminded the children of a treasure chest. They began to build forts for the treasure chest and the treasure hunts became more of a large-group activity.

Bookmaking

BOOKMAKING

English Language Arts Curriculum   *Grade:*
Kindergarten

Competency Goal 1: The learner will develop and apply enabling strategies and skills to read and write.

1.03. Demonstrate decoding and word recognition strategies and skills.
- Recognize and name upper case and lowercase letters of the alphabet.
- Recognize some words by sight, including a few common words, one's own name, and environmental print such as signs, labels, and trademarks.
- Recognize most beginning consonant letter-sound associations in one-syllable words.

Competency Goal 4: The learner will apply strategies and skills to create oral, written, and visual texts.

4.02. Use words that name and words that tell action in a variety of simple texts.

4.03. Use words that describe color, size, and location in a variety of texts (e.g., oral retelling, written stories, lists, and journal entries of personal experiences).

Competency Goal 5: The learner will apply grammar and language conventions to communicate effectively.

5.01. Develop spelling strategies and skills by:
- Representing spoken language with temporary and/or conventional spelling.
- Writing most letters of the alphabet.
- Analyzing sounds in a word and writing dominant consonant letters.

Science Curriculum   *Grade: Kindergarten*

Competency Goal 4: The learner will increase his/her understanding of how the world works by using tools.

4.02. Determine the usefulness of tools to help people: scissors, pencils, crayons, etc.

In December, many of the children began to make their own books by stapling, taping, and gluing paper together. Some children cut pictures from magazines and glued them into their books, while others drew their own pictures. Teachers capitalized on this interest and enhanced literacy skills by planning bookmaking activities related to other activity strands, such as creating a book about feelings.

The children remained primarily interested in creating their own books, and so the teachers followed their lead. Many of the children were becoming interested in learning letters and writing words/stories in their books. The children began asking the teachers to write the words in the books as they dictated the story. They also asked teachers to write words for them on separate paper, and then they copied the letters into their books. Some children who were familiar with letters asked teachers to spell the words orally while they wrote the letters. Others were ready for the teachers to help them sound out words phonetically, so that they could try to write the words on their own. Some of the children could spell many common words, and used a rich vocabulary to tell their stories.

The children used different tools to assist them in the bookmaking process. Some children cut and glued pictures from magazines, while others drew their own pictures. Some asked teachers to write dictated stories, others copied letters and words teachers wrote for them, while still others only needed the word to be spelled orally or sounded out for them. Scissors, pencils, and crayons were used by most of the children. These tools were useful in helping the children create individual products.

As the children continued to extend their own ideas, repeat similar stories, and observe others' books, they developed more advanced skills. This strand allowed the teachers to observe and naturally extend literacy skills, such as letter recognition, writing development, and top-to-bottom and left-to-right orientation. The activity also boosted children's phonetic awareness and their understanding of story development. Many of the stories were drawn from the children's personal experiences and generated a sharing of ideas and interest in the work of others.

Classroom Garden

In December the children continued to talk about a garden they had grown on the playground the previous year. They were extremely interested in using the spray bottles to water the new plants that one of the teachers had donated to the classroom. The children began to compare the different types of plants found in the classroom—how they grew, or the similarities and differences in their appearance. They also observed that certain plants produce food, and others do not.

The teachers wanted to build on the children's skills of observation and their appreciation of nature. As it was not possible to grow an outdoor garden during that time of year, they assisted the children in sprouting beans in the classroom. In January the children and teachers planted bulbs and began to chart their growth. The children's discussion of different types of seeds and uses for them led to art activities in which they used seeds to make necklaces, collages, media table experiences, etc. The class also made plans to grow a vegetable garden the next month, and they began to plant some of the plants in the classroom. The children discussed when they needed to plant indoors and why, as well as when plants could be planted outdoors.

GROWING THINGS

Science Curriculum   ***Grade: Kindergarten***

Competency Goal 1: The learner will build an understanding of similarities and differences in plants and animals.

1.01. Identify the similarities and differences in plants: appearance, growth, change, and uses.

1.02. Identify the similarities and differences in animals: appearance, growth, change, and purpose.

1.03 Observe the different ways that animals move from place to place, and how plants move in different ways.

1.04. Observe similarities of humans to other animals, such as basic needs. Observe how humans grow and change.

Competency Goal 2: The learner will build an understanding of weather concepts.

2.03. Observe the seasonal and daily changes in weather (e.g., temperature changes).

Competency Goal 3: The learner will build an understanding of the properties/movement of common objects and organisms.

3.03. Describe motion when an object, a person, an animal, or other living creature moves from one place to another.

Grade: One

Competency Goal 1: The learner will build an understanding of the needs of living organisms.

1.01. Learn why plants need air, water, nutrients, and light.

Competency Goal 2: The learner will build an understanding of solid earth materials.

2.03. Determine the properties of soil (e.g., its capacity to retain water and ability to support life).

Grade: Two

Competency Goal 1: The learner will build an understanding of plant and animal life cycles.

1.01. Analyze the life cycle of plants, including reproduction, maturation, and death.

Grade: Three

Competency Goal 1: The learner will build an understanding of plant growth and adaptations.

1.03. Analyze plant structures for specific functions: growth, survival, and reproduction.

1.04. Determine that new plants can be generated from such things as seeds and bulbs.

As a result of these activities, the children gained an understanding that without water, light, and nutrients, the plants and sprouts would not thrive. They also began to understand the properties of soil (e.g., how the soil absorbed or retained water, and how soil supports plant life). By taking care of the plants, the children could observe how the plants grew from day to day and week to week. They could observe whether the plant survived, and when or if it reproduced. As they cared for the plants, the children observed the life cycle of a plant: how a plant grew more leaves as it reproduced, how it matured, and how some eventually died.

Discussions about growing things eventually extended to people and animals. One of the student teachers provided a butterfly habitat, through which children were able to observe the development of butterflies from larvae. The children compared one state of growth to another as the larvae became caterpillars, then butterflies. Caterpillars grown from larvae and chrysalises developed into butterflies. By watching these processes, the children could identify similarities and differences (appearance, growth, change, and purpose) in animals. Comparisons were suggested for consideration, such as human babies and caterpillars need kinds of food that older humans and butterflies may not need to eat. Every living thing, however, needs a source of food or nutrients to sustain life. Also, those needs change at different times or stages in life. The children were able to observe these stages and the requirements of each stage. The butterfly habitat allowed the children to observe not only the development of a butterfly, but also its movement in different states. The butterfly habitat also allowed the children to observe and chart how butterflies and caterpillars move differently to get from one place to another. The class eventually released the butterflies.

Discussing Feelings

In November the teachers initiated several group meeting discussions regarding feelings, with the purpose of helping the children develop a set of classroom rules. They believed that helping the children understand and recognize their own feelings would provide a base on which the children could develop relevant, functional guidelines for classroom behavior. Group-time discussions about feelings and their causes led to the creation of classroom books about feelings in which children used literacy skills and creativity. The children either drew or cut out magazine pictures and dictated the text of their stories to the teachers. During group time, the students made lists and charts, so they could compare and contrast their opinions.

Discussions about different feelings and personal reactions led to comparisons of physical characteristics. The children worked on life-sized "Me" pictures for several days in December. In February, they were still talking about their similarities and differences, so the teachers planned an activity in which the children mixed paints to develop colors that would most closely resemble their skin colors, and then again worked on self-portraits.

The children had enjoyed earlier activities that involved tape recording their voices and then identifying each voice. The teachers

FEELINGS/AWARENESS OF SELF AND OTHERS

Healthful Living Curriculum   *Grade: Kindergarten*

Competency Goal 2: Stress management.

2.1. Naming feelings.

2.2. Verbalizing feelings.

2.3. Accepting the normalcy of feelings.

Social Studies Curriculum   *Grade: Kindergarten*

Competency Goal 2: The learner will infer that individuals and families are alike and different.

2.1. Describe aspects of families.

2.2. Distinguish likenesses and differences among individuals and families (particularly with reference to cultural differences and skin color).

Competency Goal 6: The learner will characterize change in different settings.

6.1. Describe changes in oneself.

Science Curriculum   *Grade: Kindergarten*

Competency Goal 1: The learner will build an understanding of the similarities and differences in plants and animals.

1.04. Observe how humans grow and change.

---

planned another activity in which each child read a book into a tape recorder. As a group, over several days, the children listened to the tapes and discussed the voices, as well as the story. By February, the children were able to recognize that they were not static; they began to view themselves as growing and changing beings. A growth chart that was updated over the course of the year recorded changes in height, so that the children would have further concrete evidence of change over time.

Conclusions

It is clear that play in this classroom addressed many of the goals for children's learning in kindergarten, as well as those for 1st and 2nd grade. The children were enthusiastic about the activities because the teachers built and planned them around the children's interests. The curriculum in this classroom was not only developmentally appropriate and child-centered, it also served to prepare children for kindergarten. With experience in a high-quality, developmentally appropriate classroom such as this one, children will more likely be adequately prepared for the ever-increasing rigor of kindergarten competencies.

Regardless of the curriculum adopted in the pre-kindergarten or child care classroom, however, exposure to appropriate and stimulating curriculum does not ensure that all children will master concepts. It is critical that a developmentally appropriate curriculum be coupled with a developmentally appropriate assessment system that documents the progress of each child in the classroom. Many children will fail in a kindergarten or preschool environment that favors a rigid pass/fail system, attempts to measure only "facts," and in which assessment is conducted in artificial and unnatural settings. Indeed, the only way for children to be successful under such circumstances is for teachers to teach to the test under typical test-taking conditions. Under such conditions, however, it will be difficult to determine what children really know, especially if they are unaccustomed to such environments, as is often the case for children who come from developmentally appropriate classrooms. Only through developmentally appropriate curriculum and assessment, such as portfolio documentation, can we be assured that each child is adequately prepared for kindergarten.

Furthermore, three other essential components must be in place to effectively meet the needs of preschoolers:

- Teachers must be knowledgeable and able to facilitate learning for each child. They must possess a keen understanding of children's development and how the young child learns. An ability to determine the children's abilities, individual personalities, family cultures, and priorities also is critical. Teachers' role in observing the children's interests and ongoing play was the catalyst for creating this educationally stimulating environment. Their ability to capture crucial information that was relevant to this group of children, and to utilize it as the basis of their curriculum, transformed "ordinary" preschool activities into an extremely rich and stimulating learning environment.

- Communication with parents is essential in helping them understand how a play-based curriculum prepares children for kindergarten. Because play is such an enjoyable and engaging experience for children, it is sometimes difficult for parents to see how children learn through a play-based curriculum, particularly when many adults view play as fun but superfluous, and "work" as valuable but not usually enjoyable.

- Communicating with kindergarten teachers and administrators about best practices in preschool education, and its relationship to kindergarten entry, also is critical. Many public school personnel are unfamiliar with best practices in preschool education and need articulate preschool teachers to explain the relationship between play and the competencies and expectations of kindergarten.

With the guidance of knowledgeable teachers, these children were truly prepared for kindergarten and enjoyed learning during their preschool years. Teachers can educate parents and administrators about how a child-centered curriculum is also a readiness curriculum.

Summary

Much has been written, discussed, and opined about kindergarten readiness. Unfortunately, a recurrent underlying assumption places the burden of becoming ready solely on young children and their families. All too often, children are forced to be "ready" for an inappropriate environment that contains few of the components that would make it "ready" for them. Children *can* be "ready" for kindergarten, given an early education environment that 1) is engaging, age-appropriate, and child-centered; 2) includes a curriculum and assessments system that provides for individual differences; and 3) provides knowledgeable teachers who are responsive and capable of facilitating learning.

References

Cassidy, D. J., & Lancaster, C. (1993). The grassroots curriculum: A dialogue between children and teachers. *Young Children, 48*(6), 47-51.

Cassidy, D. J., & Myers, B. K. (1987). Early childhood planning: A developmental perspective. *Childhood Education, 64,* 2-8.

Cost, Quality, & Child Outcomes Study Team. (1995). *Cost, quality, and child outcomes in child care centers. Public report* (2nd ed.). Denver, CO: Economics Department, University of Colorado at Denver.

Marcon, R. A. (1999). Differential impact of preschool models on development and early learning of inner-city children: A three cohort study. *Developmental Psychology, 2,* 358-375.

National Research Council. (2000). *Eager to learn.* Washington, DC: National Academy Press.

North Carolina State Department of Public Instruction. *North Carolina Standard Course of Study.* Retrieved December 15, 2002, from www.dpi.state.nc.us/Curriculum

North Carolina School Improvement Goal Panel Ready for School Goal Team. (2000). *School readiness in North Carolina: Strategies for defining, measuring, and promoting success for all children.* Raleigh, NC: North Carolina State Board of Education.

Schweinhart, L., & Weikart, D. (1998). Why curriculum matters in early childhood education. *Educational Leadership, 55,* 57-60.

Shore, R. (1998) *Ready schools.* Washington, DC: Goal 1 Ready Schools Resource Group, National Education Goals Panel.

Deborah J. Cassidy is Associate Professor, Department of Human Development and Family Studies, and Sharon Mims is Director, Child Care Education Program, University of North Carolina at Greensboro. Lia Rucker is Training Coordinator and Sheresa Boone is Outreach Training Coordinator, North Carolina Rated License Assessment Project.

EARLY LITERACY AND VERY YOUNG CHILDREN

This article was adapted from Before the ABCs: Promoting School Readiness in Infants and Toddlers, a publication written by Rebecca Parlakian for ZERO TO THREE's Center for Program Excellence.

REBECCA PARLAKIAN

Early (or emergent) literacy is what children know about reading and writing before they can actually read and write. It encompasses all the experiences—good and bad—that children have had with books, language, and print from birth onward. Because these experiences unfold in the context of relationships, they are linked to and dependent on social–emotional development.

When one imagines an infant or toddler, it is often difficult to conceptualize what early literacy "looks like" for such young children. Schickedanz (1999) has identified several commonly observed early literacy behaviors for infants and toddlers that providers may use to recognize the emergence and progression of very young children's early literacy skill development. These behaviors include:

1. *Handling books* Physically manipulating books (e.g., page turning and chewing).
2. *Looking and recognizing:* Paying attention to and interacting with pictures in books (e.g., laughing at a picture); recognizing and beginning to understand pictures in books (e.g., pointing to pictures of familiar objects).
3. *Comprehending pictures and stories:* Understanding pictures and events in a book (e.g., imitating an action seen in a picture or talking about the events told in a story.
4. *Reading stories:* Verbally interacting with books and demonstrating an increased understanding of print in books (e.g., babbling in imitation of reading or running fingers along printed words).

What does research tell us about early literacy development in the first 3 years of life? The short answer is, not enough. There are several significant gaps in our understanding of the antecedents of early literacy skills, one being the period from birth to 3. Few longitudinal studies follow children into kindergarten or elementary school to confirm the ways and extent to which early interventions, either in the home or caregiving setting, shape later competencies in reading and writing.

The National Early Literacy Panel (NELP), funded by the National Institute for Learning and administered by the National Center for Family Literacy, has been charged with synthesizing the existing research regarding the development of early literacy in children ages birth to 5. The NELP does plan to analyze preschool children separately from kindergarten children. Although the NELP's report is not yet released, researchers Strickland and Shanahan recently shared preliminary findings highlighting the skills and abilities that "have direct links to children's eventual success in early literacy development" (2004). These skills included oral language ability, alphabetic knowledge, and print knowledge.

---

at a glance

- [F]or infants and toddlers, education and care are "two sides of the same coin."

- Instructional strategies that are most appropriate to the early years include *intentionality* and *scaffolding*.

- Intentionality means thoughtfully providing children with the experiences they need to achieve developmentally appropriate skills in early literacy.

- Scaffolding is the continuum of supportive learning experiences that more competent others (adults or peers) offer to children as they master a new strategy or skill.

Oral Language Development and Literacy

Language development provides the foundation for the development of literacy skills. Speaking, reading aloud, and singing all stimulate a child's understanding and use of language. Studies linking oral language to literacy address vocabulary growth and listening comprehension. Oral language development is facilitated (a) when children have many opportunities to use language in interactions with adults, and (b) when they listen and respond to stories that are read and told to them (Strickland & Shanahan, 2004). A growing body of research affirms this link between children's early language skills and later reading abilities (Strickland & Shanahan, 2004).

Parents are essential supports of their children s language development. The more time that parents spend talking with their children, the more rapidly their children's vocabulary will grow (Hart & Risley, 1999). Listening to books being read—and having the opportunity to discuss illustrations, characters, and storylines—is also important. The experience of shared reading, whether with parents or other caring partners, is integral to language development. Research in this area finds that the repeated reading and discussion of a story enhances a child's receptive and expressive vocabulary (Senechal, 1997).

> **Being able to communicate and being understood by those around them is a powerful achievement for very young children.**

Language development occurs gradually across the first 3 years of life, and indeed, throughout childhood. Speaking, reading, and writing are reciprocal, interactive skills, each supporting the other's development. For example, toddlers engaged in a pretend-play dramatic scenario (e.g., talking into a plastic banana "phone") possess not only the oral language skills required for this "conversation" but also the ability for symbolic thought, which is integral to understanding that letter symbols can represent sounds and vice versa.

Being able to communicate and being understood by those around them is a powerful achievement for very young children. It is also a critical social–emotional skill originating in the reflexive communication (such as crying, cooing, body and facial movements) that is apparent from birth. Intentional communication emerges as very young children are increasingly able to use gestures and words to convey needs, desires, and ideas. Most important expressive language (such as spoken speech) helps children communicate, to connect with another: to request, protest, greet or take leave of someone, respond to a comment, ask a question, solve a problem, and share their feelings and ideas (Weitzman & Greenberg, 2002). These interactions form the basis of the child's relationships with family members and the outside world.

Alphabetic Knowledge and Literacy

By listening to others and speaking themselves, children develop phonemic awareness—the insight that every spoken word can be conceived as a sequence of phonemes (Snow, Burns, & Griffin, 1998). An example of phonemic awareness is recognizing that *bug, bear*, and *button* all start with "b." Because phonemes are the units of sound that are represented by the letters of an alphabet, an awareness of phonemes is key to understanding the logic of the alphabetic principle. Learning the letters of the alphabet and recognizing the sounds within words are two skills that form the foundation for later decoding and spelling—which is linked to learning to read. Research has shown that phonemic awareness and alphabetic knowledge (an understanding of the names and shapes of the alphabet) predict whether a child will learn to read during his first 2 years of school (National Reading Panel, 2000).

Print Knowledge and Literacy

Print knowledge is a recognition of the many uses of the printed word and an understanding of how printed language works. The research base here emphasizes the importance of infusing the caregiving environment with print. For example, when children are provided literacy "props" (menus, newspapers, magazines, tablets, writing utensils, etc.), they will incorporate these items into their play (e.g., "reading" a menu and playing restaurant; Neuman & Roskos, 1992). This play offers repeated opportunities for children to practice and expand early literacy skills.

Exposure to environmental print—the print that appears on signs, labels, and products in our everyday environment—also contributes to a child's early literacy skills (Kuby, Goodstadt-Killoran, Aldridge, & Kirkland, 1999). Often, awareness of environmental print emerges organically in a child's life—for example, when a toddler learns to "read" a fast-food sign or recognizes the meaning behind a stop sign. Infant-family professionals can promote children's awareness of and facility with recognizing environmental print by pointing it out, discussing it with children, or integrating it into play activities (e.g., pointing out street signs on walks or noting labeled play spaces).

Social–Emotional Development and Literacy

For babies and toddlers, all learning happens within a relationship. The social–emotional context of a child's most important relationships—parents, family members, and infant–family professionals—directly affects young children's motivation to learn to read and write. In short, for infants and toddlers, the learning of a new skill and the emotional context in which the learning takes place are equally important (National Research Council, 2001).

Social–emotional skills are an integral part of school readiness because they give very young children the skills they need to communicate, cooperate, and cope in new environments. Over the long term, social–emotional skills contribute to a successful first year of school. For example, research has shown that the quality of children's relationships with their kindergarten teachers predicts how well those children adapt and learn, that year *and* the next (Bowman, 2001). In addition, at the end of the kindergarten year, the children who were considered to have made a positive adjustment to school also had the most friends, were able to maintain those friendships over time, and established new friendships across that first year (National Education Goals Panel, 1997). A positive adjustment to kindergarten is an important achievement: Children who are not successful in the early years of school often fall behind from the start (Peth-Pierce, 2000).

> # Children who are not successful in the early years of school often fall behind from the start.

School readiness means that children enter the classroom able to form relationships with teachers and peers, listen and communicate, cooperate with others, cope with challenges, persist when faced with difficult tasks, and believe in their own competence. The relationship between school readiness and social–emotional development can be summarized in five key points (adapted from Bowman, 2001):

1. Responsive, supportive relationships with parents, caregivers, and other significant adults nurture a child's desire to learn.

2. Learning requires a solid foundation of social–emotional skills.

3. The development of social–emotional skills depends on, and is responsive to, experience.

4. Children acquire new experiences within the context of relationships with the significant adults in their lives; this is why, for infants and toddlers, education and care are "two sides of the same coin."

5. Social–emotional development and academic achievement *are united priorities*. They represent a developmental continuum, a gathering-up of all the skills, abilities, and attributes that children need to succeed in school and, later, in life.

Social–emotional skills help children to adapt and be resilient, to resolve conflict, to make sense of their feelings, and to establish a new network of supportive satisfying relationships to depend on and grow within. Social–emotional skills enable children to concentrate on learning.

Cognitive Development and Literacy

Cognitive development—a crucial part of school readiness—is the natural product of warm and loving families, experienced and well-trained caregivers and enriching environments. Infants and toddlers do not need organized instruction to develop their cognitive skills. Young children's everyday activities and experiences provide ample opportunity for infusing learning into play.

It is possible to introduce cognitive skills such as literacy during the infant and toddler years. Rote learning, flash cards, and one-size-fits-all approaches, however, are developmentally inappropriate for very young children. Drill and practice may reduce children's natural curiosity and enthusiasm for the learning process and so undermine their interest in learning. Toddlers who feel pushed to read, for example, may become frustrated and fearful, and they may begin to associate those negative feelings with books. Although introducing emergent literacy skills is important, these abilities are unlikely to flourish in very young children when presented out of context as isolated skills (National Association for the Education of Young Children, 1995).

Until the body of research on the early learning skills of the birth-to-3 population becomes more robust, infant–family professionals are challenged to "translate" successful, research-based instructional strategies for older children to meet the needs of infants and toddlers. Instructional strategies that are most appropriate to the early years include *intentionality* and *scaffolding* (Collins, 2004). Rather than use a didactic approach, adults who work with infants and toddlers can creatively integrate these strategies into the day-to-day "teachable moments" that unfold during their natural interactions with very young children.

Intentionality, in this context, means thoughtfully providing children with the support and experiences they need to achieve developmentally appropriate skills in early literacy (and other domains). For example, an intentional provider may offer 14-month-olds the opportunity to pick up raisins and cereal by themselves (which builds fine motor skills critical to writing) and then later offer children crayons to experiment with (which gives them direct experience with writing and drawing). Intentionality is at play here when the provider recognizes the relationship between these experiences, offers these experiences purposefully, and understands the shared developmental goal they both support.

Infants and toddlers learn best when the adults in their lives provide opportunities for exploration and learning in their everyday routines and interactions. The concept of intentionality underscores the role that planning, knowledge, and expertise play in devising and introducing these opportunities. It is the cumulative effect of intentional teaching—the thoughtful repetition of early literacy experiences, the introduction of literacy props into play, modified teacher behavior (e.g., pointing to words on the page), and the creation of language-rich, stimulating environments—that yields the early and important learning that takes place in very young children ages birth to 3.

Scaffolding, a concept introduced by Vygotsky (1962), refers to the continuum of supportive learning experiences that more competent others (adults or other children) offer to children as they master a new strategy or skill (Kemple, Batey, & Hartie, 2004). Children need engaged, responsive adults in their lives who offer them appropriate opportunities to question and problem solve, to hypothesize and take action, to (safely) fail and try again. The richest opportunity for learning—in which children experience a challenge as they pursue a task but do not struggle so intensely as to become frustrated—is called the one of proximal development (Vygotsky, 1962). To help children perform in this zone, teachers must provide scaffolding that incorporates the development of new skills and concepts on the foundation of established ones. This scaffolding requires that teachers know each child in their care—their skills, achievements, and needs—and offer a careful balance of planned, teacher-initiated activities and child-initiated ones, as well. In working with infants and toddlers, a teacher could initiate the practice of reading to children one-on-one each day while placing books at the child's level to enable child-initiated, spontaneous exploration, as well.

> **The more time that parents spend talking with their children, the more rapidly their children's vocabulary will grow.**

In working with older toddlers, skilled teachers can combine a child-initiated interest that arises in the classroom—for example, a passion for castles—and create a series of teacher-initiated early literacy activities that are responsive and flexible. Using the castle example, such activities might include:

- drawing pictures of castles (which helps build fine motor skills for writing);
- reading books about castles; asking older toddlers to dictate stories to the teacher about castles; and
- making a cardboard box castle for the classroom and encouraging children to "act out" storylines using the castle prop (which creates opportunities to expand vocabulary—*moat, knight, king, queen, drawbridge,* etc.).

This "castle" project may last for several days (or weeks), depending on the children's intensity of interest. By remaining observant and responsive to the children's engagement with the topic and activities, teachers can gauge when the children's interest has shifted and when it might be time to introduce a set of early literacy-based activities around a new theme.

Supporting and nurturing early literacy and language skills in infants and toddlers is complex. These skills cannot be developed in isolation but, rather, emerge together with a child's growing competency in all domains—including the social–emotional, motor, and cognitive domains. When providers can recognize and observe each child's current stage of development, they are better positioned to use the strategies above to appropriately extend and build upon a child's existing skills and abilities.

Parents, School Readiness, and Early Literacy

Relationships—especially those between parent and child—play a critical role in ensuring that infants and toddlers are adequately prepared for school. Parents' beliefs about the appropriate ways to express emotion, resolve conflict, persuade, and cooperate with others have a profound influence on toddlers' abilities to get along with peers, follow rules, and cooperate with adults—and ultimately, to be ready for school (Morisset, 1994). In addition, children's positive, satisfying relationships with parents set the tone for equally positive, secure relationships with preschool teachers (DeMulder, Denham, Schmidt, & Mitchell, 2000). This crucial achievement is an important predictor of a successful transition to early education environments (Bowman, 2001).

Parents are the most important people in a child's life. Parents' attitudes toward education, their aspirations for children, the language models and literacy materials they provide, and the activities they encourage all contribute to children's language development. Parental behaviors also influence children's early learning. For example, research shows that the type of at-home language environment is the most powerful influence on children's language growth (Educational Research Service, 1998). Preschool children who live in homes where literacy is supported amass 1,000 to 1,700 hours of informal reading and writing encounters before entering school, whereas children without similar family support may enter school with only about 25 hours of literacy experiences (Adams,1990). Not surprisingly, most children who have difficulties learning to read have been read to one tenth as much as those who are the most successful with acquiring this skill (Adams, 1990).

When infants and very young children receive what they need from their parents, they learn to believe that the world is a good place, that it is safe to explore, and that loving adults will provide comfort, affection, and security. Children who do not receive this loving care expend a great deal of energy trying to ensure that these needs are fulfilled by someone, sometime. How much energy do these children have left for learning and exploration—and, later, for the new concepts and challenges that are a part of going to school?

The Role of Infant–Family Professionals in Supporting Early Literacy

The adults who populate the lives of very young children (including family members and the professionals who support them) make important contributions to children's school readiness. In working with infants and toddlers, teachers and child-care providers are reminded that care and education are not separate activities. They unfold together—one leading to the other, one supporting the other.

Children begin kindergarten with 5 years of accumulated life experiences. Because each set of experiences is unique, children have different perspectives on education, different approaches to relationships with adults and peers, and different levels of competency with social–emotional and academic skills. The ability of direct-service professionals to individualize their approaches to specific children and families is crucial to ensuring that services are meaningful and effective.

Infant–family professionals can support the development of very young children's school readiness skills in several ways.

Responding to children's individual needs and temperaments. Staff members in all infant–family fields can respond to children as individuals, build on their strengths, and support their development. Staff members in infant–family programs must be excellent observers of children. Responsive staff members search for the meaning behind infants' and toddlers' gestures, gurgles, cries, and glances. They wonder why particular behaviors

INTRODUCING LITERACY CONCEPTS TO YOUNG CHILDREN

Teachers can introduce early literacy concepts to infants and toddlers in a variety of fun, meaningful, and developmentally appropriate ways.

Oral Language

Read to very young children: The most important thing that providers can do to support children's emerging literacy skills is read to them and discuss the stories, at the children's pace and based on their cues.

Talk to children: Children learn language when adults talk to them and with them.

Rhyme and sing: Rhyming activities such as songs and poems promote very young children's knowledge of sounds of speech.

"Narrate" the child's day: Providers can describe what happened that day, which creates opportunities to expand children's vocabulary.

Alphabetic Knowledge

Repeat letter sounds: Providers can point out and say the letters they see in signs or books.

Make a game of repetition: Children love knowing what comes next in a story and anticipating a picture or phrase.

Sing the ABC song and read alphabet books: Both verbal and visual experience with letters help children learn the alphabet.

Play with letters: Arranging and rearranging magnetic letters, alphabet blocks, and puzzles help children with letter recognition and letter sounds.

Use the child's name: Providers can teach children their own names and the sounds that make up their names.

Print Awareness

Make literacy part of playtime: Providers can stock children's play spaces with literacy "props."

Encourage children's own writing: Make paper and writing utensils (markers, crayons, fingerpaint, chalk) available to children. Let infants "write" in applesauce or yogurt.

Point out signs in your neighborhood: When taking walks, providers can look for opportunities to point out stop signs, street signs, and school crossing signs.

Show how adults use writing: Providers can encourage children to watch as they write notes to themselves or colleagues, make a shopping list, or compose the class's weekly update for parents. Providers can also give older toddlers the opportunity to "write" (dictate) notes to one another and family members.

Help children "read" their food: When preparing meals and snacks, providers should read children the words on the food labels, or ask them to "read" the labels to themselves.

Read while you're out and about: Pointing out and reading the signs that say "women" and "men," "exit" and "entrance," and "open" and "closed" are easy ways of sensitizing children to environmental print. Point to the words while reading them aloud to children.

occur, come up with educated guesses to explain why, and interact with children to determine whether their guesses are correct.

Encouraging children's curiosity and exploration. If caregivers select all the "lessons" that are to be learned or provide an environment that is not stimulating, children will push to do activities that interest them or to create their own stimulation. Often children are told "No," "Stop," or "Bad"—not because these children are not learning, but because they are following their own learning agenda or searching for experiences that interest them. Although setting some limits is important and helps keep children safe, it is equally important to allow children to engage in self-directed learning—that is, to follow their interests and allow them to become immersed in new ideas. This approach supports their development of persistence, motivation, critical thinking, and logical thinking skills.

Introducing early literacy and numeracy concepts in developmentally appropriate ways. A program that serves infants and toddlers can introduce literacy concepts in ways that are fun, meaningful, and developmentally appropriate for very young children (Collins, 2004). (See the sidebar on this page for examples.)

Appreciating the magic of everyday moments'. Children often develop social–emotional skills not in specially planned lessons but in the context of their daily interactions and experiences—such as napping, eating, playing, and diapering (Lerner, Dambra, & Levine, 2000). When staff members use these everyday moments to support and expand children's current repertoire of social–emotional skills, they help prepare young ones to enter the larger world with all of its demands.

To help parents do the same, staff members should emphasize the important learning that takes place in everyday interactions. For example, the give-and-take of parents imitating their babies' babbling teaches children about turn-taking and communication and, from a social–emotional perspective, that they are important, loved, and listened to. Observing this ongoing, daily learning also encourage parents' pride in and enjoyment of their children.

Establishing strong working relationships with families. When interactions between parents and staff members are open and collaborative, parents receive the support they need to learn and grow in their new roles as mothers and fathers. Parents are then better able to support their children's development with affection, responsiveness, and sensitivity. Staff members can provide parents with an outlet in which to explore the questions and challenges associated with child rearing; wonder about their children's behavior, needs, and motivations; and brainstorm about how best to respond.

Recognizing and respecting family culture. By entering a dialogue with parents about how they want their child raised and what family or cultural practices they value, staff members let families know that they are respected

partners in the program. If it is difficult to incorporate families' wishes into program practices, a solid foundation of respect and openness makes negotiating these differences easier and more helpful for everyone.

Reducing parents' anxiety about school success. A newborn does not need expensive "developmental" toys or flash cards to become intellectually curious and academically successful. Staff members can help parents understand that the foundation of school readiness is in supportive, nurturing relationships that provide children with a safe "home base" from which they can explore, learn, and grow. This close parent–child bond also helps children develop the key social–emotional competencies that are necessary for a successful transition to school.

Providing anticipatory guidance. When staff members help parents anticipate their children's developmental changes, parents are better prepared to support their children's learning. Armed with accurate information, parents can respond to their children's changing developmental needs in appropriate ways. Parents' ability to meet their children's needs contributes to a greater sense of competency and confidence, which in turn strengthens the family as a whole.

> **Speaking, reading, and writing are reciprocal, interactive skills, each supporting the other's development.**

Supporting inclusive environments. Very young children with special needs may face unique challenges in achieving the skills (social–emotional or otherwise) necessary to enter school. Inclusion is an important intervention because it draws children with disabilities into the mainstream. Ongoing interactions with typically developing children may help support the development of children with disabilities. Inclusion is also important for children whose development is more typical, because diversity helps them to broaden their experiences and learning and to develop empathy.

Conclusion

Developing early literacy skills across the first 3 years of life is a critical ingredient in ensuring that children are school-ready at age 5. By using all domains of development as well as all their senses, children develop the foundational skills necessary for cultivating a lifelong love of literacy. Supported by healthy relationships formed early in life with parents and caregivers, children experience the world as both safe and exhilarating, they view new challenges as exciting, and they believe themselves to be competent learners. In short, infants and toddlers have a lust for life and learning. When we reject the notion of children as passive "sponges," we are able to truly follow in "the wake of a curious, motivated, social child who is dying to learn" (Lally, 2001).

REFERENCES

Adams. M. J. (1990). *Beginning to read: Thinking and learning about print*. Cambridge, MA: MIT Press.

Bowman. B. (2001. December). *Eager to learn*. Plenary presentation at the 16th Annual National Training Institute of ZERO TO THREE, San Diego, CA.

Collins, R. (2004, April). *Early steps to language and literacy*. Workshop presented at the meeting of the National Head Start Association, Anaheim, CA.

DeMulder, E. K., Denham, S., Schmidt, M., & Mitchell, J. (2000). Q-Sort assessment of attachment security during the preschool years: Links from home to school *Developmental Psychology, 36*(2), 274–282.

Educational Research Service. (1998). *Reading aloud to children*. ERS Info-File #F1-342. Arlington, VA: Author.

Hart, B., & Risley, T. R. (1999). *The social world of children learning to talk*. Baltimore: Paul H. Brookes.

Kemple, K. M., Batey, J. J., & Hartie, L. C. (2004). Music play: Creating centers for musical play and exploration. *Young Children, 59*(4), 30–37.

Kuby, P., Goodstadt-Killoran, I., Aldridge, J., & Kirkland, L. (1999). A review of the research on environmental print. *Journal of Instructional Psychology, 26*(3), 173–183.

Lally, R. (2001, December). *School readiness*. Plenary presentation at the 6th Annual National Training Institute of ZERO TO THREE, San Diego, CA.

Lerner, C., Dombro, L., & Levine, K. (2000). *The magic of everyday moments'* [series]. Washington, DC: ZERO TO THREE.

Morisset, C. E. (1994, October). *School readiness: Parents and professionals speak on social and emotional needs of young children* [Report No. 26]. Center on Families, Communities, Schools, and Children's Learning. Retrieved January 25, 2002, from `http://readyweb.crc.uiuc.edu/library/1994/cfam-sr/cfam-sr.html`

National Association for the Education of Young Children. (1995). *NAEYC position statement on school readiness*. Revived January 24, 2002, from `www.naeyc.org/resources/position_statements/psredy98.htm`

National Education Goals Panel. (1997). *Getting a good start in school*. Retrieved January 23, 2002, from `http://www.negp.gov/Reports/good-sta.htm`

National Reading Panel. (2000). *Report of the National Reading Panel. Teaching children to read: An evidence-based assessment of the scientific research literature on reading and its implications for reading instruction*.

THE ESSENTIALS OF EARLY LITERACY INSTRUCTION

Kathleen A. Roskos, James F. Christie, and Donald J. Richgels

*T*he cumulative and growing research on literacy development in young children is rapidly becoming a body of knowledge that can serve as the basis for the everyday practice of early literacy education (IRA & NAEYC 1998; National Research Council 1998; Yaden, Rowe, & MacGillivary 2000; Neuman & Dickinson 2001; NAEYC & NAECS/SDE 2002). Although preliminary, the knowledge base outlines children's developmental patterns in critical areas, such as phonological and print awareness. It serves as a resource for designing early literacy programs and specific instructional practices. In addition, it offers reliable and valid observational data for grounding approaches to early reading assessment.

That we know more about literacy development and acquisition, however, does not let us escape a central issue of all early education: What *should* young children be learning and doing before they go to kindergarten? What early literacy instruction should children receive? What should it emphasize—head (cognition) or heart (motivation) or both?

Real-life answers to these questions rarely point directly to this or that, but rather they are somewhere in the middle, including both empirical evidence and professional wisdom. While we will continue to wrestle with these complicated questions, we must take practical action so that our growing understanding in early literacy supports the young child as a wholesome, developing person.

What then are the essentials of early literacy instruction? What content should be included, and how should it be taught in early education settings? Our first response to these complex questions is described below in a skeletal framework for action. We briefly define early literacy, so as to identify what young children need to know and be able to do if they are to enjoy the fruits of literacy, including valuable dispositions that strengthen their literacy interactions. Then we describe two examples of instruction that support children's reading and writing learning before they enter the primary grades.

With the imagery of Pip's remark from *Great Expectations* in mind, we hope to show that well-considered early literacy instruction is certainly not a bramble-bush for our very young children, but rather a welcoming environment in which to learn to read and write.

THE LEARNING DOMAIN

Today a variety of terms are used to refer to the preschool phase of literacy development—emerging literacy, emergent reading, emergent writing, early reading, symbolic tools, and so on. We have adopted the term *early literacy* as the most comprehensive yet concise description of the knowledge, skills, and dispositions that precede learning to read and write in the primary grades (K–3). We chose this term because, in the earliest phases of literacy development, forming reading and writing concepts and skills is a dynamic process (National Research Council 1998, 2000).

Young children's grasp of print as a tool for making meaning and as a way to communicate combines both oral and written language. Children draw and scribble and "read" their marks by attributing meaning to them through their talk and action. They listen to stories read aloud and learn how to orient their bodies and minds to the technicalities of books and print.

When adults say, "Here, help me hold the book and turn the pages," they teach children basic conventions of book handling and the left-to-right, top-to-bottom orientation of English. When they guide children's small hands and eyes to printed words on the page, they show them that this is the source of the reading and that the marks have meaning. When they explain, "This says 'goldfish'. Do you remember our goldfish? We named it Baby Flipper. We put its name on the fishbowl," they help children understand the connection between printed words, speech, and real experience.

Children's early reading and writing learning, in other words, is embedded in a larger developing system of oral communication. Early literacy is an emerging set of relationships between reading and writing. These relationships are situated in a broader communication network of speaking and listening, whose components work together to help the learner negotiate the world and make sense of experience (Thelen & Smith 1995; Lewis 2000; Siegler 2000). Young children need

Essential Early Literacy Teaching Strategies

Effective early literacy instruction provides preschool children with developmentally appropriate settings, materials, experiences, and social support that encourage early forms of reading and writing to flourish and develop into conventional literacy. These basics can be broken down into eight specific strategies with strong research links to early literacy skills and, in some cases, with later elementary-grade reading achievement. Note that play has a prominent role in strategies 5, 6, and 8. Linking literacy and play is one of the most effective ways to make literacy activities meaningful and enjoyable for children.

1. Rich teacher talk

Engage children in rich conversations in large group, small group, and one-to-one settings. When talking with children,

- use rare words—words that children are unlikely to encounter in everyday conversations;
- extend children's comments into more descriptive, grammatically mature statements;
- discuss cognitively challenging content—topics that are not immediately present, that involve knowledge about the world, or that encourage children to reflect on language as an object;
- listen and respond to what children have to say.

2. Storybook reading

Read aloud to your class once or twice a day, exposing children to numerous enjoyable stories, poems, and information books. Provide supportive conversations and activities before, during, and after reading. Repeated reading of favorite books builds familiarity, increasing the likelihood that children will attempt to read those books on their own.

3. Phonological awareness activities

Provide activities that increase children's awareness of the sounds of language. These activities include playing games and listening to stories, poems, and songs that involve *rhyme*—identifying words that end with the same sound (e.g., Jack and Jill went up the hill);
alliteration—recognizing when several words begin with the same sound (e.g., Peter Piper picked a peck of pickled peppers);
sound matching—deciding which of several words begins with a specific sound (e.g., show a child pictures of a bird, a dog, and a cat and ask which one starts with the /d/ sound).
Try to make these activities fun and enjoyable.

4. Alphabet activities

Engage children with materials that promote identification of the letters of the alphabet, including

- ABC books
- magnetic letters
- alphabet blocks and puzzles
- alphabet charts

Use direct instruction to teach letter names that have personal meaning to children ("Look, Jennifer's and Joey's names both start with the same letter. What is the letter's name? That's right, they both start with j").

5. Support for emergent reading

Encourage children to attempt to read books and other types of print by providing

- a well-designed library center, stocked with lots of good books;
- repeated readings of favorite books (to familiarize children with books and encourage independent reading);
- functional print linked to class activities (e.g., daily schedules, helper charts, toy shelf labels);
- play-related print (e.g., signs, menus, employee name tags in a restaurant play center).

6. Support for emergent writing

Encourage children to use emergent forms of writing, such as scribble writing, random letter strings, and invented spelling, by providing

- a writing center stocked with pens, pencils, markers, paper, and book-making materials;
- shared writing demonstrations in which the teacher writes down text dictated by children;
- functional writing opportunities that are connected to class activities (e.g., sign-up sheets for popular centers, library book check-out slips, Do not touch! signs);
- play-related writing materials (e.g., pencils and notepads for taking orders in a restaurant play center).

7. Shared book experience

Read Big Books and other enlarged texts to children, and point to the print as it is read. While introducing and reading the text, draw children's attention to basic concepts of print such as

- the distinction between pictures and print;
- left-to-right, top-to-bottom sequence;
- book concepts (cover, title, page).

Read favorite stories repeatedly, and encourage children to read along on the parts of the story they remember.

8. Integrated, content-focused activities

Provide opportunities for children to investigate topics that are of interest to them. The objective is for children to use oral language, reading, and writing to learn about the world. Once a topic has been identified, children can

- listen to the teacher read topic-related information books and look at the books on their own;
- gather data using observation, experiments, interviews, and such;
- use emergent writing to record observations and information; and
- engage in dramatic play to consolidate and express what they have learned.

As a result of such projects, children's language and literacy skills are advanced, and they gain valuable background knowledge.

writing to help them learn about reading, they need reading to help them learn about writing; and they need oral language to help them learn about both.

What early literacy instruction should children receive? What should it emphasize—head (cognition) or heart (motivation) or both?

Young children need writing to help them learn about reading, they need reading to help them learn about writing; and they need oral language to help them learn about both.

NECESSARY CONTENT AND DISPOSITIONS IN EARLY LITERACY

Early literacy holds much that young children might learn. Yet we cannot teach everything and must make choices about what content to teach and which dispositions to encourage. High-quality research provides our best evidence for setting priorities for what to address and how.

Recent reviews of research indicate at least three critical content categories in early literacy: oral language comprehension, phonological awareness, and print knowledge. They also identify at least one important disposition, print motivation—the frequency of requests for shared reading and engagement in print-related activities, such as pretend writing (Senechal et al. 2001; Layzer 2002; Neuman 2002; Lonigan & Whitehurst in press).

Children need to learn mainstay concepts and skills of written language from which more complex and elaborated understandings and motivations arise, such as grasp of

the alphabetic principle, recognition of basic text structures, sense of genre, and a strong desire to know. They need to learn phonological awareness, alphabet letter knowledge, the functions of written language, a sense of meaning making from texts, vocabulary, rudimentary print knowledge (e.g., developmental spelling), and the sheer persistence to investigate print as a meaning-making tool.

Content of Early Literacy Instruction

Teaching preschool children
- what reading and writing can do
- to name and write alphabet letters
- to hear rhymes and sounds in words
- to spell simple words
- to recognize and write their own names
- new words from stories, work, and play
- to listen to stories for meaning

Valuable Dispositions of Early Literacy Instruction

Cultivating preschool children's
- willingness to listen to stories
- desire to be read to
- curiosity about words and letters
- exploration of print forms
- playfulness with words
- enjoyment of songs, poems, rhymes, jingles, books, and dramatic play

---

WRITTEN LANGUAGE IS HARDER TO LEARN THAN ORAL

Learning an alphabetic writing system requires extra work. Both spoken and written language are symbol systems for representing and retrieving meanings. In spoken language, meaning making depends on

phonemes or sounds. As children gain experience with the language of their community, they learn which words (or sequences of phonemes) stand for which concepts in that language. For example, children learn that the spoken word *table* in English or *mesa* in Spanish names a four-legged, flat-topped piece of furniture.

Writing and reading with an alphabetic system involve an extra layer of symbols, where the phonemes are represented by letters. This means that beginners must both learn the extra symbols—the letters of the alphabet—and raise their consciousness of the phonemes (because, while speaking and understanding speech, we unconsciously sequence and contrast phonemes).

Speakers, for example, understand the two very different concepts named by the words *nail* and *lane* without consciously noticing that those words are constructed from the same three phonemes (/n/, /A/, and /l/), but in different sequences. When children learn to read, however, they must pay attention to those three phonemes, how they are sequenced, and what letters represent them.

Invented spelling is a phonemic awareness activity that has the added advantage of being meaningful and functional (Richgels 2001). Children nonconventionally but systematically match sounds in words that they want to write with letters that they know. For example, they may use letter names and sounds in letter names (/ch/ in H, /A/ as the name of the letter A, and /r/ in R) when spelling *chair* as *HAR*. Invented spelling begins before children's phonemic awareness is completely developed and before they know all the names of the letters of the alphabet. With encouragement from adults, it develops through stages that culminate in conventional spelling.

The meanings of both spoken and written language serve real purposes in our daily lives (Halliday

1975). We usually do not speak without wanting to accomplish something useful. For example, we might want to influence others' behavior ("Would you turn that down, please?"), express our feelings ("I hate loud music"), or convey information ("Habitual listening to loud music is a danger to one's hearing"). Similarly, with written messages we can influence behavior (NO SMOKING), express feelings (I ♥ NY), and inform (Boston 24 mi) while serving such added purposes as communicating across distances or preserving a message as a record or a reminder.

These added purposes require that written messages be able to stand on their own (Olson 1977). Written language is decontextualized; that is, the sender and receiver of a written communication usually do not share the same time and space. The writer is not present to clarify and extend his or her message for the reader. This means that young readers' and writers' extra work includes, in addition to dealing with phonemes and letters, dealing with decontextualization.

WHY DO THE EXTRA WORK?

Historically, societies have found the extra work of writing and reading to be worthwhile. The extra functions of written language, especially preserving messages and communicating across distances, have enabled a tremendous growth of knowledge. Individual children can experience similar benefits if teachers help them to acquire the knowledge and skill involved in the extra work of reading and writing while always making real to them the extra purposes that written language serves. We must cultivate their dispositions (curiosity, desire, play) to actively seek, explore, and use books and print. As they learn what letters look like and how they match up with phonemes, which strings of letters represent which words, and how to represent their meanings in print and retrieve

others' meanings from print, they must see also how the fruits of those labors empower them by multiplying the functionality of language.

With speech, children can influence the behavior of others, express their feelings, and convey information. A big part of motivating them to take on the extra work of reading and writing must be letting them see how the permanence and portability of writing can widen the scope of that influencing, expressing, and informing. Young children who can say "No! Don't!" experience the power of spoken words to influence what others do or don't do—but only when the speakers are present. Being able to write *No* extends the exercise of that power to situations in which they are not present, as morning kindergartners Eric, Jeff, Zack, and Ben realized when they wrote *NOStPN* (No stepping) to keep afternoon kindergartners from disturbing a large dinosaur puzzle they had assembled on the classroom floor (McGee & Richgels 2000, 233–34).

Written language is decontextualized; that is, the sender and receiver of a written communication usually do not share the same time and space.

THE PRACTICE OF EARLY LITERACY INSTRUCTION: TWO EXAMPLES

Unlike the very real and immediate sounds and meanings of talk, print is silent; it is obscure; it is not of the here and now. Consequently, early literacy instruction must often be explicit and direct, which is not to say that it must be scriptlike, prescriptive, and rigid (Schickedanz 2003). Rather it should be embedded in the basic activities of early learning long embraced by early education practice and research. These include

reading aloud, circle time, small group activities, adult-child conversations, and play.

Teachers can embed reading and writing instruction in familiar activities, to help children learn both the conventions of print and how print supports their immediate goals and needs. The two examples below show how what's new about early literacy instruction fits within tried-and-true early education practice.

INTERACTIVE STORYBOOK READING

Reading aloud has maximum learning potential when children have opportunities to actively participate and respond (Morrow & Gambrell 2001). This requires teachers to use three types of scaffolding or support: (a) before-reading activities that arouse children's interest and curiosity in the book about to be read; (b) during-reading prompts and questions that keep children actively engaged with the text being read; and (c) after-reading questions and activities that give children an opportunity to discuss and respond to the books that have been read.

Instruction can be easily integrated into any of these three phases of story reading. This highly contextualized instruction should be guided by children's literacy learning needs and by the nature of the book being read:

- information books, such as Byron Barton's *Airport*, can teach children new vocabulary and concepts;

- books, songs, and poems with strong rhymes, such as Raffi's *Down by the Bay*, promote phonological awareness; and

- stories with strong narrative plots, such as *There's an Alligator under My Bed*, by Mercer Mayer, are ideal for generating predictions and acquainting children with narrative structure, both of which lay a foundation for reading comprehension.

Shared Reading to Learn about Story Plot

Here is how one teacher reads *There's an Alligator under My Bed*, by Mercer Mayer, to a group of four-year-olds.

Before reading. The teacher begins by saying, "Let's look at the picture on the cover of the book. [Shows a boy in bed with an alligator sticking out from beneath] The boy in this story has a *big* problem. Can anyone guess what that problem is?"

After the children make their guesses, the teacher points to the title and says, "The title of this book is *There's an Alligator under My Bed*. So Suzy and Joey were correct in guessing what the boy's problem is. How do you think the boy will get rid of the alligator?"

After several children share their predictions, the teacher begins reading the book aloud.

During reading. After reading the first section of the book, which introduces the boy's problem, the teacher pauses and asks, "Do you have any other ideas about how the boy might get rid of the alligator?"

The teacher reads the next two pages, which detail the boy's plan to leave a trail of bait to the garage, and then pauses to ask the children what the word bait means.

After reading the next section, in which the boy lays out a trail of food, the teacher asks, "What do you think the alligator is going to do?"

Finally, after reading the rest of the story, in which the alligator gets trapped in the garage, the teacher points to the note the boy left on the door to the garage and asks, "What do you think the boy wrote in his note?"

After reading. The teacher sparks a discussion of the book by asking several open-ended questions, such as "What did you like best about the story?" and "How would *you* have gotten rid of that alligator?"

Later, the teacher does a follow-up small group activity—to reinforce a sense of story plot, she helps children sequence a few pictures of the main story events.

In addition, most books can be used to teach print recognition, book concepts (e.g., cover, page), and concepts of print (e.g., print vs. pictures). Of course, instruction should be limited to several brief teaching points per reading so children can enjoy the read-aloud experience. Enjoyment and building positive dispositions should always be given high priority when reading aloud. For an example of how a teacher might do an interactive story reading session with *There's an Alligator under My Bed*, see "Shared Reading to Learn about Story Plot."

LITERACY IN PLAY

The general benefits of play for children's literacy development are well documented, showing that a literacy-enriched play environment exposes children to valuable print experiences and lets them practice narrative skills (Christie & Roskos 2003). In the following example, two preschoolers are playing in a restaurant activity center equipped with wall signs (Springville Restaurant), menus, pencils, and a notepad:

Food server: Can I take your order?

Customer: [Looks over the menu] Let's see, I'd like some cereal. And

how about some orange juice. And how about the coffee with that too.

Food server: We don't have coffee. We're all runned out.

Customer: Okay, well . . . I'll just take orange juice.

Food server: [Writes down order, using scribble writing] Okay. I'll be right back with your order. (Roskos et al. 1995)

Here, the customer is using the literacy routine of looking at a menu and then placing an order. If the menu is familiar and contains picture cues, some emergent reading might also be taking place. The food server is using another routine—writing down customer orders—and is practicing emergent writing. In addition, the children have constructed a simple narrative story, complete with a problem (an item is not available) and a resolution (drop that item from the order).

A Vygotskian approach to developing mature dramatic play also illustrates the value of tangible play plans for helping children to self-regulate their behaviors, to remember on purpose, and to deliberately focus their attention on play activity—foundational cognitive skills of reading and writing (Bodrova & Leong 1998). We have found that preschoolers often spend more time

preparing for their dramatizations than they spend acting out the stories. For example, one group of four-year-olds spent more than 30 minutes preparing for a pizza parlor story (organizing felt pizza ingredients, arranging furniture for the pizza kitchen, making play money, and deciding on roles) and less than 10 minutes acting out the cooking, serving, and eating of the pizza meal. One would be hard pressed to find another type of activity that can keep young children focused and "on task" for this length of time.

Specific to early literacy, descriptive research shows that a literacy-in-play strategy is effective in increasing the range and amount of literacy behaviors during play, thus allowing children to practice their emerging skills and show what they have learned (Neuman & Roskos 1992). Evidence is also accumulating that this strategy helps children learn important literacy concepts and skills, such as knowledge about the functions of writing (Vukelich 1993), the ability to recognize play-related print (Neuman & Roskos 1993), and comprehension strategies such as self-checking and self-correction (Neuman & Roskos 1997). Like storybook reading, the literacy learning potential of play can be increased when it includes before, during, and after types of scaffolding as illustrated in "Guided Play to Explore New Words and Their Sounds."

Guided Play to Explore New Words and Their Sounds

With the teacher's help, the children are creating a gas station/garage play center as part of an ongoing unit on transportation.

Before play. The teacher provides background knowledge by reading *Sylvia's Garage*, by Debra Lee, an information book about a woman mechanic. She discusses new words, such as *mechanic, engine, dipstick, oil.*

Next, the teacher helps the children plan the play center. She asks children about the roles they can play (e.g., gas station attendant, mechanic, customer) and records their ideas on a piece of chart paper. She then asks the children to brainstorm some props that they could use in their center (e.g., signs, cardboard gas pump, oil can, tire pressure gauge) and jots these down on another piece of chart paper. The children then decide which props they will make in class and which will be brought from home, and the teacher or a child places an *m* after each make-in-class item and an *h* after each from home item.

During the next several days, the teacher helps the children construct some of the make-in-class props, such as a sign for the gas station ("Let's see…*gas* starts with a *g.* Gary, your name also starts with a *g.* Can you show us how to write a *g?*).

The list of props from home is included in the classroom newsletter and sent to families.

During play. The teacher first observes the children at play to learn about their current play interests and activities. Then she provides scaffolding that extends and enriches children's play and at the same time teaches important literacy skills. She notices, for example, that the mechanics are not writing out service orders or bills for the customers, so she takes on a role as an assistant mechanic and models how to write out a bill for fixing a customer's car. She monitors her involvement to ensure close alignment with children's ongoing activity.

After play. During small group activity time, the teacher helps children with a picture-sort that includes pictures of people and objects from their garage play. They sort the pictures into labeled columns according to beginning sounds—/m/ (*mechanic, man, map, motor*); /t/ (*tire, tank, top, taillight*); and /g/ (*gas, gallon, garden, goat*). They explore the different feel of these sounds in the different parts of their mouths. They think of other words they know that feel the same way.

After modeling, the teacher gives the children a small deck of picture cards to sort, providing direct supervision and feedback.

CLOSING

We are gaining empirical ground in understanding early literacy learning well enough to identify essential content that belongs in an early childhood curriculum. Increasingly, the field can articulate key concepts and skills that are significant and foundational, necessary for literacy development and growth, research-based, and motivational to arouse and engage children's minds. The need to broadly distribute this knowledge is great—but the need to act on it consistently and carefully in instructional practice is even greater, especially if we are to steer children clear of the bramble-bushes and on to be successful readers and writers.

REFERENCES

Bodrova, E., & D. Leong. 1998. Development of dramatic play in young children and its effects on self-regulation: The Vygotskian approach. *Journal of Early Childhood Teacher Education* 19 (2): 115–24.

Christie, J., & K. Roskos. 2003. Literacy in play. In *Literacy in America: An encyclopedia of history, theory and practice,* ed. B. Guzzetti, 318–23. Denver, CO: ABC-CLIO.

Halliday, M.A.K. 1975. *Learning how to mean.* New York: Elsevier.

IRA & NAEYC. 1998. Joint Position Statement. Learning to read and write: Developmentally appropriate practices for young children. *Young Children* 53 (4): 30–46. Online (overview): www.naeyc.org/resources/position_statements/psread0.htm

Layzer, C. 2002. Adding ABCs to apple juice, blocks and circle time. Paper presented at the conference, Assessing Instructional Practices in Early Literacy and Numeracy, September, in Cambridge, Massachusetts.

Lewis, M. 2000. The promise of dynamic systems approaches for an integrated account of human development. *Child Development* 71: 36–43.

Lonigan, C., & G. Whitehurst. In press. Getting ready to read: Emergent literacy and family literacy. In "Family literacy programs: Current status and future directions," ed. B. Wasik. New York: Guilford.

McGee, L.M., & D.J. Richgels. 2000. *Literacy's beginnings: Supporting young readers and writers.* 3d ed. Needham, MA: Allyn & Bacon.

Morrow, L., & L. Gambrell. 2001. Literature-based instruction in the early years. In *Handbook of early literacy research,* eds. S. Neuman & D. Dickinson, 348–60. New York: Guilford.

NAEYC & NAECS/SDE (National Association of Early Childhood Specialists in State Departments of Education). 2002. Joint Position Statement. Early learning standards: Creating the conditions for success. Online: naeyc.org/resources/position_statements/earlylearn.pdf

National Research Council. 1998. *Preventing reading difficulties in young children.* Washington, DC: National Academy Press.

National Research Council. 2000. *From neurons to neighborhoods: The science of early childhood development.* Washington, DC: National Academy Press.

Neuman, S.B. 2002. What research reveals: Foundations for reading instruction in preschool and primary education. Handout of the U.S. Department of Education's Early Educator Academy, 14–15 November, in Los Angleles.

Neuman, S.B., & D. Dickinson, eds. 2001. *The handbook of early literacy research.* New York: Guilford.

Neuman, S.B., & K. Roskos. 1992. Literacy objects as cultural tools: Effects on children's literacy behaviors in play. *Reading Research Quarterly* 27 (3): 202–35.

Neuman, S.B., & K. Roskos. 1993. Access to print for children of poverty: Differential effects of adult mediation and literacy-enriched play settings on environmental and functional print tasks, *American Educational Research Journal* 30 (91): 95–122.

Neuman, S.B., & K. Roskos. 1997. Literacy knowledge in practice: Contexts of participation for young writers and readers. *Reading Research Quarterly* 32 (1): 10–33.

Olson, D.R. 1977. From utterance to text: The bias of language in speech and writing. *Harvard Educational Review* (47): 257–81.

Richgels, D.J. 2001. Invented spelling, phonemic awareness, and reading and writing instruction. In *Handbook of early literacy research*, eds. S.B. Neuman & D. Dickinson, 142–55. New York: Guilford.

Roskos, K., C. Vukelich, J. Christie, B. Enz, & S. Neuman. 1995. Linking literacy and play. Videotape (12 min.) and facilitator's guide. International Reading Association.

Schickedanz. J. 2003. Engaging preschoolers in code learning. *In Literacy and young children*, eds. D. Barone & L. Morrow, 121–39. Newark, DE: International Reading Association.

Senechal. M., J. LeFevre, K.V. Colton, & B.L. Smith. 2000. On refining theoretical models of emergent literacy. *Journal of School Psychology* 39 (5): 439–60.

Siegler, R. 2000. The rebirth of children's learning. *Child Development* 71 (1): 26–35.

Thelen, E., & L.B. Smith. 1995. *A dynamic systems approach to the development of cognition and action.* Cambridge, MA: The MIT Press.

Vukelich, C. 1993. Play: A context for exploring the functions, features, and meaning of writing with peers. *Language Arts* 70: 386–92.

Yaden, D., D. Rowe, & L. MacGillivary. 2000. Emergent literacy: A matter (polophony) of perspectives. In *The handbook of reading research*, vol. 3, eds. M. Kamil, P.B. Mosenthal, P.D. Pearson, & R. Barr, 425–54. Mahwah, NJ: Erlbaum.

Kathleen A. Roskos, Ph.D., is the director of the Ohio Literacy Initiative at the Ohio Department of Education and is a professor at John Carroll University in Cleveland. She coordinated Bridges and Links, one of the first public preschools in Ohio, and is instrumental in the development of content guidelines in early literacy. Kathleen studies early literacy development, teacher cognition, and the design of professional education for teachers.

James F. Christie, Ph.D., is a professor of curriculum and instruction at Arizona State University in Tempe, where he teaches courses in language, literacy, and early childhood education. His research interests include children's play and early literacy development. James is the president of the Association for the Study of Play.

Donald J. Richgels, Ph.D., is a professor in the literacy education department at Northern Illinois University in DeKalb, where he teaches graduate and undergraduate courses in language development, reading, and language arts.

Beyond the Journal. This article also appears on NAEYC's Website: www.naeyc.org.

Illustrations © Diane Greenseid.

Educating Early Childhood Teachers about Computers

Cynthia J. Bewick and Marjorie Kostelnik

Our new computers arrived yesterday, but I don't know where to start. I can write a short letter on my computer at home, but this one has different software. I'm frightened that I'll do something awful to it. Besides, everyone else knows lots more than I do, including the children.

—Preschool Teacher

Each time I enter the kindergarten classroom, the teacher has her computer covered with a sheet. She tells me this is "just temporary." Families want their children to use computers. All our classrooms have computers now, but this teacher doesn't seem interested.

—Elementary School Principal

Look into many early childhood classrooms and among the blocks, the art supplies, and the storybooks, you are likely to see a computer. Computers have become commonplace at home and in classrooms. Also commonplace is the assumption that most early childhood teachers have enough working knowledge of computers to use them effectively with young children. The research, however, is to the contrary. In fact, there is strong evidence that many teachers basically ignore the computers in their classrooms or use them only in a limited fashion (Landerholm 1995; Cuban 2001; Guthrie 2003). However, teachers can be the facilitators who organize and create the relationships between children, computers, and the classroom.

Teachers may not use computers for a variety of reasons. Some have limited experience with technology. Others believe there are more appropriate activities for young children. Early childhood programs may not offer technology training, teachers may lack sufficient time to

learn new computer skills, or directors may assume teachers know more about computers than they actually do (Thouvenelle & Bewick 2003). Sometimes when funds are limited the hardware used by teachers and children does not work all of the time and technical support might be lacking. Yet, computers are a significant part of today's society. When teachers help young children learn to use these important tools in a developmentally appropriate manner, they offer them strategies for their educational future (NAEYC 1996). Each professional must set a good example by continuing to increase her or his technological skills.

> There is strong evidence that many teachers basically ignore the computers in their classrooms or use them only in a limited fashion.

What do teachers need to know about using computers?

Access to computer hardware and software is not a problem for most educators. Ninety-nine percent of public schools have at least one computer; 94 percent of kindergarten teachers have computers in their classrooms (U.S. Department of Education 2003). A random sample of Head Start teachers in one state finds that 88 percent also had at least one available computer (Bewick 2000, 88). Many libraries and community centers also have computers that the public may use. Increasing one's knowledge therefore does not require owning a personal computer.

Teacher Technology Assessment

Basic operation of the computer and related components
- Do you know how to turn everything on and off?
- Can you make the computer do what you want it to do?
- Do you know how to troubleshoot solutions when a problem occurs?
- Can you use software shortcuts that save you time?

Choosing appropriate software for young children
- How does the software support children's age-appropriate developmental skills?
- In what ways does the software reflect your organization's curriculum goals and objectives?
- How does the software avoid gender, racial, and ethnic stereotypes?
- Will the software easily integrate with ongoing curriculum activities and materials?
- What characteristics does the software share with other quality early childhood materials?
- How does the software serve as a learning tool, rather than as an electronic worksheet?
- How does the software support English-language learners?

Using the computer for instruction with young children
- How does your current curriculum support learning with computers?
- What would you say if a parent or colleague asked about controversial issues regarding technology and children, such as teaching toddlers about computers?
- How does the physical environment affect children's social, emotional, and cognitive development when they use computers: Does the arrangement and location of the computer center support peer learning and teaching? Can children easily collaborate with each other?
- Are you familiar with basic research related to young children's learning with computers?
- What strategies do you use to effectively introduce the computer to young children so that it becomes an ongoing and independent learning center?
- How do you plan and implement curriculum activities based on the computer?

Using computers for instructional support
- Do you know how to make instructional materials (labels, games, pictures, newsletters, stories, and so forth)?
- Can you keep records and create reports about the children or classroom activities?
- How does your computer help you assess children's learning?
- Can you communicate with parents and/or other professionals via e-mail?
- Can you locate Internet resources for lesson planning and ideas for best teaching practices?
- Can you create or add educational information to a classroom-based Web site?
- Can you develop and print photographs from digital cameras?

Watching other computer users and talking with children, students, or other teachers are productive learning activities.

Learning about computers is a continuous process. No one will have every skill or piece of knowledge after taking one course, talking to another teacher, or receiving individual training. Teachers might find the ongoing nature of computer education frustrating as new products appear almost daily. It is important to remember that increasing computer competency is not dependent upon purchasing the latest gadgets. Teachers

can use the "Teacher Technology Assessment" to review their computer knowledge and learning needs.

How can teachers learn to use computers?

Early childhood professionals learn about computers through different types of education and training. Research suggests that many prefer individual experimentation in addition to interactions with others (Bewick 2000). This means that watching other computer users and talking with children, students, or other teachers are productive learning activities. Some educators learn about computers in more formal settings—a college class, professional conference, or specific computer workshop. Others may read books and manuals before attempting new skills. Many people find the following ideas helpful.

Talk with other teachers and anyone else who uses computers. Ask them how they learned to use computers, what they would do differently, and which one tip they believe is most useful. Most people are willing to share their expertise. Also, ask the children for help. They often have less anxiety and fewer misconceptions than do adults.

Experiment and explore! Discover what happens when trying new techniques or different keyboard combinations. Many adults are fearful that they will severely damage a computer during normal operations. This is incorrect. Routine keyboarding will not create serious problems.

Take a computer class through an adult education program or college. Recognize that the other students can be resources. Use the class as an opportunity to learn from them as well as from the instructor.

Use critical thinking. Teachers must be able to distinguish what is and is not important to know when using computers with children.

Continue the learning process. There is a never ending stream of new information about technology.

How can administrators support teacher learning about computers?

Administrators and supervisors can help teachers increase their computer skills by providing the appropriate tools, training experiences, and time to get to know and practice using different software. Here are some helpful things managers can do.

1. Include sufficient funds in the budget for technical support, replacement of outdated hardware, and purchase of additional hardware to enhance computer capability. Technological tools must operate properly and have adequate capacity for them to be useful for learning and planning.

2. Ensure sufficient time for teachers to learn about computers by experimenting and sharing ideas with each other (Bewick 2000). Adults with limited computer experiences must increase their competence and decrease their anxiety. Offer informal and formal interactions that use shared problem solving as well as demonstration and practice of new skills.

3. Choose and monitor carefully the types of software teachers use with children. Research suggests that software characteristics are one of the key elements

of appropriate computer use by children (Clements 1994; Haugland & Wright 1997).

4. Remind teachers that by learning about computers, they can improve their skills, make their job easier, and teach children how to use them (Bewick 2000). These factors may motivate any skeptics.

5. Select computer software that supports curriculum guidelines. Staff are likely to be frustrated when software presentations conflict with program standards, such as depictions of ethnic or gender stereotypes instead of recognition and tolerance of diversity among peers.

6. Distribute free and low-cost publications on computer use in early childhood education. Share NAEYC's position statement on technology (NAEYC 1996) and other journal articles about technology. *Computers in Head Start Classrooms* (Mobius Corporation 1994) contains recommendations from the Head Start/IBM Partnership Project and is useful for all preschool programs. The Milken Exchange, a nonprofit organization, offers a variety of computer-related publications based on research in public schools. Most documents are available at **www.mff.org/edtech**.

Administrators and supervisors can help by providing the appropriate tools, training experiences, and time to get to know and practice using different software.

Conclusion

Teachers set the stage for all types of learning in preschool and primary classrooms. Guided by state and local curriculum standards, they have the immediate responsibility for children's learning. When programs presume that teachers have a working knowledge of computers, children may not have an effective model for technology use. With the support of administrators, teachers can continue to learn about computers and build their technology skills. Children will receive the ultimate benefit—preparation for the technological twenty-first century.

References

Bewick, C.J. 2000. The adoption of computers as an instructional tool by Michigan Head Start teachers. PhD dissertation, Michigan State University.

Clements, D.H. 1994. The uniqueness of the computer as a learning tool: Insights from research and practice. In *Young children: Active learners in a technological age*, eds. J.L. Wright & D.D. Shade, 31–49. Washington, DC: NAEYC.

Cuban, L. 2001. *Oversold and underused: Computers in classrooms.* Cambridge: Harvard University Press.

Guthrie, J. 2003. Computers idle in public schools. *USA Today*, March 18, A15.

Haugland, S.W., & J.L. Wright. 1997. *Young children and technology: A world of discovery*. Boston: Allyn & Bacon.

Landerholm, E. 1995. Early childhood teachers' computer attitudes, knowledge, and practices. *Early Child Development and Care* 109: 43–60.

MOBIUS Corporation. 1994. *Computers in Head Start classrooms: Recommendations from the Head Start/IBM Partnership Project*. 2nd ed. Alexandria, VA: Author. Online: **www.kidware.com/Mobius/compinhs.pdf.**

NAEYC. 1996. Position Statement: Technology and young children—Ages three through eight. *Young Children* 51 (6): 11–16.

Thouvenelle, S., & C.J. Bewick. 2003. *Completing the computer puzzle: A guide for early childhood educators*. Boston: Allyn & Bacon.

U.S. Department of Education, National Center for Education Statistics. 2003. *Young children's access to computers in the home and at school in 1999 and 2000*. Washington, DC: Author. Online: **www.nces.ed.gov/pubs2003/quarterly/spring/q3_1.asp.**

Cynthia J. Bewick, PhD, is the education services manager for Tri-County Head Start in Paw Paw, Michigan. Her interests are technology and professional development of teachers, curricula, and assessment, which she pursues actively including through university teaching and consulting. She is coauthor of *Completing the Computer Puzzle: A Guide for Early Childhood Educators.*

Marjorie Kostelnik, PhD, is dean of the College of Education and Human Sciences at the University of Nebraska—Lincoln. She began as a Head Start teacher and has worked with children, families, early childhood professionals, and college students ever since. She serves on the advisory board for T.E.A.C.H. Nebraska.

From *Young Children*, 59(3) May 2004, pp. 26-29. Copyright © 2004 by National Association for the Education of Young Children. Reprinted with permission from the National Association for the Education of Young Children.

Movement and *Learning:* A Valuable Connection

Deborah Stevens-Smith

Making a Connection

Physical educators enjoy teaching because they understand the value and purpose physical education can bring into the lives of children. Physical educators, who connect with classroom educators to help them understand the value of movement and physical activity to learning, can be even more effective. Classroom and physical educators share common teaching characteristics, but educate in different ways. Physical educators need to ensure that academic instruction is also taking place during sport and physical activity instruction. Many principals and classroom educators believe they have nothing in common with the physical educator, nor have they been involved in or taken the time to observe a quality physical education program. Those who do see and understand what goes on in the gym are able to connect the value of movement to learning. It is when the education community understands the value of movement to learning that goals can be established that contributes to a complete education for all students. Brain research appears to validate the concept of movement's contribution to learning.

How We Learn

The process of learning involves basic nerve cells that transmit information and create numerous neural connections essential to learning. Developmental movements in babies and young children evolve from these neural connections in the brain (Hannaford, 1995). The neurons in a child's brain make many more connections than an adult's brain as they respond to their environment; the greater the stimulation, the greater number of neural interconnections. The process is greatest between the ages of two and eleven. As a child approaches puberty, the connections his/her brain finds useful become permanent, and those connections not used, are eliminated. All of this neural stimulation takes place in response to movement (Hannaford, 1995).

What does all this mean? The greater the movement and stimulation, the greater the number of synaptic nerves interconnections, and therefore, the greater capacity to learn. Synaptic connections are created when a child moves or performs skills. The more a skill is practiced, the faster and better the neurons become at processing the response (Hannaford, 1995). The process makes practice during and after school highly significant, in terms of skill development.

One way to increase learning is to encourage creation of more synaptic connections in the brain through movement (Hannaford, 1995). The more connections one has, the better and faster one becomes at assimilating information, solving problems, and thinking. Brain scans show that children learn best when they are actually moving *and* learning at the same time. Hannaford found that movement stimulates the necessary neurons and electrical wiring that facilitates the child's ability to absorb information or learn.

King (2000) believes that physical movement not only strengthens the body, but is also crucial to brain and nervous system development; that learning by doing is imperative to improving a child's ability to take in data and utilize that data in effective ways. Clearly, based on the research, children need to be more physically active and spend less time sitting at both home and school!

What Encourages Learning?

The International Society of Sports Psychology (1992), King (1999) and Payne (1999) found that a positive link exists between physical activity and learning. Physical activity increases all-around vigor, promotes clearer thinking, and affects grade scores of children. The researcher cited above also found that children who are physically active are more alert and energized to learn. A study in California also found a direct correlation between academic achievement and physical fitness levels of students. (California Department of Education, 2002).

Jean Blaydes (2000), a neurokinesiologist, found in her research that physical movements not only strengthen the body, but are crucial to brain and nervous system development. She found that:

- Raising the heart rate oxygenates the brain and feeds it glucose (necessary for learning) at an increased rate.

- Repetitive gross motor movement balances brain chemicals that calm behavior and elevates self-esteem.

- Exercise triggers the growth factor that boosts the ability of neurons to communicate with one another.

- What makes us move also makes us think.

- Memory is retrieved better when learned through movement.

- Movement helps children learn.

What Inhibits Learning?

There are many issues that block a child's ability to learn, but one facet of brain research is particularly relevant for children. Often children do not learn because both sides of the brain are not integrated or working together. This block to learning can be caused by stress or a myriad of other factors. When a child is unable to utilize the left and right side of the brain in an integrated manner, i.e., is unable to "cross the midline," then learning can be blocked (Dennison & Dennison, 1994).

Crossing the midline is an important function because the brain uses the same connections to process reading, writing, and math. The right side of the brain specializes in global aspects of learning, while the left side specializes in logic functions (Hannaford, 1995). When both sides "of the brain function integrally, learning is enhanced. Physical educators can assist classroom educators in developing students' brain integration. They can begin by introducing activities that engage the right side of the body, then the left side. For instance, students can dribble a ball from the right or left side of the body, throw with the right or left hand, or catch and kick with the right or left foot. These exercises should be followed by practice skills that engage the body from the right to the left, and then vice versa. Dribbling from the right hand to the left or throwing with the right hand and catching with the left, are examples. Sport and games, such as basketball, jumping rope, juggling, rhythmic activities, tennis and soccer all facilitate this cross lateralization process.

Jenson (2000), a leader in brain research, once stated at a conference, "If learning is not in your body, you haven't learned it." He believes that those who think the brain trains the body have it backwards, and that it is "the body that trains the brain."

Doctors and kinesiologists are beginning to realize the importance movement plays in the life of a child. Brain research shows that without movement and physical activity, the process of learning is weakened (Hannaford, 1995). When physical education class time is reduced, it affects the ability of the child to learn in a more complete way. School administrators and classroom educators aware of the research that links movement to learning can greatly increase the benefits of classroom learning by using movement to teach academic concepts to students through integrated lessons. PE Central provides an excellent website/resource for teaching academic concepts using physical activity. Learning by doing allows children to take in information and utilize it in more efficient ways (Dale, 1969). All educators, can incorporate the findings of brain research by introducing skills and movements that utilize both the right and left sides of the body, increasing the number of activities that cross the midline of the body, and using integrated lessons.

Resources

PE Central – **pe.central.vt.edu**
Edu-K Foundation – **www.braingym.com**
Wellness Quest – **www.BrainBoogie.com**

References

Blaydes, J. (2000). *How to make learning a moving experience.* Virginia Department of Education Video.

California Department of Education (2001). New Release, December 10, 2002. Sacramento, CA.

Dennison, P. & Dennison, G. (1994). *Brain Gym: Teacher's Edition*, Edu-Kinesthetics, Inc., Ventura, CA.

Dale, E. (1996). The cone of learning makes the case for active learning (in Audio-Visual Methods in Teaching, 3rd edition), Holt, Rinehart and Winston.

Hannaford, C. (1995) *Smart Moves: Why learning is not all in your head.* Great Ocean Publishers, Arlington, VA.

International Society of Sport Psychology. (1992). Physical activity and psychological benefits. *The Physician and Sports Medicine*, 20, pp. 179–180.

Jenson, E. (2000). Teaching with the body in mind The Brain Store, San Diego, CA.

King, D. (2000). *Exercise seen boosting children's brain function.* PELINKS4U:. **http://www.pelinks4u.org/ news/bgbrain.htm.**

National Association for Sport and Physical Education. (2002). *New study supports physically fit kids perform better academically*. Reston, VA:. NASPE.

Payne, G. (1999). *A powerful tool*. California Governor's Council on Physical Fitness & Sports: `http://mscd.edu/ 'quattocj/position_state/ tool.html.`

Deborah Stevens-Smith (Stevens@ Clemson .edu) is an Associate Professor for the College of Health, Education & Human Development at Clemson University, Clemson, SC.

From *Strategies,* Vol. 18, No. 1, September/October 2004, pp. 10-11. Copyright © 2004 by National Association for Sport and Physical Education (NASPE), 1900 Association Drive, Reston, VA 20191-1599. Reprinted by permission.

Promoting Creativity for Life Using
Open-Ended Materials

Walter F. Drew and Baji Rankin

Creative art is so many things! It is flower drawings and wire flower sculptures in clay pots created by kinder-gartners after visiting a flower show. It is a spontaneous leap for joy that shows up in a series of tempera paintings, pencil drawings of tadpoles turning into frogs, 3-D skyscrapers built from cardboard boxes or wooden blocks. It can be the movement and dance our bodies portray, the rhythmic sound of pie-pan cymbals and paper towel tube trumpets played by four-year-olds in their marching parade, the construction of spaceships and birthday cakes.

What is most important in the creative arts is that teachers, families, and children draw upon their inner resources, making possible direct and clear expression. The goal of engaging in the creative arts is to commu-nicate, think, and feel. The goal is to express thought and feeling through movement, and to express visual perception and representation through the process of play and creative art making. These forms of creative expression are important ways that children and adults express themselves, learn, and grow (Vygotsky [1930–35] 1978a, 1978b; Klugman & Smilansky 1990; Jones & Reynolds 1992; Reynolds & Jones 1997; McNiff 1998; Chalufour, Drew, & Waite-Stupiansky 2004; Zigler, Singer, & Bishop-Josef 2004).

This article is based on field research, observations, and interviews about the use of creative, open-ended materials in early childhood classrooms and how their use affects the teaching/learning process. We identify seven key principles for using open-ended materials in early childhood classrooms, and we wrap educators' stories, experiences, and ideas around these principles. Included are specific suggestions for practice.

PRINCIPLE 1
Children's spontaneous, creative self-expression increases their sense of competence and well-being now and into adulthood.

At the heart of creative art making is a playful attitude, a willingness to suspend everyday rules of cause and effect. Play is a state of mind that brings into being unexpected, unlearned forms freely expressed, gener-ating associations, representing a unique sense of order and harmony, and producing a sense of well-being.

Play and art making engender an act of courage equivalent in some ways to an act of faith, a belief in possibilities. Such an act requires and builds resilience, immediacy, presence, and the ability to focus and act with intention even while the outcome may remain unknown. Acting in the face of uncertainty and ambiguity is possible because pursuing the goal is worthwhile. These actions produce a greater sense of competence in children, who then grow up to be more capable adults (Klugman & Smilansky 1990; Reynolds & Jones 1997; McNiff 1998; Zigler, Singer, & Bishop-Josef 2004).

Children and adults who are skilled at play and art making have more "power, influence, and capacity to create meaningful lives for themselves" (Jones 1999). Those skilled at play have more ability to realize alter-native possibilities and assign meaning to experiences; those less skilled in finding order when faced with ambiguity get stuck in defending things the way they are (Jones 1999).

In Reggio Emilia, Italy, the municipal schools for young children emphasize accepting uncertainty as a regular part of education and creativity. Loris Malaguzzi, founder of the Reggio schools, points out that creativity

> Seems to emerge from multiple experiences, coupled with a well-supported development of personal resources, including a sense of freedom to venture beyond the known. (1998, 68)

Many children become adults who feel inept, untal-ented, frustrated, and in other ways unsuited to making art and expressing themselves with the full power of their innate creative potential. This is unfortunate when we know that high-quality early childhood experiences can promote children's development and learning (Schweinhart, Barnes, & Weikart 1993).

The Association for Childhood Education International (ACEI) has enriched and expanded the definition of creativity. Its 2003 position statement on creative thought clarifies that "we need to do more than prepare children to become cogs in the machinery of commerce":

> The international community needs resourceful, imaginative, inventive, and ethical problem solvers who will make a significant contribution, not only to the Information Age in which we currently live, but beyond to ages that we can barely envision. (Jalongo 2003, 218)

Eleanor Duckworth, author of *The Having of Wonderful Ideas* (1996), questions what kinds of people we as a society want to have growing up around us. She examines the connection between what happens to children when they are young and the adults they become. While some may want people who do not ask questions but rather follow commands without thinking, Duckworth emphasizes that many others want people who are confident in what they do, who do not just follow what they are told, who see potential and possibility, and who view things from different perspectives. The way to have adults who think and act on their own is to provide them with opportunities to act in these ways when they are young. Given situations with interesting activities and materials, children will come up with their own ideas. The more they grow, the more ideas they'll come up with, and the more sense they'll have of their own way of doing things (E. Duckworth, pers. comm.).

PRINCIPLE 2
Children extend and deepen their understandings through multiple, hands-on experiences with diverse materials.

This principle, familiar to many early childhood educators, is confirmed and supported by brain research that documents the importance of the early years, when the brain is rapidly developing (Jensen 1998; Eliot 2000). Rich, stimulating experiences provided in a safe, responsive environment create the best conditions for optimal brain development. the years from birth to five present us with a window of opportunity to help children develop the complex wiring of the brain. After that time, a pruning process begins, leaving the child with a brain foundation that is uniquely his or hers for life. The key to intelligence is the recognition and creation of patterns and relationships in the early years (Gardner 1983; Jensen 2000; Shonkoff & Phillips 2000; Zigler, Singer, & Bishop-Josef 2004).

Rich, stimulating experiences provided in a safe, responsive environment create the best conditions for optimal brain development.

The importance of active, hands-on experiences comes through in the stories that follow, related by several early childhood educators.

At the Wolfson Campus Child Development Center in Miami, program director Patricia Clark DeLaRosa describes how four-year-old preschool children develop some early understandings of biology and nature watching tadpoles turn into frogs. The fact that this change happens right before their eyes is key to their learning. The children make simple pencil drawings of the characteristics and changes they observe.

One day during outdoor play, the teachers in another class see that children are picking flowers from the shaded area and burying them. This leads to a discussion with the children about how to prepare a garden in which to grow flowers and vegetables. Children and teachers work together to clear weeds and plant seeds. They care for the garden and watch for signs of growth. Over time they observe the plants sprouting, leaves opening, and colorful flowers blooming. The direct, hands-on experience inspires the children to look carefully and to draw and paint what they see.

Another group of children in the same class takes walks around downtown Miami. The children then talk about what they saw, build models, look at books, and explore their new understandings in the block play area.

DeLaRosa describes a classroom that includes a number of children who display challenging behaviors. Some of the architectural drawings the children produce during a project on architecture amaze her. They demonstrate that with a concrete project in which children are deeply interested, and with teachers who guide them and prompt them with stimulating materials and related books, children's accomplishments can far exceed expectations. Because the children have direct and compelling experiences and multiple ways to express their thoughts, curiosity, and questions, the teachers are able to help them focus and produce, expressing their thoughts and feelings in a positive way.

When an architect supplies actual building plans of a house, the children become even more active. They make room drawings and maps of the house, all the while conversing and building vocabulary. They roll up the plans in paper tubes and carry them around like architects. Because the children are deeply involved in the project, DeLaRosa reports, they experience significant growth in critical thinking and creative problem solving. With questions like "How can we build it so it stands up?" and "Where's the foundation?" they show a growing understanding of the structure of buildings and a deep engagement in the learning process.

Claire Gonzales, a teacher of four- and five-year-olds in Albuquerque, points out how open-ended materials allow children choices and independence, both crucial in stimulating genuine creativity. Children make things without preconceived ideas. When teachers support authentic expression, there is no one right or wrong way—there is space to create.

Gonzales describes a child who is fascinated by a stingray he sees on a visit to an aquarium. He is inspired to make a detailed, representational drawing of the stingray that goes beyond anything he has done before. Gonzales relates how he was able to use his memory and cognition to revisit the aquarium because the stingray made such a deep impression on him. The child recalled the connection he made with the stingray and represented the creature's details—the eyes, the stinger, the gills.

Key to this kind of work by children is the teacher's respect for both the child and the materials and the availability of open-ended materials like clay, paint, and tools for drawing and writing. materials can be reusable resources—quality, unwanted, manufacturing business by-products, otherwise destined for the landfill, which can serve as much-needed, open-ended resources: cloth remnants, foam, wire, leather, rubber and wood (See "A Word about Reusable Resources.") Open-ended materials are particularly effective because they have no predetermined use (Drew, Ohlsen, & Pichierri 2000)

Margie Cooper, in Atlanta, Georgia, works with Project Infinity, a group of educators inspired by the schools of Reggio Emilia. She speaks of the values of seeing art making not as a separate area of the curriculum but rather as an extension of thinking and communication. Art making can be especially valuable for young children whose verbal skills are not well developed because the diverse materials offer a variety of ways to communicate. We can learn a lot from children who show a natural affinity for materials, gravitating to them without fear or intimidation. Cooper notes that adults often approach materials, familiar or unfamiliar, with apprehension. Learning from children's openness to materials is important so as not to teach children the fears or discomforts we as adults may have.

PRINCIPLE 3
Children's play with peers supports learning and a growing sense of competence.

Duckworth underscores the importance of this principle, emphasizing that by working and playing together in groups, children learn to appreciate not only their own ideas and ways of ding things, but also each other's. a child can learn that others have interesting methods and ideas that are worth paying attention to and that can contribute to his or her interests as well.

In a kindergarten classroom in Worcester, Massachusetts, five- and six-year-old children study flowers together before a visit to a flower show. The children see and discuss with each other pictures of flowers painted by Vincent Van Gogh, Claude Monet, and Georgia O'Keeffe. They use some of these pictures as inspiration for their own sketches and paintings. They explore flowers with different colors, paints, paper, brushes, and print making.

To give the field trip a focus, the teacher, Sue Zack, organizes a scavenger hunt. At the flower show, the children work in small groups, searching for wolves,

> By working and playing together in groups, children learn to appreciate not only their own ideas and ways of doing things, but also each other's.

sunflowers, tulips, a large fountain, waterfalls, goats, a yellow arrangement of flowers, and a Monet painting.

At school the children make flower creations using recycled materials. At first, they have difficulty making their top-heavy flowers stand up. Then one child discovers that he can use the recycled wire available on the table to hold the flower upright. Others encountering the problem use their classmate's solution.

When children discover how difficult it is to make flowers from clay, one child suggests, "We can use the clay to make a vase and put flowers in it instead." So the project turns into making clay pots. Zack describes the children as being so involved that they seem unaware of her presence nearby. They are engrossed in their flower pots, expressing their thoughts to each other while working and using adjectives such as *smooth, bigger, huge, longer, taller, bumpy, dusty, sticky*, and *cold*. All the children are proud of their work, eager to show and share with one another. "Did you make yours yet?" "Where did you put yours?" "What flowers do you have on yours?" "I have a dandelion and tulips." "My flowers go right from a side to the bottom."

Here are children excited to be working in small groups and deeply connected to a sense of themselves. They do not look for external motivation or recognition. Rather, they express something direct and clear from within themselves as individuals. This is a wonderful example of endogenous expression, where children draw on their inner resources and express themselves from within.

Learning in a social setting is extended when children use diverse materials and symbol systems such as drawing, building, talking, making, or writing. the interaction among these various symbol systems—that is, different languages children use to express themselves— promotes and extends thinking in individuals and within the group.

Promoting interaction among these expressive languages fosters children's development and learning. And the languages encompass a variety of subjects, which leads to the next principle.

PRINCIPLE 4
Children can learn literacy, science, and mathematics joyfully through active play with diverse, open-ended materials.

When children play with open-ended materials, Duckworth says, they explore the look and feel of the materials. They develop a sense of aesthetics by investigating what is beautiful and pleasing about the material. The wide variety of forms of different kinds of materials, along with suggestions of things to do and to look at, flows over into artistic and scientific creation. These experiences naturally lead to conversations among children that they can write or draw about or make into books or other literacy or science experiences. Play helps children develop a meaningful understanding of subject matter (Kamii 1982; Christie 1991; Stupiansky 1992; Althouse 1994; Owocki 1999; Jensen 2001; VanHoorn et al. 2002).

The more children use open-ended materials, the more they make them aesthetically pleasing by fiddling, sorting, and ordering, and the more they see the potential in the materials and in themselves. "Knowing your materials is the absolute basis for both science and art. You have to use your hands and your eyes and your whole body to make judgments and see potential," states Duckworth.

Cathy Weisman Topal, coauthor with Lella Gandini of *Beautiful Stuff* (1999), points out that children develop power when they build individual relationships with materials. When children have the chance to notice, collect, and sort materials, and when teachers respond to their ideas, the children become artists, designers, and engineers. When children are simply given materials to use without the chance to explore and understand them, the materials do not become part of their world. Weisman Topal relates,

> When a child says, "Oh, I need some of that red netting from onions," he demonstrates that he has experience, knowledge, and a relationship with the material, a connection. It is not somebody else's discovery; it is the child's. Whenever a child makes the discovery, it's exciting, it's fun. The child is the researcher and the inventor; this builds confidence. (Weisman Topal, pers. comm.)

Children's explorations come with stories. Histories, associations, and questions. From the questions come the next activities, investigations, and discoveries. A natural consequence is descriptive language; children naturally want to talk about—and maybe draw about—their discoveries. "Not many things can top an exciting discovery!" says Weisman Topal. Organizing and dealing with materials is a whole-learning adventure. Working in these modes, the child produces and learns mathematical patterns and rhythms, building and combining shapes and creating new forms.

When children have the chance to notice, collect, and sort materials, and when teachers respond to their ideas, the children become artists, designers, and engineers.

Teachers can promote language, literature, mathematics, and science through creative exploration. Margie Cooper points out that skill-based learning and standardized testing by themselves do not measure three qualities highly valued in our society—courage, tenacity, and a strong will. Yet these three characteristics may have more to do with success in life than the number of skills a person may have mastered.

PRINCIPLE 5
Children learn best in open-ended explorations when teachers help them make connections.

Working to strengthen a child's mind and neural network and helping the child develop an awareness of patterns and relationships are the teacher's job. Constructive, self-active, sensory play and art making help both children and adults make connections between the patterns and relationships they create and previous knowledge and experience. The brain, a pattern-seeking tool, constructs, organizes, and synthesizes new knowledge.

Teachers integrate playful, creative art making with more formal learning opportunities such as discussion, reading, writing, and storytelling. They ask questions and listen to the children so that the more formal learning activities are connected closely to the children's ideas and thinking. Teachers provide concrete experiences first: investigating, manipulating, constructing and reconstructing, painting, movement, and the drama of self-activity. Then the reflection and extension involving literacy, science, and mathematics that follow are meaningful. Zack in Massachusetts gives us a good example of this when she organizes a scavenger hunt at the flower show, encouraging children to make connections between their interests and activities at the show.

PRINCIPLE 6
Teachers are nourished by observing children's joy and learning.

A central tenet in the schools of Reggio Emilia is the idea that teachers are nourished by children's joy and intelligence. DeLaRosa clearly demonstrates this tenet as she describes teachers working with children on the architectural plans:

> Watching the teachers guide, interact, and work with the children makes me feel extremely excited—joyful just to see the gleam in their eyes. You know the children are thinking, you see them creating and producing and playing with purpose. I am proud to see teachers taking learning to higher levels, not sitting back festering about this problem or that. They could hang on to the fact that they have a hard time with some of the children … but they don't. They look at the positive and move on. (Pers. comm.)

Teachers and children learn together in a reciprocal process. The exciting work of the children inspires the teachers to go forward. Children are looking for more, and the teachers think, "What else can I do to bring learning to the next level?" "How can we entice them to go further?" "What new materials can I introduce?" and "I can see how to do this!" At times the teachers set up and move ahead of the children, and at times the children move ahead of the teachers. When teachers see what children can accomplish, they gain a greater appreciation for them and for the creative arts and materials.

In addition, the work that children do, while inspired by experiences teachers and parents provide, is at the same time an inspiration to all adults who notice. Sue Zack notes,

> The flower unit forced me to make the time to listen, reflect, and write down observations of the children. It felt good! It is what I need and what the class needs in order to be a group that communicates, experiences life, creates, learns, and cares about each other. (Pers. comm.)

PRINCIPLE 7
Ongoing self-reflection among teachers in community is needed to support these practices.

It is vital for teachers to work and plan together to promote children's creativity and thinking. By meeting together regularly over a few years, teachers connected with Project Infinity in Atlanta have developed the trust to have honest conversations with each other regarding observations of children and classroom experience—not an easy task. They are doing research and constructing knowledge together about how children build relationships (M. Cooper, pers. comm.). Just as children learn and grow in community, so do their teachers (Fosnot 1989).

Conclusion

Play and the creative arts in early childhood programs are essential ways children communicate, think, feel, and express themselves. Art making, fiddling around with bits of wood and fabric or pieces of plastic and leather, reveals the gentle spirit creating simple forms and arrangements, touching the hands, hearts, and minds of young children—and adults.

Children will succeed when they have access to a wide variety of art-making materials such as reusable resources, and when they are surrounded by adults who see and believe in the creative competence of all children and are committed to their success in expressing themselves. As we trust the process, as we encourage and observe the emerging self-initiative and choice making of the children, we come to more fully understand the intimate connection between the spirit of play and the art-making process.

Word about Reusable Resources

Many of the materials used in art-making and play experiences can be discards donated by local businesses. Fabric, yarn, foam, plastic moldings, gold and silver Mylar, paper products, wood, wire, and a world of other reusable materials provides early childhood teachers and families with hands-on resources for creative learning.

Most businesses generate an abundance of unwanted by-products, overruns, rejects, obsolete parts, and discontinued items and pay costly fees to dispose of them. Throughout the nation, manufacturers dispose of their discarded materials in landfills and incinerators.

Through the establishment of a local Reusable Resource Center, high-quality, unwanted materials serve much-needed resources for creative play, the arts, mathematics, science, and other creative problem-solving activities for early childhood education.

In this way businesses become a powerful force to improve early childhood education while reducing disposal costs, improving their bottom line, helping their community, and communicating a strong message that they are in business not just to make a profit but also to make a difference.

(For information on Reusable Resource Centers near you or for training and technical assistance in developing a reuse program in your community contact Reusable Resource Association, P.O. Box 511001, Melbourne Beach, FL 32951, or visit **www.reusableresources.org**.)

Given these optimum circumstances, children surprise and delight us—they create structures and thoughts no one has seen or heard before. We adults develop a greater appreciation for the children and for the power of creative art making and materials, thus providing a strong motivation for adults to continue teaching and children to continue learning in this way.

In this era of performance standards and skill-based/outcome-based education, it is more important than ever for educators and families to articulate the values and support the creativity of play and exploration as ways to meet the standards—and to go beyond them.

References

Althouse, R. 1994. *Investigating mathematics with young children*. New York: Teachers College Press.

Chalufour, I., W. Drew, & S. Waite-Stupiansky, 2004. Learning to play again. In *Spotlight on young children and play*, ed. D. Koralek, 50–58. Washington, DC: NAEYC.

Christie, J.F., ed. 1991. *Play and early literacy development*. Albany: State University of New York Press.

Drew, K., M. Ohlsen, & M. Pichierri. 2000. *How to create a reusable resource center: A guidebook for champions*. Melbourne, FL: Institute for Self Active Education.

Duckworth, E. 1996. *The having of wonderful ideas and other essays on teaching and learning*. 2nd ed. New York: Teachers College Press.

Eliot, L. 2000. *What's going on in there? How the brain and mind develop in the first five years of life*. New York: Bantam.

Fosnot, C.T. 1989. *Enquiring teachers, enquiring learners: A constructivist approach for teaching*. New York: Teachers College Press.

Gardner, H. 1983. *Frames of mind: The theory of multiple intelligences*. New York: Basic Books.

Jalongo, M.J. 2003. The child's right to creative thought and expression. *Childhood Education* 79: 218–28.

Jensen, E. 1998. *Teaching with the brain in mind*. Alexandria, VA: Association for Supervision and Curriculum Development.

Jensen, E. 2000. *Brain-based learning*. San Diego, CA: Brain Store.

Jensen, E. 2001. *Arts with the brain in mind*. Alexandria, VA: Association for Supervision and Curriculum Development.

Jones, E. 1999. The importance of play. Presentation for "The Play Experience: Constructing Knowledge and a Community of Commitment," symposium at the NAEYC Annual Conference, New Orleans.

Jones, E., & G. Reynolds. 1992. *The play's the thing: Teachers' roles in children's play*. New York: Teachers College Press.

Kamii, C. 1982. *Number in preschool and kindergarten: Educational implications of Piaget's theory*. Washington, DC: NAEYC.

Klugman, E., & S. Smilansky, eds. 1990. *Children's play and learning: Perspectives and policy implications*. New York: Teachers College Press.

Malaguzzi, L. 1998. History, ideas, and basic philosophy: Interview with Lella Gandini. In *The hundred languages of children: The Reggio Emilia approach—Advanced reflections*, 2nd ed., eds. C. Edwards, L. Gandini, & G. Forman, 49–97. Greenwich, CT: Ablex.

McNiff, S. 1998. *Trust the process: An artist's guide to letting go*. Boston, MA: Shambhala.

Owocki, G. 1999. *Literacy through play*. Portsmouth, NH: Heinemann. Available from NAEYC.

Reynolds, G., & E. Jones. 1997. Master players: Learning from children at play. New York: Teachers College Press.

Schweinhart, L.J., H.V. Barnes, & D.P. Weikart. 1993. *Significant benefits: The High/Scope Perry Preschool Study through age 27*. Monographs of the High/Scope Educational Research Foundation, no. 10. Ypsilanti, MI: High/Scope Press.

Shonkoff, J.P., & D.A. Phillips, eds. 2000. *From neurons to neighborhoods: The Science of early childhood development*. Report of the National Research Council, Washington, DC: National Academies Press.

Stupiansky, S.W. 1992. *Math: Learning through play*. New York: Scholastic.

VanHoorn, J., P. Nourot, B. Scales, & K. Alward. 2002. *Play at the center of the curriculum*. 3rd ed. Upper Saddle River, NJ: Merrill/Prentice Hall.

Vygotsky, L. [1930–35] 1978a. The role of play in development. in *Mind in society: The development of higher psychological processes*, eds. M. Cole, V. John-Steiner, S. Scribner, & E. Souberman, 92–104. Cambridge, MA: Harvard University Press.

Vygotsky, L. [1930–35] 1978b. The prehistory of written language. In *Mind in society: The development of higher psychological processes*, eds. M. Cole, V. John-Steiner, S. Scribner, & E. Souberman, 105–20. Cambridge, MA: Harvard University Press.

Weisman Topal, C., & L. Gandini. 1999. *Beautiful stuff: Learning with found materials*. New York: Sterling.

Zigler, E., D.G. Singer, & S.J. Bishop-Josef, eds. 2004. *Children's play: The roots of reading*. Washington, DC: Zero to Three Press.

Walter F. Drew, EdD, is a nationally known early childhood consultant whose inspiring workshops feature hands-on creative play with open-ended reusable resources. As founder of the Reusable Resource Association and the Institute for Self Active Education, he has pioneered the development of Reusable Resource Centers as community-building initiatives to provide creative materials for early childhood programs. He is an early childhood adjunct faculty member at Brevard Community College in Melbourne, Florida, and creator of Dr. Drew's Discovery Blocks.

Baji Rankin, EdD, is executive director of NMAEYC, lead agency for T.E.A.C.H. Early Childhood New Mexico. Baji studies the Reggio Emilia approach and is committed to building early childhood programs with well-educated and -compensated teachers who find renewal through promoting children's creativity.

From *Young Children*, July 2004, pp. 38-45. Copyright © 2004 by National Association for the Education of Young Children. Reprinted by permission.

BUILDING CULTURALLY & LINGUISTICALLY COMPETENT SERVICES

Kathy Seitzinger Hepburn, M.S.
Georgetown University Center for Child and Human Development

A. Curriculum

OVERVIEW OF THE ISSUE

For young children, their family is their first "developmental niche" and learning environment. From the anticipated birth, delivery and arrival, through daily routines and relationships with family and caregivers, children are influenced by the culture—or values, beliefs, practices, customs, etc., of their home environment. A greater number of children enter childcare and early out-of-home settings than ever before. These numbers include those of culturally and linguistically diverse families and challenge the capacity of these settings to support school readiness for each child.

The early care and education environments where young children continue to grow and learn can also support learning about culture—and diversity. Childcare settings must be responsive to each child and whenever possible adapt practices and routines to assure continuity of care and culture between home and the early care setting (Chang & Pulido, 1994). Similarly, as the young child moves into the pre-school and school setting, the early education environment can value diversity, teach from a multicultural perspective, and promote anti-bias and tolerance for differences. By doing so, the early care and education environments can demonstrate respect for the strengths of families, the value of cultural and linguistic differences, and honor the uniqueness of each individual child and family.

The multicultural perspective is for everyone. Offering culturally and linguistically competent care and teaching with a multicultural perspective require knowledge about the meaning of culture and the impact on child development; attitudes and behaviors that value respectful and open discovery of differences; and skills to design and implement learning experiences that support multicultural learning. Flexibility in caregiving and early teaching and instruction practices—offering multiple ways for children to explore their world, to demonstrate their learning, to participate in classroom activities, and to interact with adults and other children—may be particularly conducive to teaching diverse groups of children (National Research Council and Institute of Medicine, 1994). Numerous research studies about the early process of identity and attitude development conclude that children learn by observing the differences and similarities among people and by absorbing the spoken and unspoken messages about those differences. By teaching children to respect different cultures, children gain positive feelings about themselves and learn to live and work together respectfully. Enriching early care and education environments is one way that communities can participate in nurturing culturally and linguistically competent services and supports.

Strategies for caregiving and technical tools for teaching with a multicultural perspective in a childcare or classroom environment include provider preparation, involving families, and utilizing developmentally appropriate curricula, educational materials (books, toys, games), and other childcare and classroom helps.

Critical Questions for Communities

- *What is the level of value and commitment to adapting to diversity and a multicultural, anti-bias approach in early care and education?*
- *What do we need to learn about diversity and implications for learning, caregiving, and working with young children and families to support school readiness?*
- *How can the daily routine, curriculum and the early care or classroom environment support diversity, multiculturalism and represent movement toward cultural and linguistic competence?*
- *How can multiculturalism be infused into learning rather than held separate as a "special" learning event?*
- *What resources exist to support this effort and what strategies might be most accessible and affordable for early care and classroom settings?*

Key Strategies for Families, Providers, and Administrators

What families can do:

- *Support multicultural and anti-bias education by sharing their own cultural perspective and experience.*
- *Encourage their children's learning outside of the classroom by answering questions about their own identity and background, exposing them to children and adults of other backgrounds, and discussing differences and similarities.*
- *Model the behaviors and attitudes they want their children to adopt.*

What providers can do:

- *Support multicultural and anti-bias education by raising personal awareness of cultural and linguistic diversity and anti-bias issues as well as committing to the value of human diversity and the fair treatment of all people.*
- *Observe and evaluate one's own behavior and the early care and/or classroom environment for messages about multicultural diversity.*
- *Use the whole learning environment and curriculum for "teachable moments" to explore diversity—not just one lesson plan at a time.*

What administrators can do:

- *Establish agency or organization-wide policy that supports respect for diversity and multiculturalism.*
- *Make resources available for early care environment or classroom curricula and materials to support in-classroom learning as well as facility-wide promotion activities.*
- *Establish support structures and strategies (teamwork, training, coaching, mentoring, counseling) to help staff maintain the vision and commitment to this effort.*

The Goals and Common Pitfalls of a Multicultural Anti-Bias Curriculum

Goals

In the big picture, the goal of multicultural education is to empower all students (children) to become knowledgeable, caring and active citizens in a multicultural and linguistically diverse world around them. (Banks, 1993)

For each student, the goals of a multicultural and anti-bias curriculum are to foster each child's:

- Construction of a knowledgeable, confident self-identity;

- Comfortable, empathic interaction with people from diverse backgrounds;

- Critical thinking about bias; and

- Ability to stand up for herself or himself, and for others, in the face of bias (Hohensee & Derman-Sparks, 1992).

While these may appear to be lofty goals when thinking about young children, it is clear that acquiring self-identity, perceptions of differences in others, developing self-esteem, and having empathy toward and engaging in empathic interactions with others are very early developmental tasks.

Common Implementation Pitfalls

- **Viewing cultural is an "add on":** Providing care and education through a multicultural approach is not something that is added on top of other teaching. It is about understanding and integrating an approach that makes all learning experiences more complete, accurate, and sensitive. It ties the learning experiences of young children to their everyday world of family and community.

- **Believing that talking openly about differences and diversity will create conflict and divide children:** Talking about differences AND how children and families are similar enriches the point of view of children and families as well as early care and education providers. It can teach the values of understanding and negotiating differences toward mutual understanding and getting along.

- **Reinforcing differences and stereotyping:** Stereotypes can be reinforced by focusing on differences between cultural groups. For example, making broad statements and comparisons between Asians and Americans or African Americans and Latinos, can lead to assumptions about individuals within a cultural group. Instead, teaching a multicultural perspective reinforces learning about individuals and families and their unique cultural experience.

- **Taking the tourist approach:** This approach to multicultural learning offers a limited view where children "visit" a culture for a special occasion. For example, by focusing on holidays rather than on integrating cultural perspectives into everyday learning in

Continued

The Goals and Common Pitfalls of a Multicultural Anti-Bias Curriculum Continued

early care and education, there is the risk of trivializing cultural and linguistic differences rather than magnifying the similarities and everyday nature of cultural and linguistic influences.

- **Implementing the "Culture Curriculum":** Similar to the tourist curriculum, this pitfall keeps the study of diverse cultures as separate lessons, rather than integrating the multicultural approach into an everyday, every-lesson learning experience.

- **Thinking the curriculum is "in place":** Implementing multicultural learning is never complete. Like culture itself, it evolves through continued dialogue, learning, and reflection. Keeping families involved in the early care and education setting and understanding their unique cultural perspective is essential and has an ever-evolving impact on multicultural learning within the early care and education setting.

Adapted from:

Banks, J. (1993). Multicultural education: Development, dimensions, and challenges. *Phi Delta Kappan, 75*(1), 22-28.

Hohensee, J., & Derman-Sparks, L. (1992). *Implementing an anti-bias curriculum in early childhood.* Retrieved June 23, 2003, from the ERIC EECE Clearinghouse on Elementary and Early Childhood Education, U.S. Department of Education Web site: http://ecap.crc.uiuc.edu/eecearchive/digests/1992/hohens92.html

Menkart, D. (1993). Multicultural education: Strategies for linguistically diverse schools and classrooms. National Center for Bilingual Education: Program Information Guide Series, Number 16. Retrieved June 19, 2003, from www.ncela.gwu.edu/pubs/pigs/pig16.htm

North Central Regional Educational Laboratory. (1998). *Critical issue: Meeting the diverse needs of young children.* Retrieved June 2, 2003, from www.ncrel.org/sdrs/areas/issues/students/earlycld/ea400.htm

Checklist for Implementing a Multicultural Anti-Bias Curriculum in Early Childhood Education

Personnel Preparation

☐ Teachers and early care providers understand the rationale for and benefits to implementing a multicultural curriculum.

☐ Teachers and early care providers are committed to a multicultural approach.

☐ Teachers and early care providers are aware and knowledgeable of their own biases.

☐ There are strategies in place for teachers and early care providers to learn about cultures different from their own.

☐ Teachers are familiar with and prepared to implement a multicultural approach.

☐ There are strategies in place for involving parents and families in the preparation and implementation of the curriculum.

☐ There are continuous learning and support opportunities for teachers and early care providers to build self-awareness, learn new skills, problem solve and evaluate implementation.

Curriculum

☐ A curriculum development/selection and review process is in place.

☐ The curriculum is developmentally appropriate.

☐ Cultural and linguistic diversity permeates the curriculum.

☐ The curriculum portrays culture as a dynamic characteristic that is shaped by new learning and experiences as well as social, political, and economic conditions.

☐ The curriculum includes people of various cultural and class backgrounds throughout.

☐ The curriculum shows respect and offers affirmation for each child's cultural and linguistic background.

☐ The curriculum helps children learn to understand experiences and multiple perspectives other than their own.

Continued

Checklist for Implementing a Multicultural Anti-Bias Curriculum in Early Childhood Education Continued

Classroom Practices and Activities

☐ There are various types of learning situations available—working in groups, pairs, or individually.

☐ Language use and communication style (verbal and nonverbal) is tailored to be culturally and linguistically sensitive.

☐ All children are equally encouraged to participate in classroom activities and discussion.

☐ The classroom models a democratic and equitable decision making process.

☐ Teachers and early care providers have integrated the curriculum so that "teachable moments" can be used to reinforce concepts from the formal curriculum.

☐ Parents are involved in classroom practices and activities to bring their cultural and linguistic strengths into the learning environment.

Materials

☐ Books, textbooks, and other written or picture materials reflect the culture of the students in the program.

☐ Play materials (blocks, dolls, musical instruments, dramatic play etc.) represent the culture of the students in the program and are relevant to each child's life and experiences.

☐ Display materials reflect the culture of all the students in the program and include pictures of people like themselves.

☐ Bi-lingual materials (books, signs, posters, etc.) are available for those who are English Language Learners.

Adapted from:
Hohensee, J., & Derman-Sparks, L. (1992). *Implementing an anti-bias curriculum in early childhood.* Retrieved June 23, 2003, from the ERIC EECE Clearinghouse on Elementary and Early Childhood Education, U.S. Department of Education Web site: http://ecap.crc.uiuc.edu/eecearchive/digests/1992/hohens92.html

Menkart, D. (1993). Multicultural education: Strategies for linguistically diverse schools and classrooms. National Center for Bilingual Education: Program Information Guide Series, Number 16. Retrieved June 19, 2003, from www.ncela.gwu.edu/pubs/pigs/pig16.htm

Seattle Public Schools. (2003). *Standards for instruction in multicultural settings.* Retrieved August 27, 2003, from the Seattle Public Schools Web site: www.seattleschools.org/area/acastan/stan/socstud/ISMCS.xml

Caregiving: Transferring Culture through Daily Routines—A Quick Checklist

For very young children, the curriculum for learning and development is deeply embedded in the daily routines and caregiver-child interaction. Within the family home or early care and education setting, caring for young children conveys cultural messages. The continuity of care and the continuity of these messages is critical to infants and toddlers.

Build on Parenting Knowledge from the Family's Own Culture

In order to better serve the infants and toddlers in our care, we:

☐ Provide a warm and accepting environment for families of diverse cultures.

☐ Engage in sensitive family information gathering to inform us about the family's beliefs, values, and customary care of their young child.

☐ Try to match families with staff who are from or have knowledge of the family's culture.

☐ Draw upon the cultural experience of the staff.

☐ Invite parents to continue to guide us in the care of their infants and toddlers.

☐ Engage in dialogue and a process where we 1) ask for information, 2) reflect to understand, 3) offer a different perspective, and 4) negotiate with families when we reach a point of cultural difference or conflicting views in the care of their child.

Adapt Early Care Practices

Whenever possible and in keeping with developmentally appropriate practices, we:

☐ Encourage provision of services in the families' preferred language; especially comforting phrases to help soothe each child.

☐ Adapt feeding and eating practices to accommodate those that are practiced in the home and most effective with the child.

☐ Support attachment by carrying the child in the ways that are most familiar and comforting to that child.

☐ Use touch and display of physical affection in ways that are known to, acceptable, and comfortable for each child.

☐ Arrange for sleeping accommodations that are most familiar and effective for each child.

Child and Caregiver Interaction

To support relationships and early learning in keeping with developmentally appropriate practices, we:

☐ Encourage provision of services in the families' preferred language.

☐ Design activities based on input from families about their culture and common teaching interactions with toddlers.

☐ Use familiar songs, music, and lap games from their culture to engage infants and toddlers.

☐ Use picture books and other materials that represent children and families that look like them and represent their culture.

Adapted from:

Chang H., & Pulido, D. (1994, October/November). The critical importance of cultural and linguistic continuity for infants and toddlers. *Bulletin of ZERO TO THREE, 15*(2), 13-17.

Pulido-Tobiassen, D., & Gonzalez-Mena, J. (1999). *A place to begin: Working with parents on issues of diversity.* Oakland, CA: California Tomorrow.

Reebye, P., Ross, S., Jamieson, K., & Clark, J. (1999). *Sharing attachment practices across cultures: Learning from immigrants and refugees.* Toronto, CA: St. Joseph's Women's Health Center, Parkdale Parents' Primary Prevention Project. Retrieved September 15, 2003, from www.attachmentacrosscultures.org

ANNOTATED RESOURCES

BOOKS AND PRINT

Anti-Bias Curriculum: Tools for Empowering Young Children

(1989, SEVENTH PRINTING 1993) DERMAN-SPARKS, L., AND THE A.B.C. TASK FORCE.

This classic text offers a rationale and steps to creating an anti-bias environment by practicing anti-bias curriculum. It suggests ways that early care and education staff and teachers can use materials, activities, and interaction with children, parents, and one-another to promote acceptance of cultural, linguistic, and other types of diversity. Implementation guidance also includes ways to support staff development and implement anti-bias curriculum into an early care or education program. Additional resources include lists of children's books and sources for additional curriculum materials.

National Association for the Education of Young Children, 1509 16th Street, NW, Washington, DC 20036-1426, 1-800-424-2460. ($15.00)

Bridging Cultures Between Home and School: A Guide for Teachers

(2001) TRUMBULL, E., ROTHSTEIN-FISCH, C., GREEN-FIELD, P., QUIROZ, B.

This guide for teachers provides a framework for learning about culture, along with may teacher-created strategies for making classrooms more successful for students, particularly those from immigrant backgrounds. Related texts are Bridging Cultures: Teacher Education Module and Bridging Cultures in Our Schools: New Approaches that Work, both available from WestEd.

WestEd Center for Child and Family Studies and the California Department of Education, CDE Press, Sales Office, P.O. Box 271, Sacramento, CA 95812-0271, 1-800-995-4099. ($17.50)

Creative Resources for the Anti-Bias Classroom

(1998) SADERMAN HALL, N.

This resource book for early care and education staff and teachers describes ways to integrate the anti-bias approach into all areas of curriculum. It includes hundreds of activities, grouped into four units—infant, toddler, preschool/kindergarten, and elementary age (up to age 11). Each unit has a developmental overview, ideas for interacting with parents and 20–50 ac-

tivities, outlined by skill. Includes appropriate books, finger plays, rhymes, and songs.

Redleaf Press, St. Paul, MN, 1-800-423-8309 or order online at www.redleafpress.org. ($58.95)

Developing Cultural Competence: A Guide for Working with Young Children and Their Families

(1998) LYNCH, E. W., AND HANSON, M. J.

Written for the early intervention community, this book is based on best practices in early intervention, literature on intercultural effectiveness, and insights and experience from the field. The three sections of the book introduce the issues of working with families from diverse cultural, ethnic, and language groups; some broad observations about the history, values, and beliefs of the major cultural and ethnic groups that make up the United States related to family, childrearing, and disability; and a synthesis and recommendations for enhancing the cultural competence of interventionists.

Paul H. Brookes Publishing Company, Inc., P.O. Box 106242, Baltimore, MD 21285, 1-800-638-3775 or order online at www.Brookespublishing.com. *($41.95)*

How Culture Shapes Social-Emotional Development: Implications for Practice in Infant-Family Programs

(2004) DAY, M., AND PARLAKIAN, R.

Written for program leaders and practitioners, this booklet examines how culture shapes children's fundamental learning about themselves, their emotions, and their way of interacting and relating to others. It includes recommendations for providing culturally responsive services, and an explanation of cultural reciprocity, a framework for resolving cultural dilemmas. Activities are provided that feature a range of infant-family settings.

ZERO TO THREE, National Center for Infants, Toddlers, and Families, 2000 M Street, NW, Suite 200, Washington, DC 20035-3307, (202) 638-1144. ($17.50)

Infants, Toddlers, and Caregivers, Fifth Edition

(1997) GONZALEZ-MENA, J., AND WIDMEYER EYER, D.

This book reviews infant-toddler development and quality childcare. It emphasizes the importance of addressing cultural differences in all aspects of the program, including bilingual communication and culturally appropriate curricula. The text is especially useful for caregivers, directors, and trainers.

Mountain View, CA: Mayfield Publishing Co. 1-800-433-1279. ($46.95)

Multicultural Issues: In Child Care, Third Edition

(2000) GONZALEZ-MENA, J.

This supplemental text useful to early care and education providers presents cultural differences relevant to all caregiving settings (day care, nursery, and pre-school programs). Daily caregiving routines and objectives are stressed throughout. Sensitivity, communication, and problem solving are key to meeting the needs of young children according to their individual development, their parents' beliefs, and the beliefs of the caregiver.

Columbus, OH: McGraw-Hill Co. 1-800-262-4729. ($22.50)

Roots and Wings: Affirming Culture in Early Childhood Programs, Revised Edition

(2003) YORK, S.

This updated edition presents a practical resource for early childhood teachers on current anti-bias and culturally relevant issues in educating young children. The text includes a curricular approach to supporting culture, activities for the classroom, practical examples and staff-training recommendations as well as chapters focused on bilingual education, culturally responsive teaching, and children and prejudice. The book also includes an extensive list of resources.

Redleaf Press, St. Paul, MN, 1-800-423-8309 or order online at www.redleafpress.org. ($29.95)

ON-LINE RESOURCES

¡Hola Means Hello! Resources and Ideas for Promoting Diversity in Early Childhood Settings

(1998) FENSON, C., DENNIS, B., AND PALSHA, S.

This 30-page booklet is designed to assist childcare providers, teachers, and other personnel who provide services to young children and families in creating opportunities for children to appreciate the diversity around them. It contains resources that include a list of sources and types of classroom materials for enhancing cultural awareness, teacher materials to promote cultural awareness, self-assessment checklist for personnel, extensive booklists for enriching classroom diversity, and helpful websites. Many items described are available at low cost department stores. Full text available at www.fpg.unc.edu/Hola/hola.htm

Frank Porter Graham Child Development Center, UNC-CH, Publications & Dissemination Office, Chapel Hill, NC 27599, (919) 966-0857.

The Critical Importance of Cultural and Linguistic Continuity for Infants and Toddlers

(1994, OCT./NOV.) CHANG, H., AND PULIDO, D.

This article focuses on the ability of the provider to understand, respect, and build upon the cultural as well as linguistic practices of the home to ensure a child's continued growth and development. It also offers examples and raises issues for further research and analysis. Full text available at www.california tomorrow.org/files/pdfs Cultural_Linguistic_Continuity.pdf

In Bulletin of ZERO TO THREE, 15(2). ZERO TO THREE, National Center for Infants, Toddlers, and Families, 2000 M Street, NW, Suite 200, Washington, DC 20035-3307, (202) 638-1144.

TRAINING AND TECHNICAL ASSISTANCE

In Our Own Way: How Anti-Bias Work Shapes Our Lives

(1998) CONTRIBUTIONS FROM ALVARADO, C., BURNLEY, L., DERMAN-SPARKS, L., HOFFMAN, E., JIMENEZ, L. I., LABYZON, J., RAMSEY, P., UNTEN, A., WALLACE, B., AND YASUI, B.

Filled with the personal reflections of people who have done anti-bias work in child care and early childhood settings, this text shows how the writers learned to think critically and how they learned to teach this skill in their anti-bias work. Childcare providers and teachers can learn from the experience of those who have gone before and continue to learn themselves.

Available from Redleaf Press, St. Paul, MN, 1-800-423-8309 or order online at www.redleafpress.org. ($19.95)

Program for Infant/Toddler Caregivers Module IV: Culture, Family, and Providers

(1998) PROGRAM FOR INFANT/TODDLER CAREGIVERS (PITC).

One in a series of four training modules produced by WestEd PITC, Module IV includes: The curriculum Infant/Toddler Caregiving: A Guide to Culturally Sensitive Care ($12.50), a Trainer's Guide: Module IV: Culture, Family, and Providers ($20.00), and Video: Essential Connections: Ten Keys to Culturally Sensitive

Child Care ($65.00). Articles in the curriculum guide focus on development of a child's development in the context of culture, cultural diversity, the development of cultural sensitivity, and support to a child's full participation in his or her home culture. The video supports these messages through recommending and describing ten strategies to strengthen children's connections with their family and their home culture and is available in English, Cantonese, and Spanish. Audiences would include: professional developers, social service agencies, community-based organizations, and parents.

WestEd Center for Child and Family Studies and the California Department of Education, CDE Press, Sales Office, P.O. Box 271, Sacramento, CA 95812-0271, 1-800-995-4099.

Start Seeing Diversity: The Basic Guide to an Anti-Bias Classroom

(1998) WOLPERT, E.

This study guide and accompanying video help teachers recognize and address bias by illustrating one community's effort to create a responsive childcare program. The study guide includes discussion questions and handouts. Appropriate for trainers, directors, and instructors.

Committee for Boston Public Housing, Redleaf Press, St. Paul, MN. 1-800-423-8309. (Guide and 52 minute video—$69.95)

Index

Index

Test Your Knowledge Form

We encourage you to photocopy and use this page as a tool to assess how the articles in *Annual Editions* expand on the information in your textbook. By reflecting on the articles you will gain enhanced text information. You can also access this useful form on a product's book support Web site at *http://www.dushkin.com/online/*.

NAME: DATE:

_____

TITLE AND NUMBER OF ARTICLE:

_____

BRIEFLY STATE THE MAIN IDEA OF THIS ARTICLE:

_____

LIST THREE IMPORTANT FACTS THAT THE AUTHOR USES TO SUPPORT THE MAIN IDEA:

_____

WHAT INFORMATION OR IDEAS DISCUSSED IN THIS ARTICLE ARE ALSO DISCUSSED IN YOUR TEXTBOOK OR OTHER READINGS THAT YOU HAVE DONE? LIST THE TEXTBOOK CHAPTERS AND PAGE NUMBERS:

_____

LIST ANY EXAMPLES OF BIAS OR FAULTY REASONING THAT YOU FOUND IN THE ARTICLE:

_____

LIST ANY NEW TERMS/CONCEPTS THAT WERE DISCUSSED IN THE ARTICLE, AND WRITE A SHORT DEFINITION:

We Want Your Advice

ANNUAL EDITIONS revisions depend on two major opinion sources: one is our Advisory Board, listed in the front of this volume, which works with us in scanning the thousands of articles published in the public press each year; the other is you—the person actually using the book. Please help us and the users of the next edition by completing the prepaid article rating form on this page and returning it to us. Thank you for your help!

ANNUAL EDITIONS: Early Childhood Education 05/06

ARTICLE RATING FORM

Here is an opportunity for you to have direct input into the next revision of this volume.
We would like you to rate each of the articles listed below, using the following scale:

1. **Excellent: should definitely be retained**
2. **Above average: should probably be retained**
3. **Below average: should probably be deleted**
4. **Poor: should definitely be deleted**

Your ratings will play a vital part in the next revision.
Please mail this prepaid form to us as soon as possible.
Thanks for your help!

RATING	ARTICLE	RATING	ARTICLE
	1. Starting Right		32. When Children Make Rules
	2. Investing in Preschool		33. Guidance & Discipline Strategies for Young Children: Time Out Is Out
	3. Preschool: The Most Important Grade		
	4. Life *Way* After Head Start		34. Beyond Banning War and Superhero Play
	5. Ready to Learn		35. Classroom Problems That Don't Go Away
	6. Class and the Classroom		36. Six Facts You Need to Know About Autism Now!
	7. Too Soon to Test		37. The Latest News on ADHD
	8. Overburdened Overwhelmed		38. Beyond the Basics: Using the Project Approach in Standards-Based Classrooms
	9. Early Education		
	10. The "Failure" of Head Start		39. Understanding Curriculum: An Umbrella View
	11. Leave No Parent Behind		40. Reggio Emilia: New Ways to Think About Schooling
	12. The Case for Staying Home		41. Emergent Curriculum and Kindergarten Readiness
	13. The Friendly Divorce		42. Early Literacy and Very Young Children
	14. The Dynamics of Families Who Are Homeless: Implications for Early Childhood Educators		43. The Essentials of Early Literacy Instruction
			44. Educating Early Childhood Teachers about Computers
	15. Skills for School Readiness—and Life		
	16. The Role of Emotional Competence in the Development of the Young Child		45. Movement and Learning: A Valuable Connection
			46. Promoting Creativity for Life Using Open-Ended Materials
	17. Childhood Obesity: The Caregiver's Role		
	18. The Allergy Epidemic		47. Building Culturally and Linguistically Competent Services
	19. Big Spenders		
	20. Achieving High Standards and Implementing Developmentally Appropriate Practice—Both ARE Possible		
	21. Second Time Around		
	22. Let's Just Play		
	23. The Importance of Being Playful		
	24. The Ultimate Guide to Preschool		
	25. Creating Home-School Partnerships		
	26. Basic Premises of Classroom Design: The Teacher's Perspective		
	27. How Safe are Child Care Playgrounds? A Progress Report		
	28. Planning Holiday Celebrations: An Ethical Approach to Developing Policy and Practices		
	29. With Boys and Girls in Mind		
	30. Building an Encouraging Classroom With Boys In Mind		
	31. Building Positive Teacher-Child Relationships		

(Continued on next page)

BUSINESS REPLY MAIL
FIRST CLASS MAIL PERMIT NO. 551 DUBUQUE IA

POSTAGE WILL BE PAID BY ADDRESEE

McGraw-Hill/Dushkin
2460 KERPER BLVD
DUBUQUE, IA 52001-9902

ABOUT YOU

Name   Date

Are you a teacher? ❑   A student? ❑
Your school's name

Department

Address   City   State   Zip

School telephone #

YOUR COMMENTS ARE IMPORTANT TO US!

Please fill in the following information:
For which course did you use this book?

Did you use a text with this ANNUAL EDITION? ❑ yes ❑ no
What was the title of the text?

What are your general reactions to the *Annual Editions* concept?

Have you read any pertinent articles recently that you think should be included in the next edition? Explain.

Are there any articles that you feel should be replaced in the next edition? Why?

Are there any World Wide Web sites that you feel should be included in the next edition? Please annotate.

May we contact you for editorial input? ❑ yes ❑ no
May we quote your comments? ❑ yes ❑ no